Viz Graphic Novel

FLAME OF RECCA ™

Vol. 10
Action Edition

Story and Art by
Nobuyuki Anzai

Flame of Recca
Vol. 10
Action Edition

Story and Art by
Nobuyuki Anzai

English Adaptation/Lance Caselman
Translation/Joe Yamazaki
Touch-up Art & Lettering/Kelle Han
Graphics & Cover Design/Sean Lee
Editor/Yuki Takagaki

Managing Editor/Annette Roman
Director of Production/Noboru Watanabe
Editorial Director/Alvin Lu
Sr. Director of Licensing & Acquisitions/Rika Inouye
Vice President of Sales & Marketing/Liza Coppola
Executive Vice President/Hyoe Narita
Publisher/Seiji Horibuchi

Published by VIZ, LLC
P.O. Box 77010
San Francisco, CA 94107

10 9 8 7 6 5 4 3 2 1
First printing, January 2005

store.viz.com

www.viz.com

ANIMERICA
ANIME & MANGA MONTHLY アニメリカ

www.animerica-mag.com

Viz Graphic Novel

FLAME OF RECCA™

Vol. 10

Story & Art by Nobuyuki Anzai

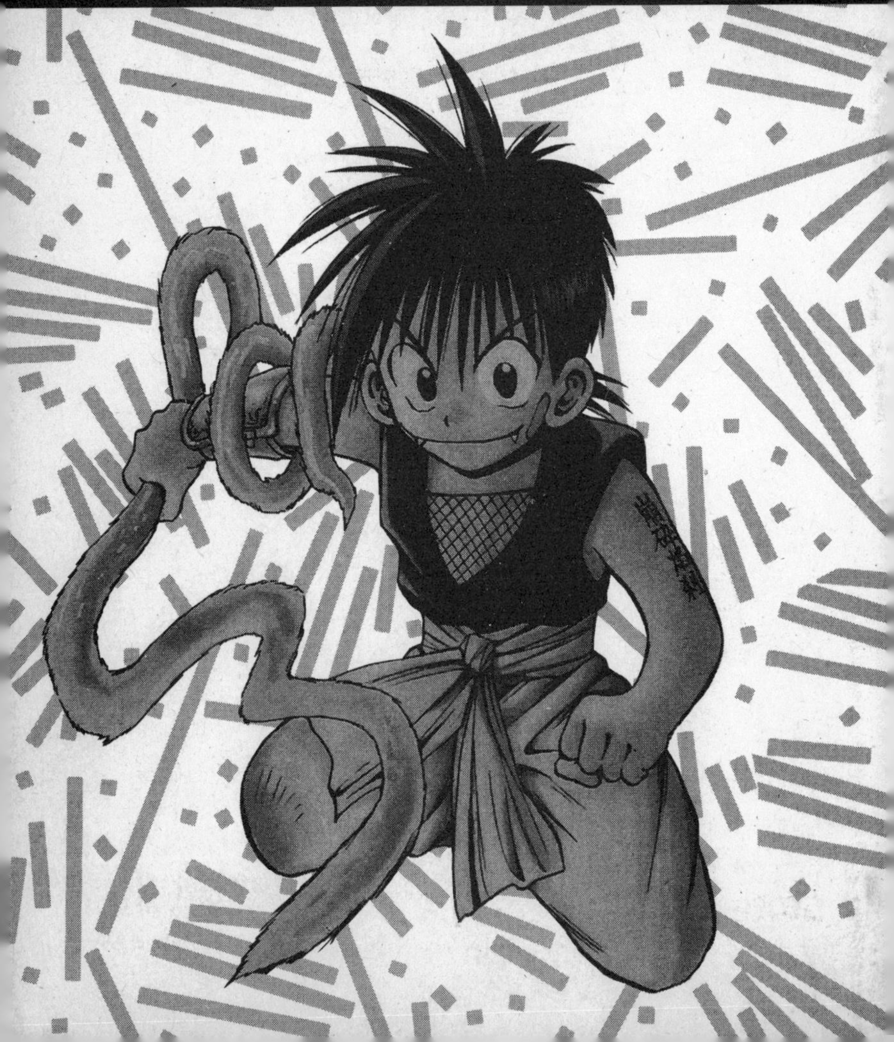

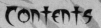

Contents

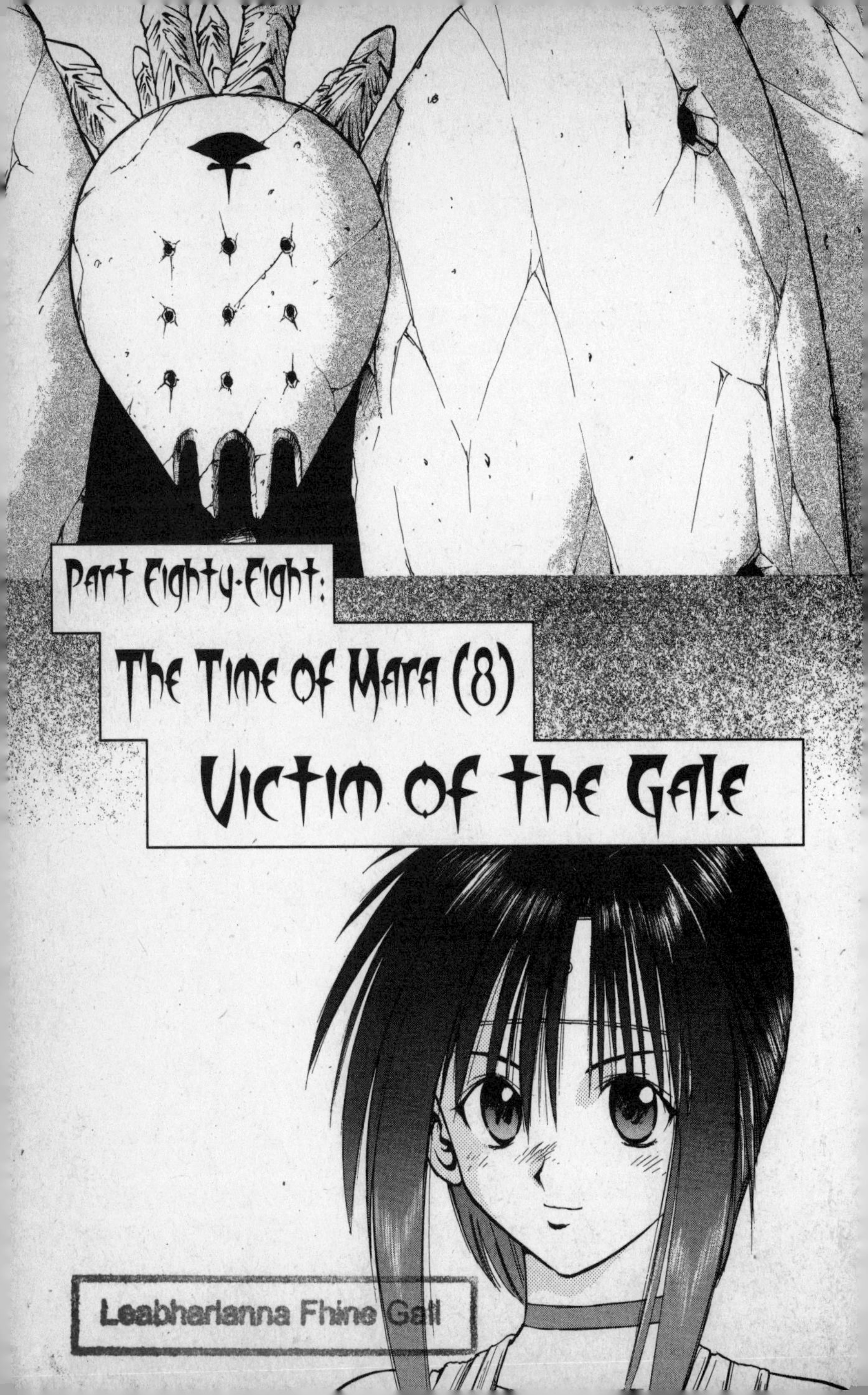
Part Eighty-Eight:
The Time of Mara (8)
Victim of the Gale

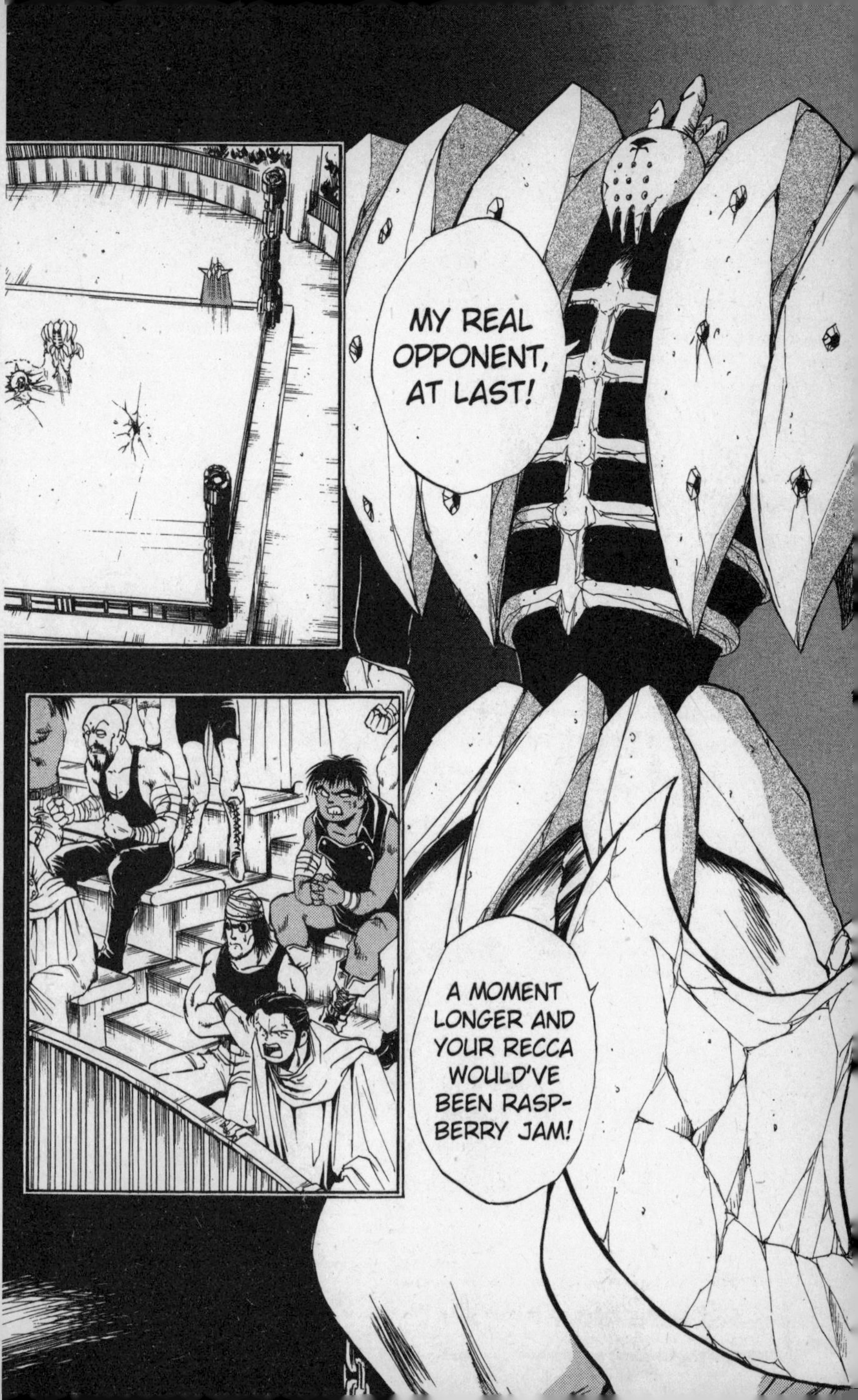
MY REAL OPPONENT, AT LAST!
A MOMENT LONGER AND YOUR RECCA WOULD'VE BEEN RASP-BERRY JAM!

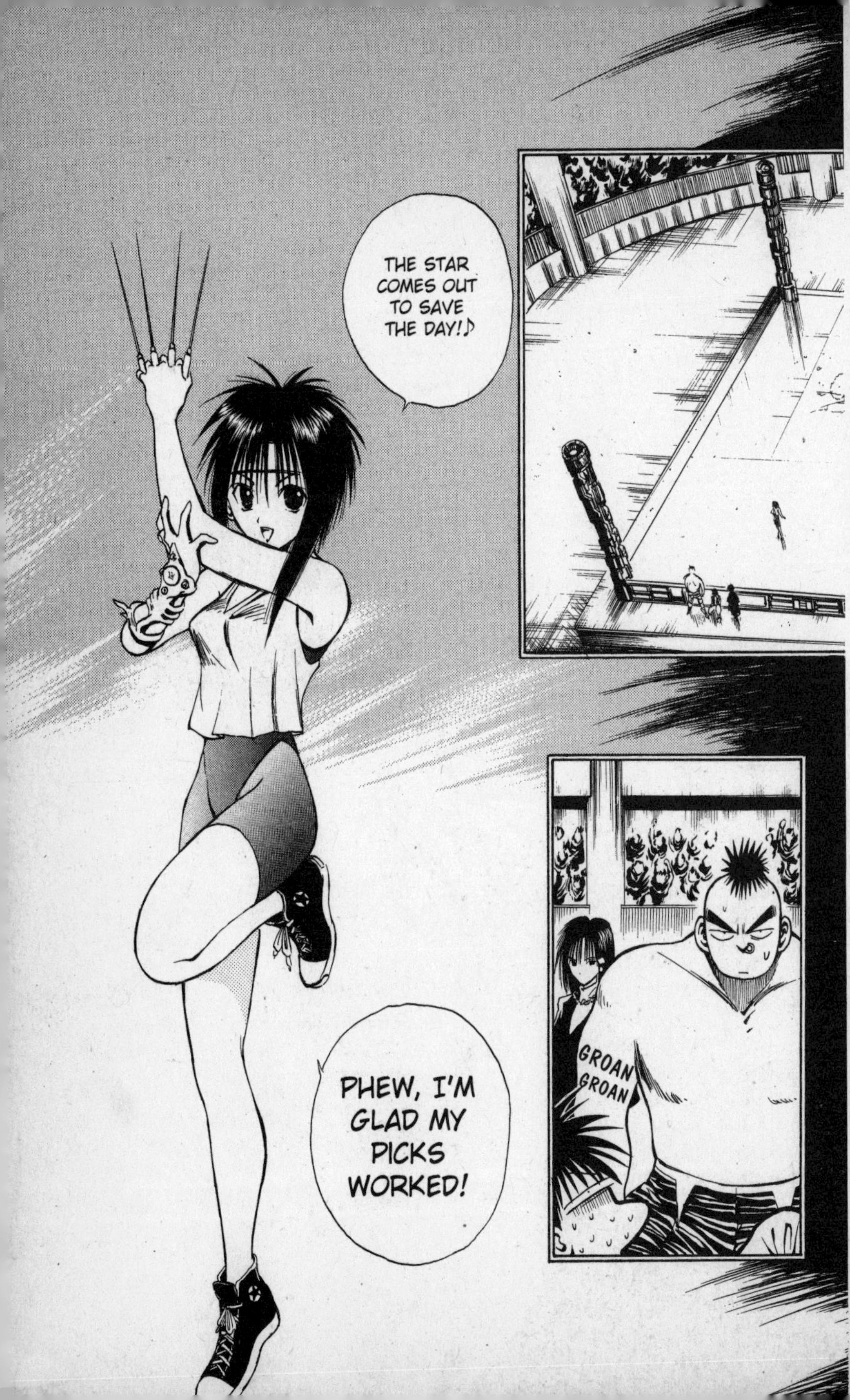
THE STAR COMES OUT TO SAVE THE DAY!♪
GROAN GROAN
PHEW, I'M GLAD MY PICKS WORKED!

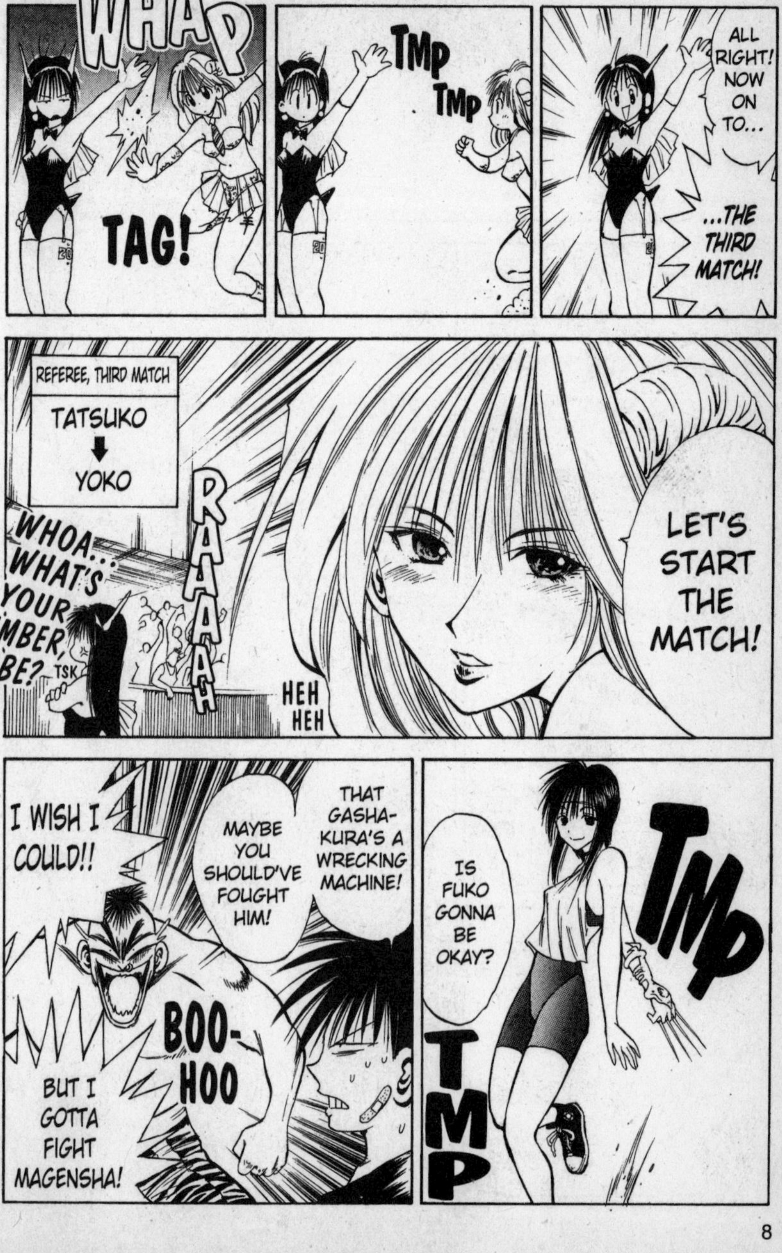
ALL RIGHT! NOW ON TO...
...THE THIRD MATCH!
TMP
TMP
WHAP
TAG!
LET'S START THE MATCH!
REFEREE, THIRD MATCH
TATSUKO ↓ YOKO
RAAAAAGH
HEH HEH
WHOA... WHAT'S YOUR NUMBER, BABE?
TSK
IS FUKO GONNA BE OKAY?
TMP
TMP
THAT GASHA-KURA'S A WRECKING MACHINE!
MAYBE YOU SHOULD'VE FOUGHT HIM!
I WISH I COULD!!
BOO-HOO
BUT I GOTTA FIGHT MAGENSHA!

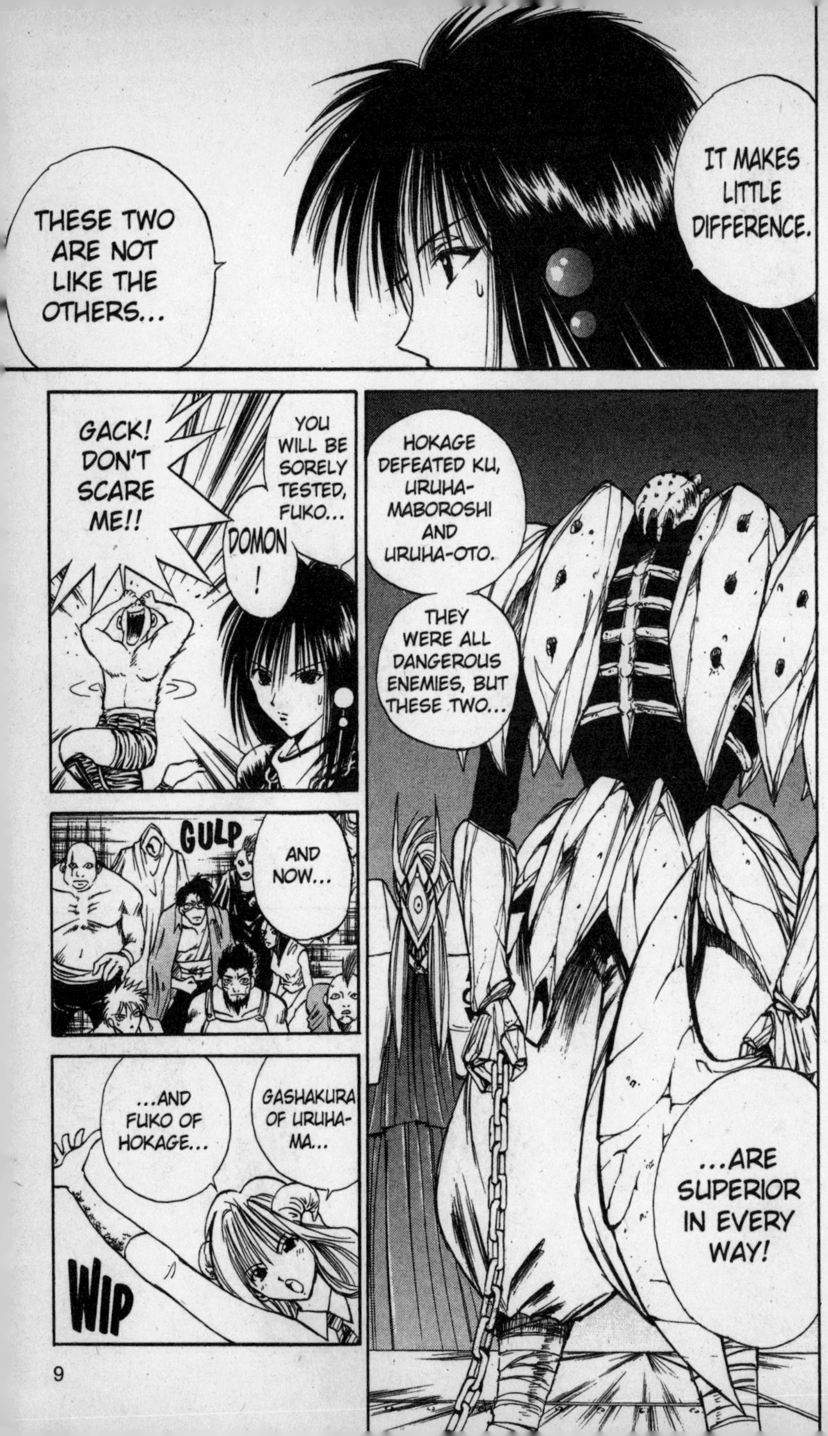
IT MAKES LITTLE DIFFERENCE.
THESE TWO ARE NOT LIKE THE OTHERS...
HOKAGE DEFEATED KU, URUHA-MABOROSHI AND URUHA-OTO.
THEY WERE ALL DANGEROUS ENEMIES, BUT THESE TWO...
...ARE SUPERIOR IN EVERY WAY!
YOU WILL BE SORELY TESTED, FUKO...
DOMON!
GACK! DON'T SCARE ME!!
AND NOW...
GULP
GASHAKURA OF URUHA-MA...
...AND FUKO OF HOKAGE...
WIP

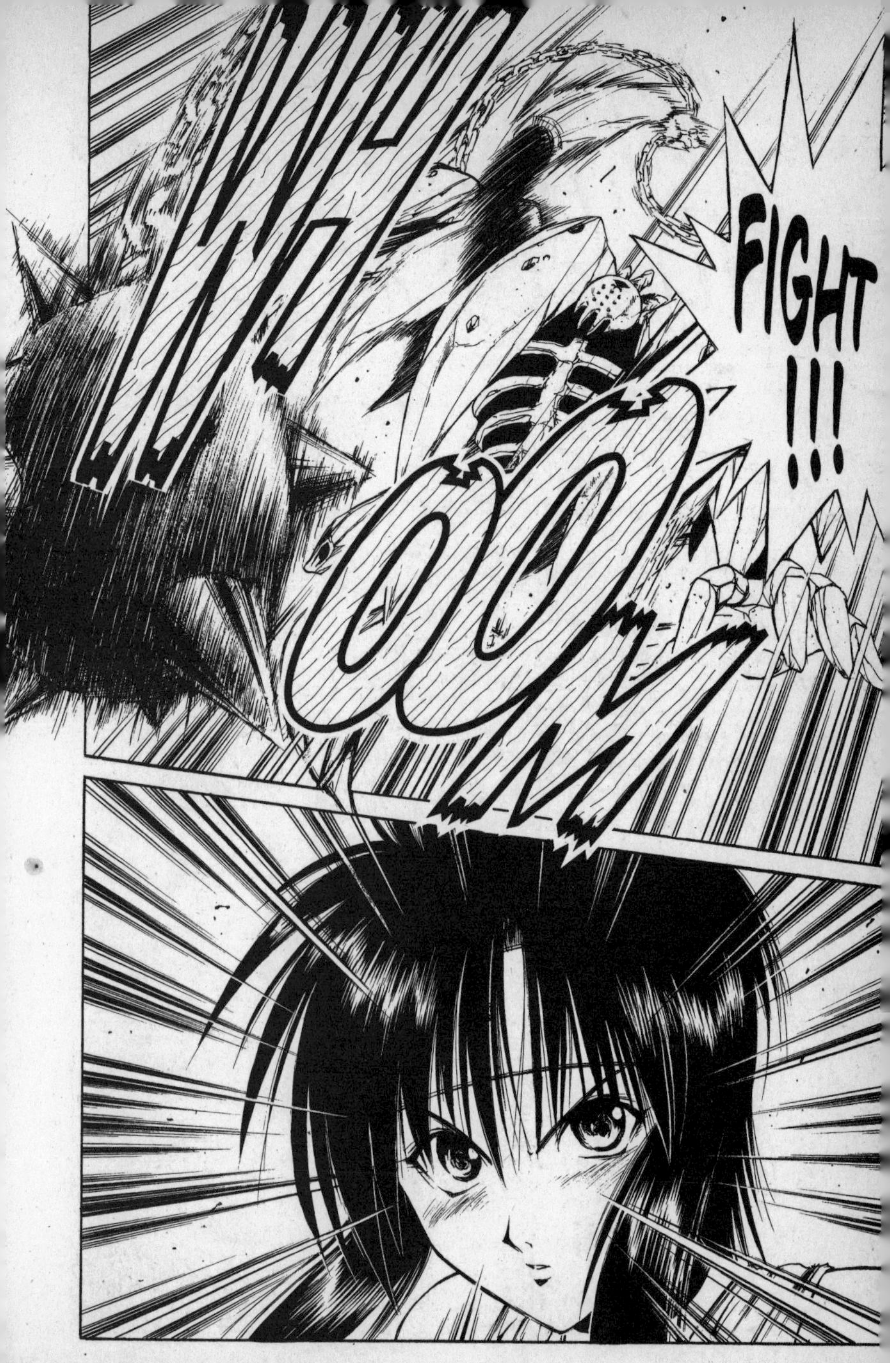
FIGHT
!!!

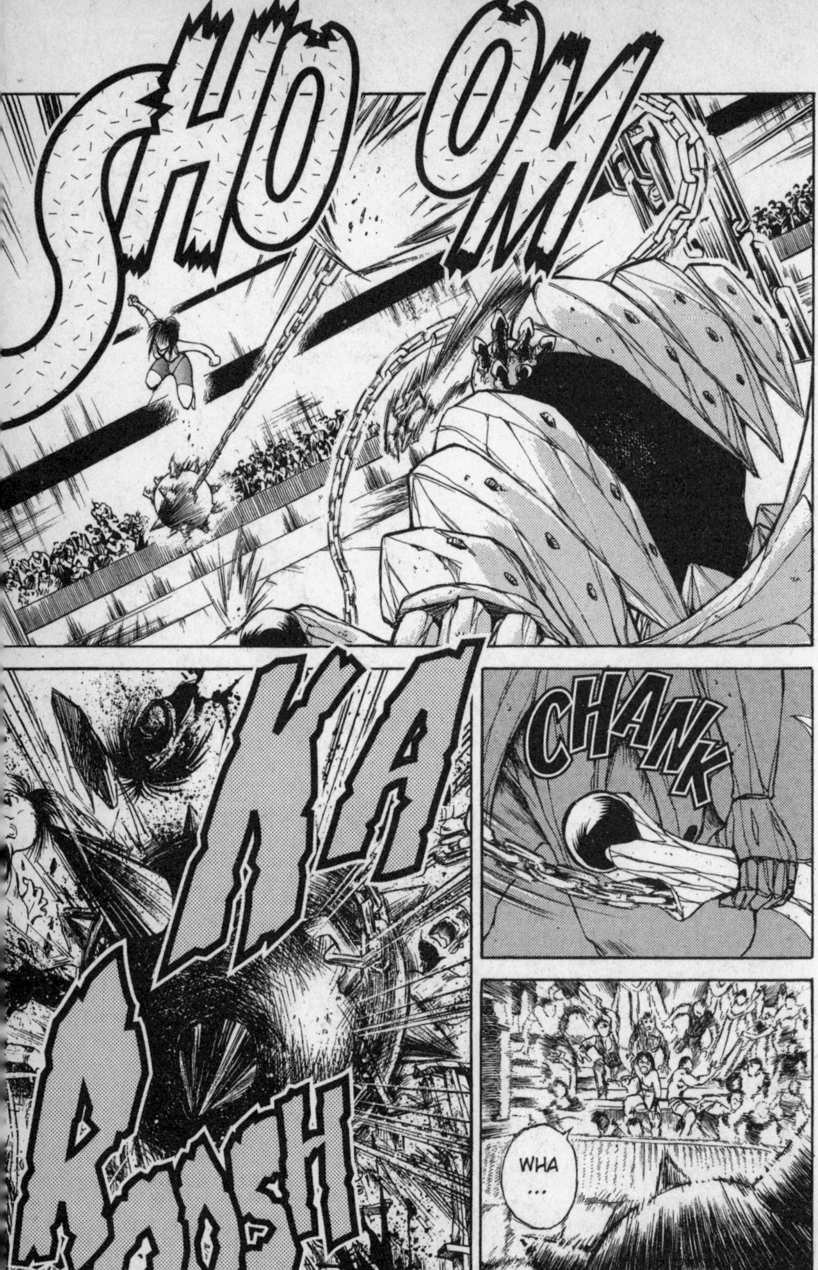
SCHOOM
CHANK
WHA
...
KABOOSH

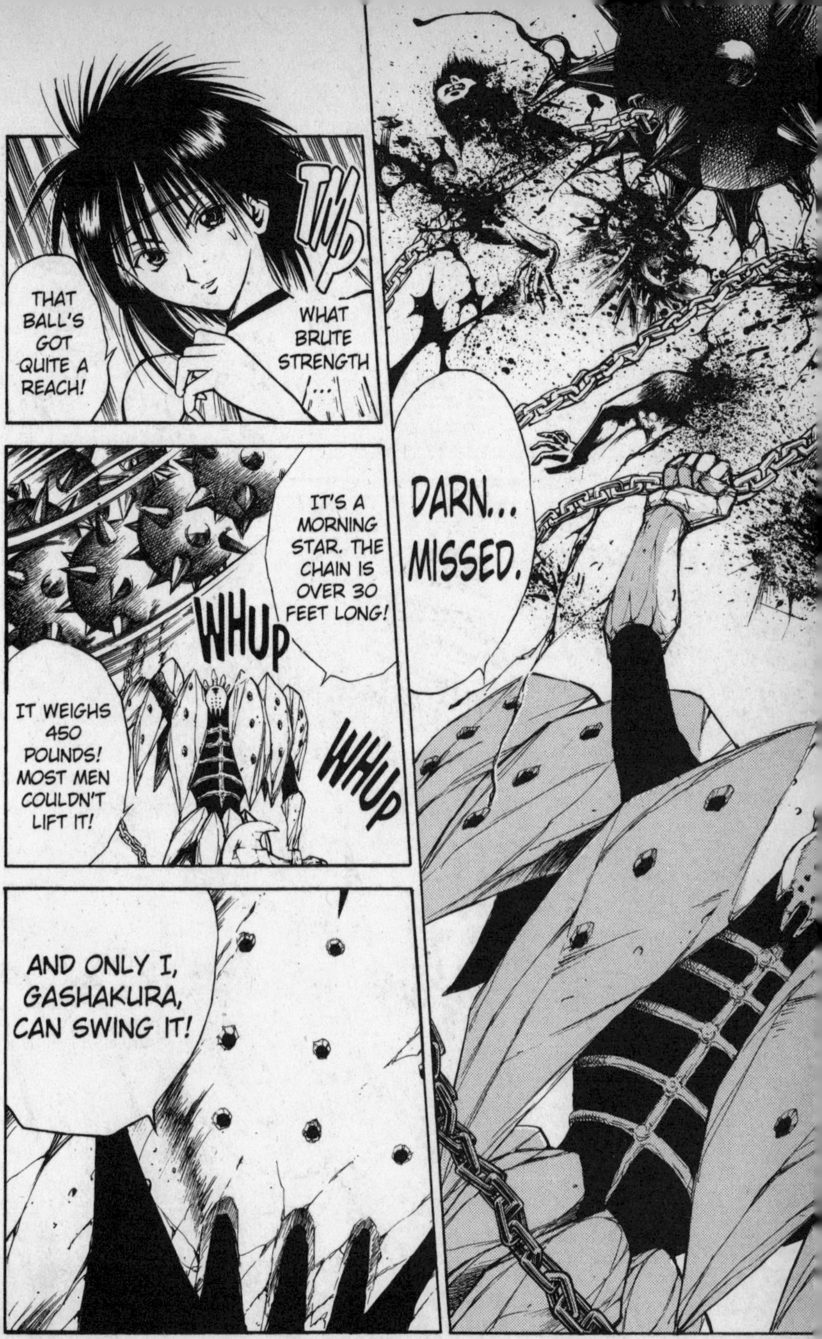
DARN... MISSED.
TMP
WHAT BRUTE STRENGTH...
THAT BALL'S GOT QUITE A REACH!
WHUP
WHUP
IT'S A MORNING STAR. THE CHAIN IS OVER 30 FEET LONG!
IT WEIGHS 450 POUNDS! MOST MEN COULDN'T LIFT IT!
AND ONLY I, GASHAKURA, CAN SWING IT!

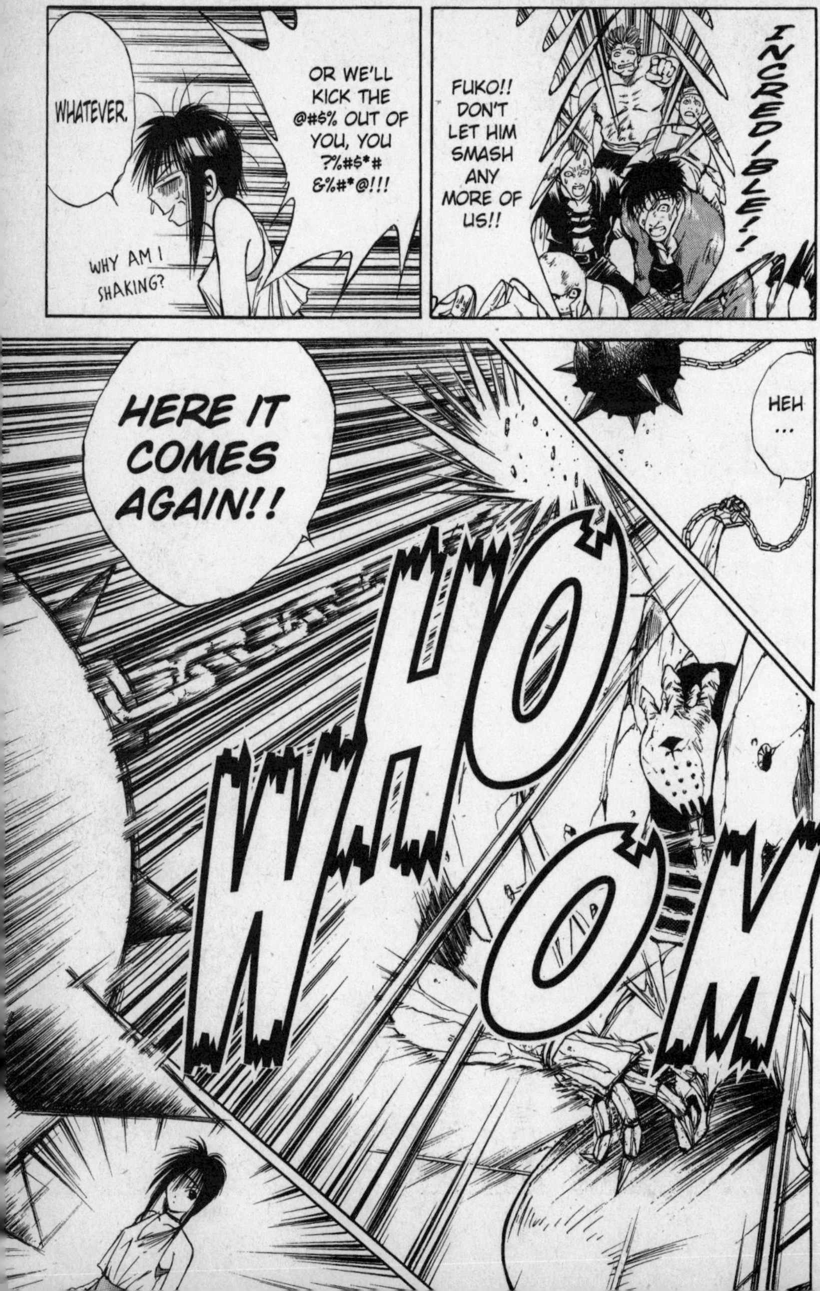
INCREDIBLE!!
FUKO!! DON'T LET HIM SMASH ANY MORE OF US!!
OR WE'LL KICK THE @#$% OUT OF YOU, YOU ?%#$*# &%#*@!!!
WHATEVER.
WHY AM I SHAKING?
HEH ...
HERE IT COMES AGAIN!!
WHOOM

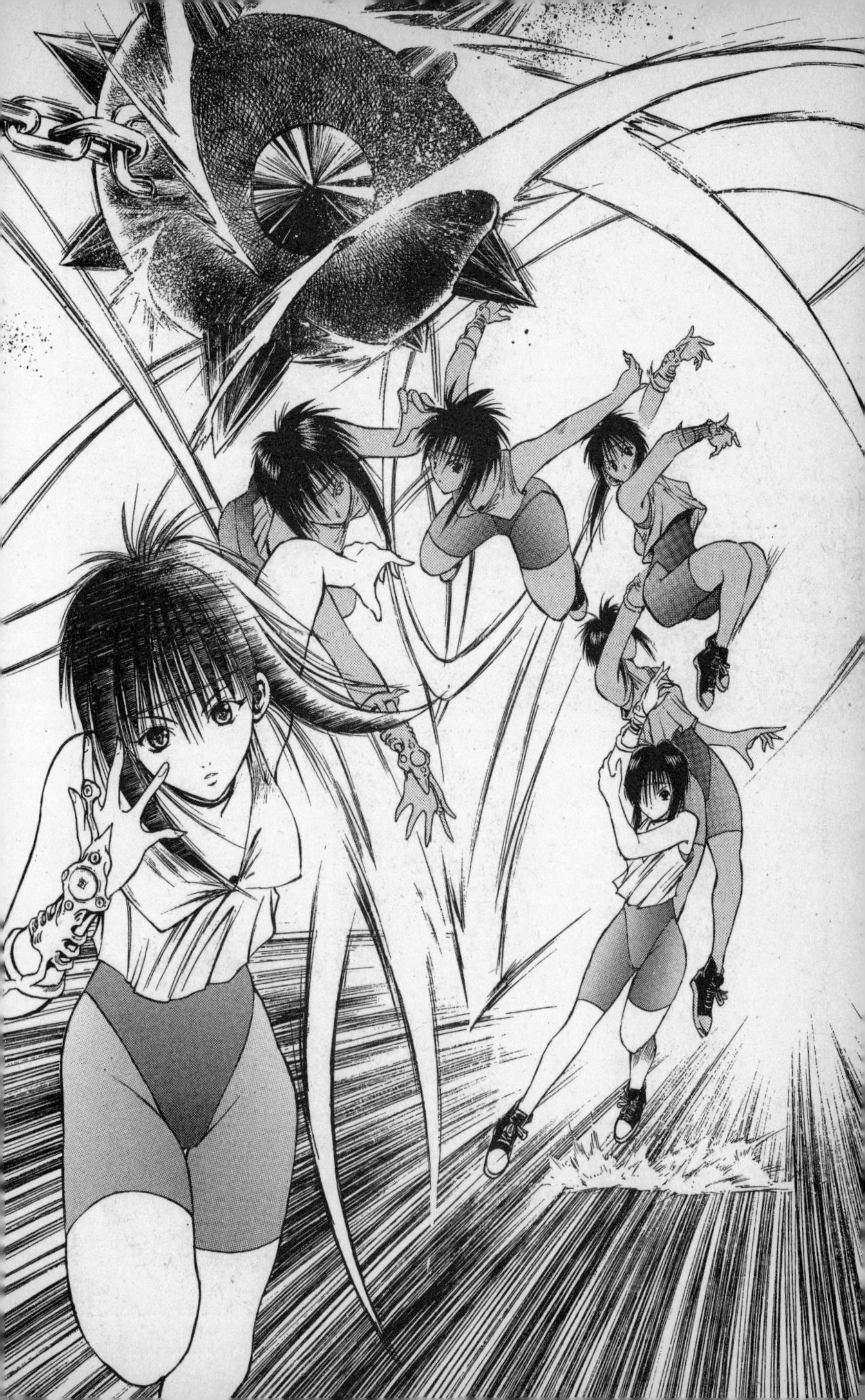

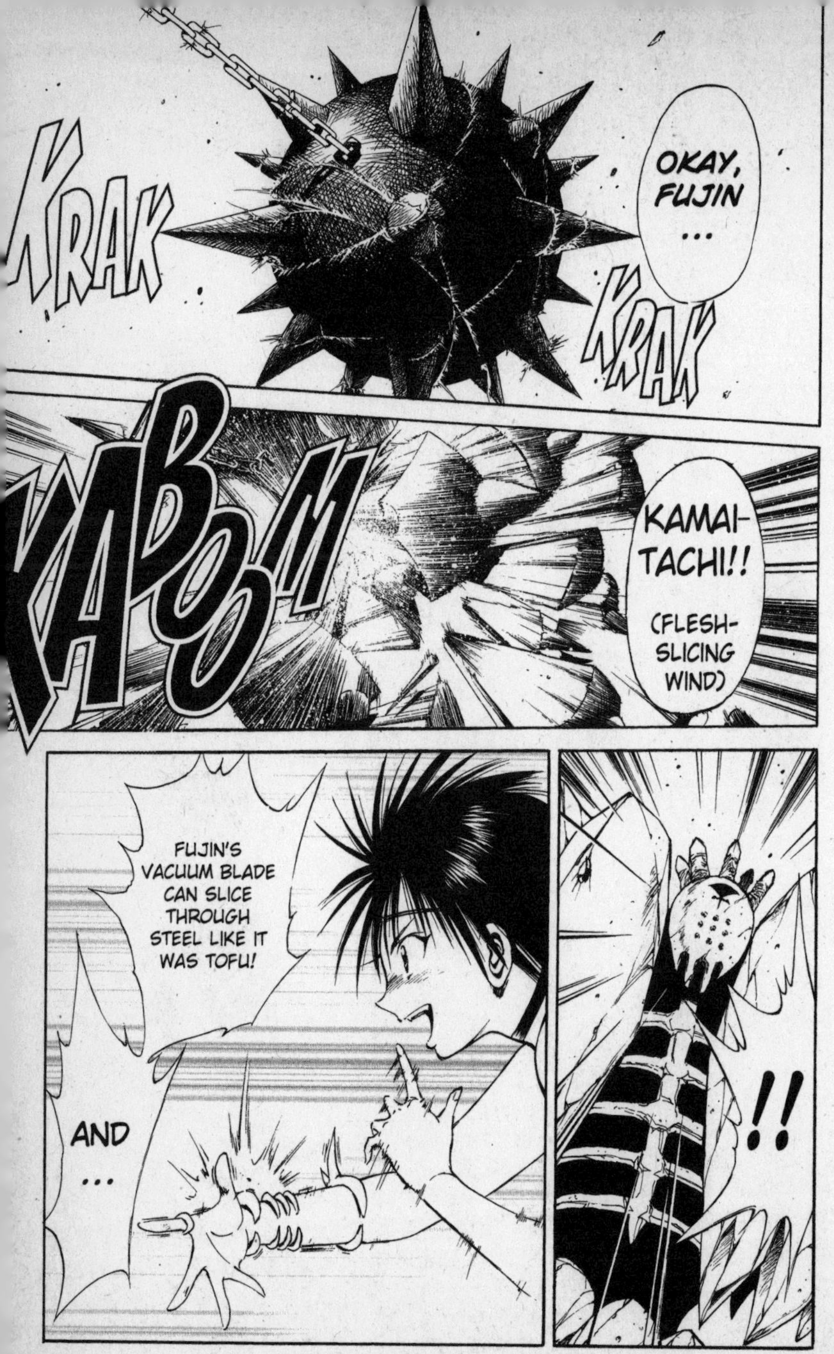
OKAY, FUJIN ...
KRAK
KRAK
KAMAI-TACHI!!
(FLESH-SLICING WIND)
KABOOM
!!
FUJIN'S VACUUM BLADE CAN SLICE THROUGH STEEL LIKE IT WAS TOFU!
AND ...

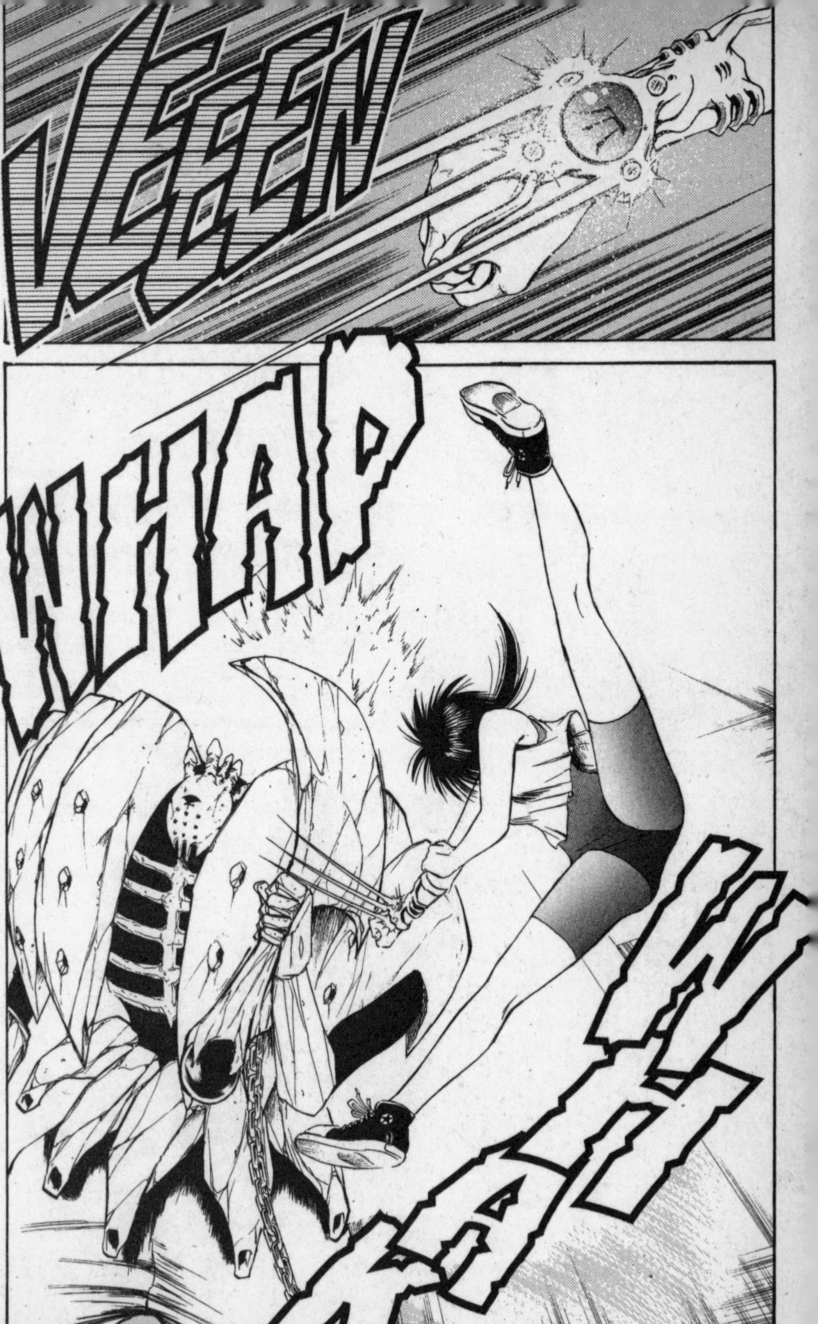
WHAP

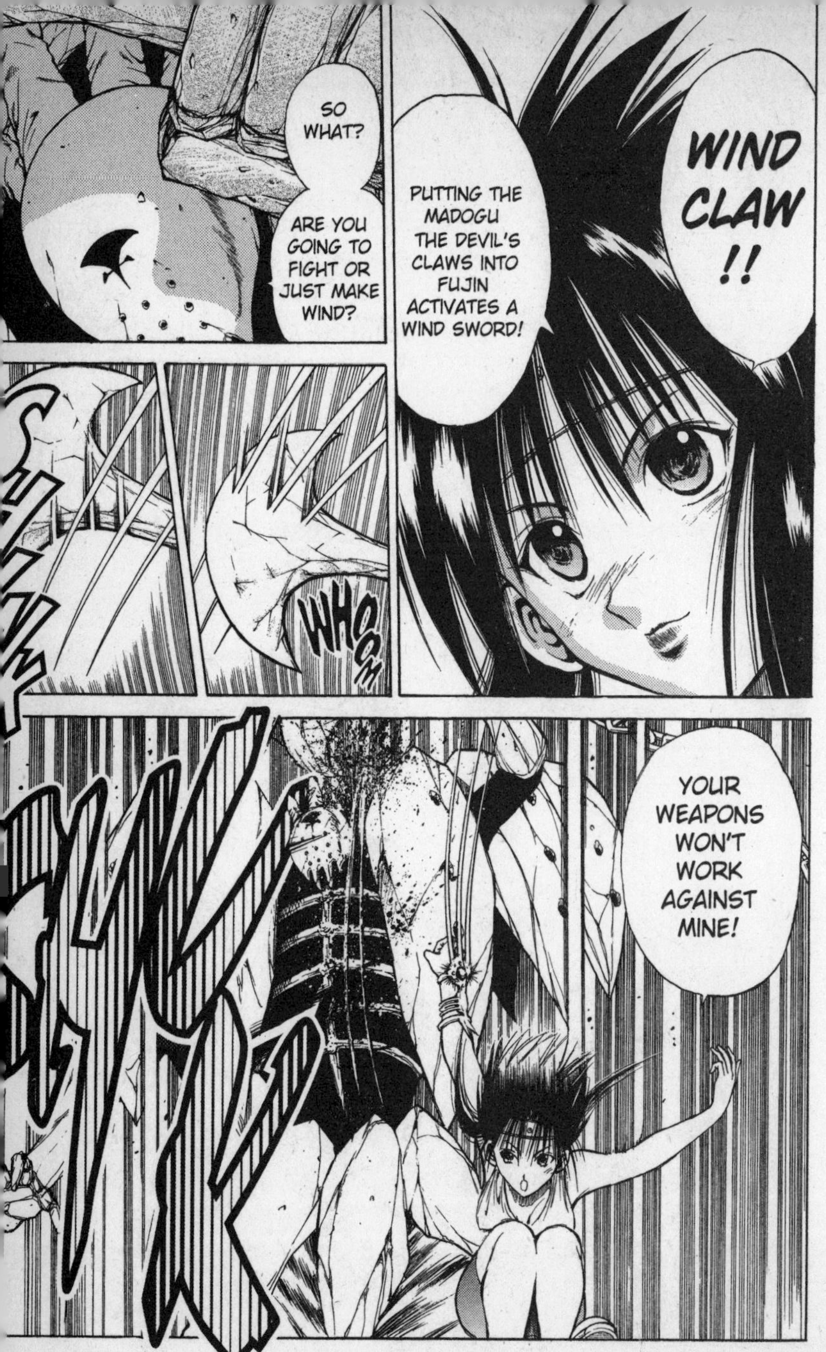
WIND CLAW !!
PUTTING THE MADOGU THE DEVIL'S CLAWS INTO FUJIN ACTIVATES A WIND SWORD!
SO WHAT?
ARE YOU GOING TO FIGHT OR JUST MAKE WIND?
WHOOM
YOUR WEAPONS WON'T WORK AGAINST MINE!

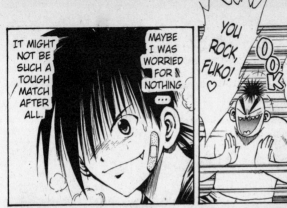

DAMN, SHE'S GOOD!
SHE MUST'VE BEEN PSYCHED FOR THIS ONE!
OOK
OOK
YOU ROCK, FUKO! ♡
MAYBE I WAS WORRIED FOR NOTHING ...
IT MIGHT NOT BE SUCH A TOUGH MATCH AFTER ALL.
...
HEH...
YOU PASS, FUKO!
NOW I'LL GET SERIOUS.

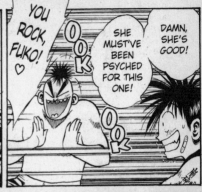

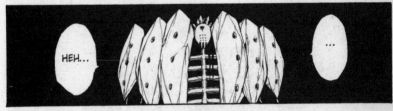

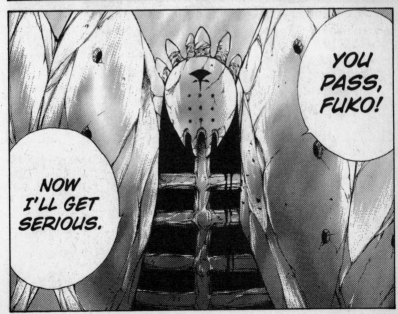

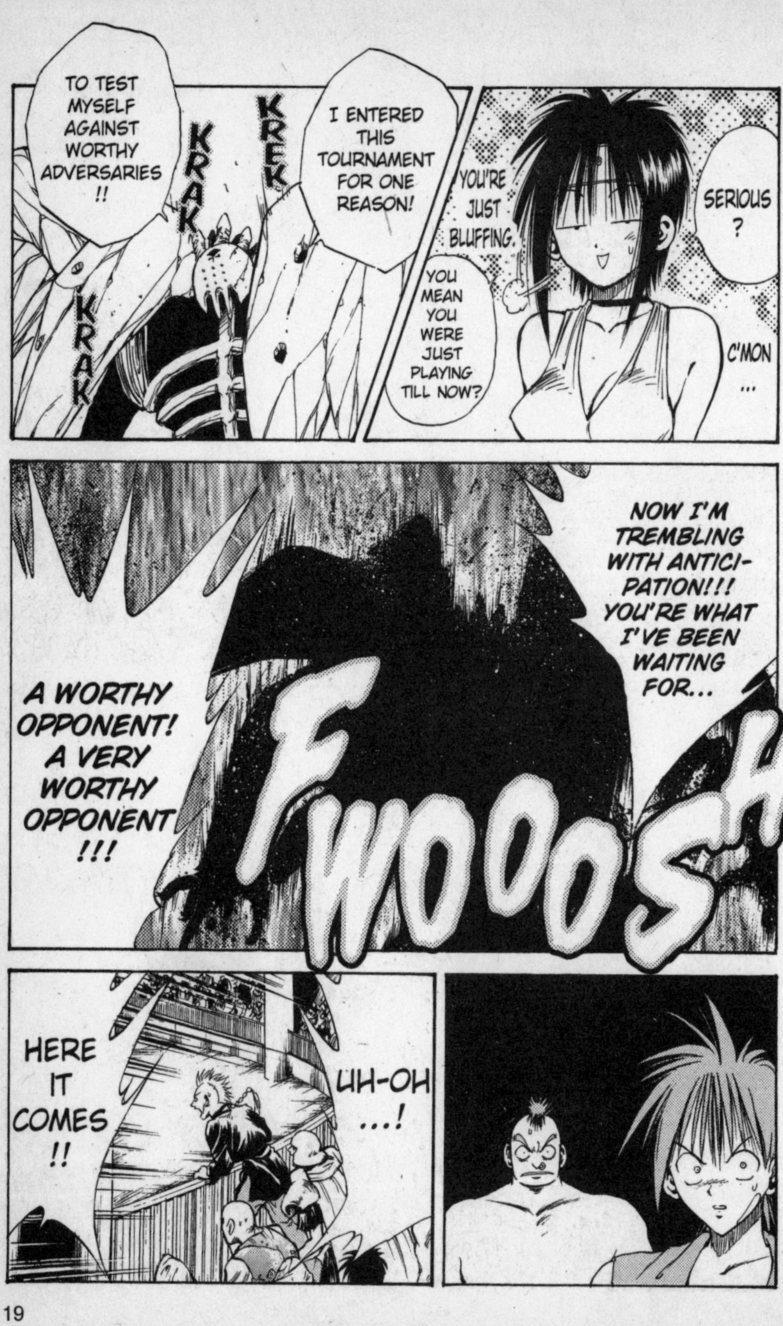
SERIOUS ?
YOU'RE JUST BLUFFING.
C'MON ...
YOU MEAN YOU WERE JUST PLAYING TILL NOW?
KREK
I ENTERED THIS TOURNAMENT FOR ONE REASON!
KRAK
TO TEST MYSELF AGAINST WORTHY ADVERSARIES !!
KRAK
NOW I'M TREMBLING WITH ANTICI-PATION!!! YOU'RE WHAT I'VE BEEN WAITING FOR...
FWOOOSH
A WORTHY OPPONENT! A VERY WORTHY OPPONENT !!!
UH-OH ...!
HERE IT COMES !!

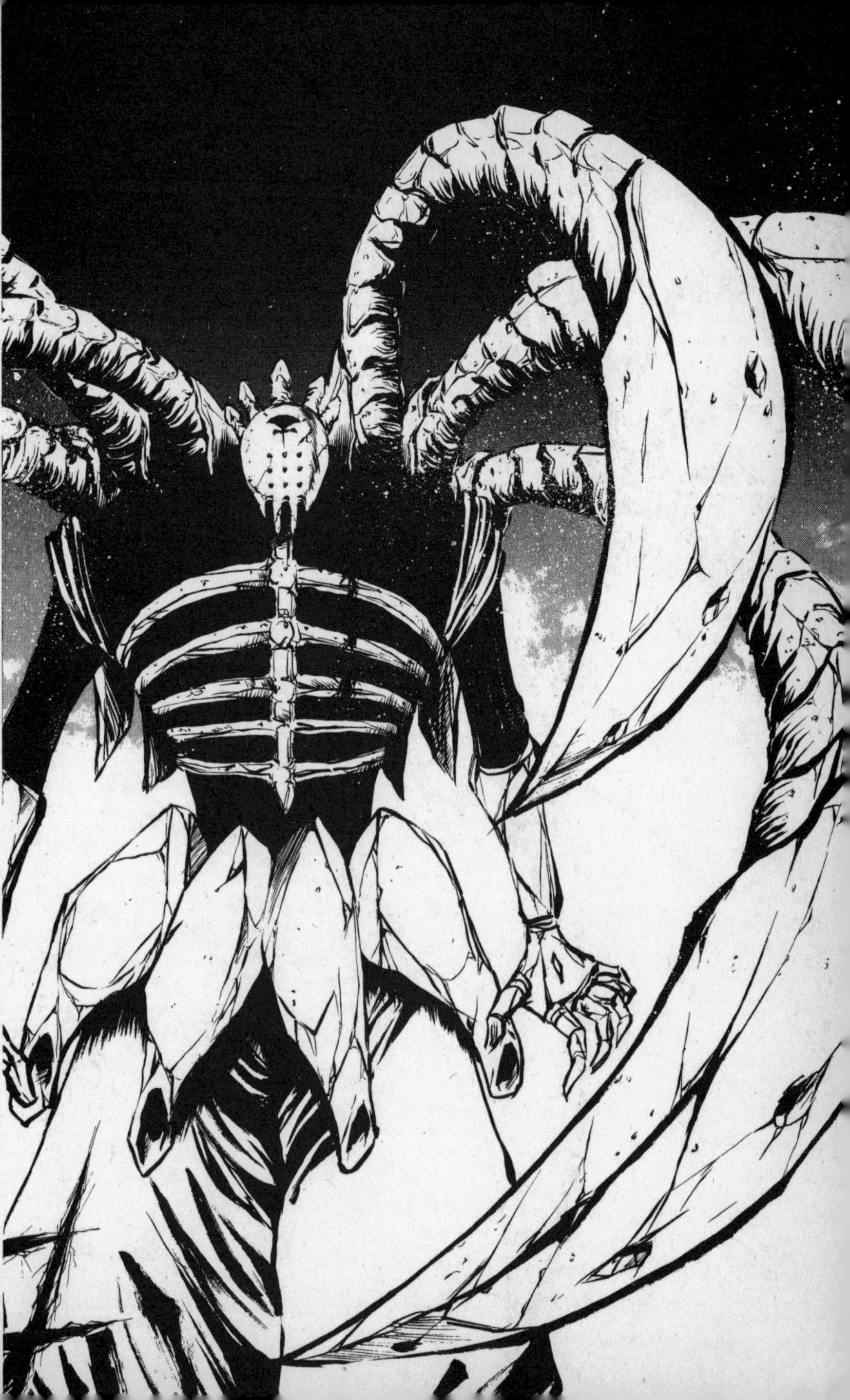

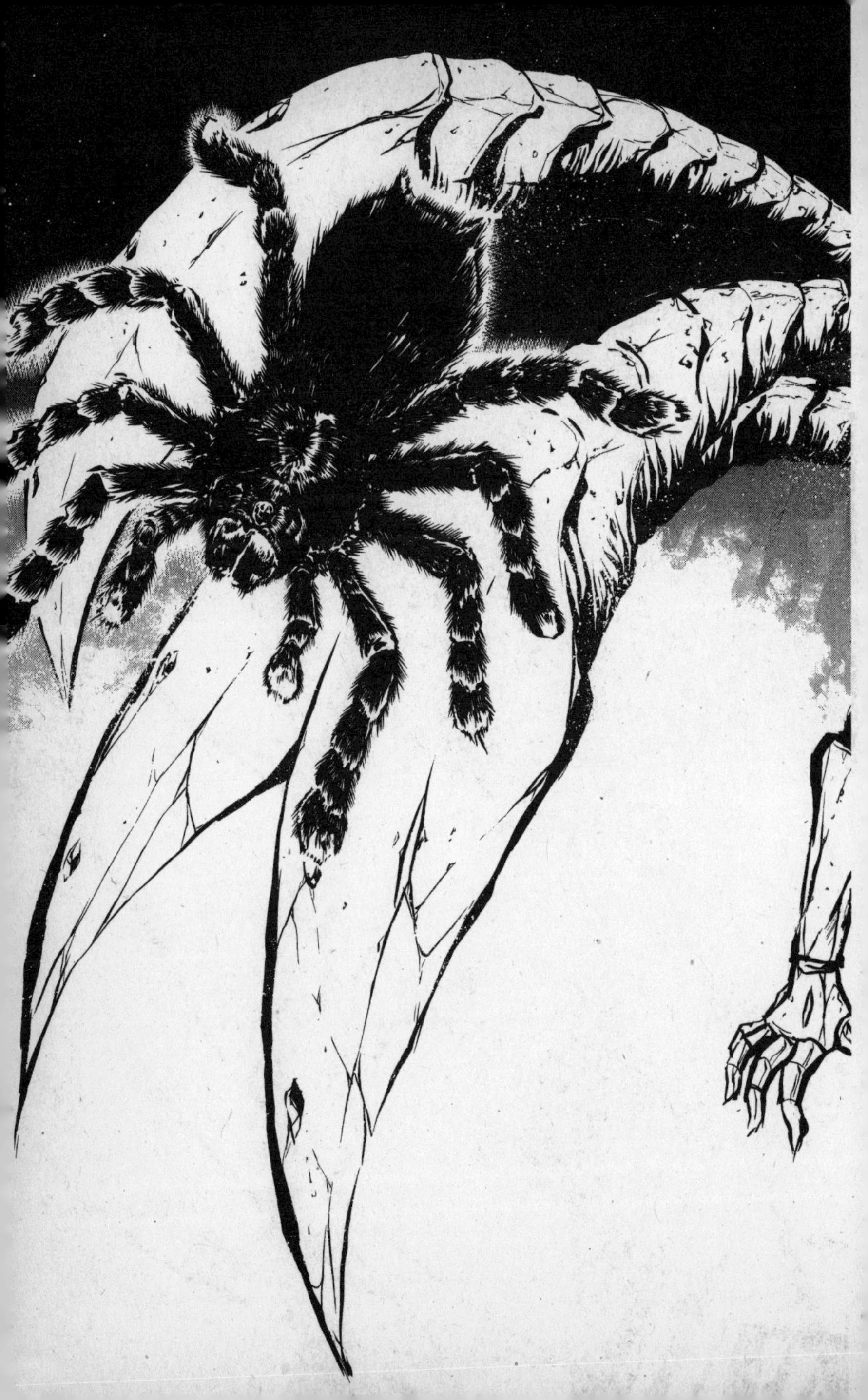

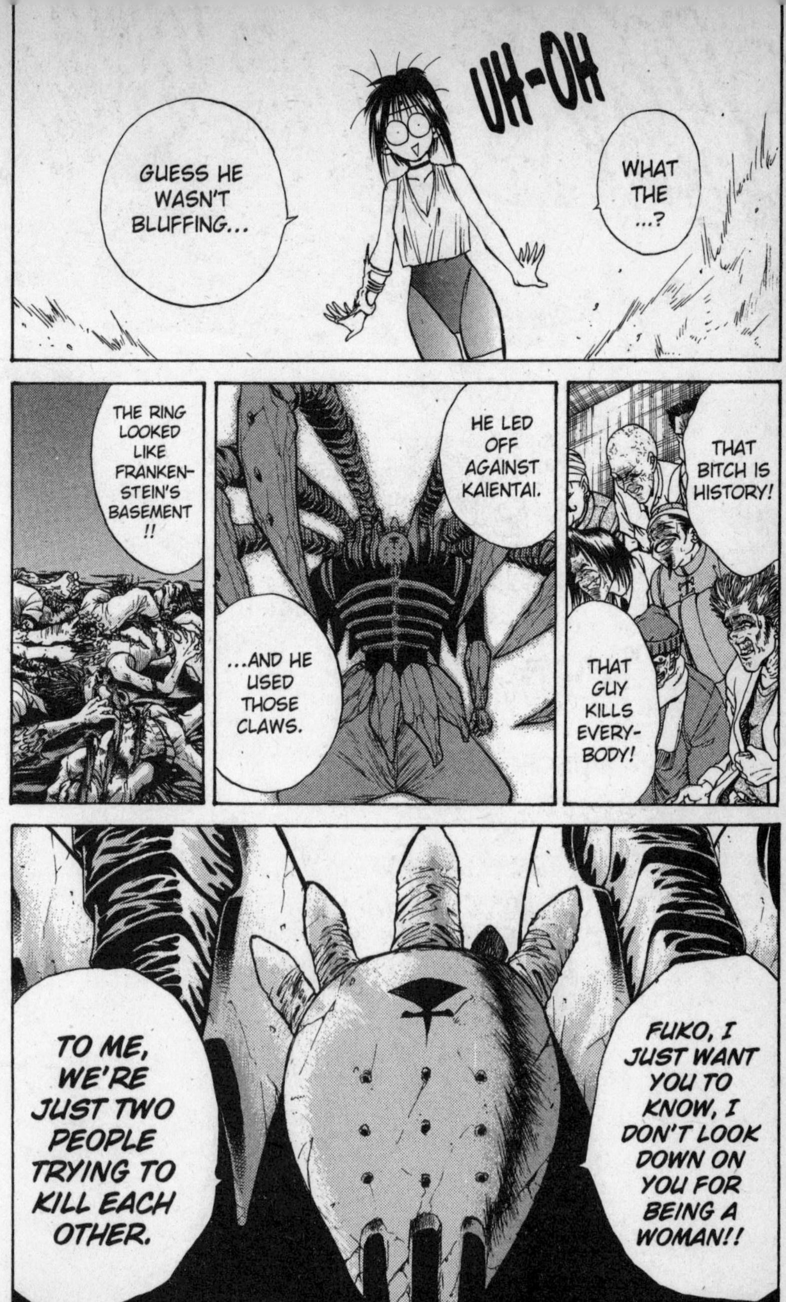
WHAT THE ...?
UH-OH
GUESS HE WASN'T BLUFFING...
THAT BITCH IS HISTORY!
THAT GUY KILLS EVERY-BODY!
HE LED OFF AGAINST KAIENTAI.
...AND HE USED THOSE CLAWS.
THE RING LOOKED LIKE FRANKEN-STEIN'S BASEMENT!!
FUKO, I JUST WANT YOU TO KNOW, I DON'T LOOK DOWN ON YOU FOR BEING A WOMAN!!
TO ME, WE'RE JUST TWO PEOPLE TRYING TO KILL EACH OTHER.

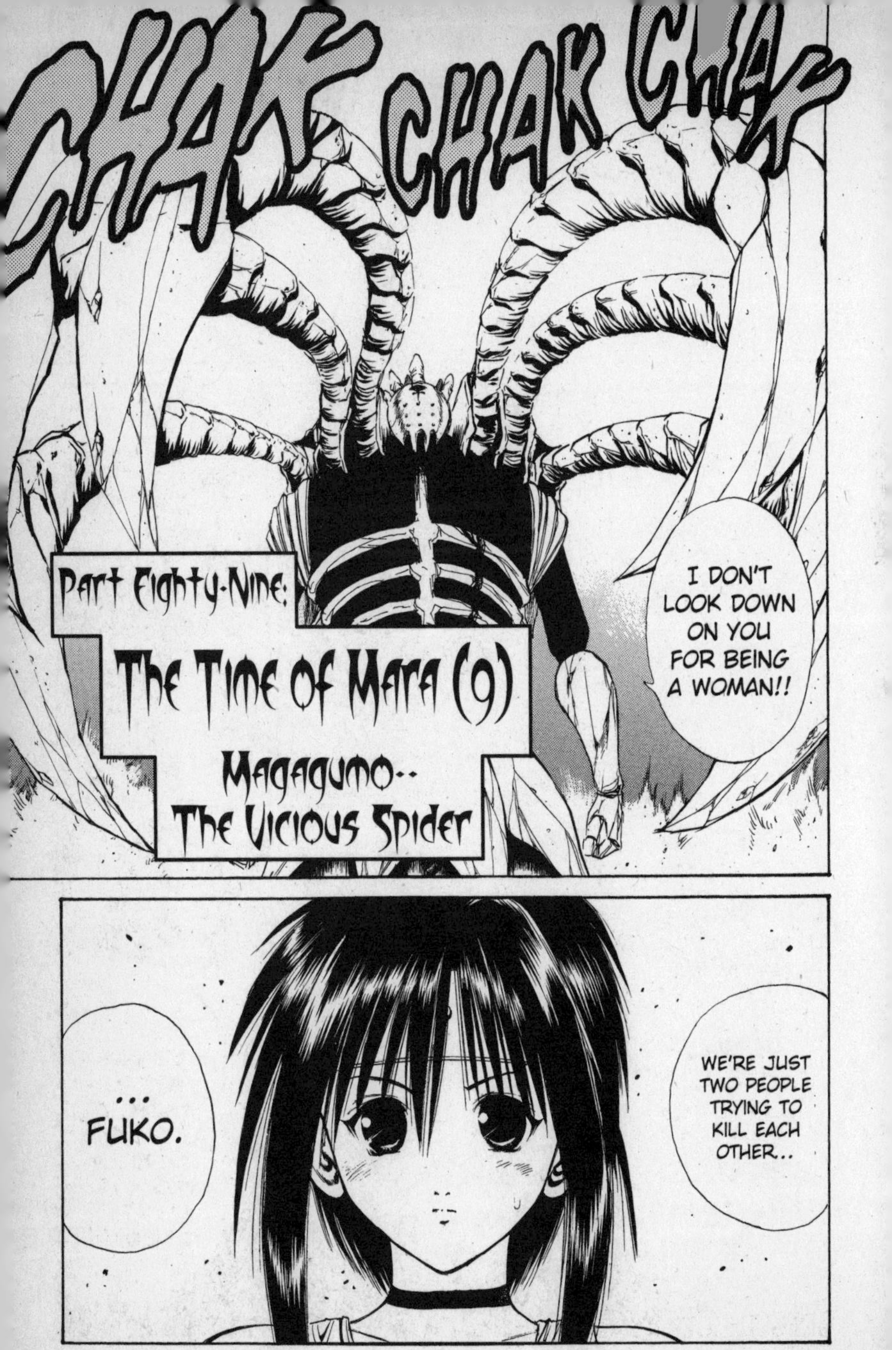
CHAK CHAK CHAK
I DON'T LOOK DOWN ON YOU FOR BEING A WOMAN!!
Part Eighty-Nine:
The Time of Mara (9)
Magagumo-- The Vicious Spider
WE'RE JUST TWO PEOPLE TRYING TO KILL EACH OTHER...
... FUKO.

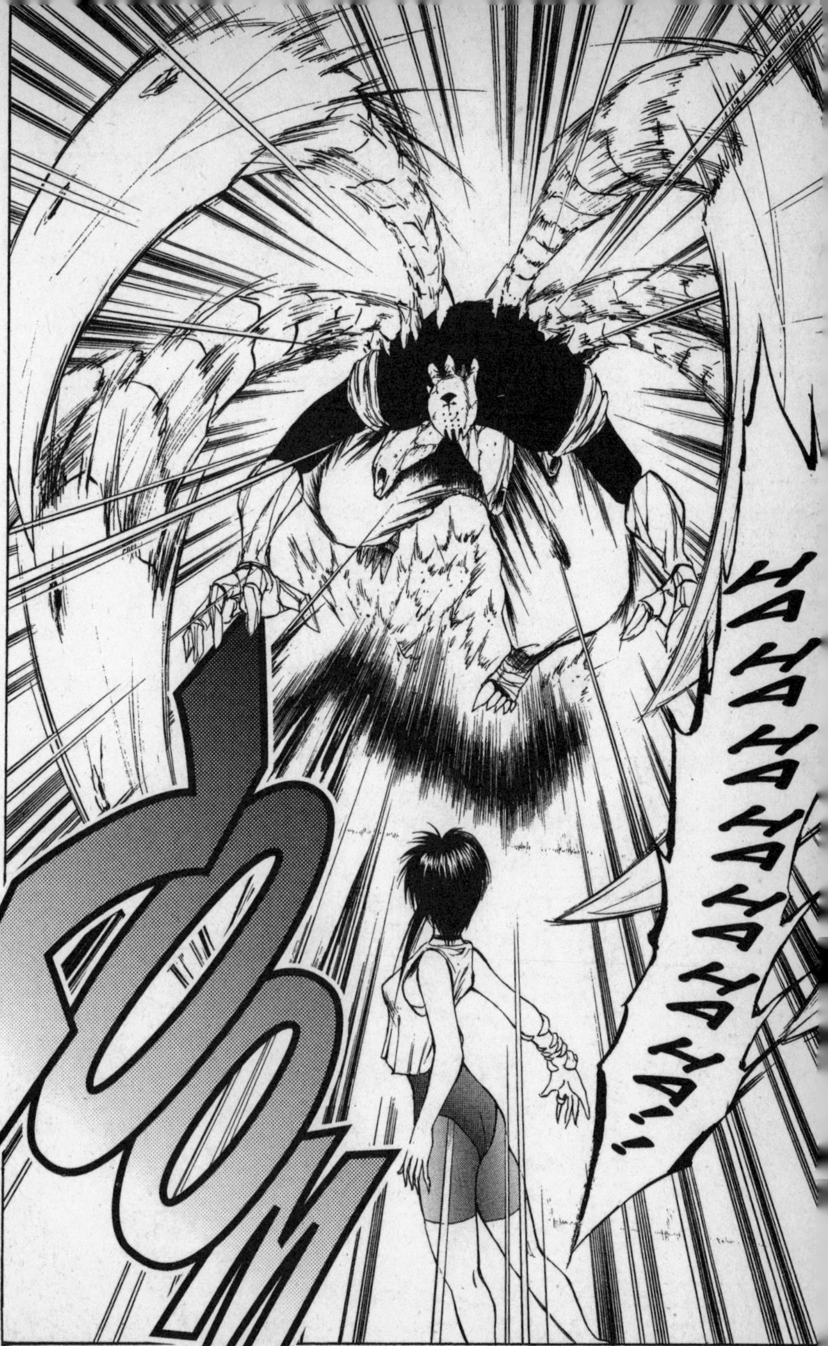
HAHAHAHAHAHAHA!!
DOOM

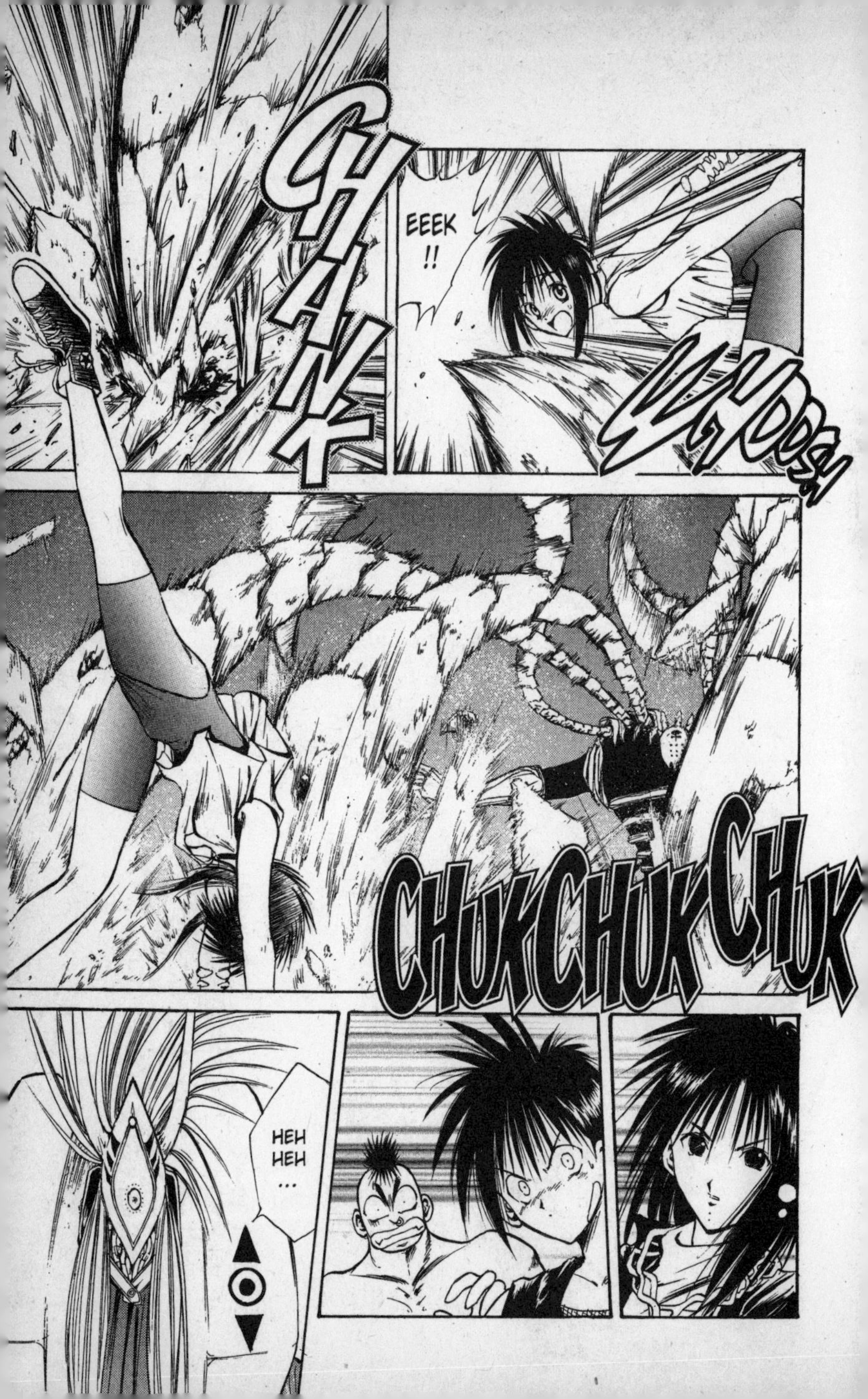
EEEK !!
WHOOSH
CHANK
CHUK CHUK CHUK
HEH HEH ...

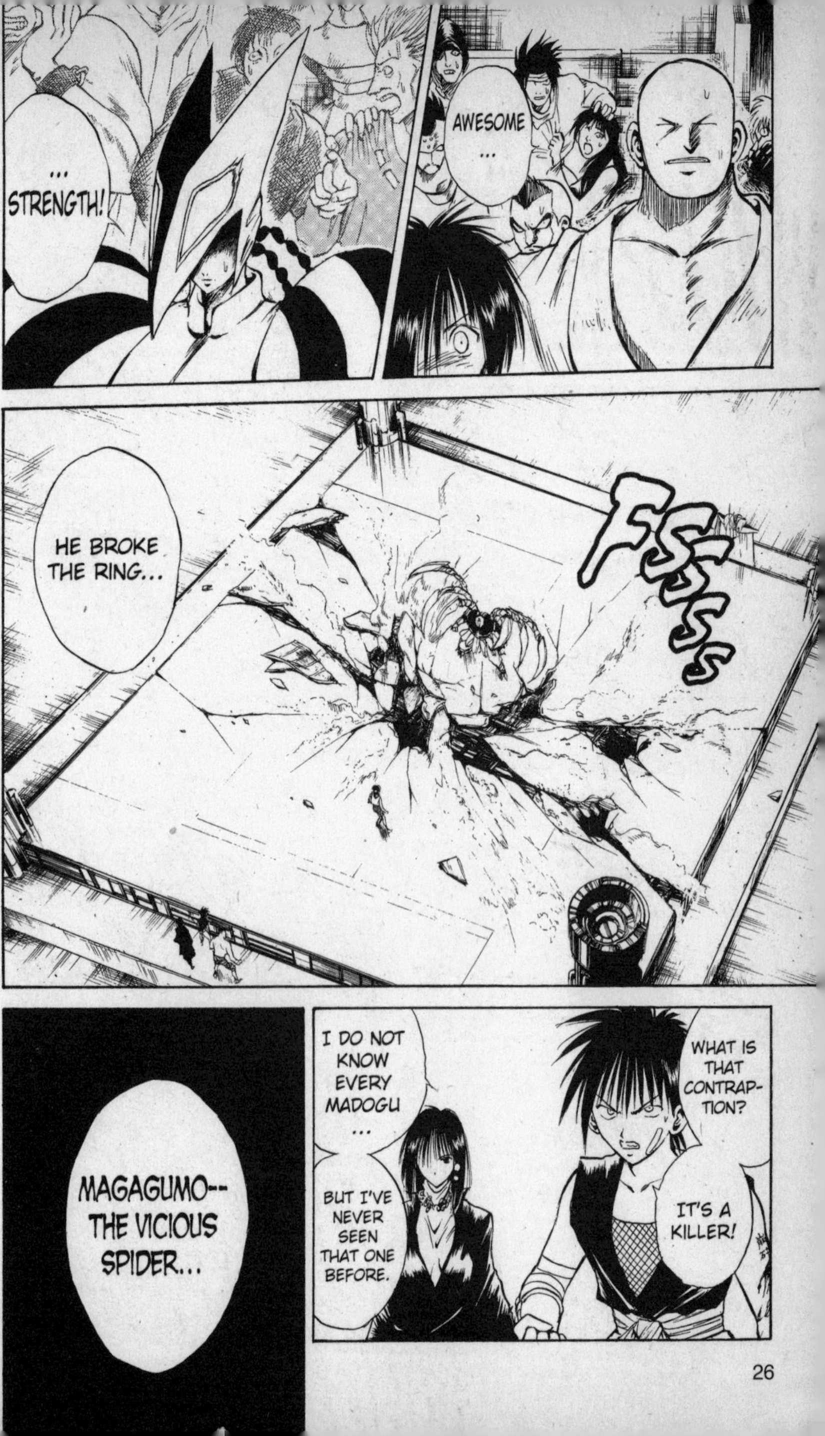
AWESOME ...
... STRENGTH!
HE BROKE THE RING...
FSSSS
WHAT IS THAT CONTRAP-TION?
I DO NOT KNOW EVERY MADOGU ...
IT'S A KILLER!
BUT I'VE NEVER SEEN THAT ONE BEFORE.
MAGAGUMO-- THE VICIOUS SPIDER...

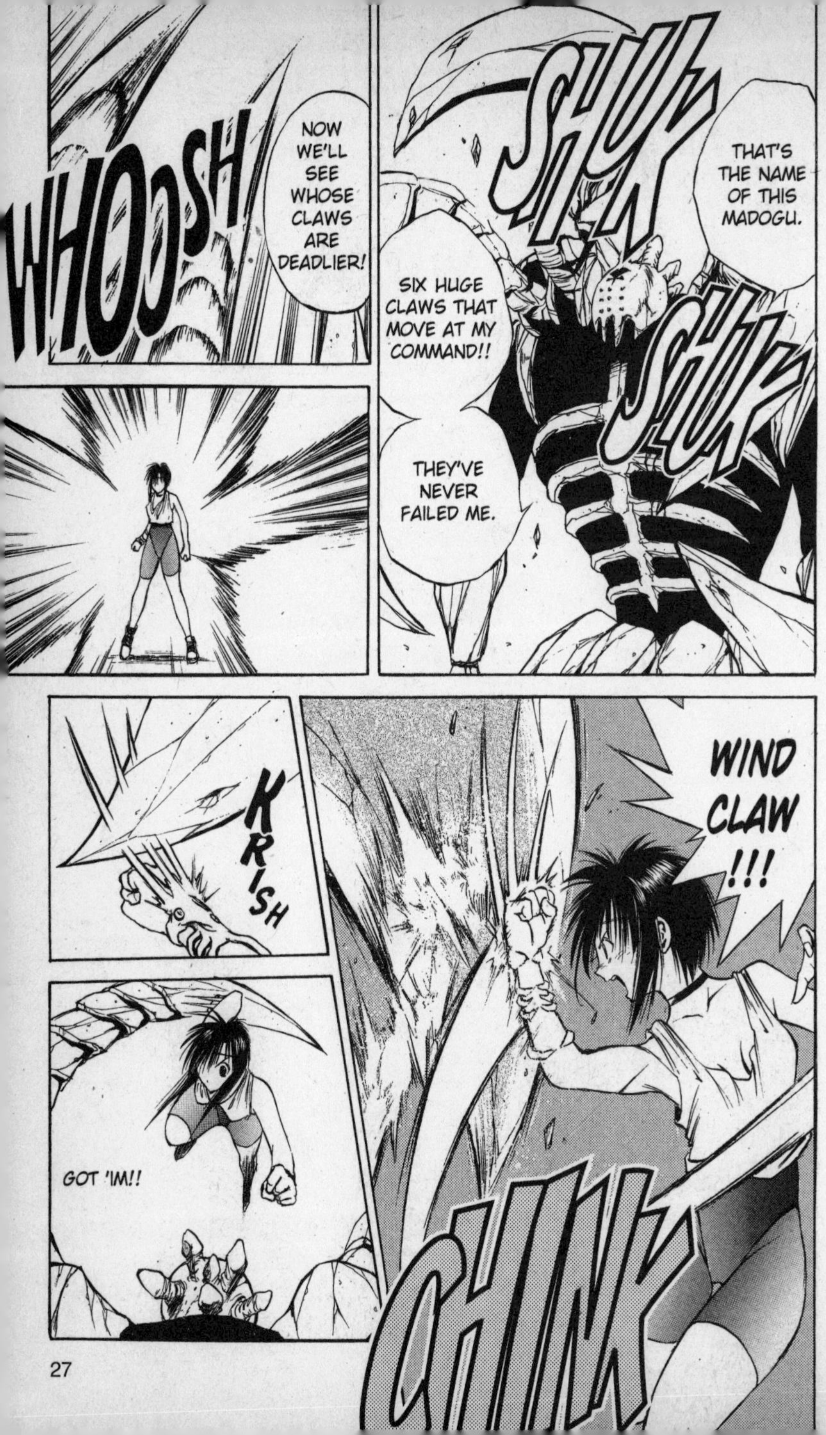

THAT'S THE NAME OF THIS MADOGU.
SHYN
SCHK
SIX HUGE CLAWS THAT MOVE AT MY COMMAND!!
THEY'VE NEVER FAILED ME.
NOW WE'LL SEE WHOSE CLAWS ARE DEADLIER!
WHOOSH
WIND CLAW!!!
CHINK
KRISH
GOT 'IM!!

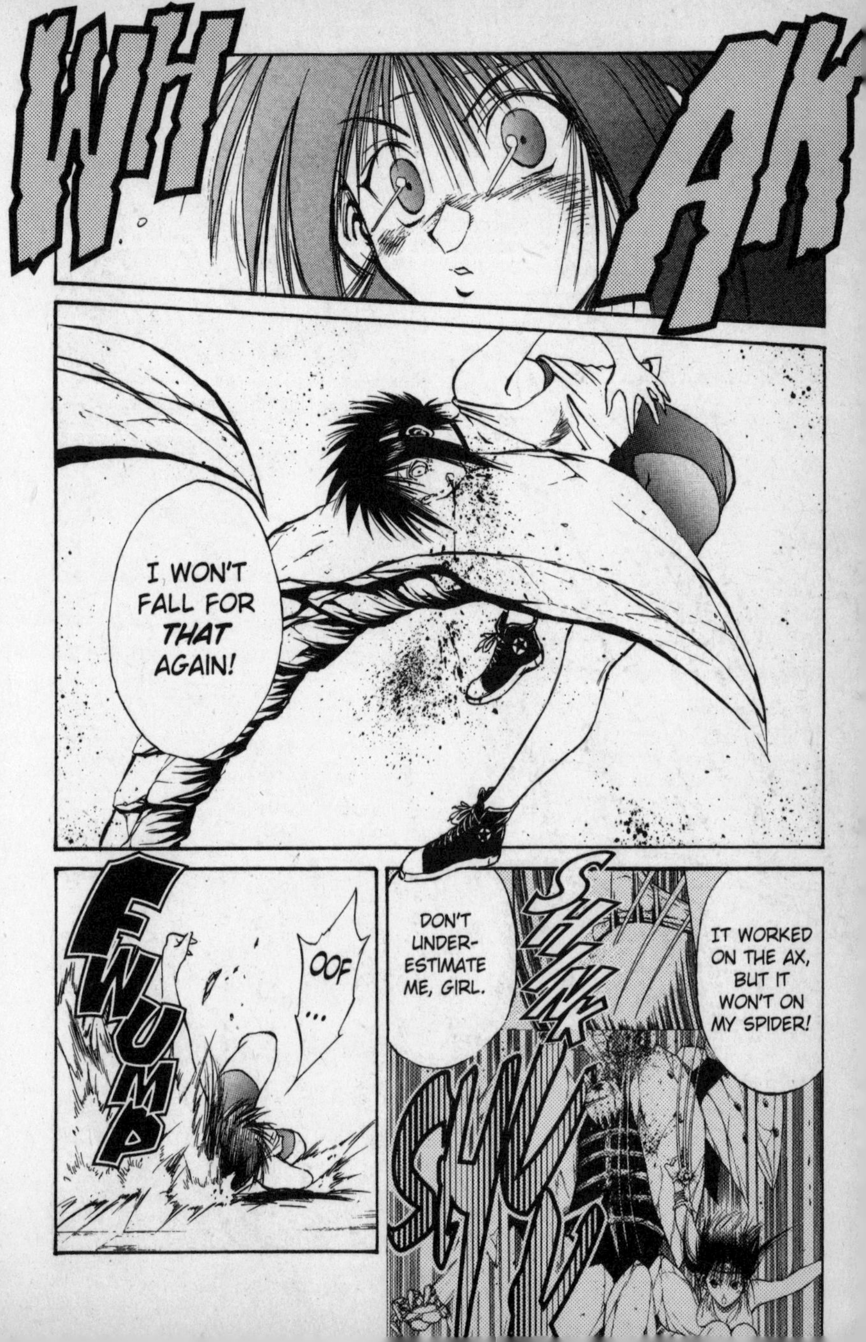
WHAK
I WON'T FALL FOR THAT AGAIN!
IT WORKED ON THE AX, BUT IT WON'T ON MY SPIDER!
DON'T UNDER-ESTIMATE ME, GIRL.
FWUMP
OOF...

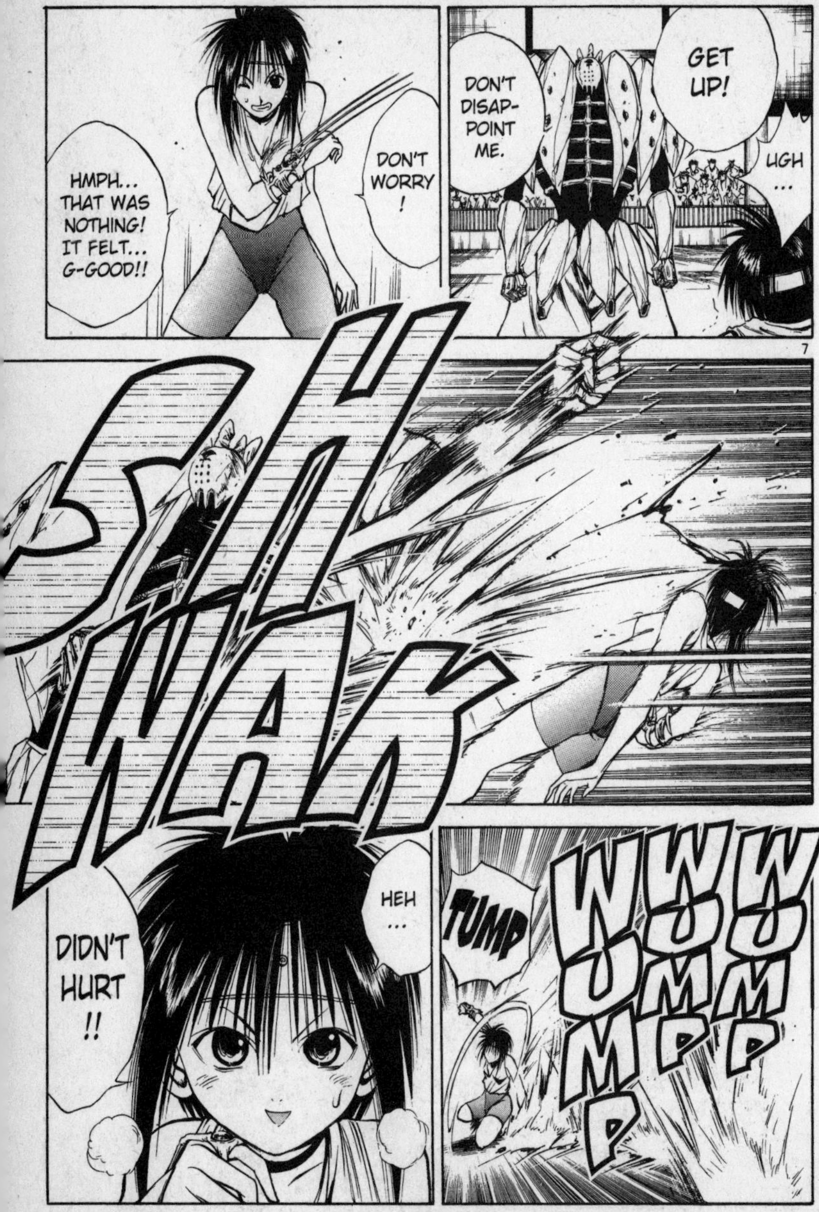
GET UP!
DON'T DISAP-POINT ME.
UGH ...
DON'T WORRY!
HMPH... THAT WAS NOTHING! IT FELT... G-GOOD!!
7
WHAK
WUMP
WUMP
WUMP
TUMP
HEH ...
DIDN'T HURT !!

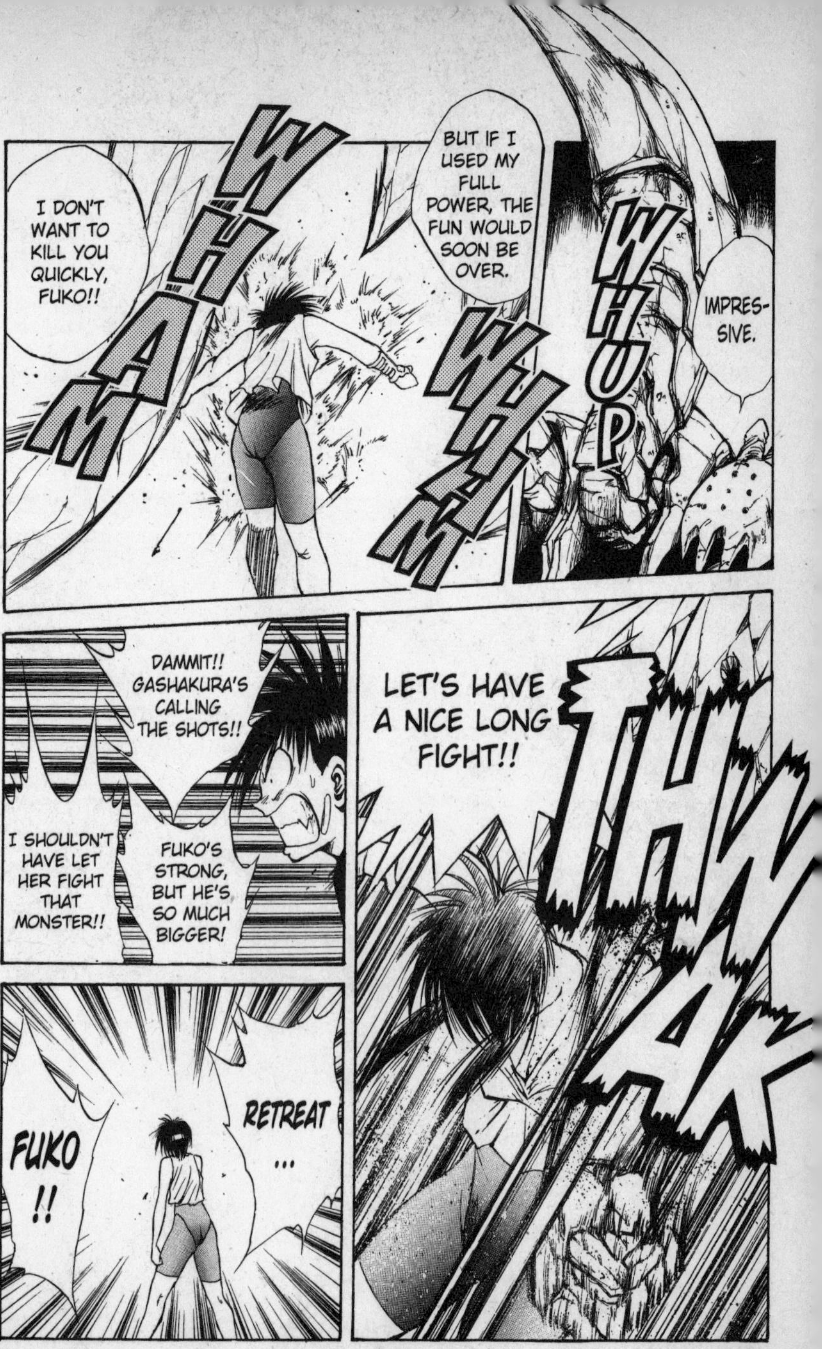
IMPRESSIVE.
WHUP
BUT IF I USED MY FULL POWER, THE FUN WOULD SOON BE OVER.
WHAM
I DON'T WANT TO KILL YOU QUICKLY, FUKO!!
WHAM
LET'S HAVE A NICE LONG FIGHT!!
THWAK
DAMMIT!! GASHAKURA'S CALLING THE SHOTS!!
FUKO'S STRONG, BUT HE'S SO MUCH BIGGER!
I SHOULDN'T HAVE LET HER FIGHT THAT MONSTER!!
RETREAT ...
FUKO !!

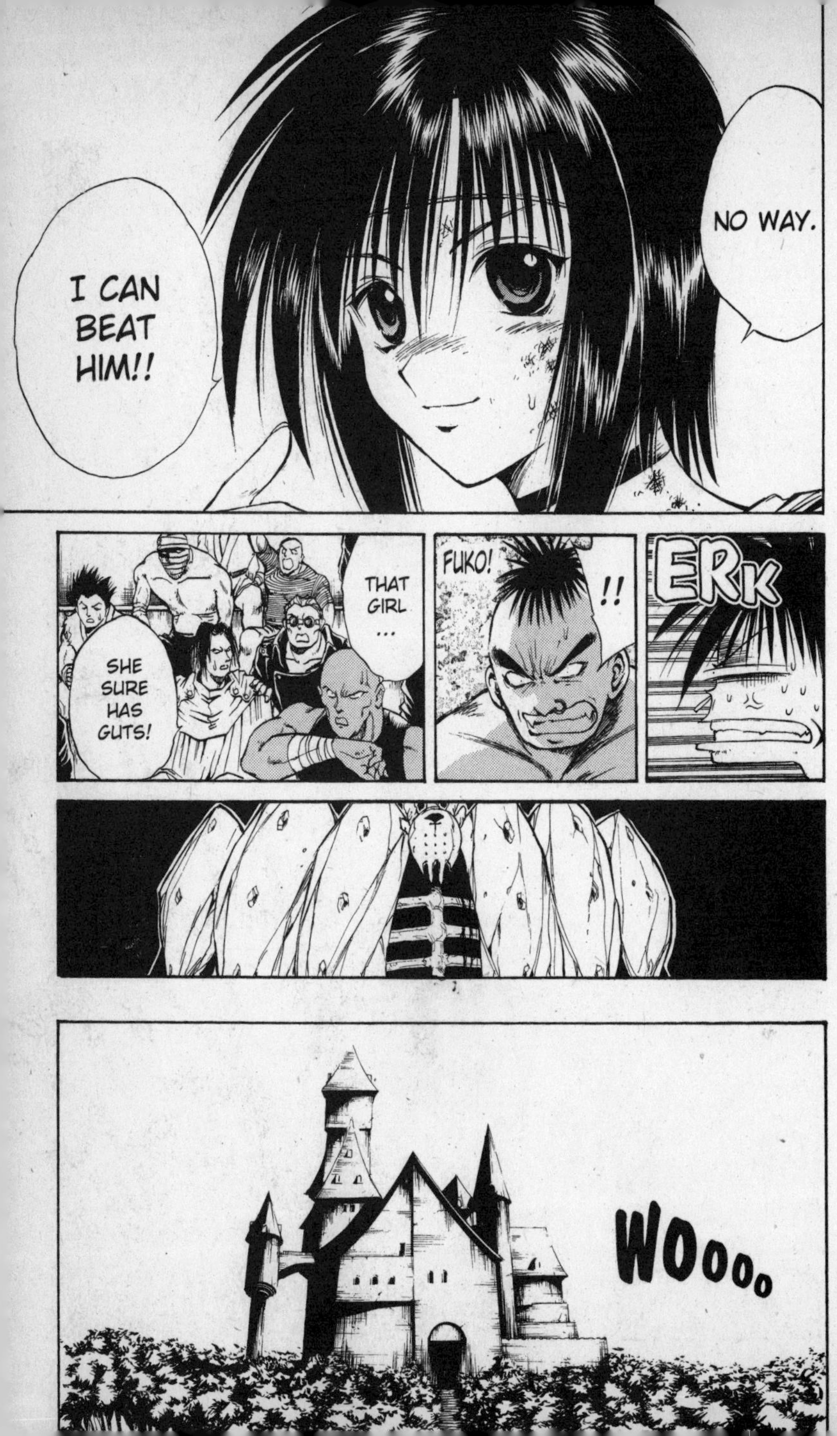
NO WAY.
I CAN BEAT HIM!!
ERK
FUKO!
!!
THAT GIRL ...
SHE SURE HAS GUTS!
WOOOO

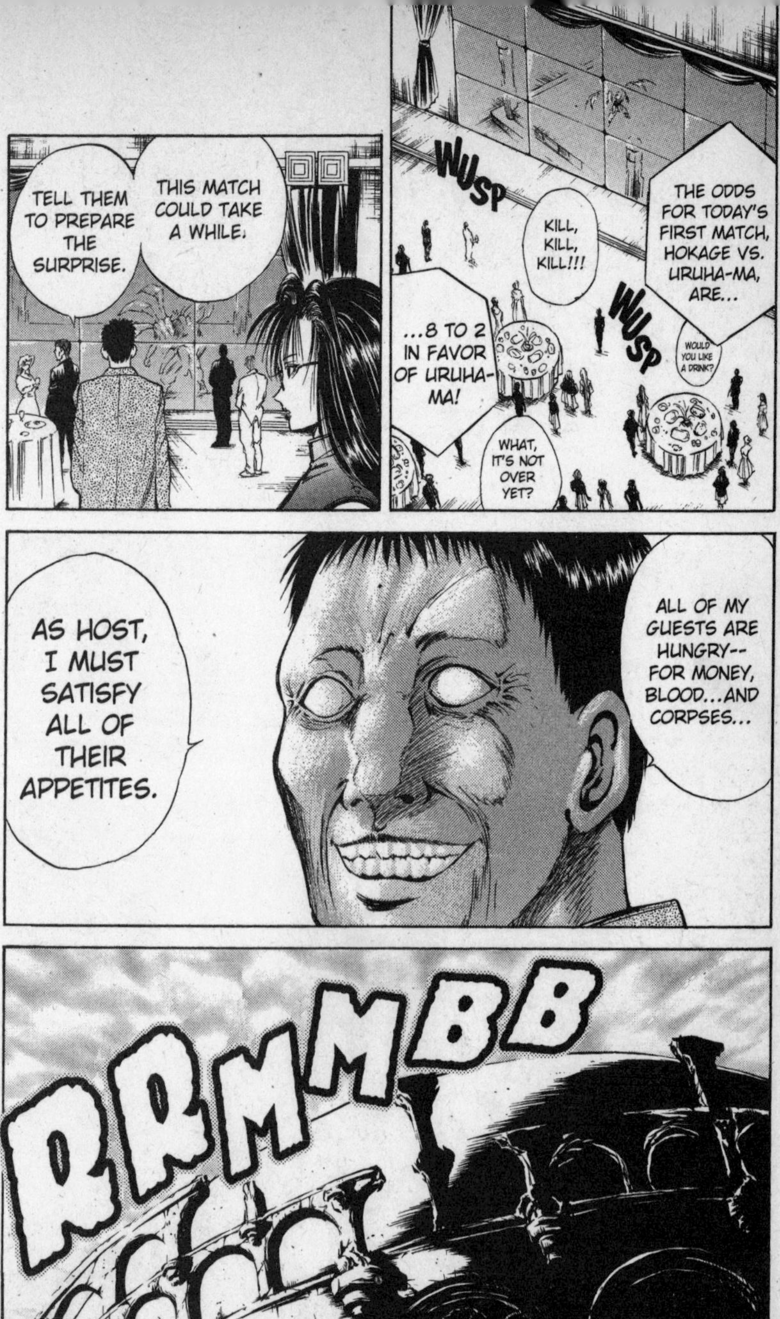

THE ODDS FOR TODAY'S FIRST MATCH, HOKAGE VS. URUHA-MA, ARE...
WUSP
KILL, KILL, KILL!!!
WUSP
WOULD YOU LIKE A DRINK?
...8 TO 2 IN FAVOR OF URUHA-MA!
WHAT, IT'S NOT OVER YET?
THIS MATCH COULD TAKE A WHILE.
TELL THEM TO PREPARE THE SURPRISE.
ALL OF MY GUESTS ARE HUNGRY-- FOR MONEY, BLOOD...AND CORPSES...
AS HOST, I MUST SATISFY ALL OF THEIR APPETITES.
RRMMBB

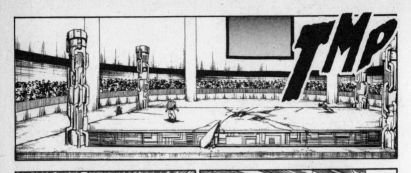

TMP

YOU CAN'T WIN!

KAMAITACHI!!

KRESH KRESH KRESH

BAM

THE MAGAGUMO IS CLAD IN STEEL ARMOR.

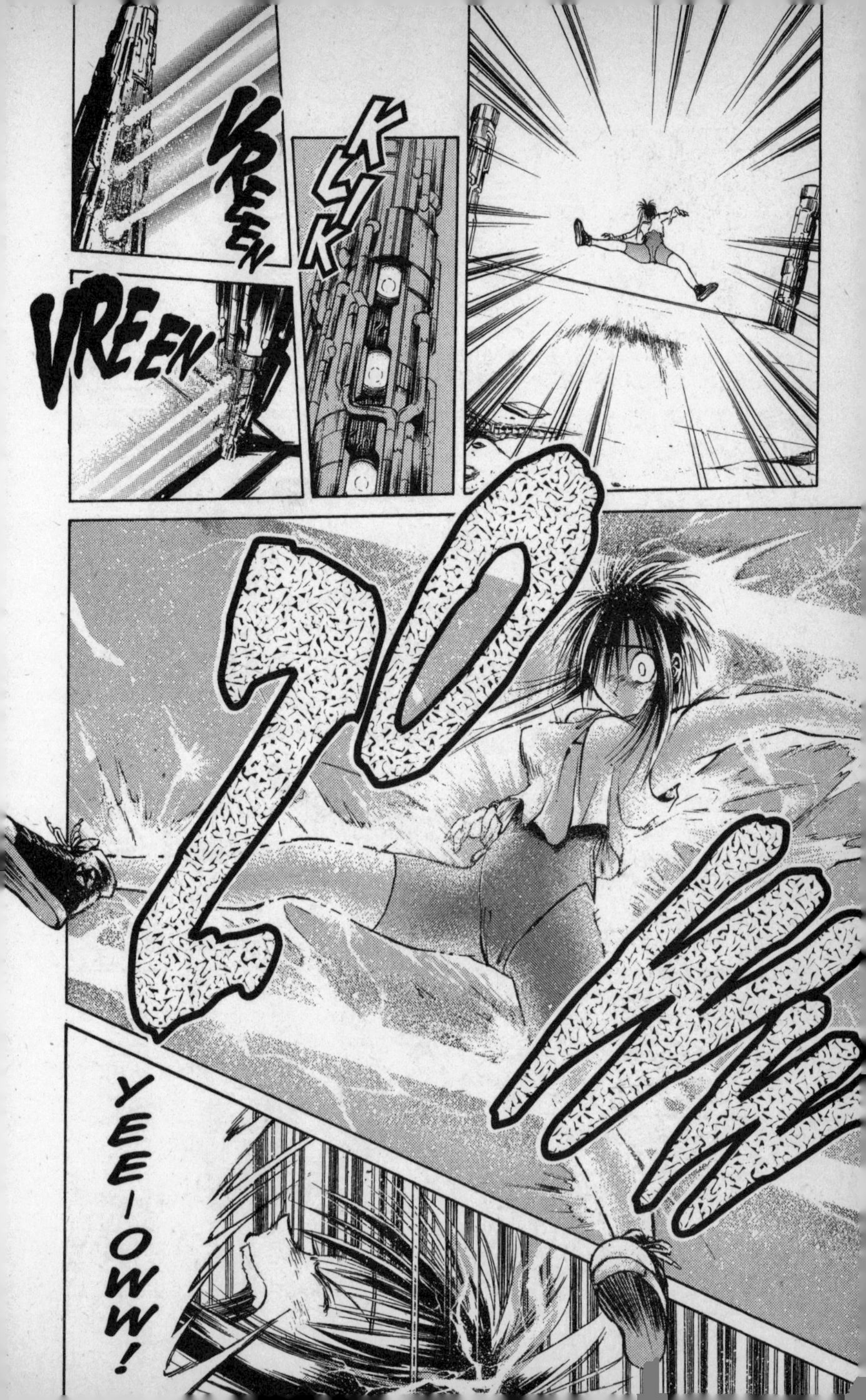
KLIK
VREEN
VREEN
YEEE-IOWW!

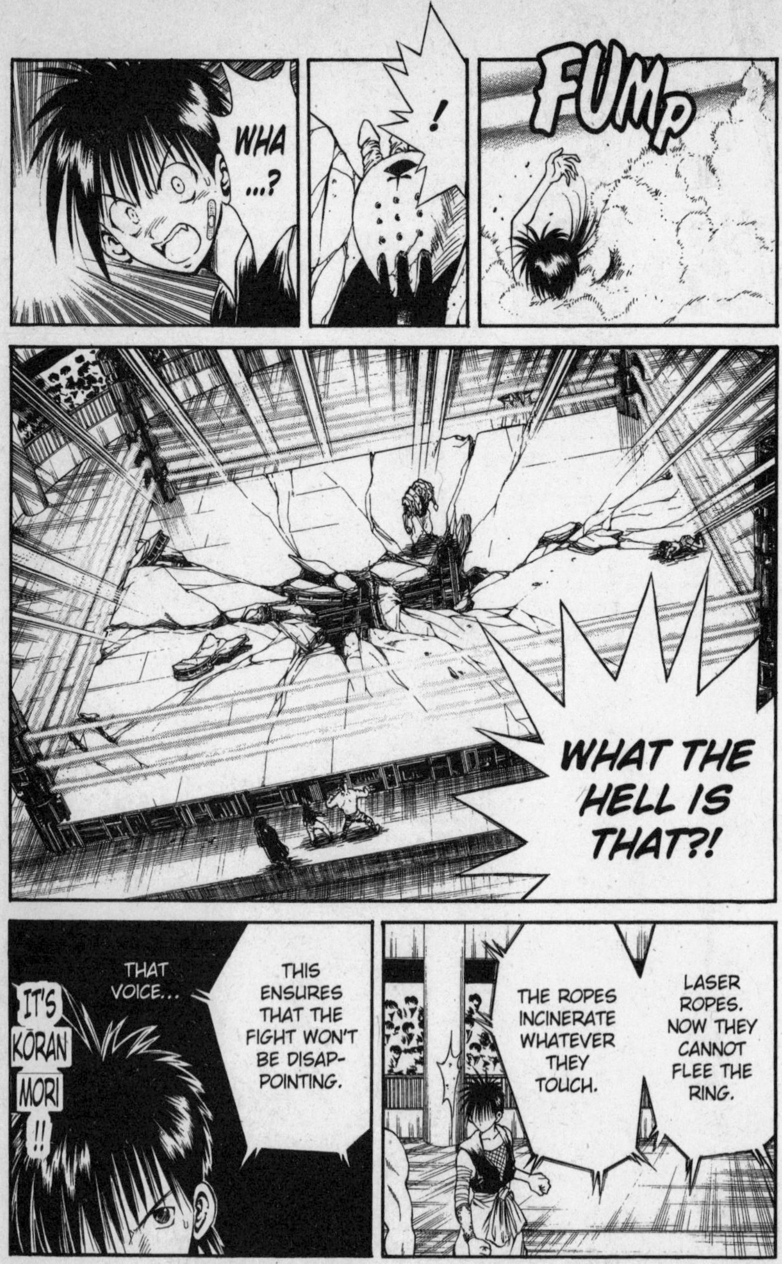
FUMP
!
WHA ...?
WHAT THE HELL IS THAT?!
LASER ROPES. NOW THEY CANNOT FLEE THE RING.
THE ROPES INCINERATE WHATEVER THEY TOUCH.
THIS ENSURES THAT THE FIGHT WON'T BE DISAP-POINTING.
THAT VOICE...
IT'S KŌRAN MORI !!

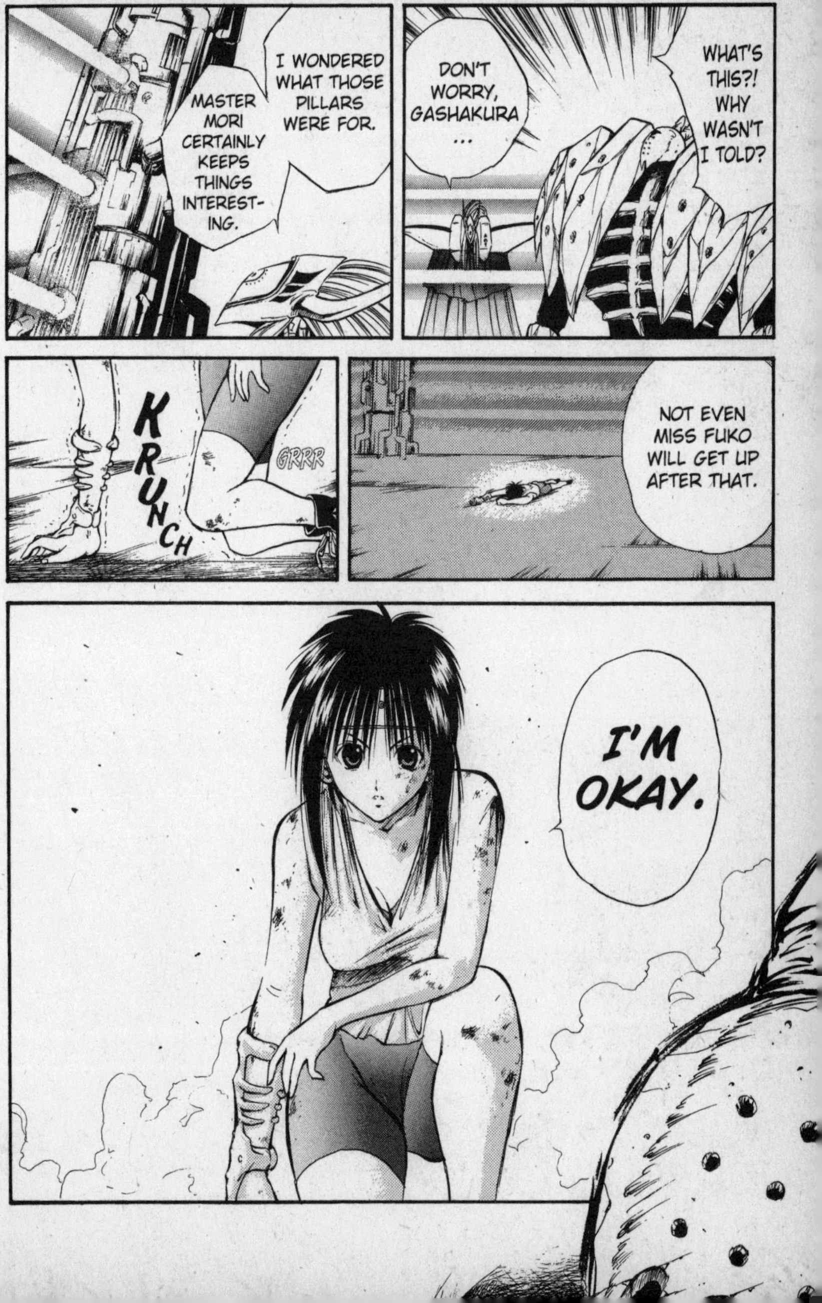
WHAT'S THIS?! WHY WASN'T I TOLD?
DON'T WORRY, GASHAKURA ...
I WONDERED WHAT THOSE PILLARS WERE FOR.
MASTER MORI CERTAINLY KEEPS THINGS INTEREST-ING.
NOT EVEN MISS FUKO WILL GET UP AFTER THAT.
KRUNCH
GRRR
I'M OKAY.

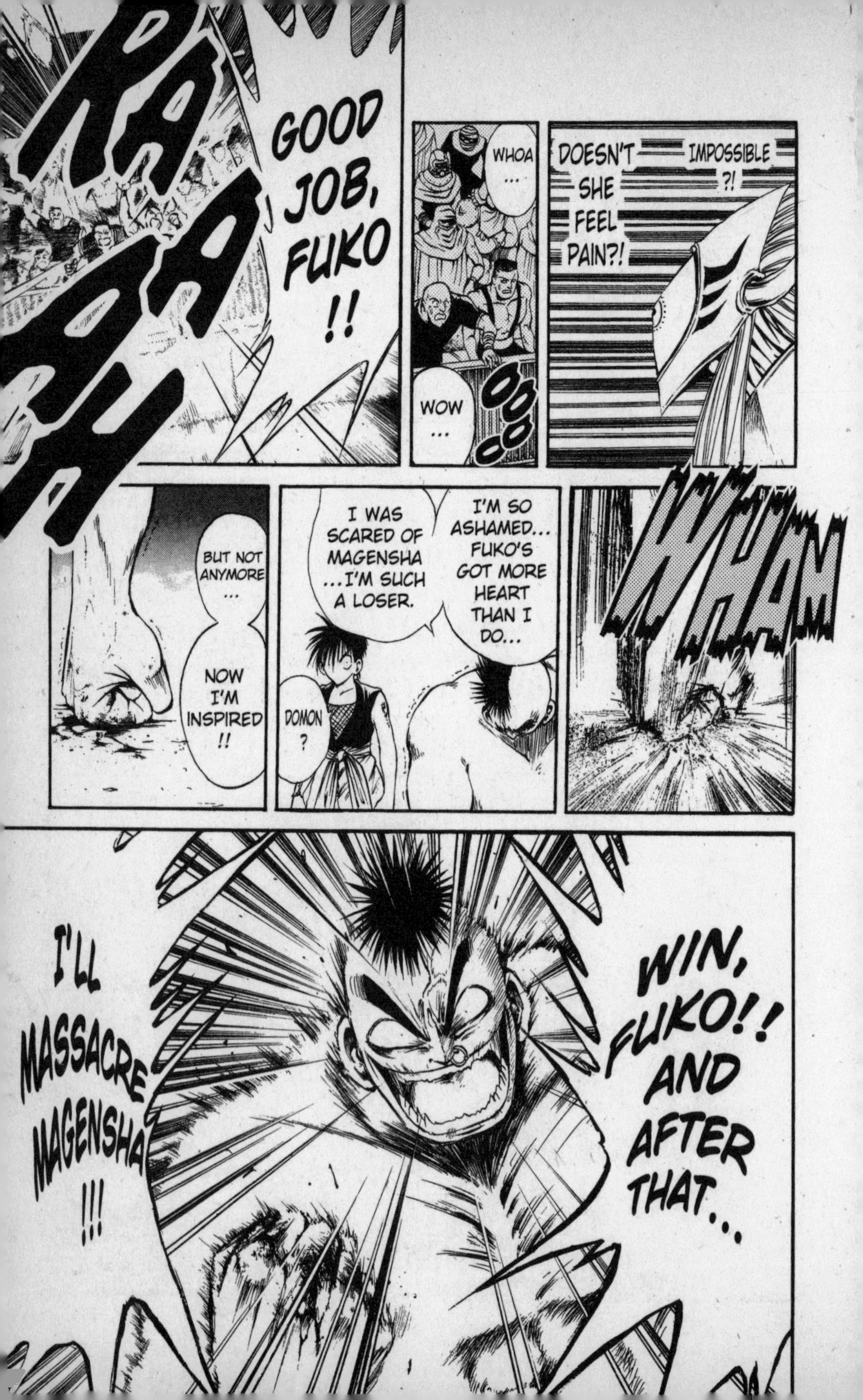
IMPOSSIBLE ?!
DOESN'T SHE FEEL PAIN?!
WHOA ...
OOOO
WOW ...
GOOD JOB, FUKO !!
WHAM
I'M SO ASHAMED... FUKO'S GOT MORE HEART THAN I DO...
I WAS SCARED OF MAGENSHA ...I'M SUCH A LOSER.
DOMON ?
BUT NOT ANYMORE ...
NOW I'M INSPIRED !!
WIN, FUKO!! AND AFTER THAT...
I'LL MASSACRE MAGENSHA !!!

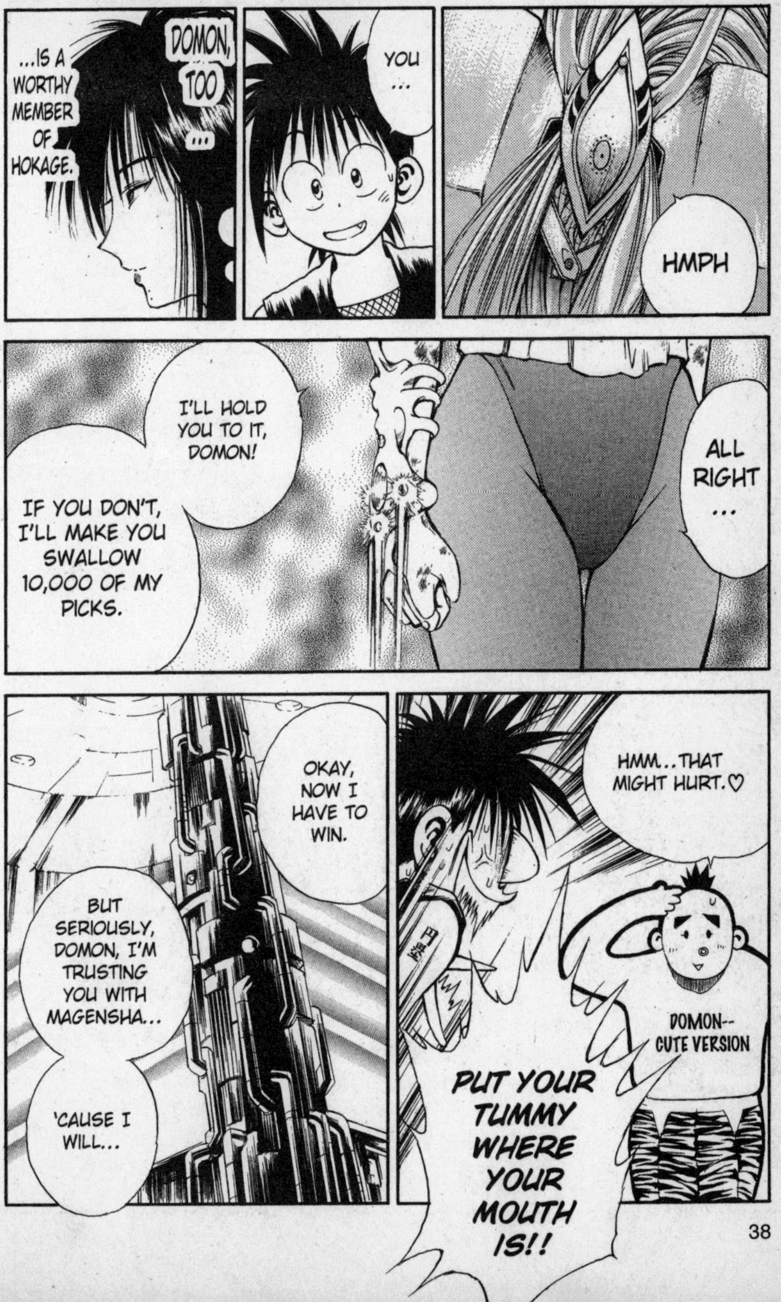
HMPH
YOU ...
DOMON, TOO ...
...IS A WORTHY MEMBER OF HOKAGE.
ALL RIGHT ...
I'LL HOLD YOU TO IT, DOMON!
IF YOU DON'T, I'LL MAKE YOU SWALLOW 10,000 OF MY PICKS.
HMM...THAT MIGHT HURT.♡
DOMON-- CUTE VERSION
PUT YOUR TUMMY WHERE YOUR MOUTH IS!!
OKAY, NOW I HAVE TO WIN.
BUT SERIOUSLY, DOMON, I'M TRUSTING YOU WITH MAGENSHA...
'CAUSE I WILL...

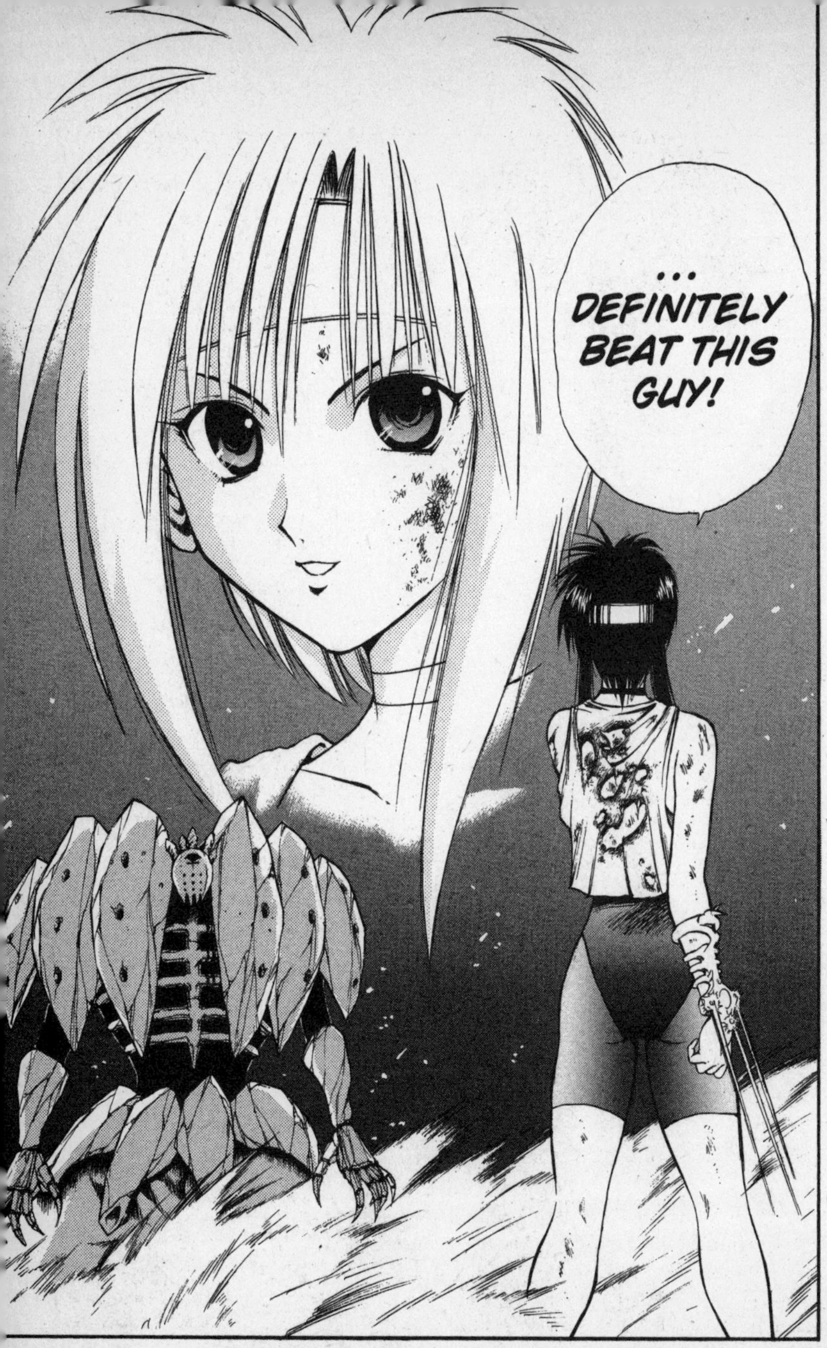
...DEFINITELY BEAT THIS GUY!

烈火の炎
~FLAME OF RECCA~

Part Ninety: The Time of Mara (10) Five Small Spheres

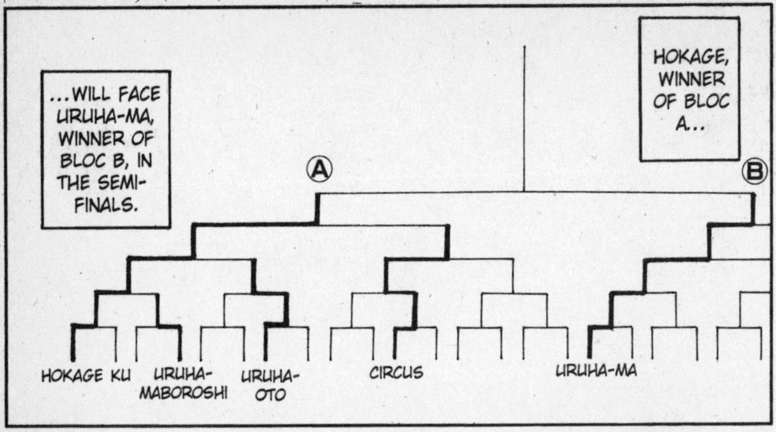
HOKAGE, WINNER OF BLOC A...
...WILL FACE URUHA-MA, WINNER OF BLOC B, IN THE SEMI-FINALS.
A
B
HOKAGE KU
URUHA-MABOROSHI
URUHA-OTO
CIRCUS
URUHA-MA

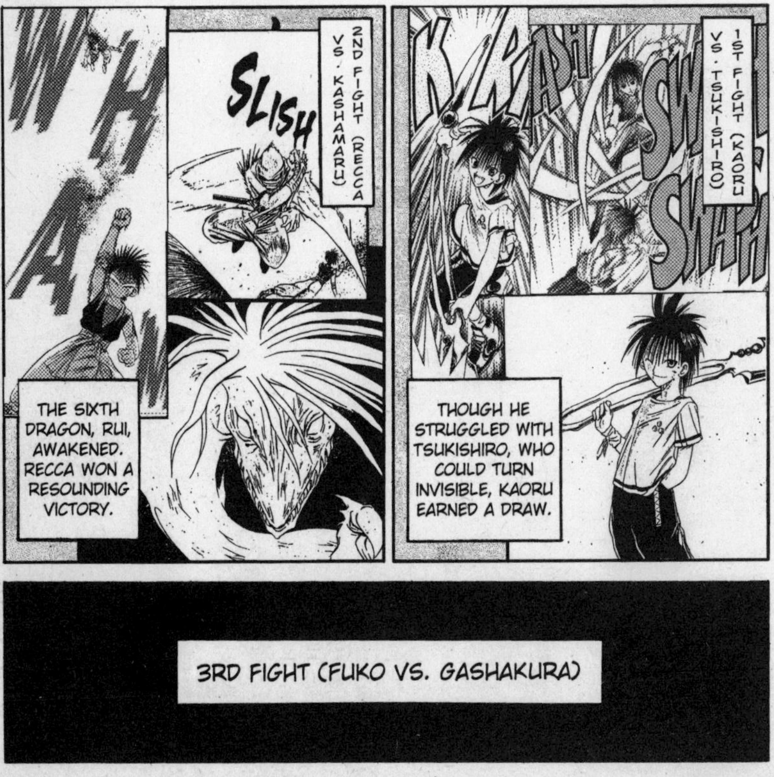
1ST FIGHT (KAORU VS. TSUKISHIRO)
THOUGH HE STRUGGLED WITH TSUKISHIRO, WHO COULD TURN INVISIBLE, KAORU EARNED A DRAW.
2ND FIGHT (RECCA VS. KASHAMARU)
SLISH
THE SIXTH DRAGON, RUI, AWAKENED. RECCA WON A RESOUNDING VICTORY.
3RD FIGHT (FUKO VS. GASHAKURA)

Part Ninety:
The Time of Mara (10)
Five Small Spheres

FUKO KIRISAWA
AGE: 16
SEX: FEMALE
BLOOD TYPE: B
BIRTHDAY: 8/2
(LEO)

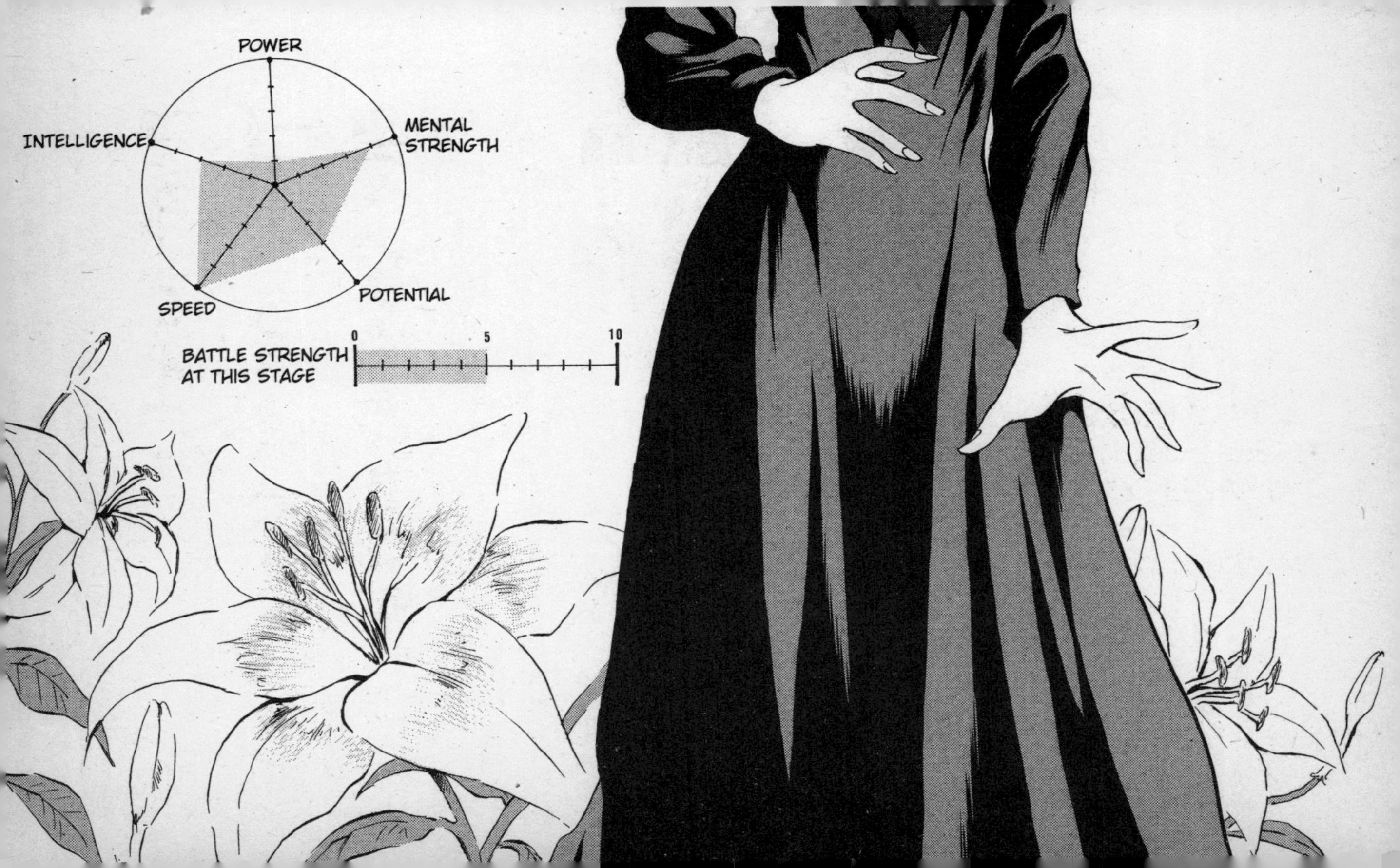
POWER
MENTAL STRENGTH
POTENTIAL
SPEED
INTELLIGENCE
BATTLE STRENGTH AT THIS STAGE
0
5
10

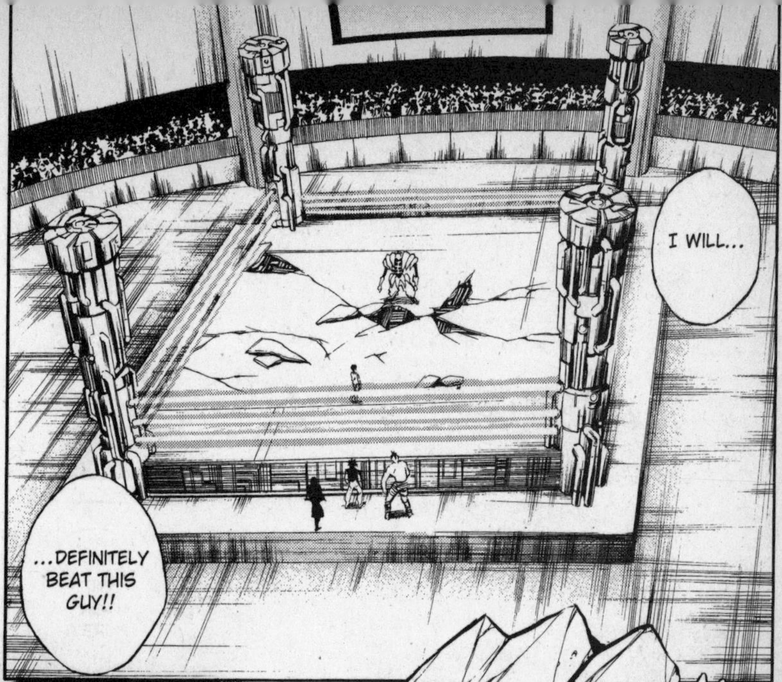
I WILL...
...DEFINITELY BEAT THIS GUY!!
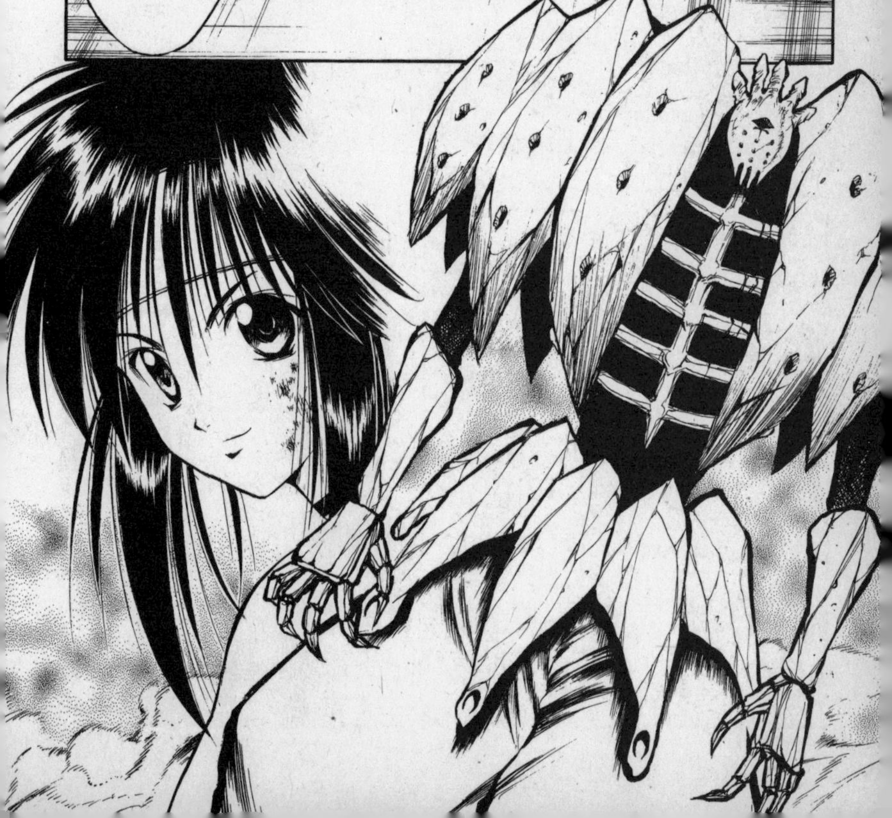

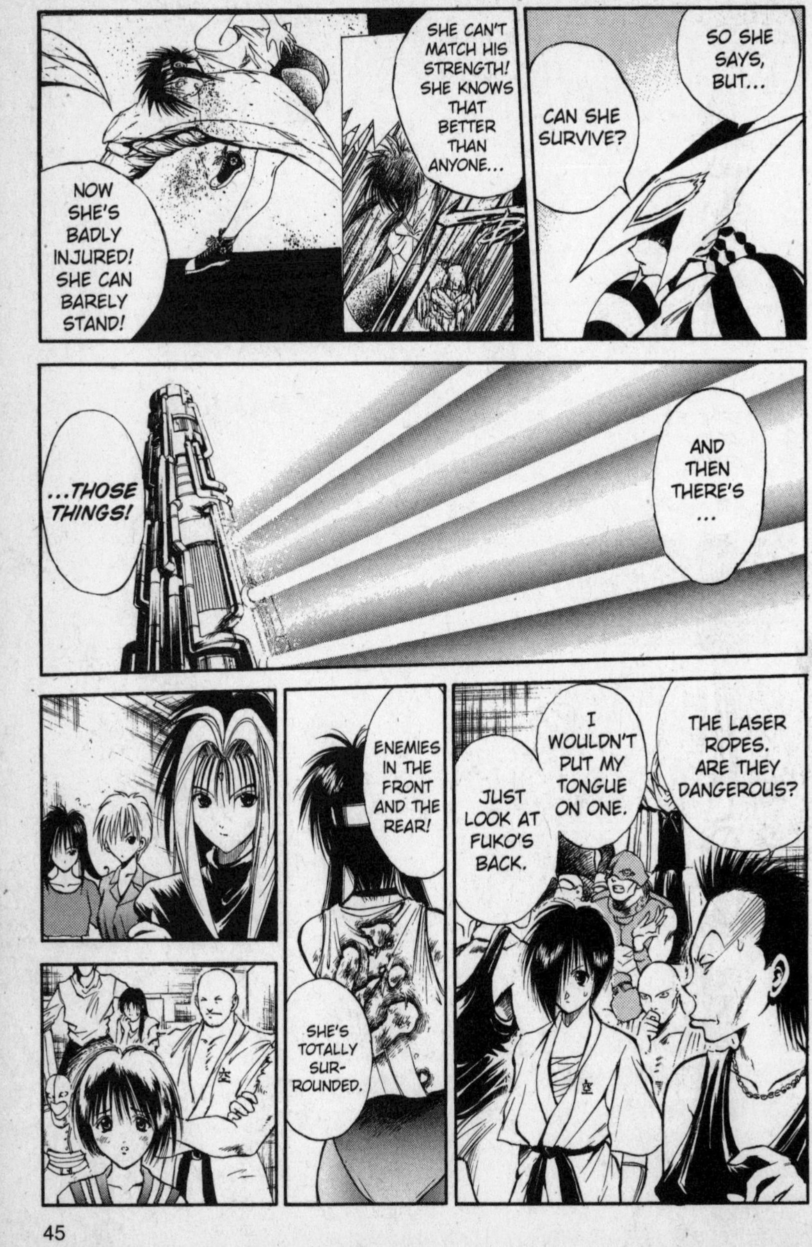
SO SHE SAYS, BUT...
CAN SHE SURVIVE?
SHE CAN'T MATCH HIS STRENGTH! SHE KNOWS THAT BETTER THAN ANYONE...
NOW SHE'S BADLY INJURED! SHE CAN BARELY STAND!
AND THEN THERE'S...
...THOSE THINGS!
THE LASER ROPES. ARE THEY DANGEROUS?
I WOULDN'T PUT MY TONGUE ON ONE.
JUST LOOK AT FUKO'S BACK.
ENEMIES IN THE FRONT AND THE REAR!
SHE'S TOTALLY SUR-ROUNDED.

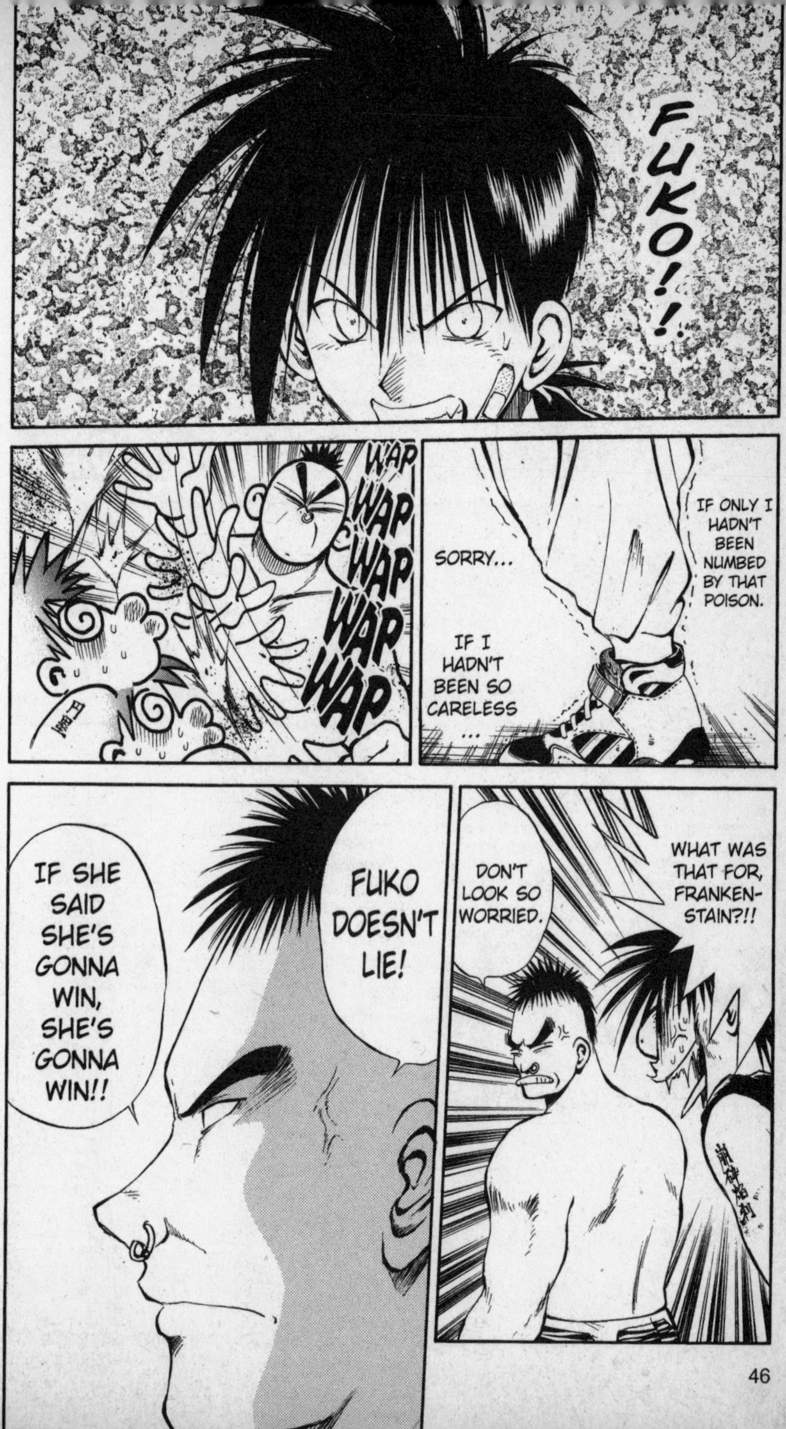
FUKO!!
IF ONLY I HADN'T BEEN NUMBED BY THAT POISON.
SORRY...
IF I HADN'T BEEN SO CARELESS ...
WAP WAP WAP WAP WAP
WHAT WAS THAT FOR, FRANKEN-STAIN?!!
DON'T LOOK SO WORRIED.
FUKO DOESN'T LIE!
IF SHE SAID SHE'S GONNA WIN, SHE'S GONNA WIN!!

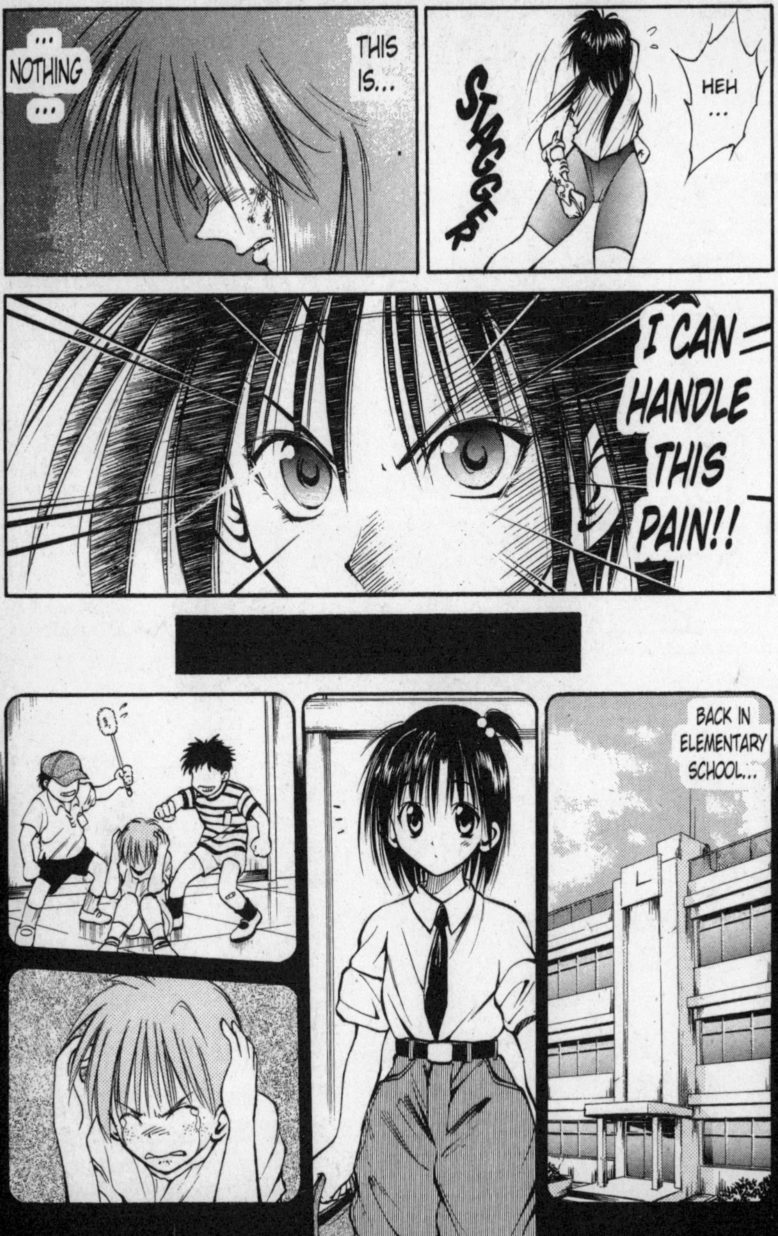
HEH ...
STAGGER
THIS IS...
... NOTHING ...
I CAN HANDLE THIS PAIN!!
BACK IN ELEMENTARY SCHOOL...

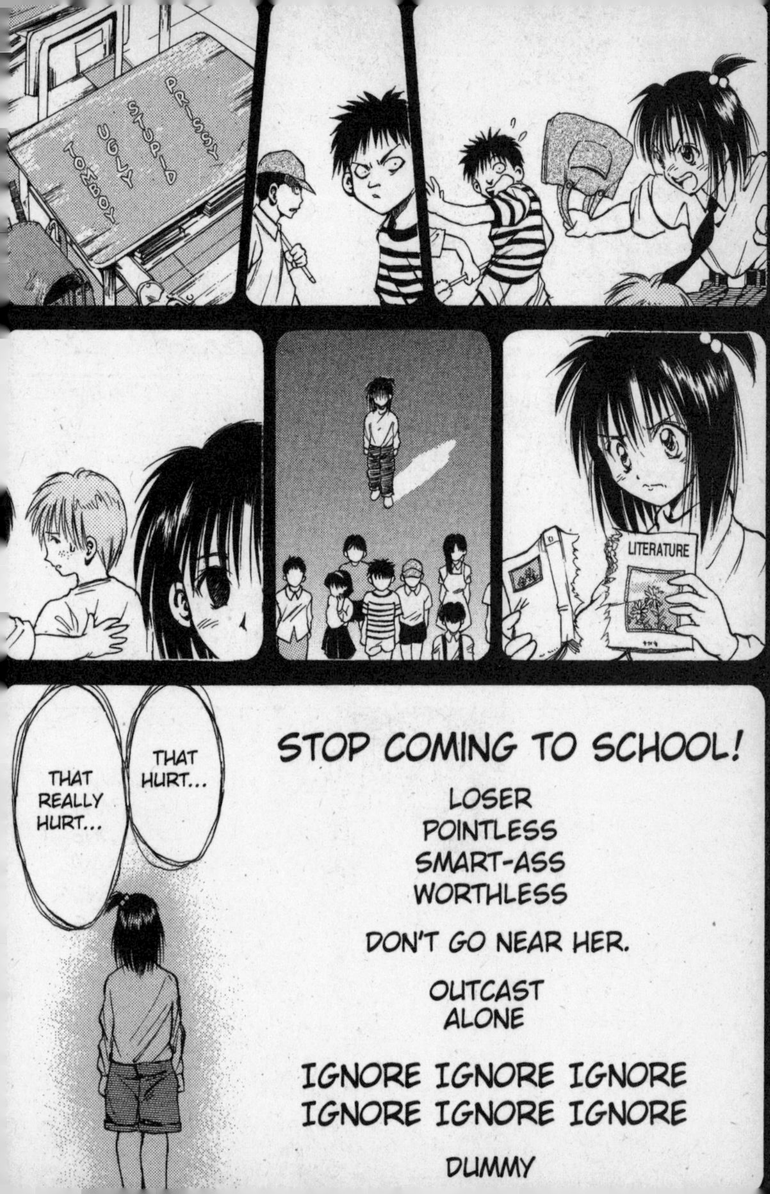
PRISSY
STUPID
UGLY
TOMBOY
LITERATURE
STOP COMING TO SCHOOL!
LOSER
POINTLESS
SMART-ASS
WORTHLESS
DON'T GO NEAR HER.
OUTCAST
ALONE
IGNORE IGNORE IGNORE
IGNORE IGNORE IGNORE
DUMMY
THAT HURT...
THAT REALLY HURT...

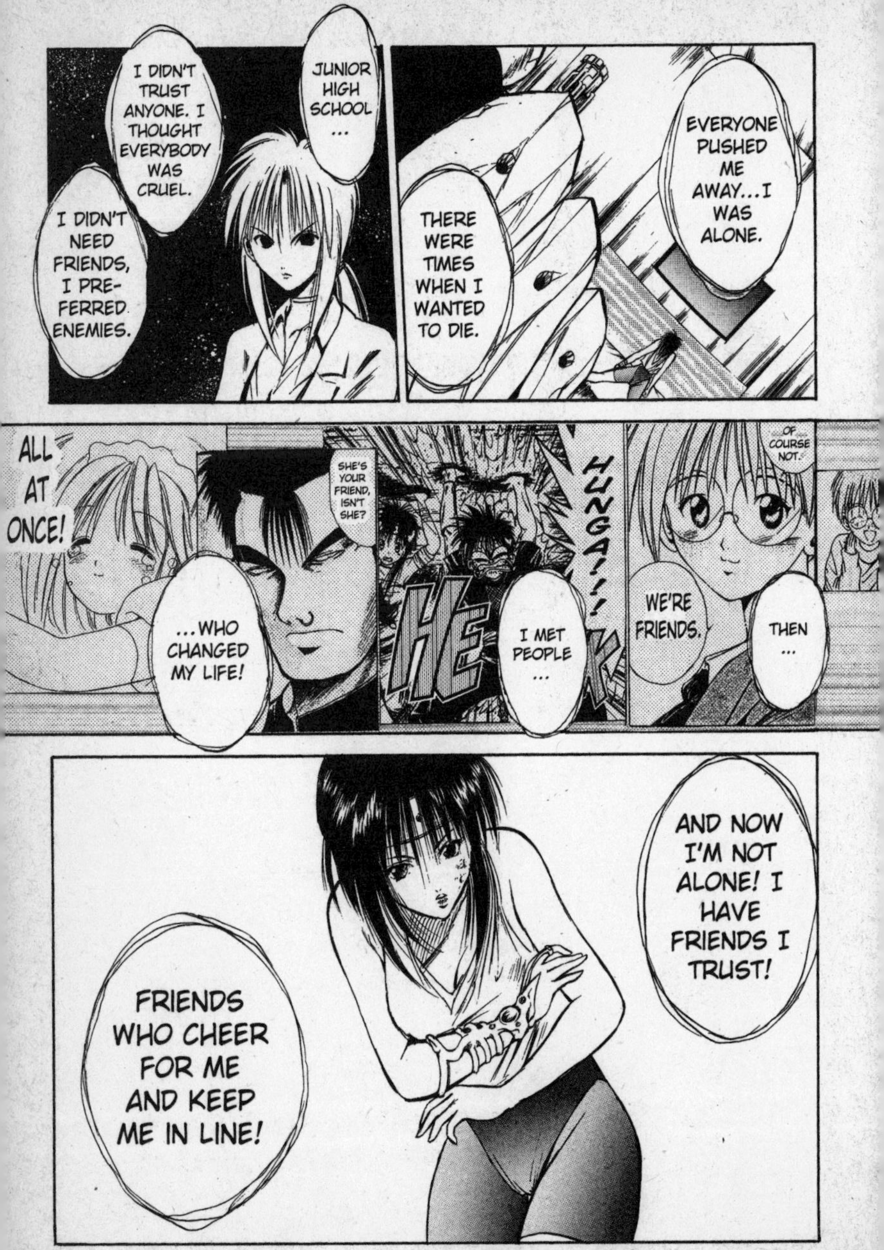
EVERYONE PUSHED ME AWAY...I WAS ALONE.
THERE WERE TIMES WHEN I WANTED TO DIE.
JUNIOR HIGH SCHOOL ...
I DIDN'T TRUST ANYONE. I THOUGHT EVERYBODY WAS CRUEL.
I DIDN'T NEED FRIENDS, I PREFERRED ENEMIES.
OF COURSE NOT.
THEN ...
WE'RE FRIENDS.
HUNGA!!!
I MET PEOPLE ...
SHE'S YOUR FRIEND, ISN'T SHE?
...WHO CHANGED MY LIFE!
ALL AT ONCE!
AND NOW I'M NOT ALONE! I HAVE FRIENDS I TRUST!
FRIENDS WHO CHEER FOR ME AND KEEP ME IN LINE!

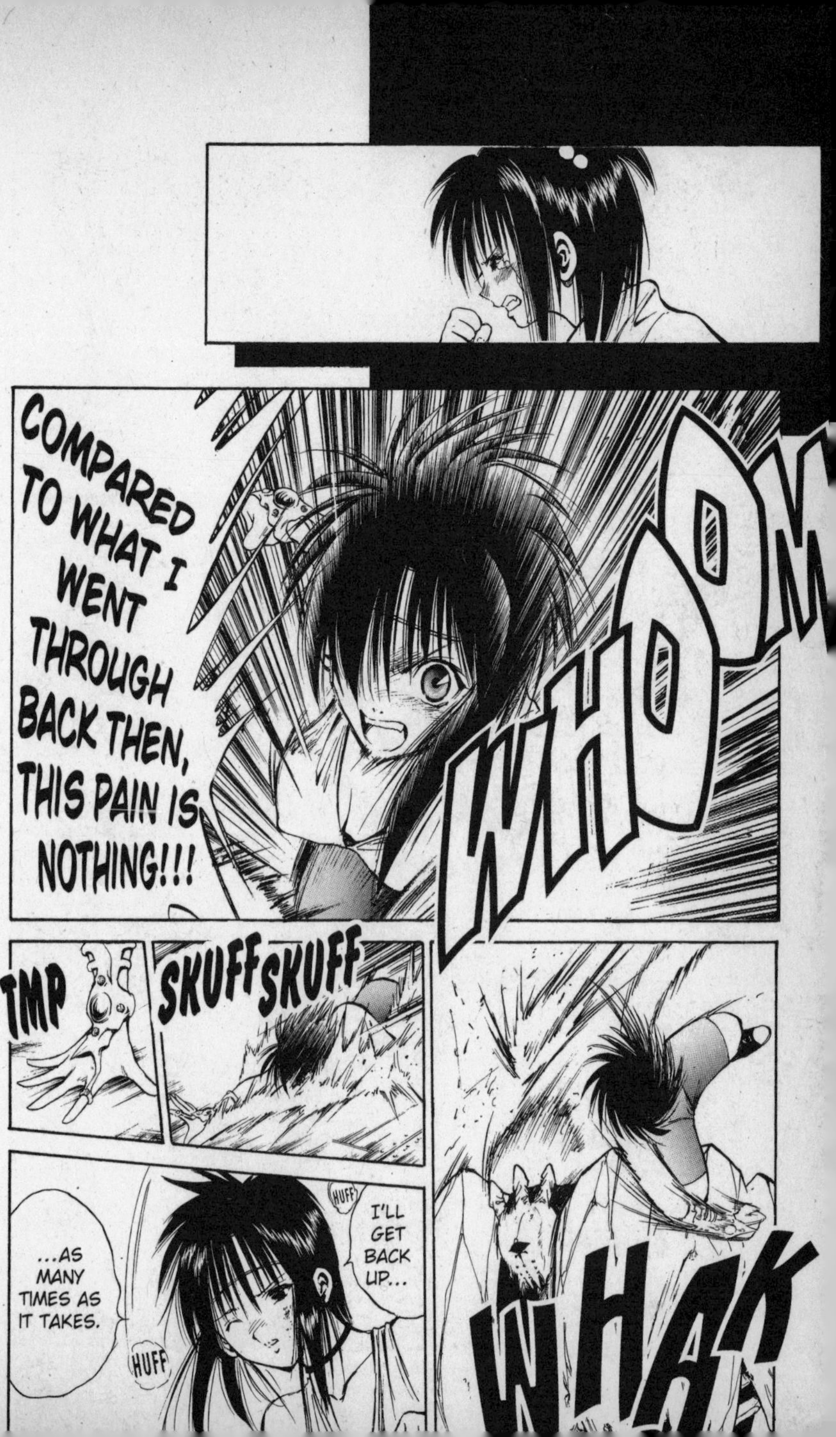
WHOOM
COMPARED TO WHAT I WENT THROUGH BACK THEN, THIS PAIN IS NOTHING!!!
WHAK
SKUFF SKUFF
TMP
HUFF
I'LL GET BACK UP...
...AS MANY TIMES AS IT TAKES.
HUFF

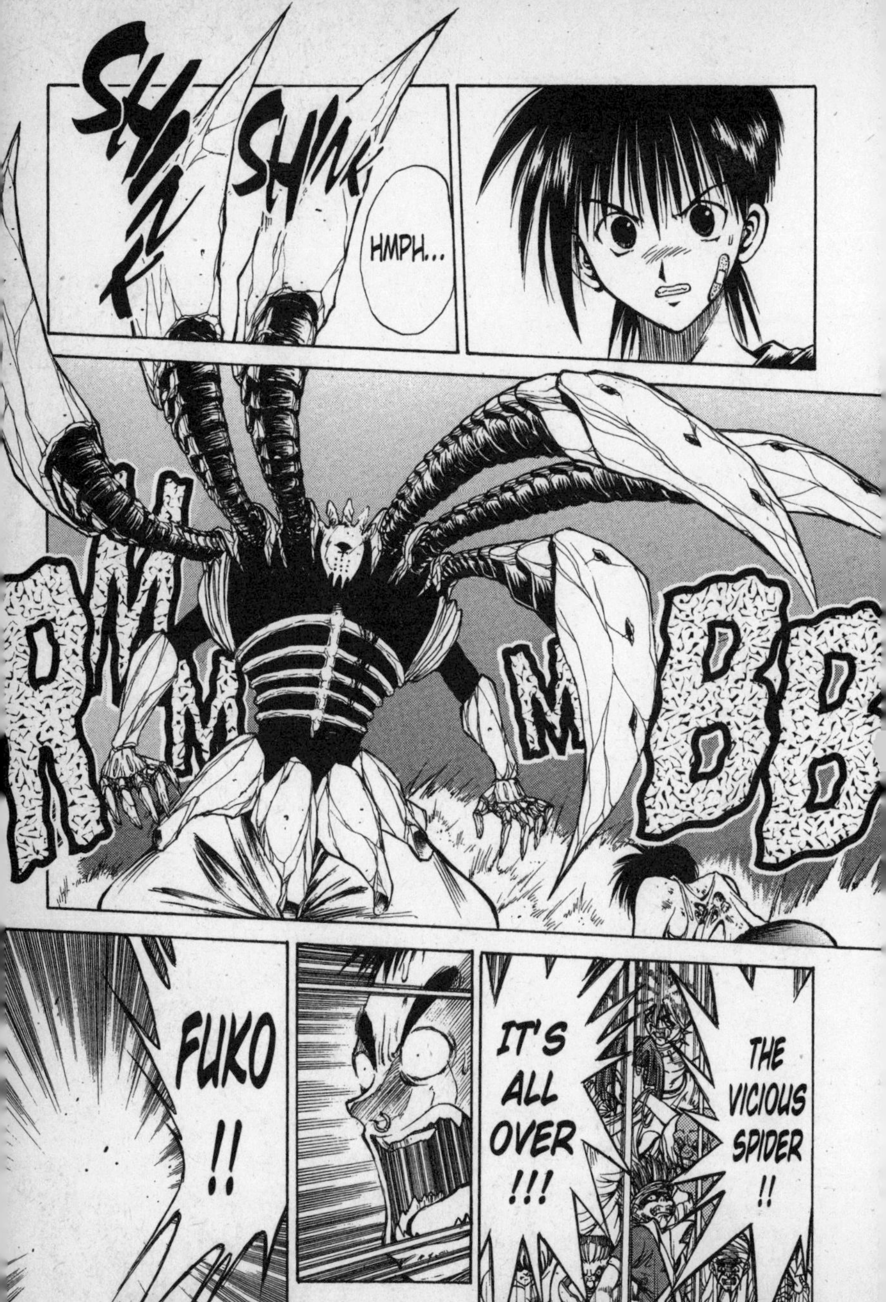
SHINK
SHINK
HMPH...
RMMBB
THE VICIOUS SPIDER !!
IT'S ALL OVER !!!
FUKO !!

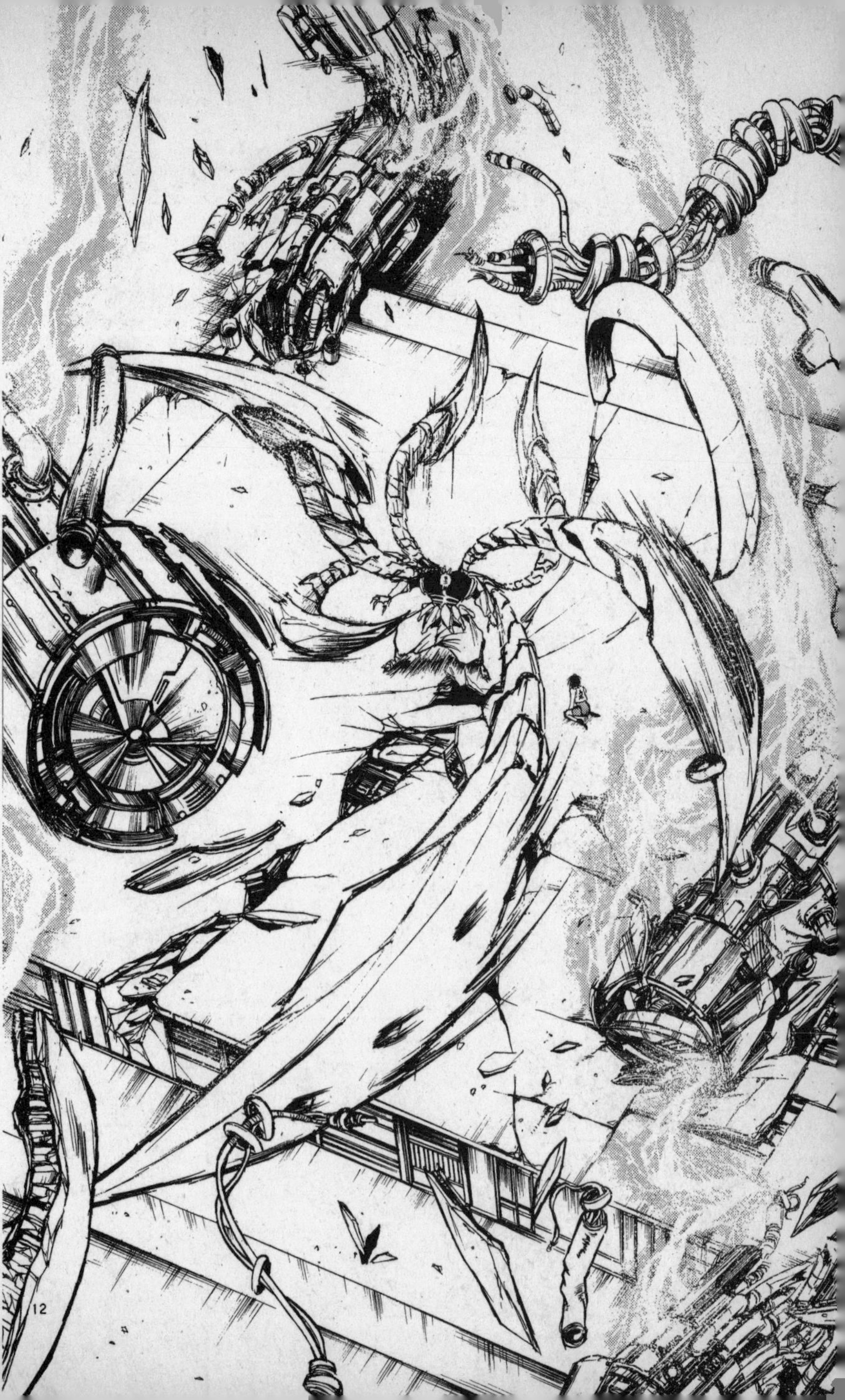

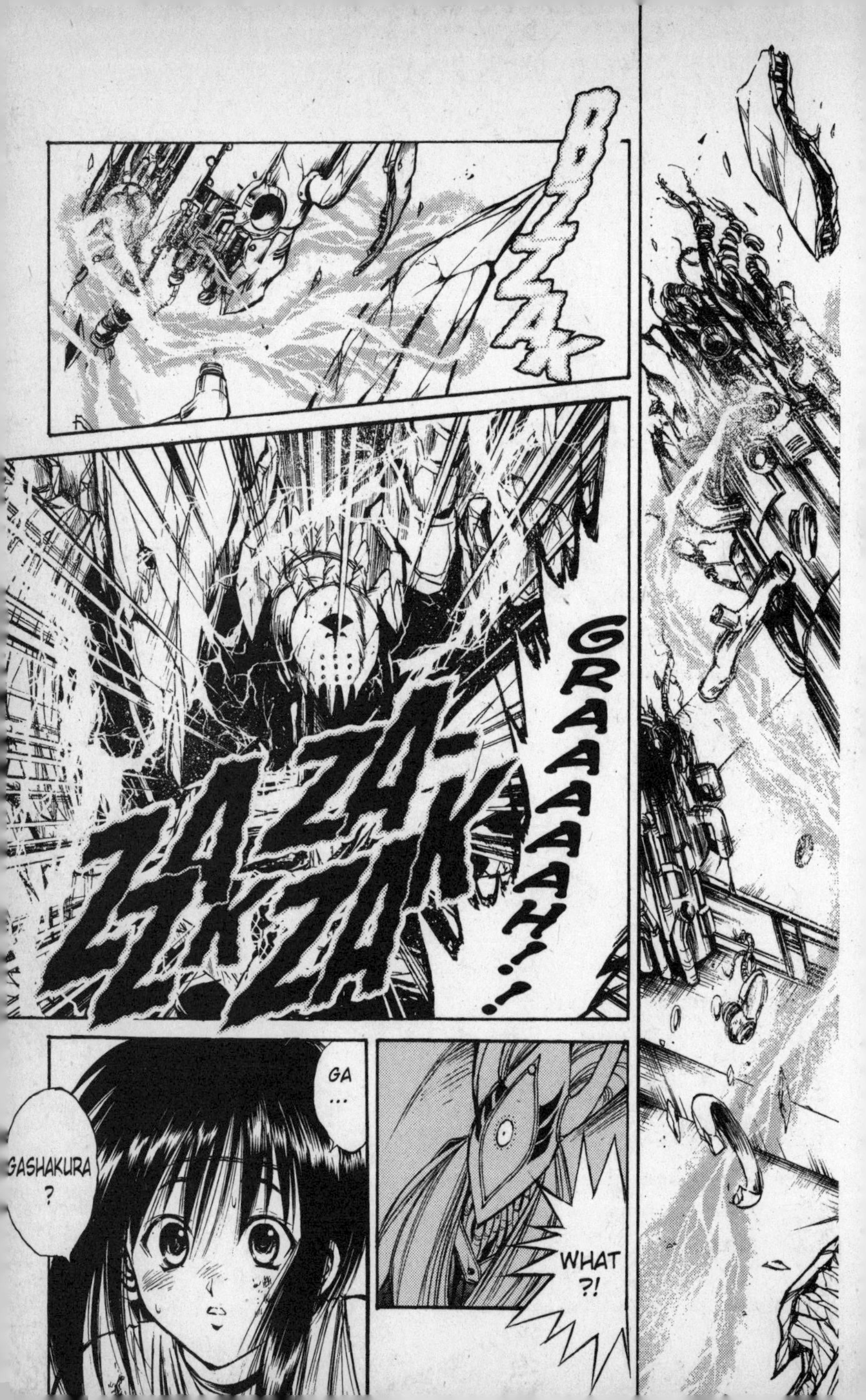
BZZAK
GRAAAAAAH!!
ZAZAK
ZAZA
GA ...
WHAT ?!
GASHAKURA ?

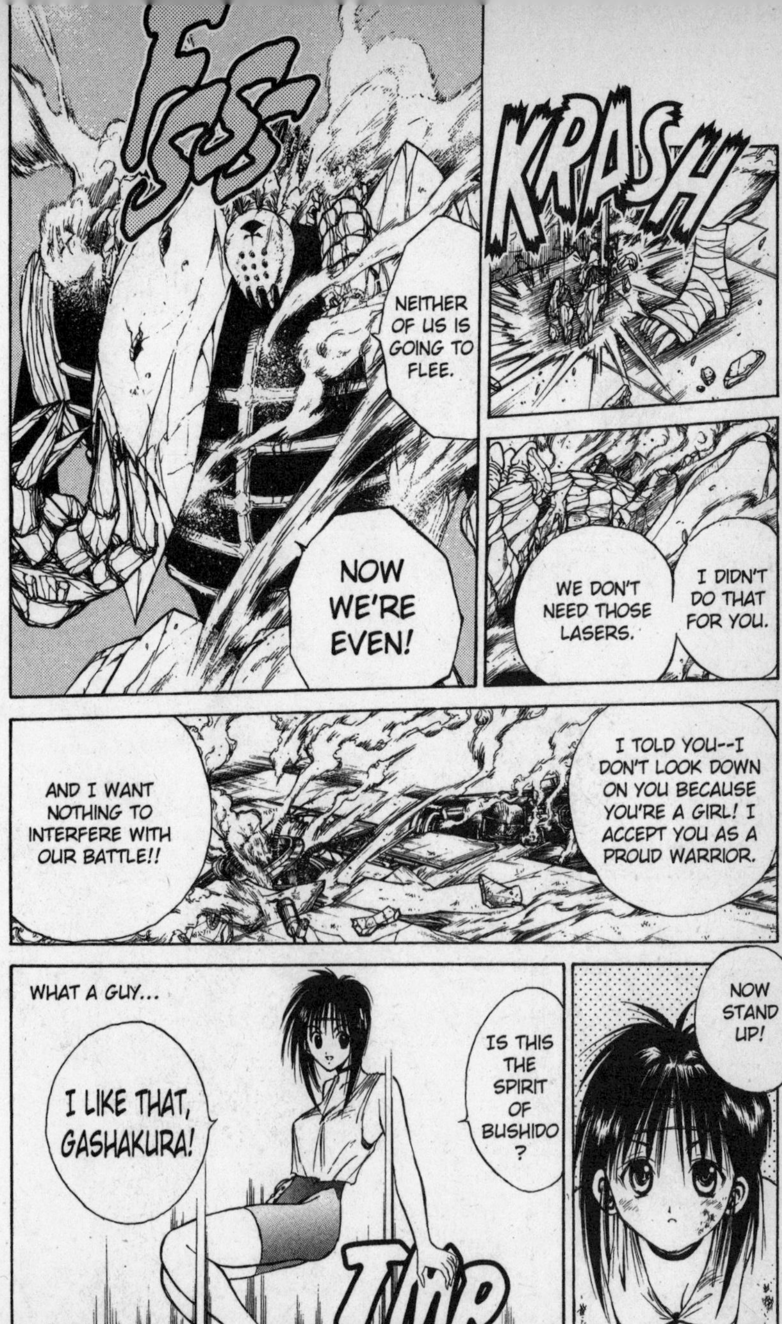
KRASH
I DIDN'T DO THAT FOR YOU.
WE DON'T NEED THOSE LASERS.
FSSS
NEITHER OF US IS GOING TO FLEE.
NOW WE'RE EVEN!
I TOLD YOU--I DON'T LOOK DOWN ON YOU BECAUSE YOU'RE A GIRL! I ACCEPT YOU AS A PROUD WARRIOR.
AND I WANT NOTHING TO INTERFERE WITH OUR BATTLE!!
NOW STAND UP!
IS THIS THE SPIRIT OF BUSHIDO ?
WHAT A GUY...
I LIKE THAT, GASHAKURA!
TMP

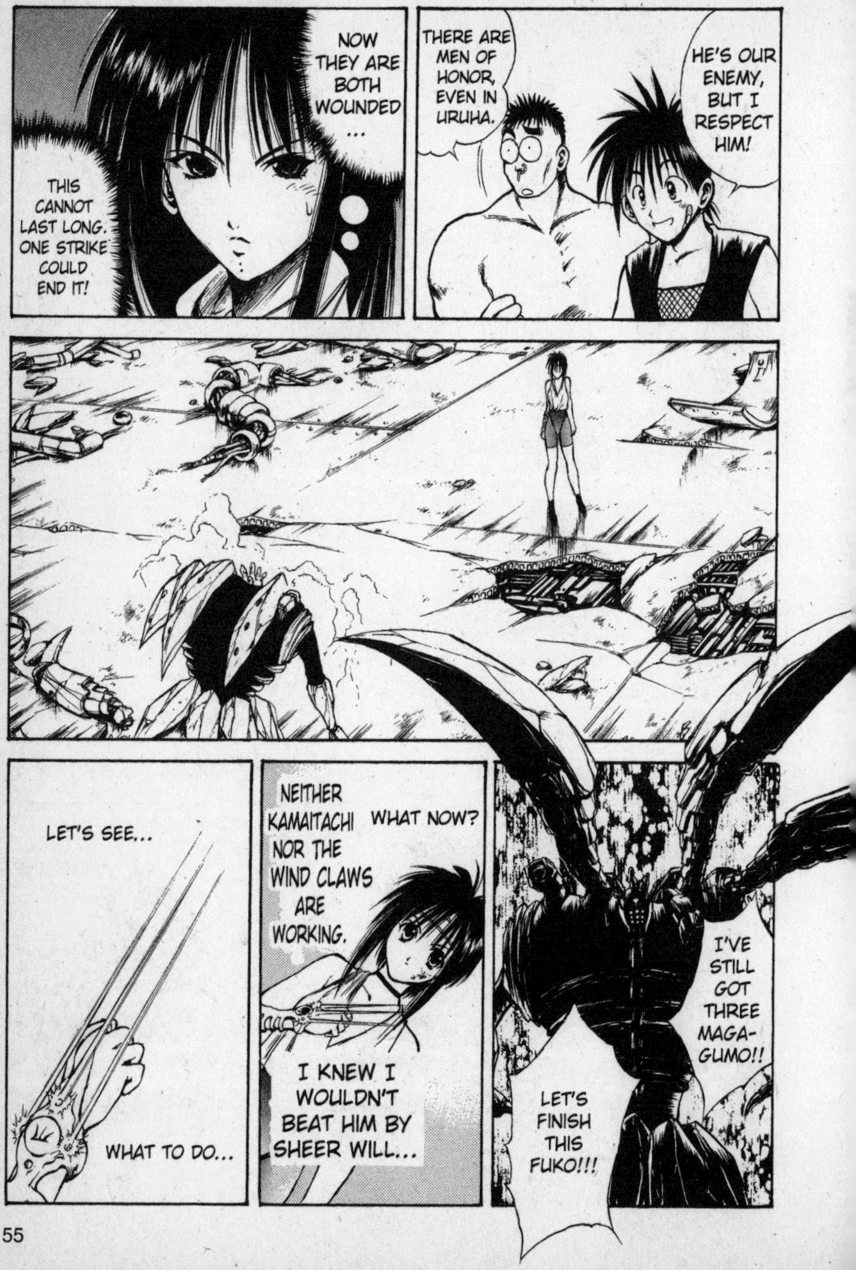
HE'S OUR ENEMY, BUT I RESPECT HIM!
THERE ARE MEN OF HONOR, EVEN IN URUHA.
NOW THEY ARE BOTH WOUNDED ...
THIS CANNOT LAST LONG. ONE STRIKE COULD END IT!
I'VE STILL GOT THREE MAGA-GUMO!!
LET'S FINISH THIS FUKO!!!
WHAT NOW?
NEITHER KAMAITACHI NOR THE WIND CLAWS ARE WORKING.
I KNEW I WOULDN'T BEAT HIM BY SHEER WILL...
LET'S SEE...
WHAT TO DO...

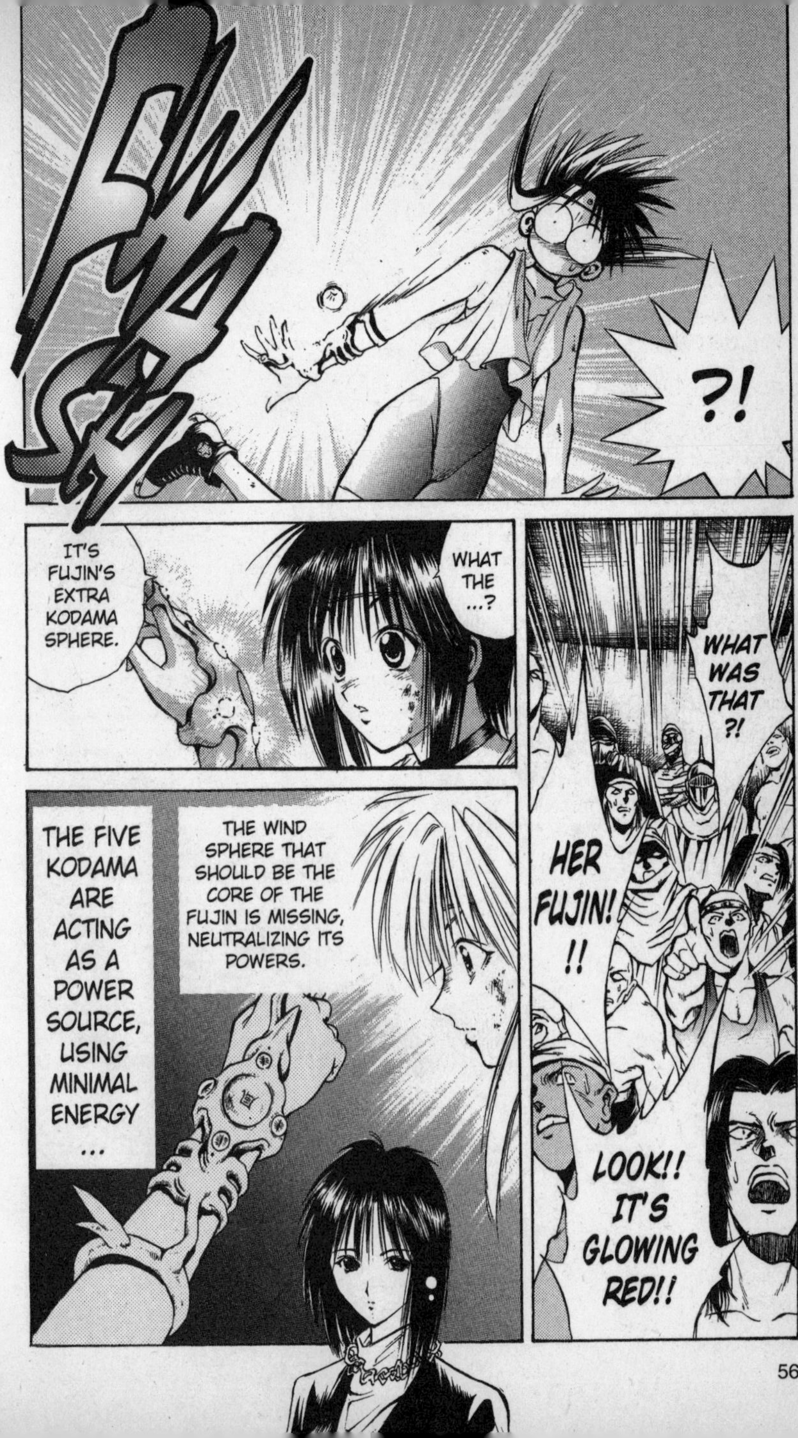
?!
WHAT WAS THAT ?!
HER FUJIN! !!
LOOK!! IT'S GLOWING RED!!
WHAT THE ...?
IT'S FUJIN'S EXTRA KODAMA SPHERE.
THE WIND SPHERE THAT SHOULD BE THE CORE OF THE FUJIN IS MISSING, NEUTRALIZING ITS POWERS.
THE FIVE KODAMA ARE ACTING AS A POWER SOURCE, USING MINIMAL ENERGY ...

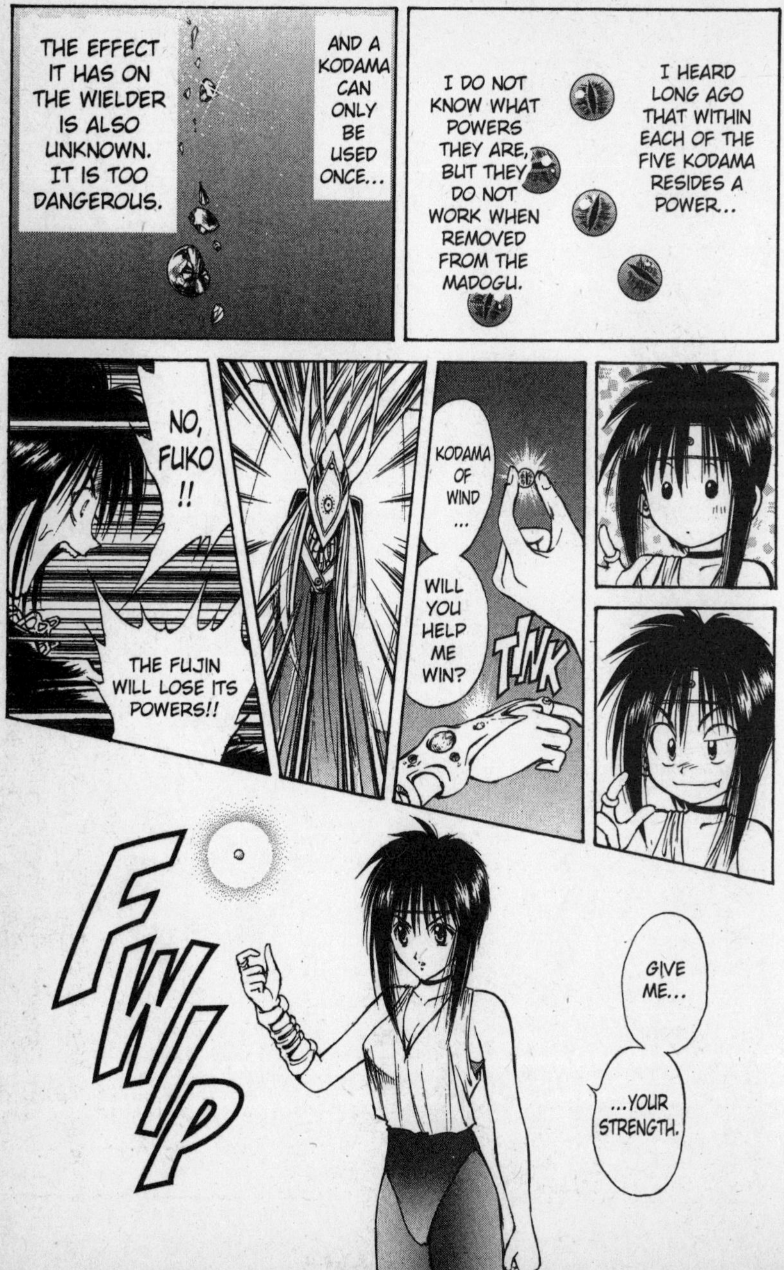
I HEARD LONG AGO THAT WITHIN EACH OF THE FIVE KODAMA RESIDES A POWER...
I DO NOT KNOW WHAT POWERS THEY ARE, BUT THEY DO NOT WORK WHEN REMOVED FROM THE MADOGU.
AND A KODAMA CAN ONLY BE USED ONCE...
THE EFFECT IT HAS ON THE WIELDER IS ALSO UNKNOWN. IT IS TOO DANGEROUS.
KODAMA OF WIND...
WILL YOU HELP ME WIN?
TINK
NO, FUKO!!
THE FUJIN WILL LOSE ITS POWERS!!
GIVE ME...
...YOUR STRENGTH.
FWIP

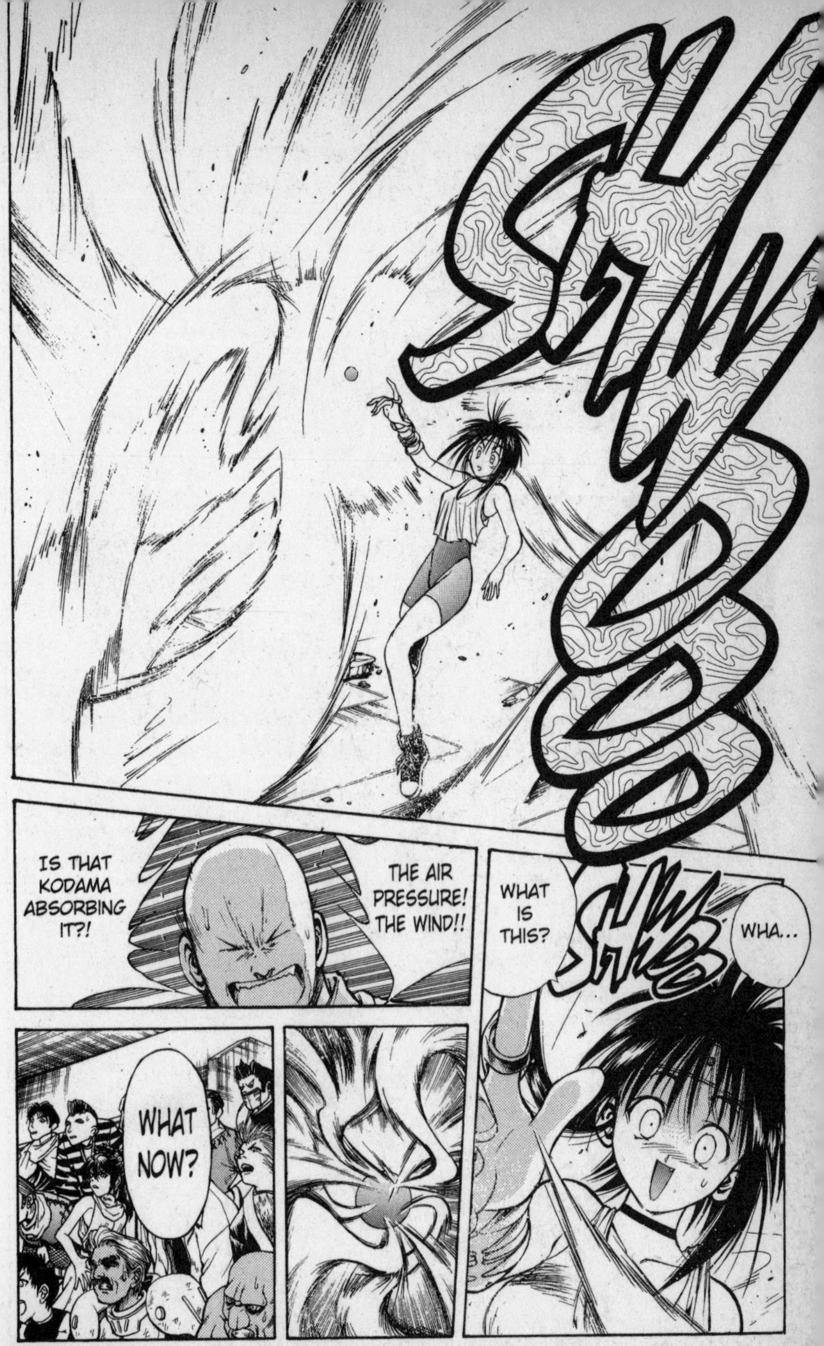
WHA...
WHAT IS THIS?
THE AIR PRESSURE! THE WIND!!
IS THAT KODAMA ABSORBING IT?!
WHAT NOW?

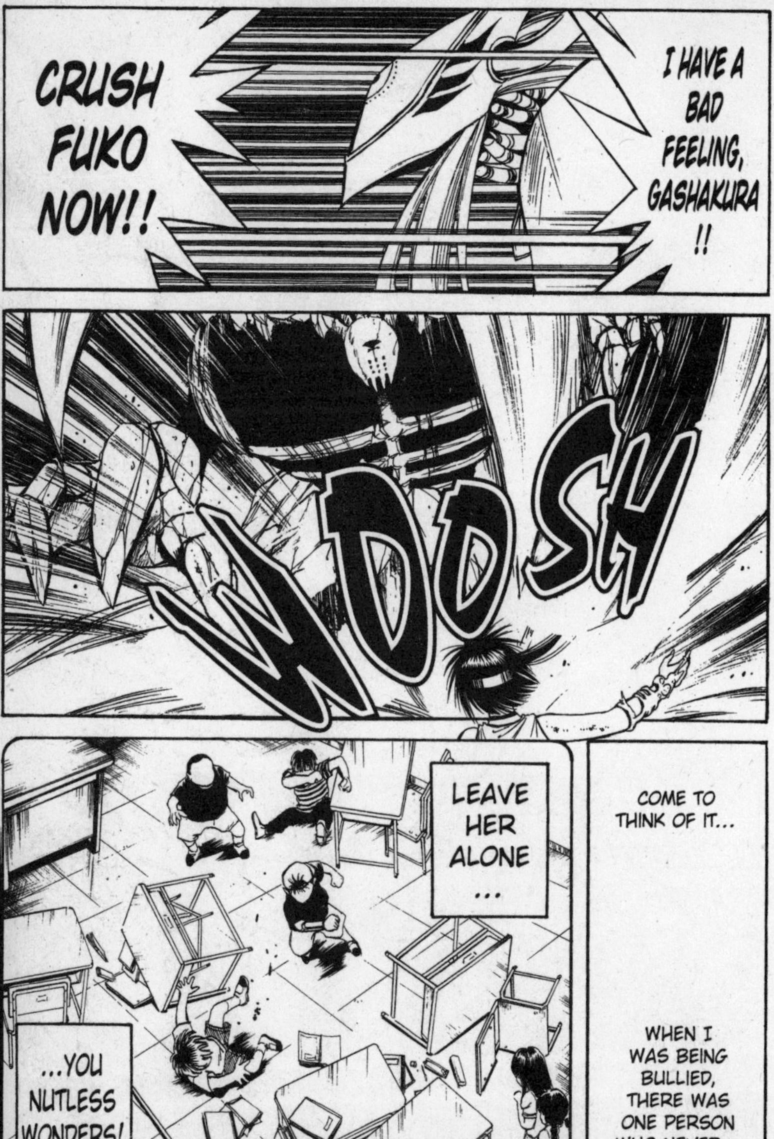
I HAVE A BAD FEELING, GASHAKURA !!
CRUSH FUKO NOW!!
WOOSH
COME TO THINK OF IT...
WHEN I WAS BEING BULLIED, THERE WAS ONE PERSON WHO NEVER...
LEAVE HER ALONE ...
...YOU NUTLESS WONDERS!

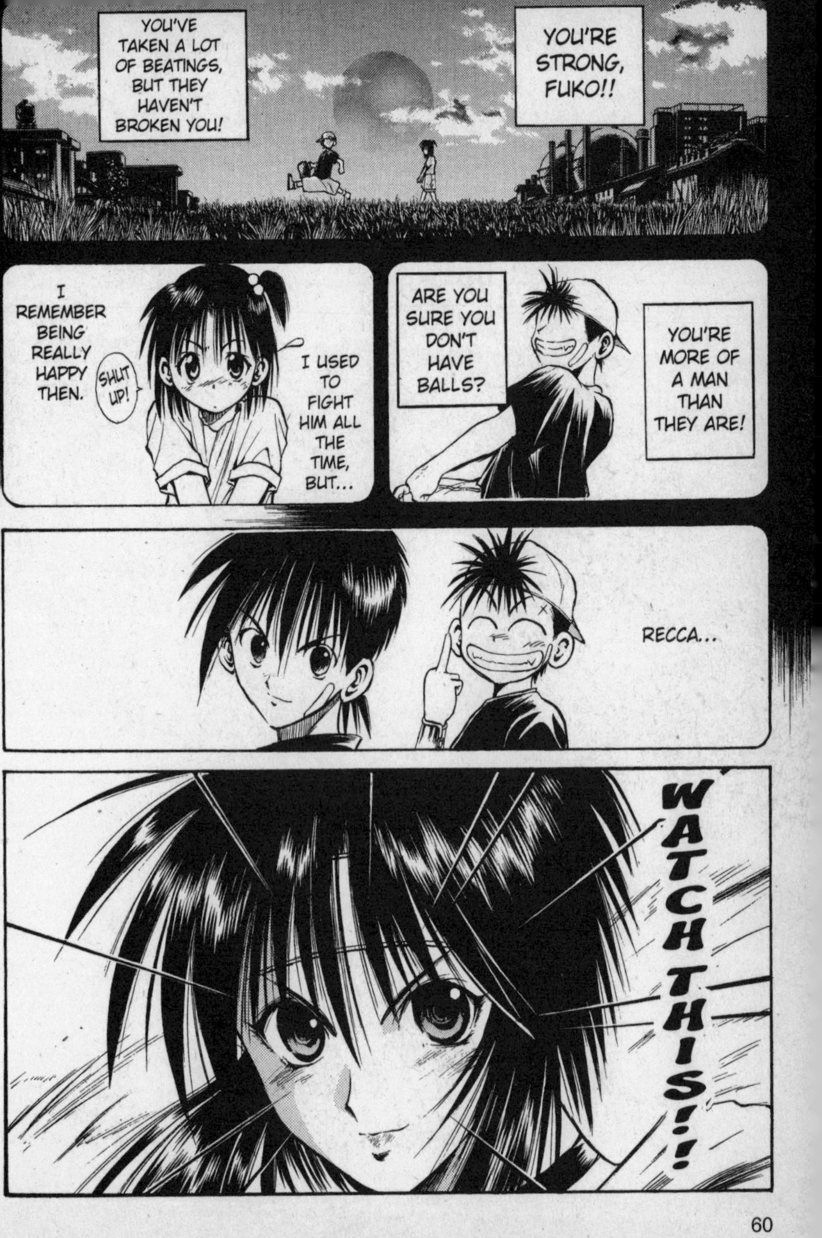
YOU'RE STRONG, FUKO!!
YOU'VE TAKEN A LOT OF BEATINGS, BUT THEY HAVEN'T BROKEN YOU!
ARE YOU SURE YOU DON'T HAVE BALLS?
YOU'RE MORE OF A MAN THAN THEY ARE!
I USED TO FIGHT HIM ALL THE TIME, BUT...
SHUT UP!
I REMEMBER BEING REALLY HAPPY THEN.
RECCA...
WATCH THIS!!!

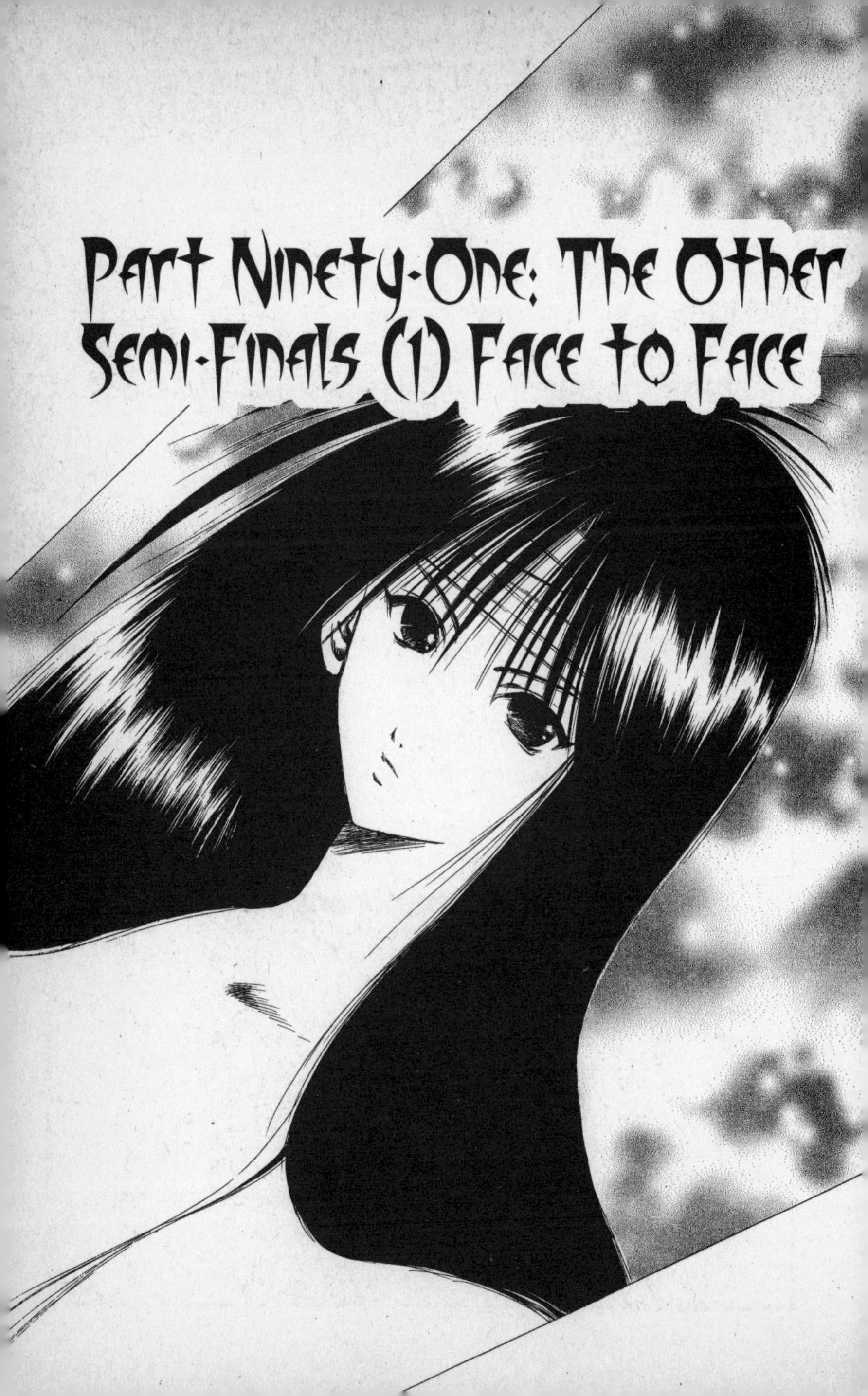
Part Ninety-One: The Other Semi-Finals (1) Face to Face

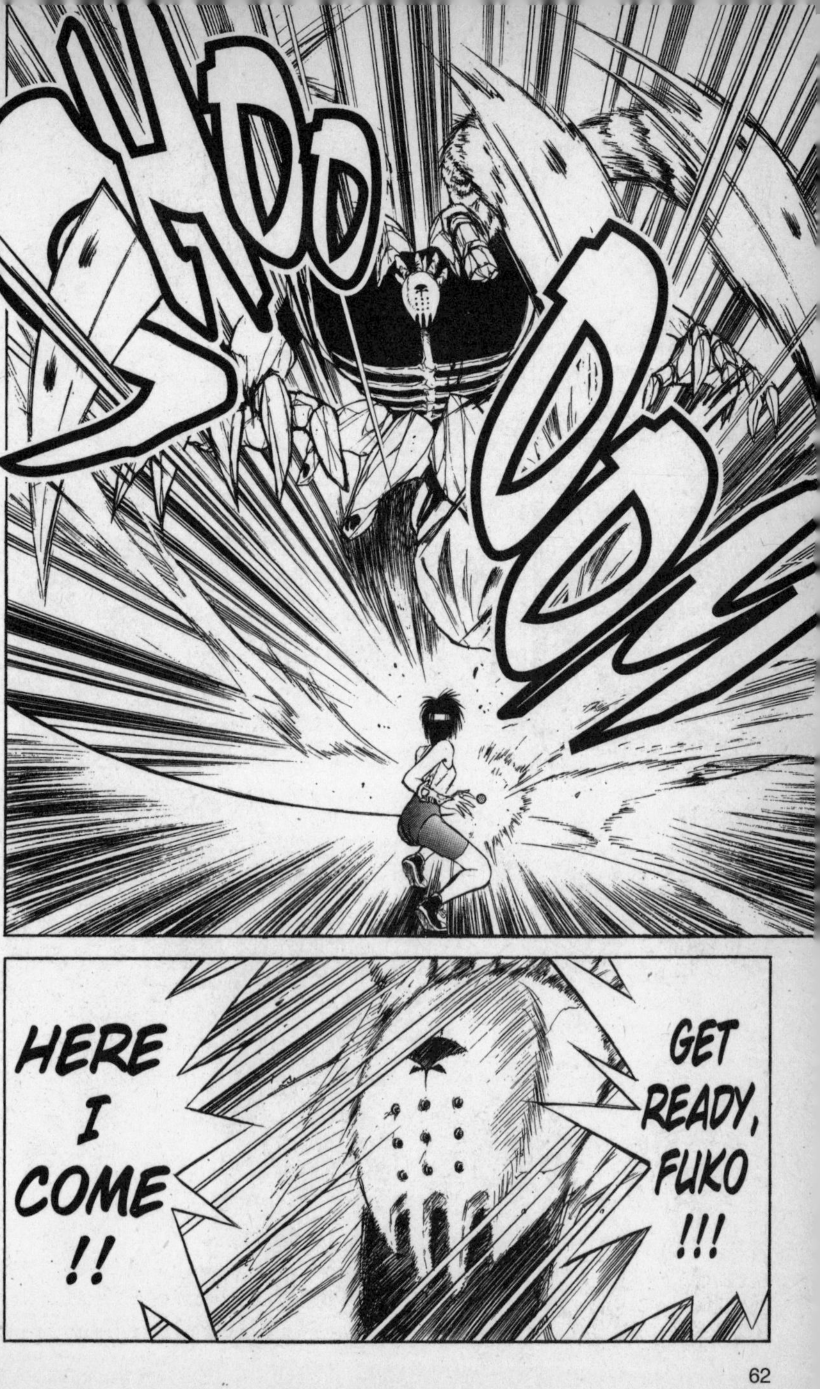
GET READY, FUKO!!!
HERE I COME!!

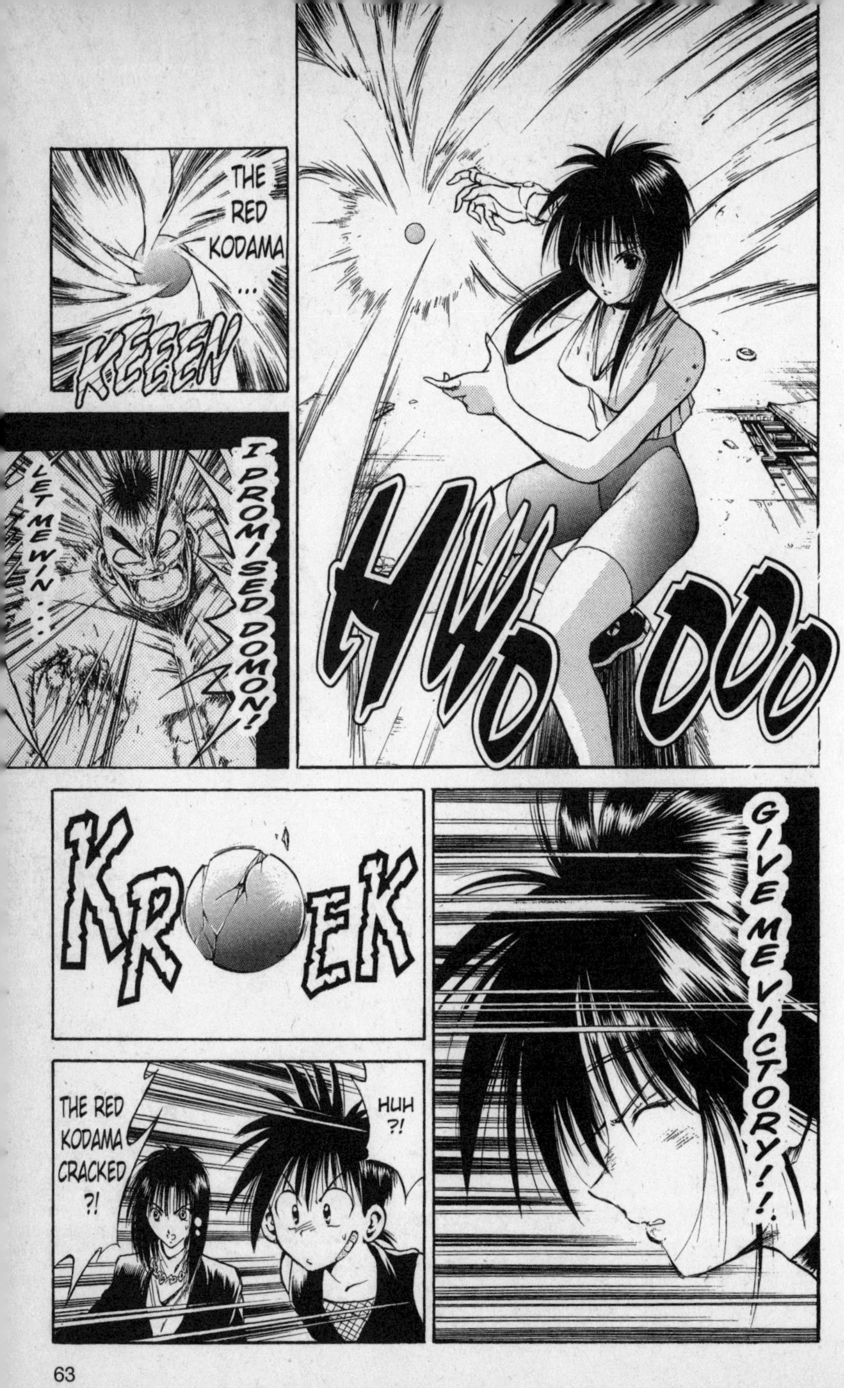
HWOOOO
THE RED KODAMA ...
KEEEN
I PROMISED DOMON!
LET ME WIN...
GIVE ME VICTORY!!
KROEK
HUH ?!
THE RED KODAMA CRACKED ?!

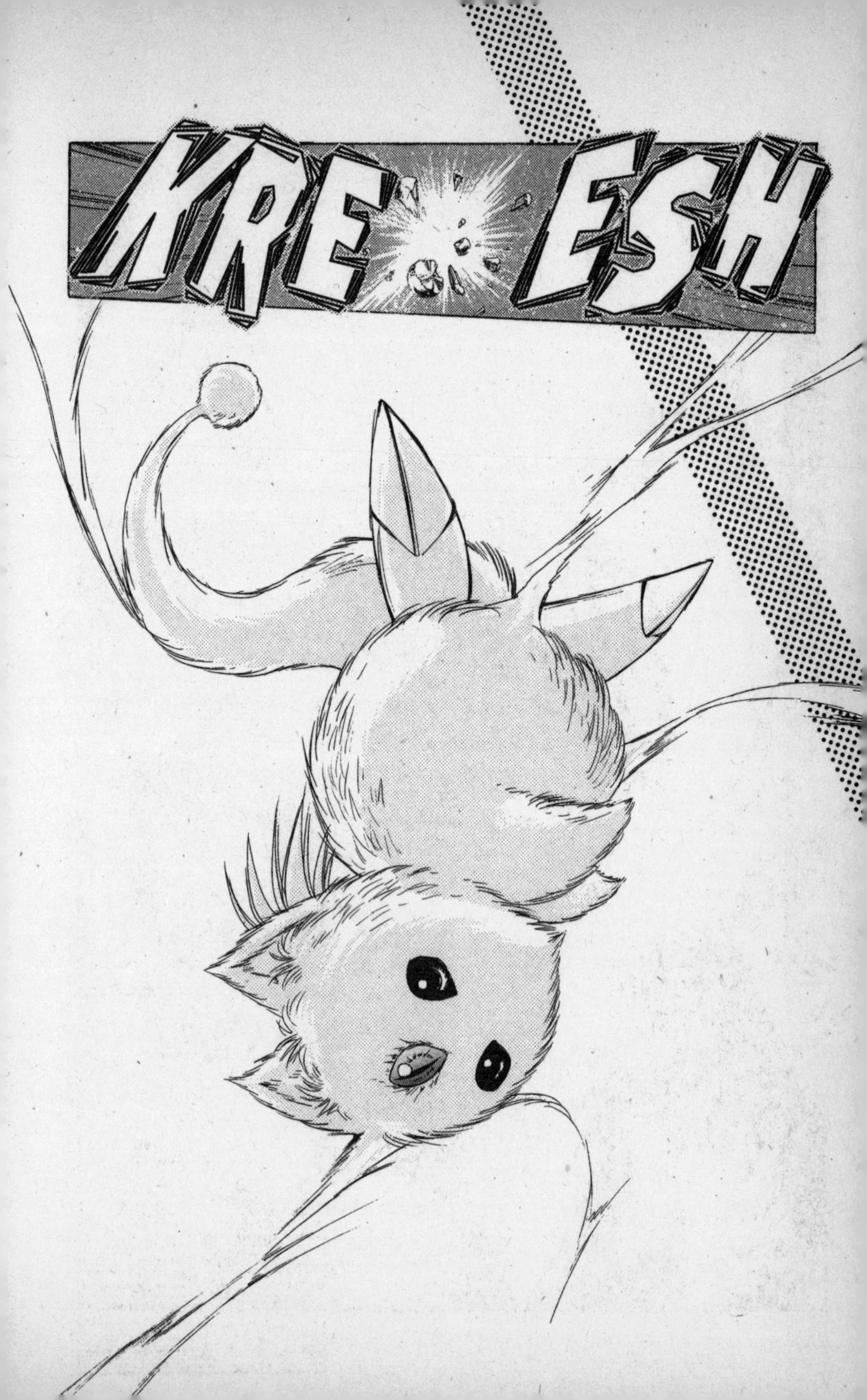
KRE ESH

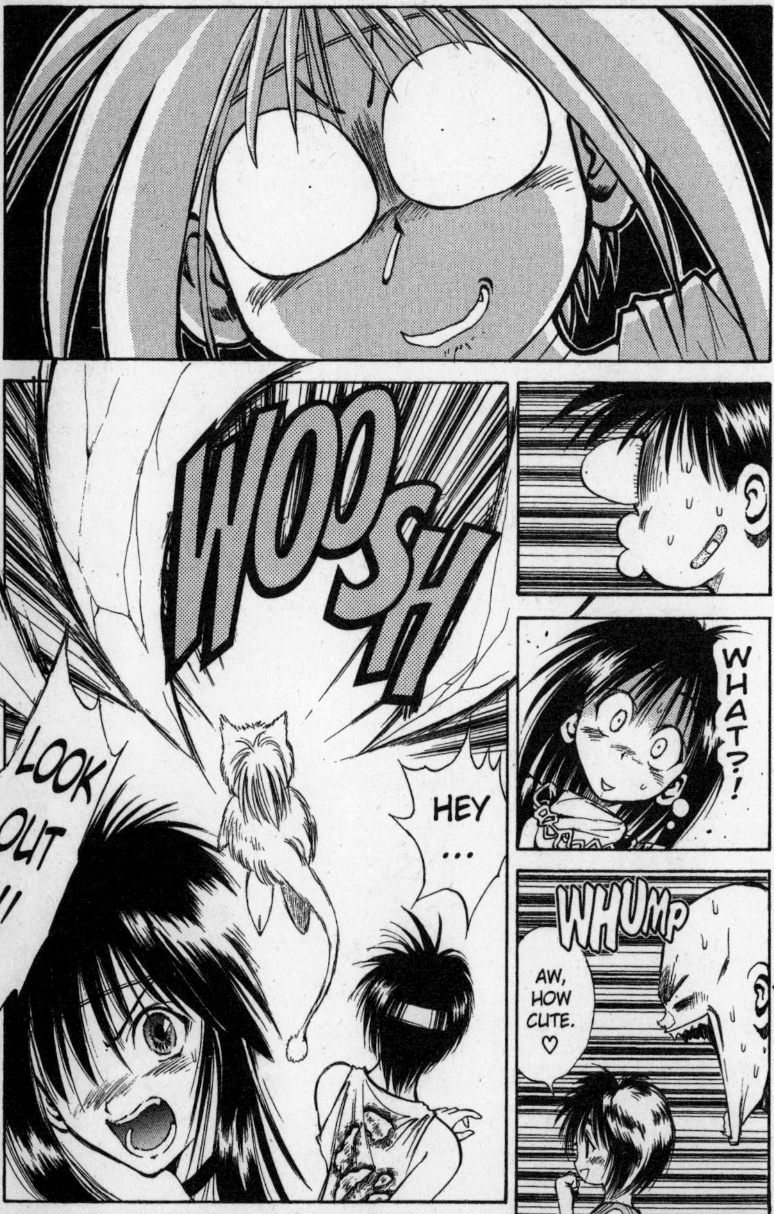
WHAT?!
WHUMP
AW, HOW CUTE. ♡
← KUKAI
WOOSH
HEY ...
LOOK OUT!!!

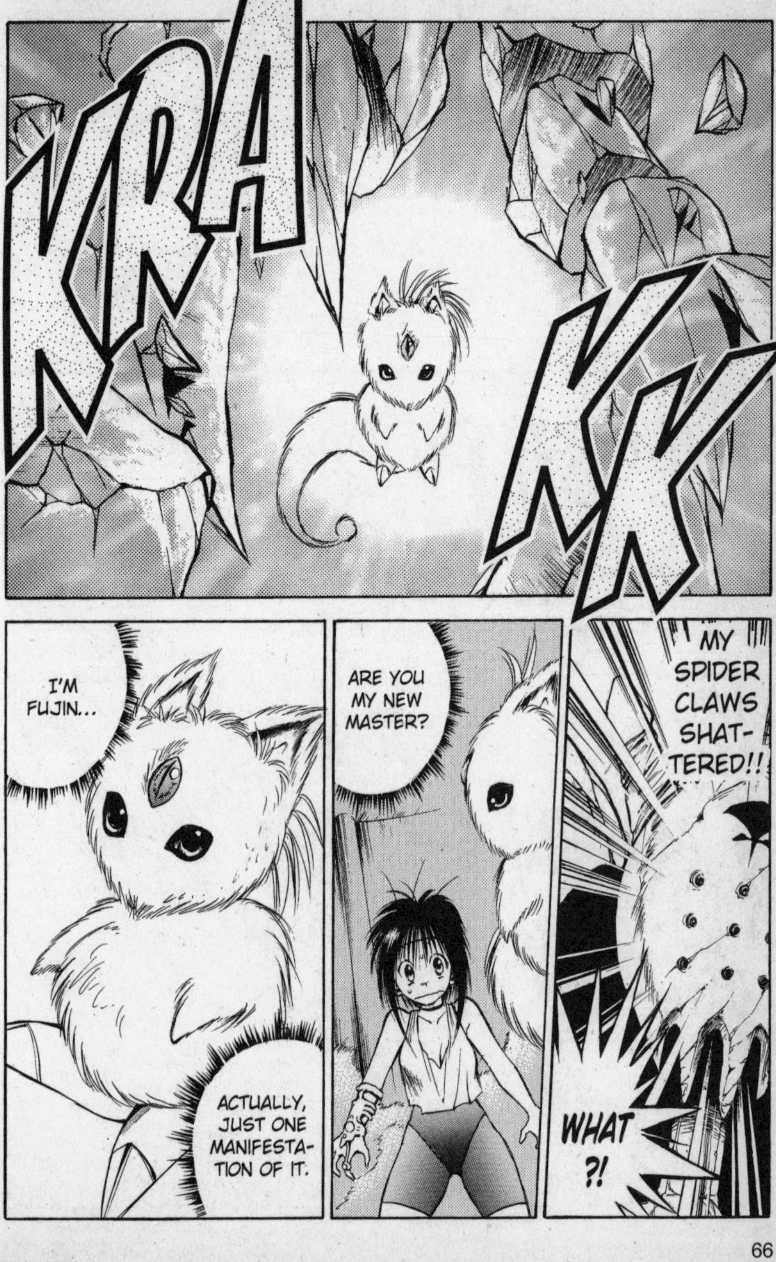
KRA
KK
MY SPIDER CLAWS SHAT-TERED!!
WHAT?!
ARE YOU MY NEW MASTER?
I'M FUJIN...
ACTUALLY, JUST ONE MANIFESTA-TION OF IT.

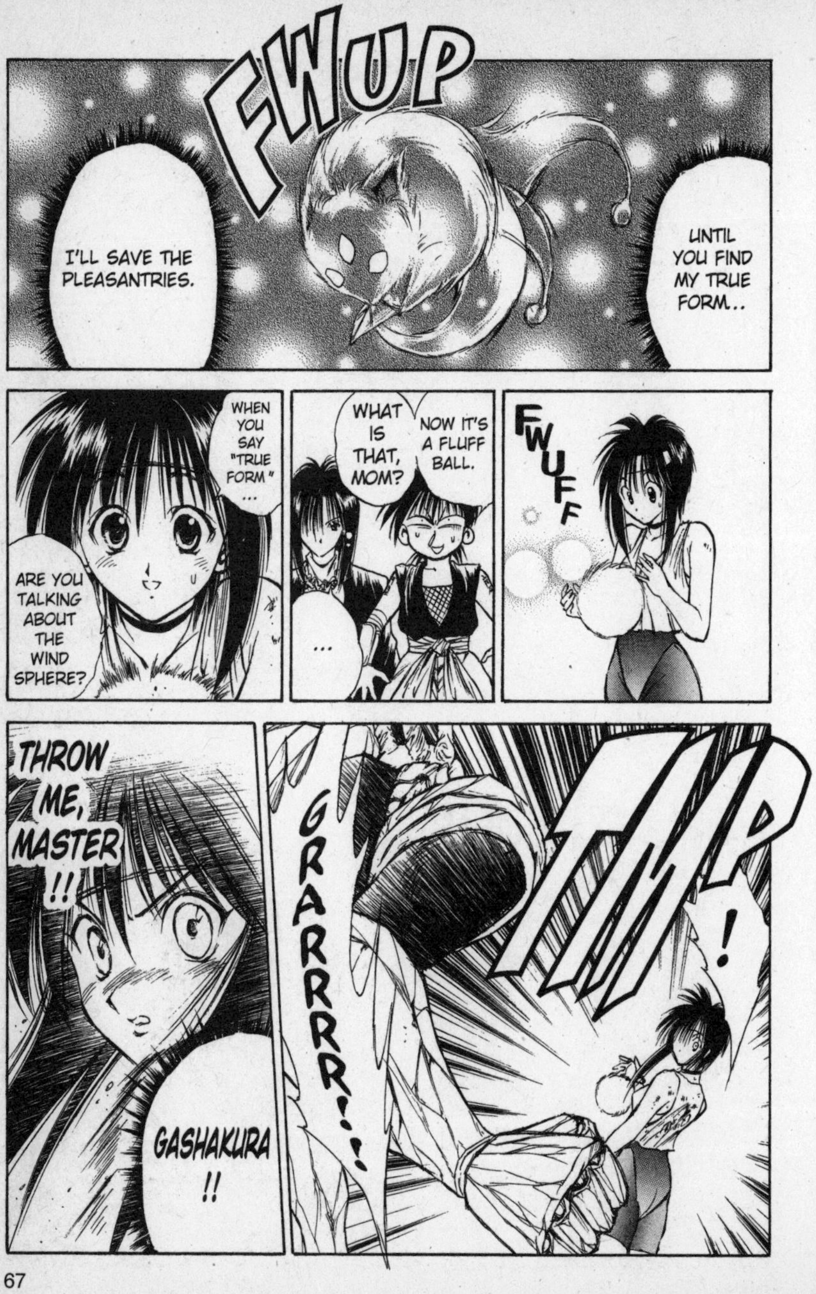
UNTIL YOU FIND MY TRUE FORM..
FWUP
I'LL SAVE THE PLEASANTRIES.
FWUFF
NOW IT'S A FLUFF BALL.
WHAT IS THAT, MOM?
...
WHEN YOU SAY "TRUE FORM" ...
ARE YOU TALKING ABOUT THE WIND SPHERE?
THP!
GRARRRRR!!!
THROW ME, MASTER!!
GASHAKURA!!

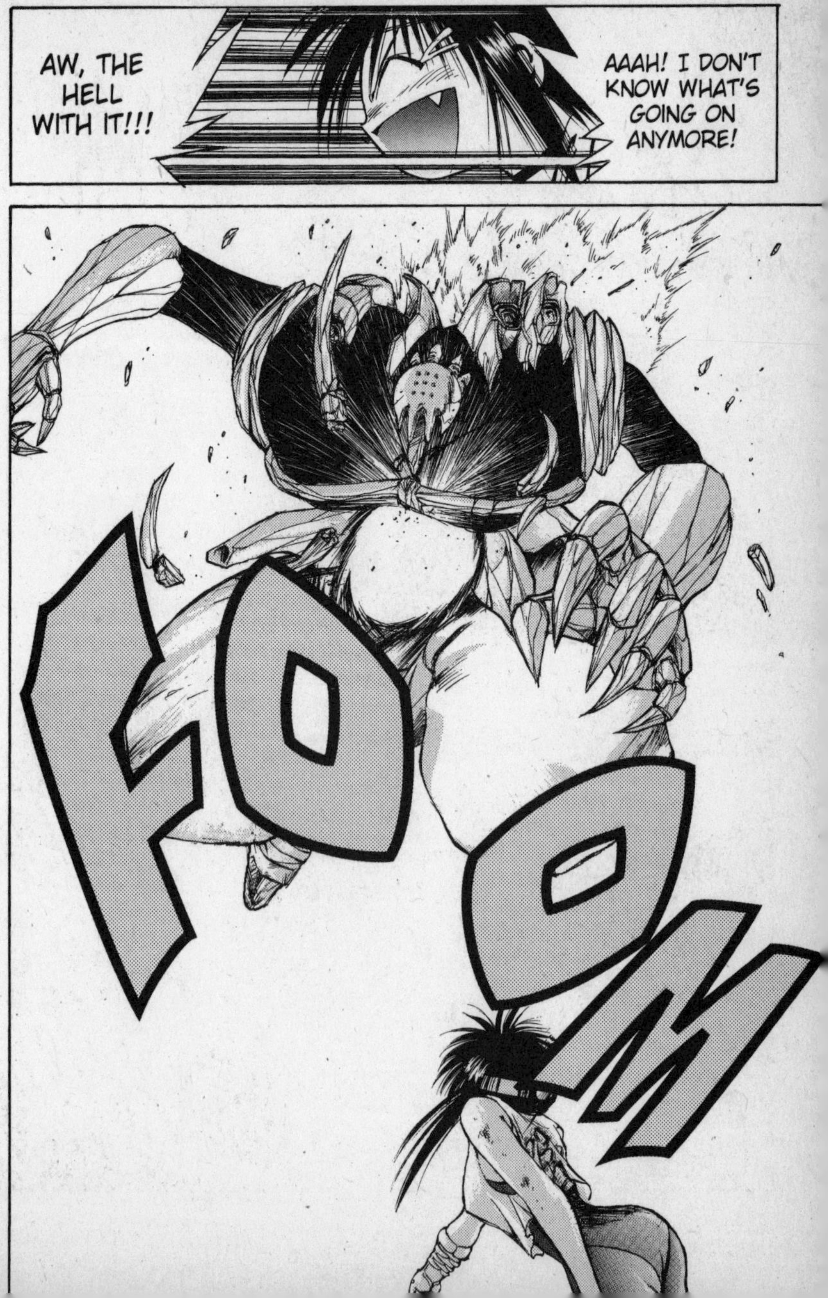
AAAH! I DON'T KNOW WHAT'S GOING ON ANYMORE!
AW, THE HELL WITH IT!!!
FOOM

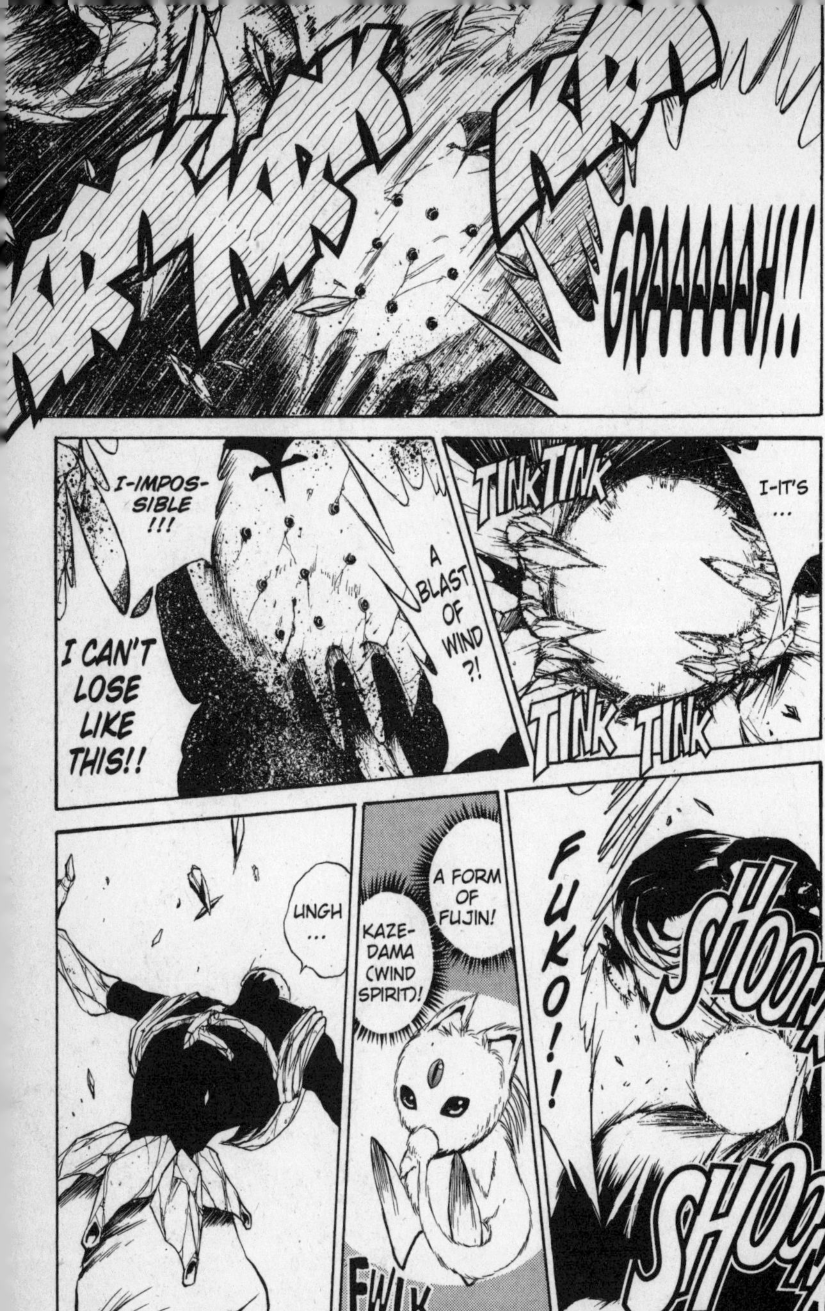
GRAAAAH!!!
I-IT'S ...
TINK TINK
TINK TINK
A BLAST OF WIND ?!
I-IMPOSSIBLE !!!
I CAN'T LOSE LIKE THIS!!
FUKO!!
SHOOOK
SHOOOK
A FORM OF FUJIN!
KAZE-DAMA (WIND SPIRIT)!
FWIK
UNGH ...

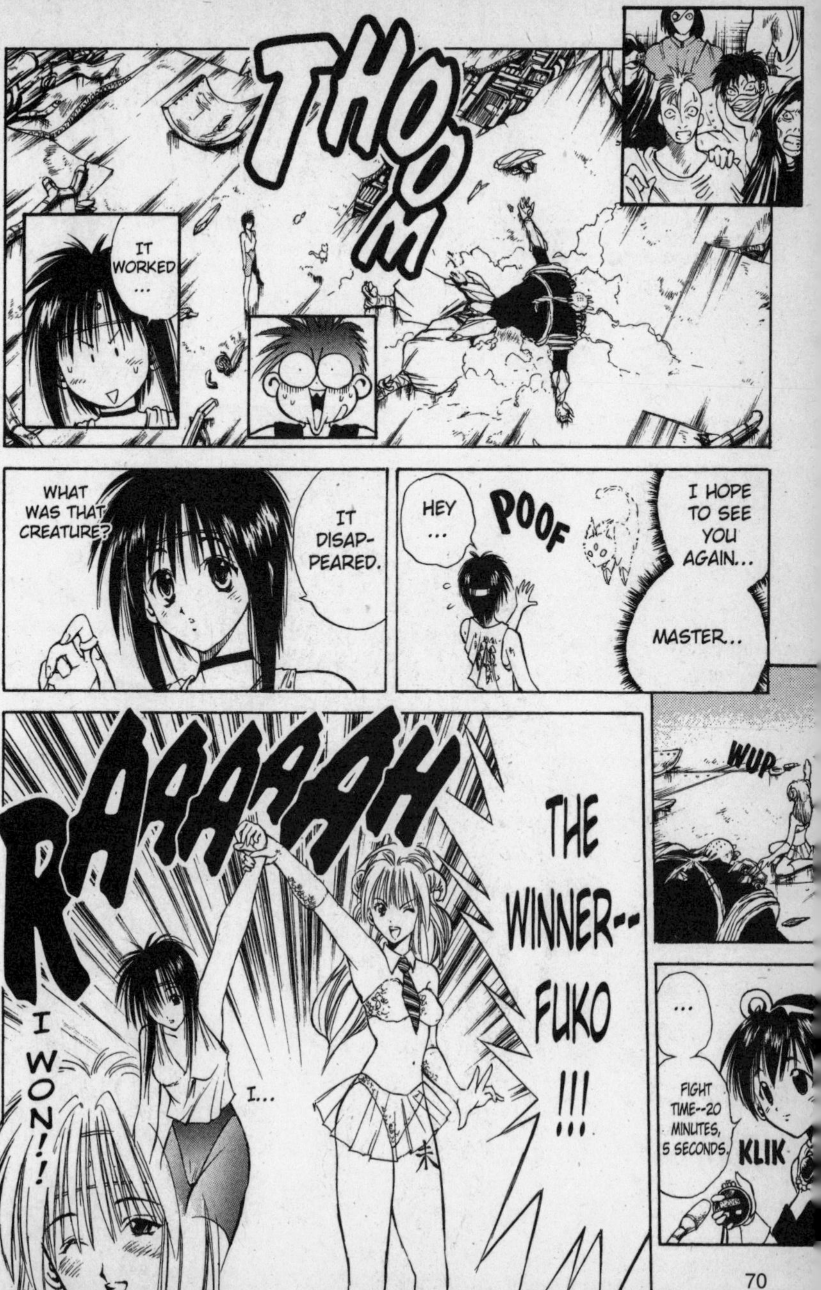
THOOM
IT WORKED...
I HOPE TO SEE YOU AGAIN...
MASTER...
POOF
HEY...
IT DISAPPEARED.
WHAT WAS THAT CREATURE?
WUP
...
FIGHT TIME--20 MINUTES, 5 SECONDS.
KLIK
RAAAAAH
THE WINNER--FUKO!!!
I...
I WON!!!

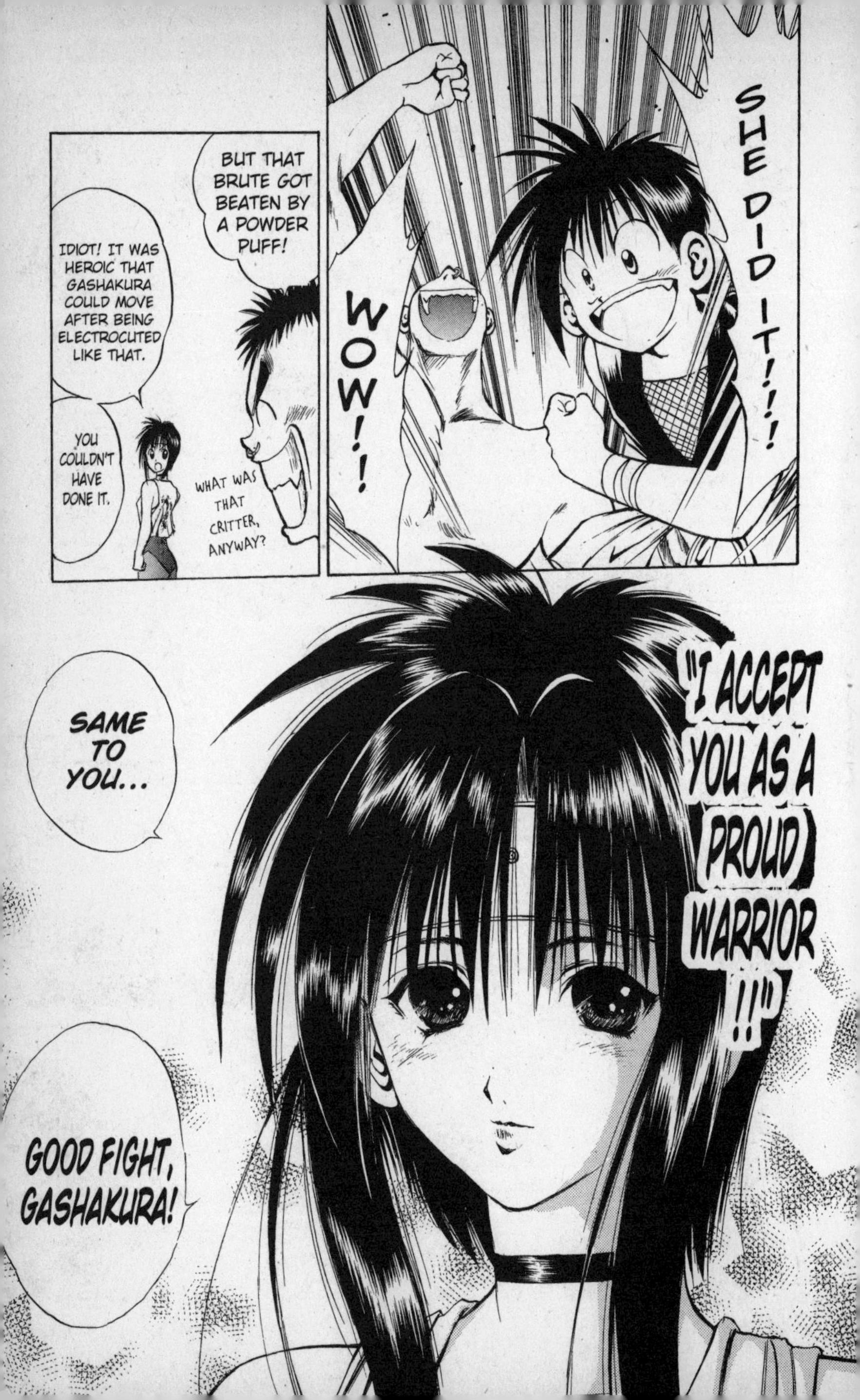
SHE DID IT!!!
WOW!!
BUT THAT BRUTE GOT BEATEN BY A POWDER PUFF!
WHAT WAS THAT CRITTER, ANYWAY?
IDIOT! IT WAS HEROIC THAT GASHAKURA COULD MOVE AFTER BEING ELECTROCUTED LIKE THAT.
YOU COULDN'T HAVE DONE IT.
"I ACCEPT YOU AS A PROUD WARRIOR!!"
SAME TO YOU...
GOOD FIGHT, GASHAKURA!

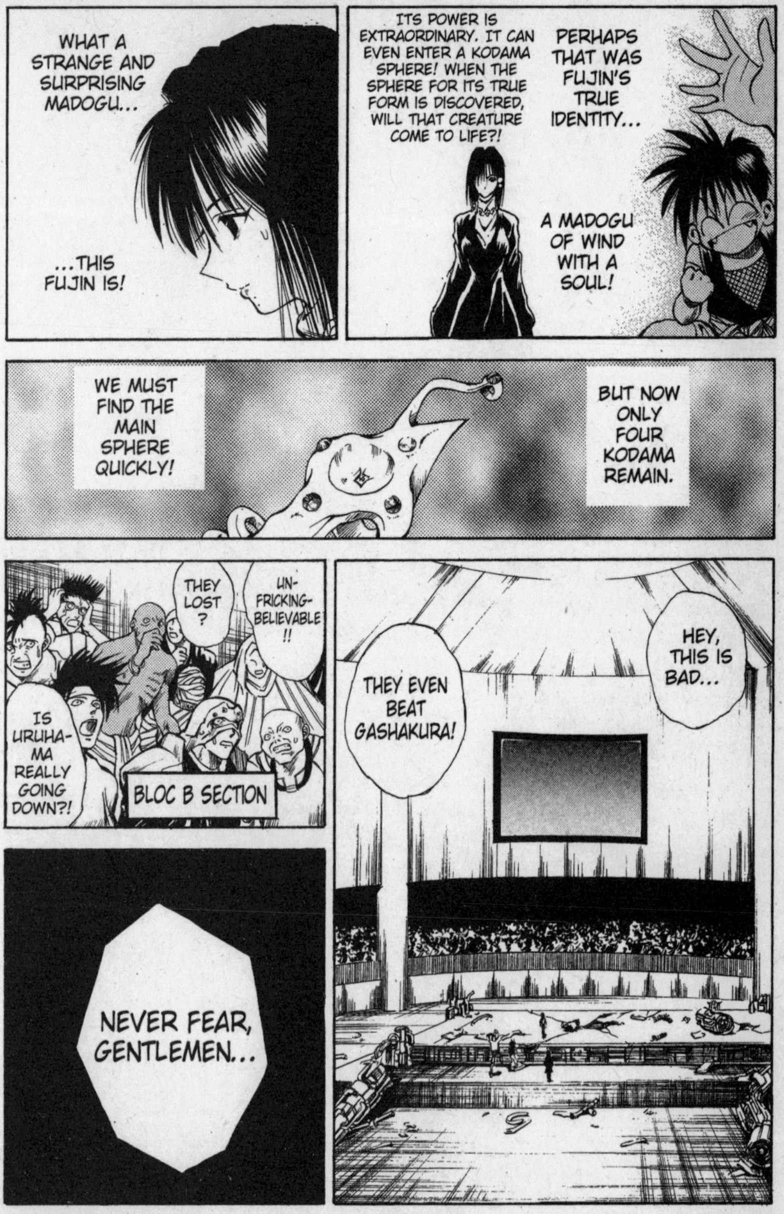
PERHAPS THAT WAS FUJIN'S TRUE IDENTITY...
A MADOGU OF WIND WITH A SOUL!
ITS POWER IS EXTRAORDINARY. IT CAN EVEN ENTER A KODAMA SPHERE! WHEN THE SPHERE FOR ITS TRUE FORM IS DISCOVERED, WILL THAT CREATURE COME TO LIFE?!
WHAT A STRANGE AND SURPRISING MADOGU...
...THIS FUJIN IS!
BUT NOW ONLY FOUR KODAMA REMAIN.
WE MUST FIND THE MAIN SPHERE QUICKLY!
HEY, THIS IS BAD...
THEY EVEN BEAT GASHAKURA!
UN-FRICKING-BELIEVABLE!!
THEY LOST?
IS URUHAMA REALLY GOING DOWN?!
BLOC B SECTION
NEVER FEAR, GENTLEMEN...

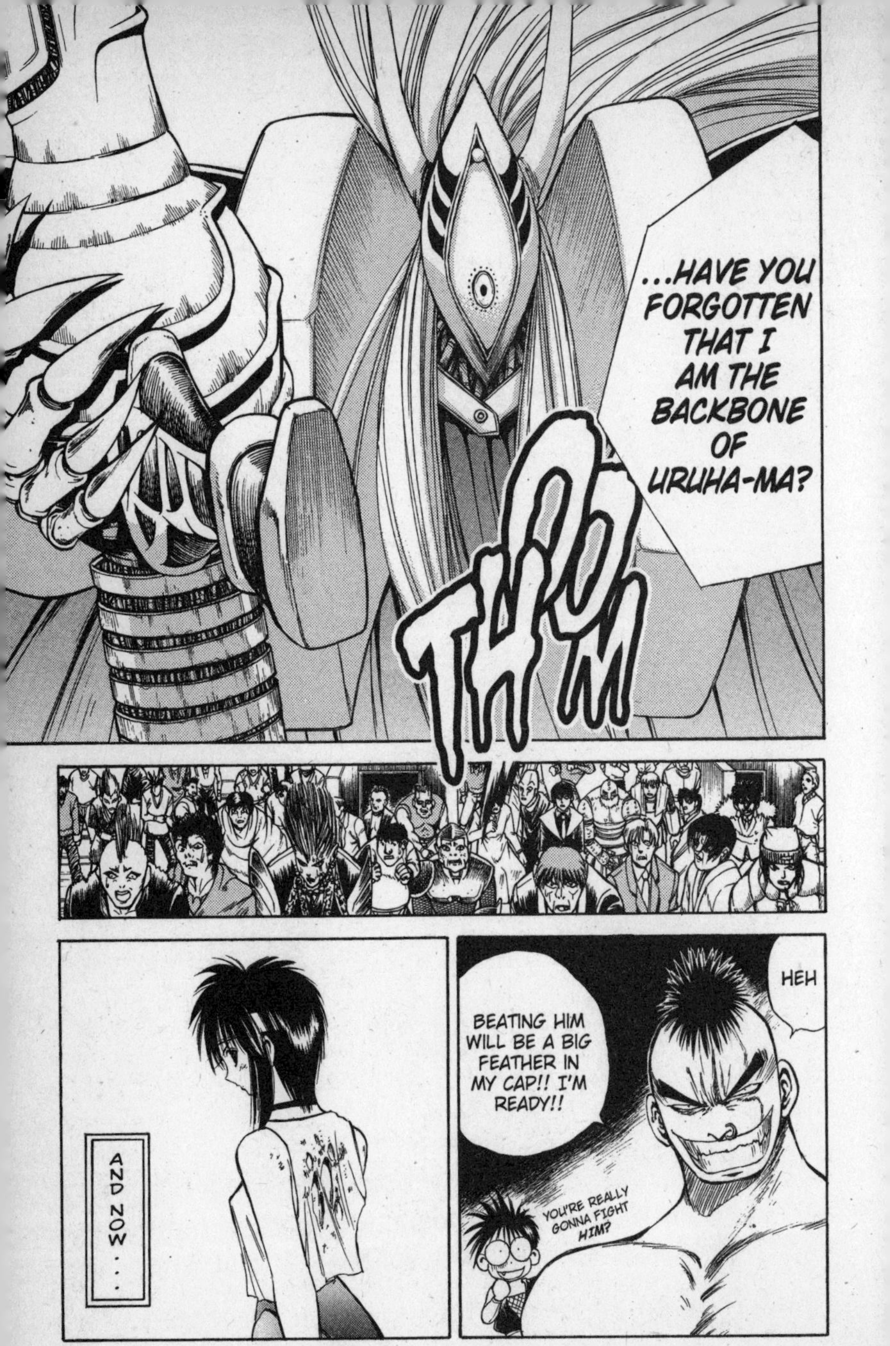
...HAVE YOU FORGOTTEN THAT I AM THE BACKBONE OF URUHA-MA?
THOOM
HEH
BEATING HIM WILL BE A BIG FEATHER IN MY CAP!! I'M READY!!
YOU'RE REALLY GONNA FIGHT HIM?
AND NOW...

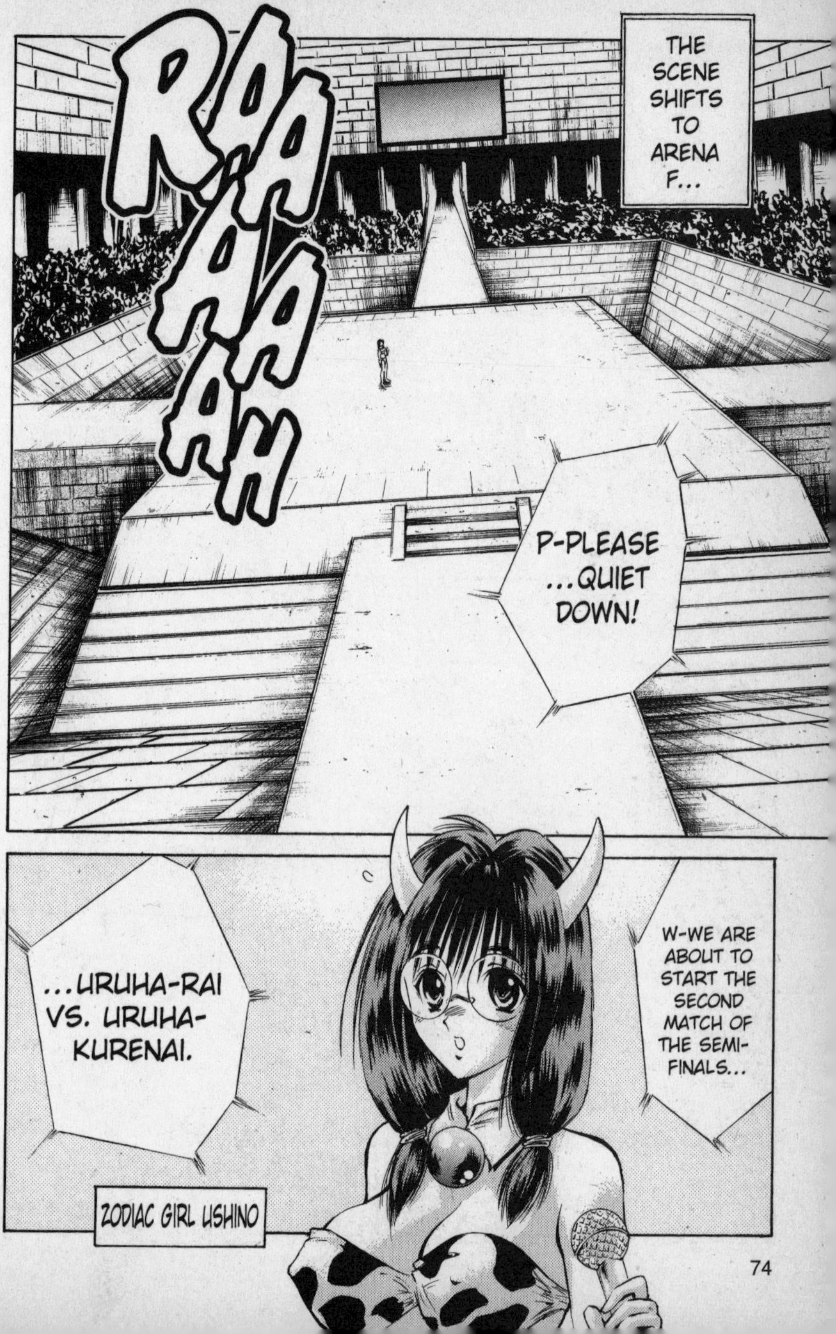
THE SCENE SHIFTS TO ARENA F...
RAAAAAH
P-PLEASE ...QUIET DOWN!
W-WE ARE ABOUT TO START THE SECOND MATCH OF THE SEMI-FINALS...
...URUHA-RAI VS. URUHA-KURENAI.
ZODIAC GIRL USHINO

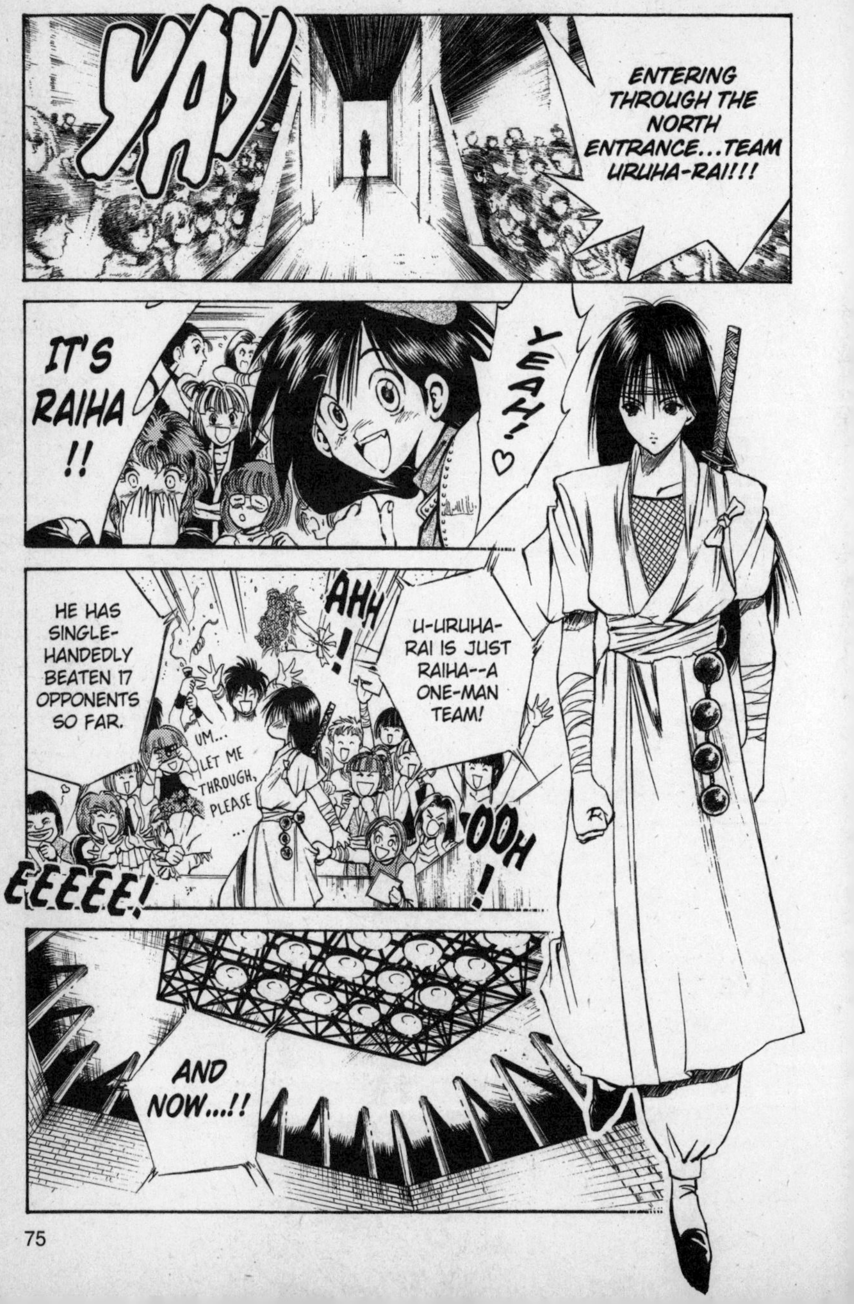
ENTERING THROUGH THE NORTH ENTRANCE...TEAM URUHA-RAI!!!
YAY
YEAH! ♡
IT'S RAIHA !!
U-URUHA-RAI IS JUST RAIHA--A ONE-MAN TEAM!
AHH!
HE HAS SINGLE-HANDEDLY BEATEN 17 OPPONENTS SO FAR.
UM... LET ME THROUGH, PLEASE...
OOH!
EEEEE!
AND NOW...!!

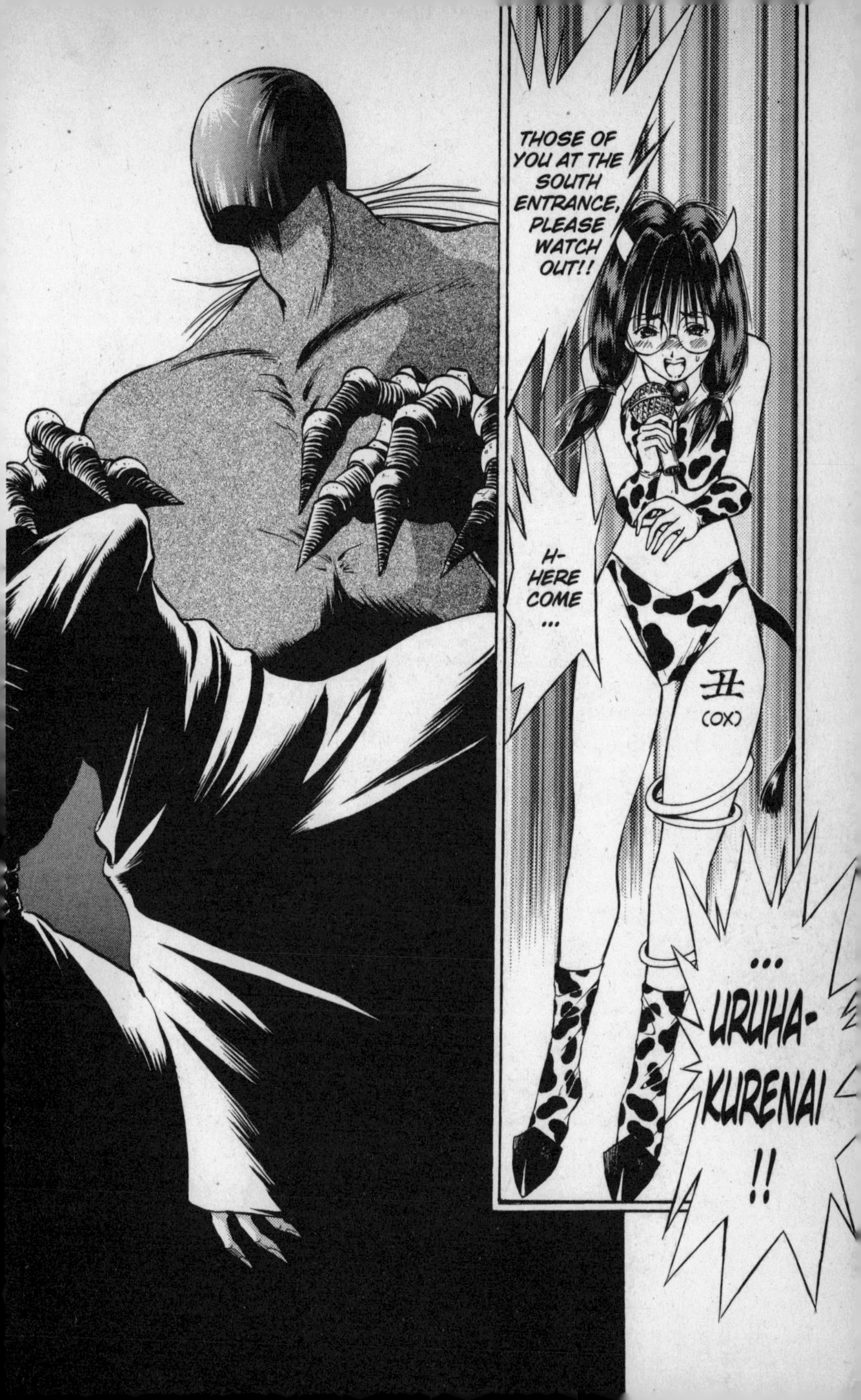
THOSE OF YOU AT THE SOUTH ENTRANCE, PLEASE WATCH OUT!!
H-HERE COME ...
丑
(OX)
... URUHA-KURENAI !!

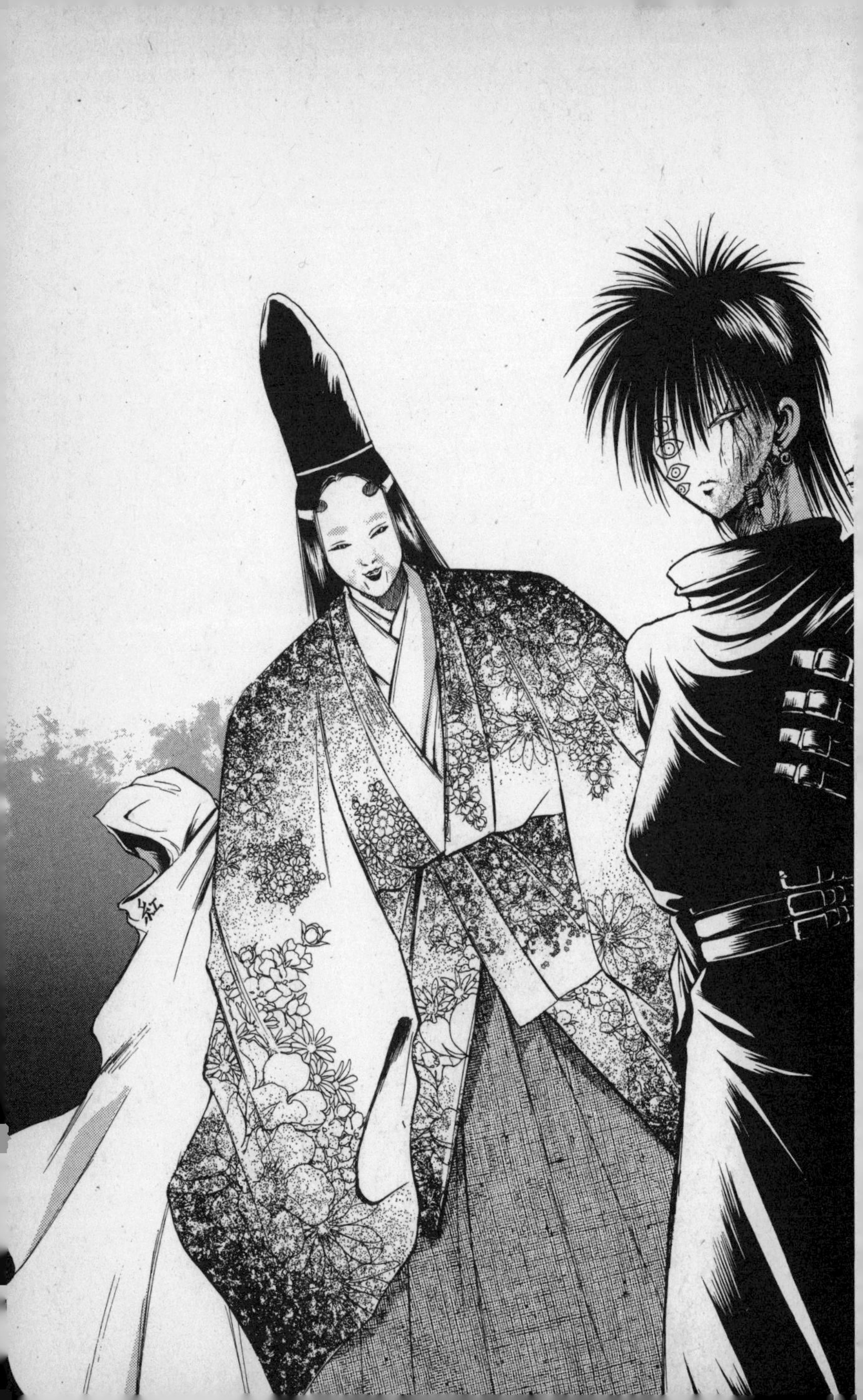
紅

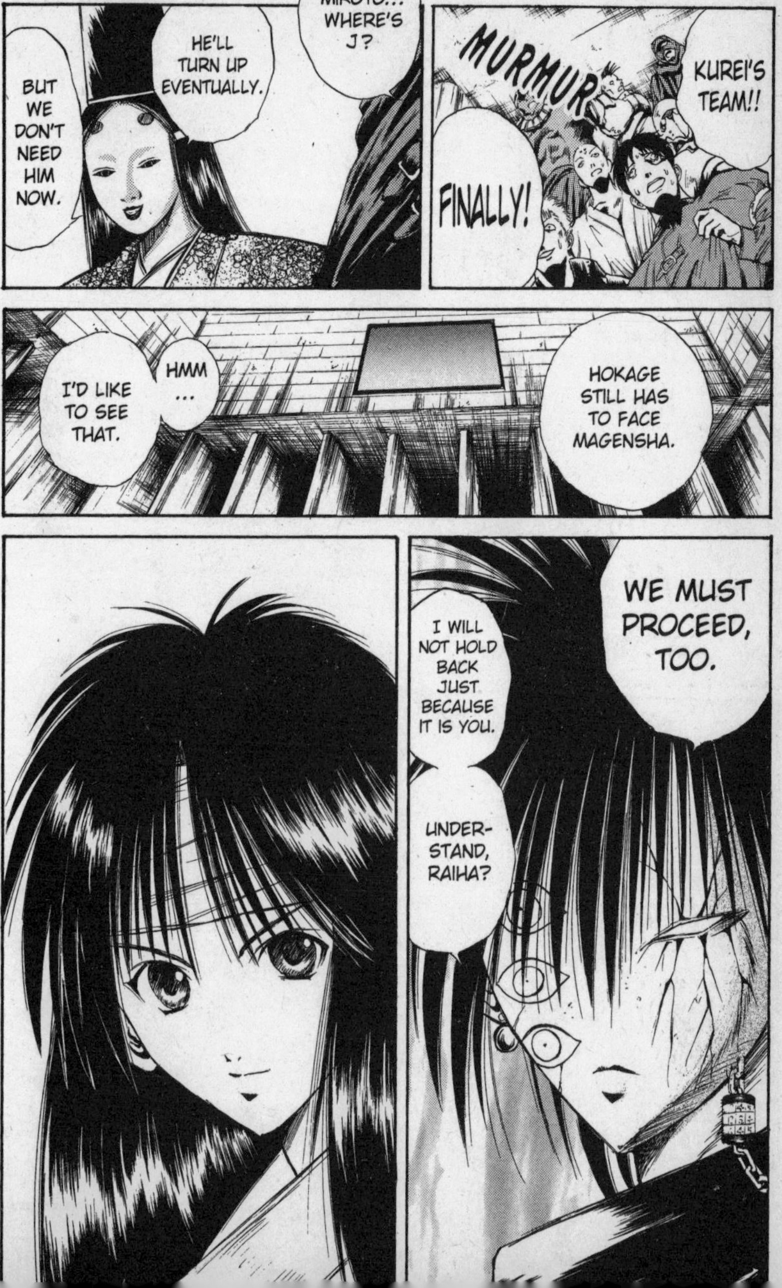
MURMUR
KUREI'S TEAM!!
FINALLY!
MIKOTO... WHERE'S J?
HE'LL TURN UP EVENTUALLY.
BUT WE DON'T NEED HIM NOW.
HOKAGE STILL HAS TO FACE MAGENSHA.
HMM...
I'D LIKE TO SEE THAT.
WE MUST PROCEED, TOO.
I WILL NOT HOLD BACK JUST BECAUSE IT IS YOU.
UNDERSTAND, RAIHA?

Part Ninety two: The Other Semi-Finals (2) A Lamp At Noon

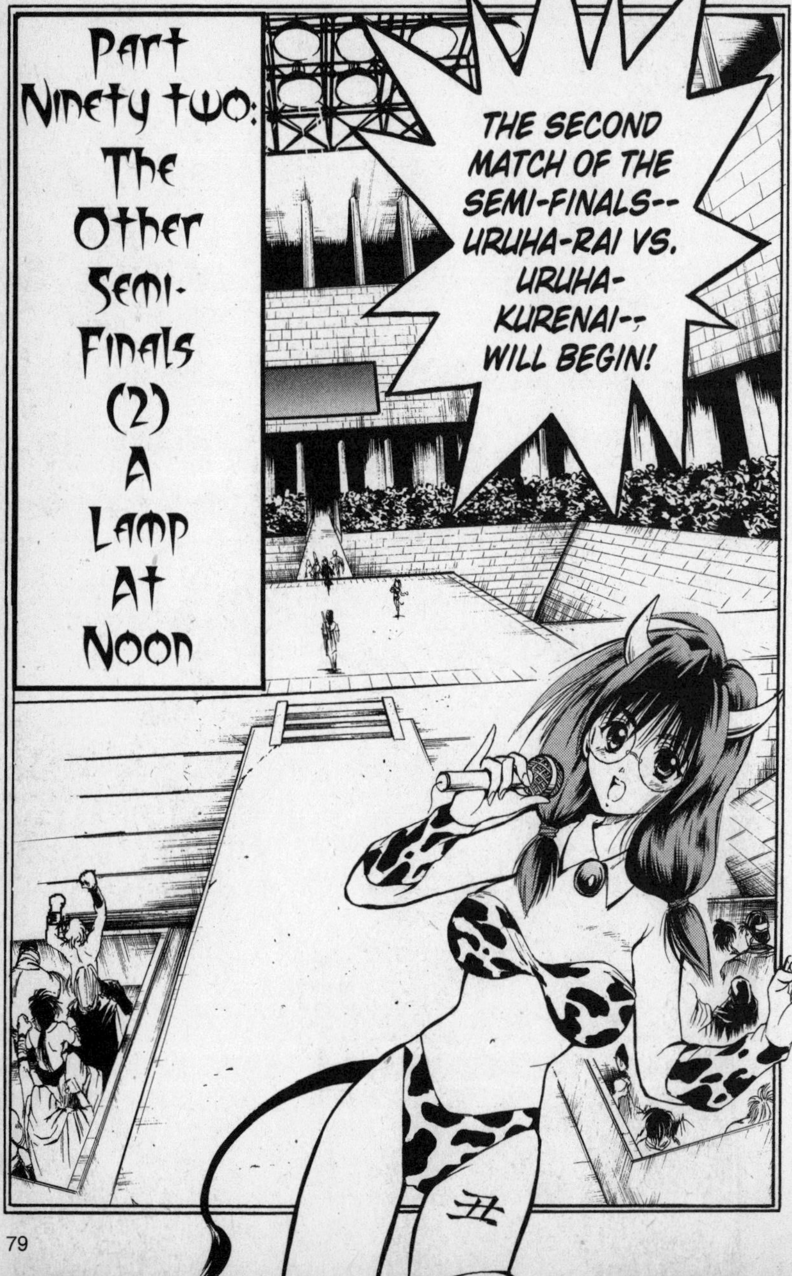
THE SECOND MATCH OF THE SEMI-FINALS-- URUHA-RAI VS. URUHA-KURENAI-- WILL BEGIN!

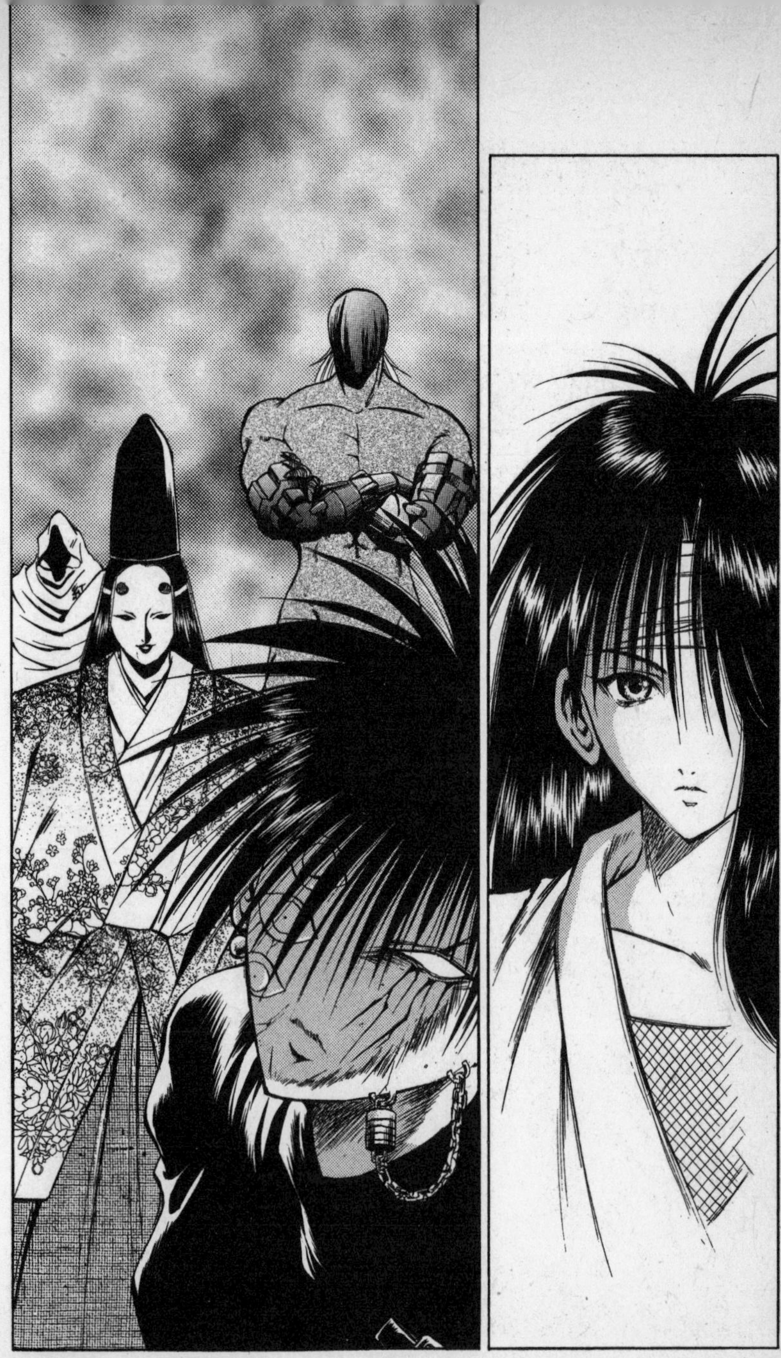

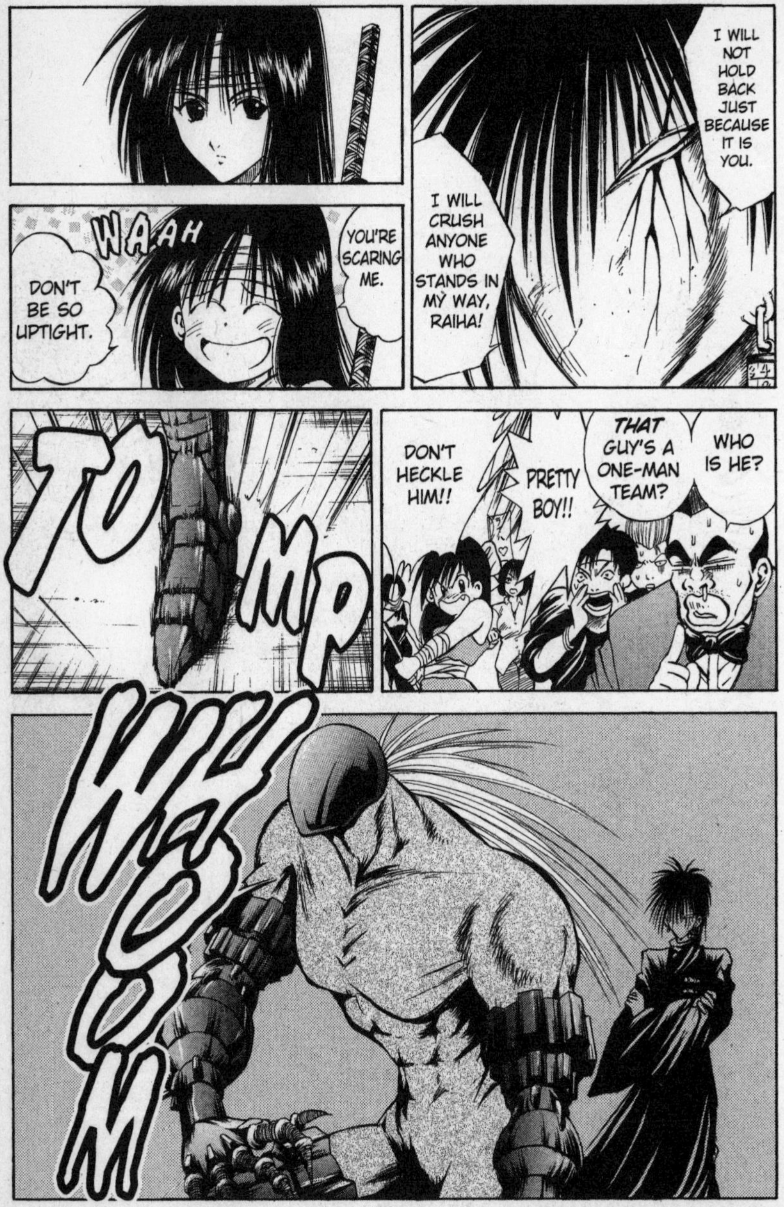
I WILL NOT HOLD BACK JUST BECAUSE IT IS YOU.
I WILL CRUSH ANYONE WHO STANDS IN MY WAY, RAIHA!
YOU'RE SCARING ME.
WAAH
DON'T BE SO UPTIGHT.
WHO IS HE?
THAT GUY'S A ONE-MAN TEAM?
PRETTY BOY!!
DON'T HECKLE HIM!!
TOMP
WHOOOM

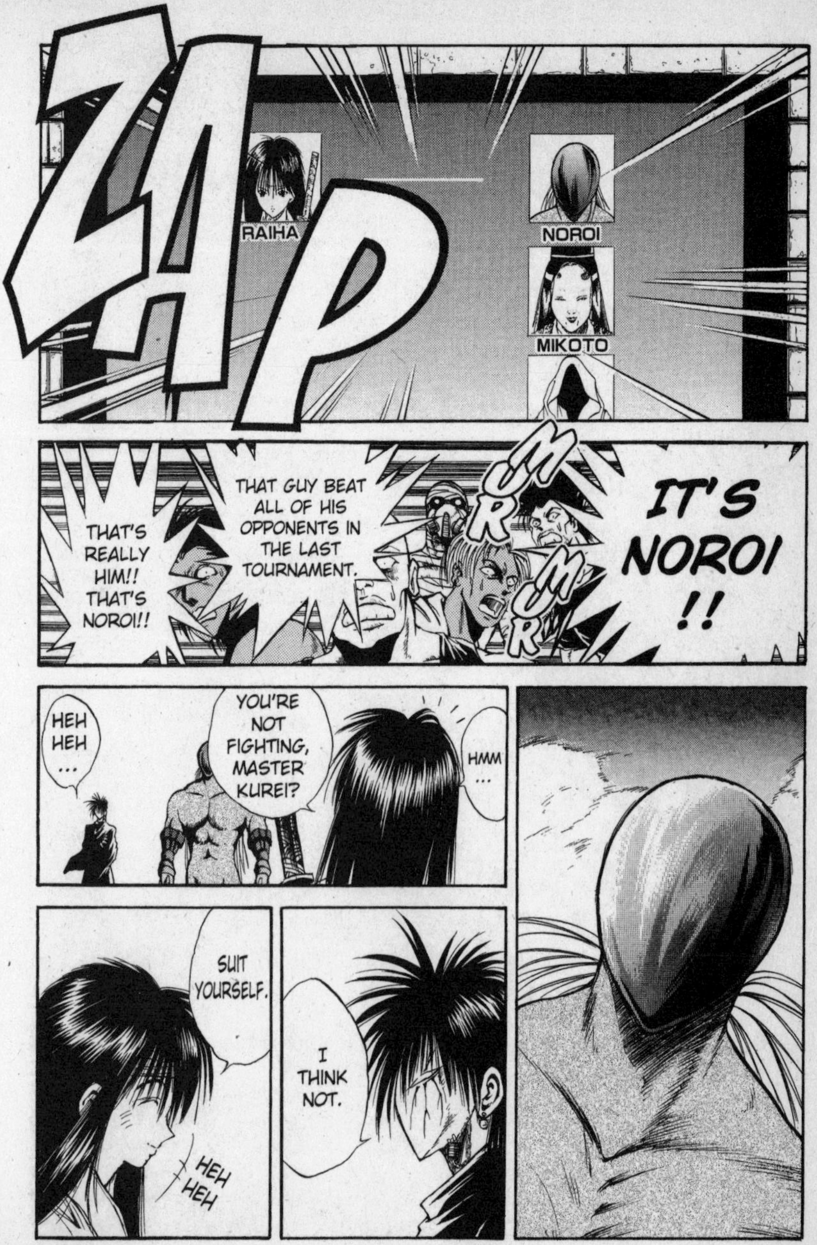
NOROI
MIKOTO
RAIHA
ZAP
IT'S NOROI!!
MURMUR
THAT GUY BEAT ALL OF HIS OPPONENTS IN THE LAST TOURNAMENT.
THAT'S REALLY HIM!! THAT'S NOROI!!
HMM ...
YOU'RE NOT FIGHTING, MASTER KUREI?
HEH HEH ...
I THINK NOT.
SUIT YOURSELF.
HEH HEH

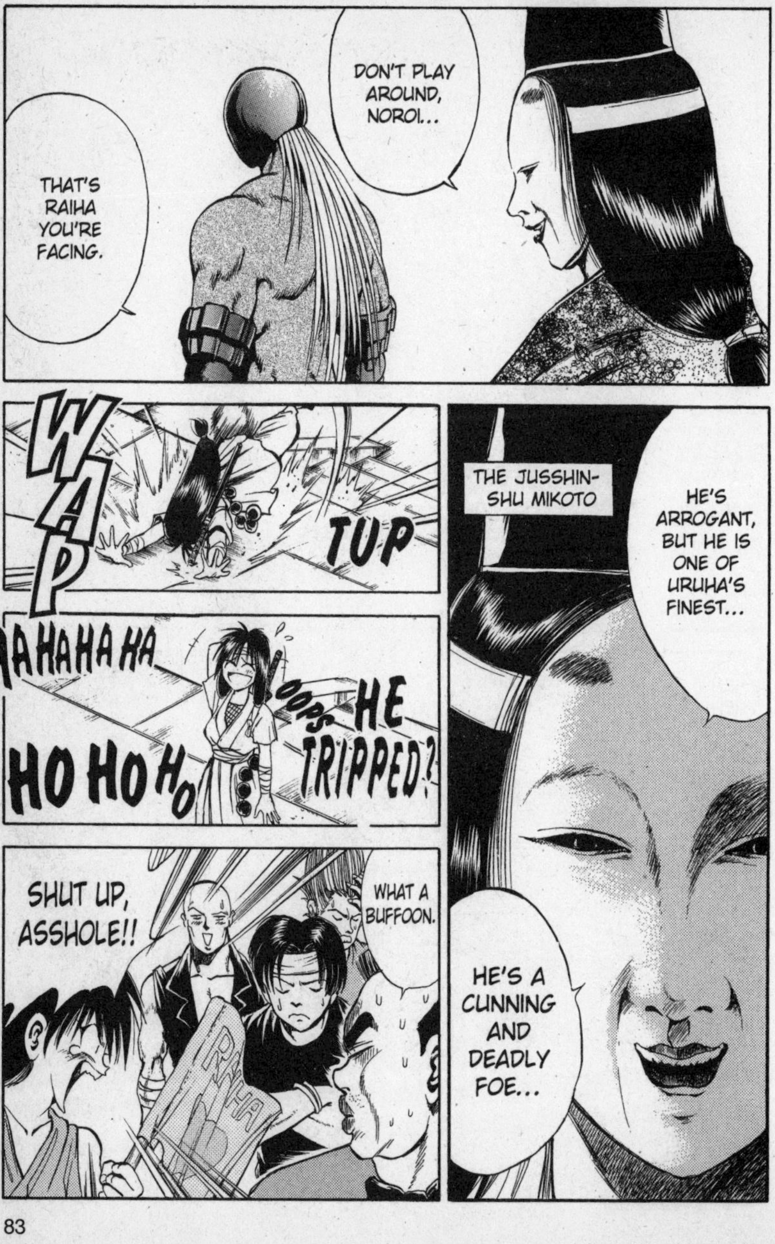
DON'T PLAY AROUND, NOROI...
THAT'S RAIHA YOU'RE FACING.
THE JUSSHIN-SHU MIKOTO
HE'S ARROGANT, BUT HE IS ONE OF URUHA'S FINEST...
HE'S A CUNNING AND DEADLY FOE...
TUP
WAP
HE TRIPPED?
OOPS
HAHAHAHA
HO HO HO HO
WHAT A BUFFOON.
SHUT UP, ASSHOLE!!

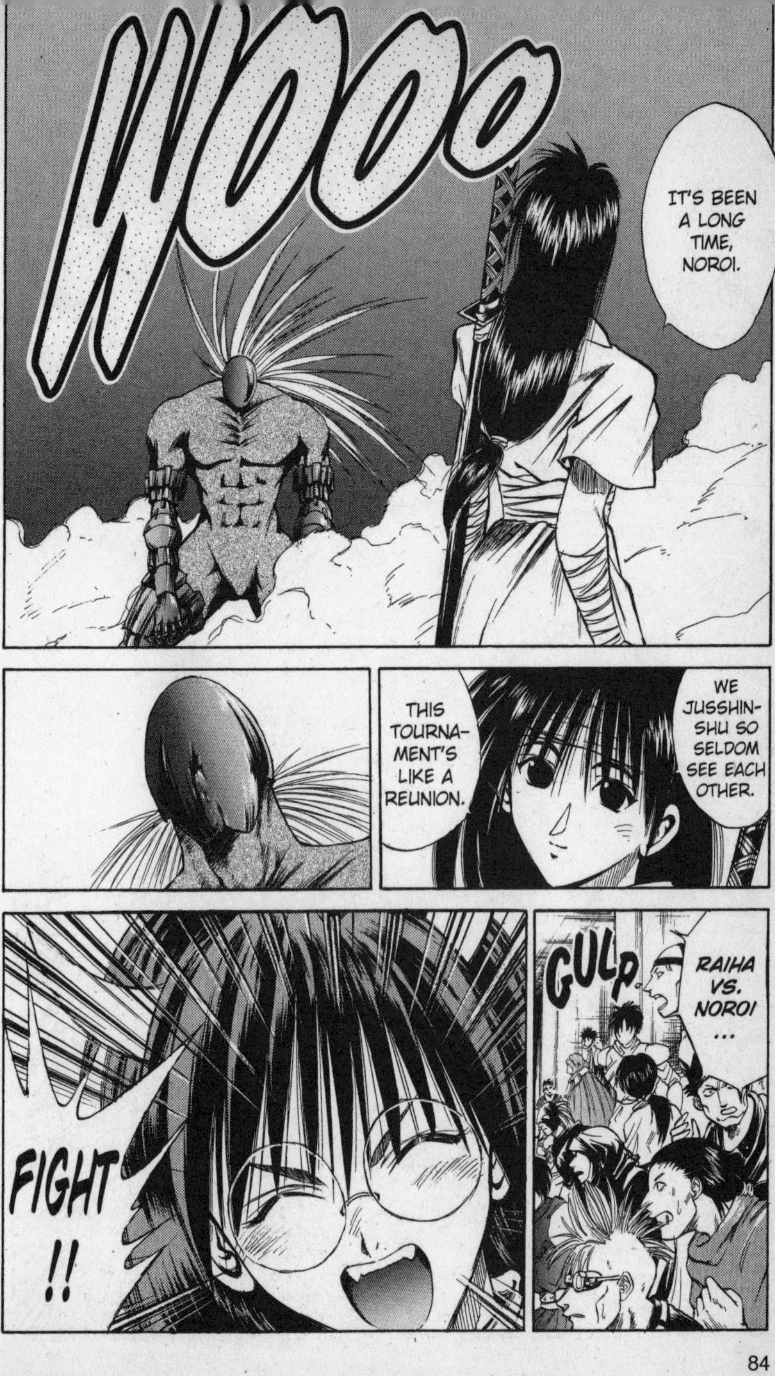
IT'S BEEN A LONG TIME, NOROI.
YOOOO
WE JUSSHIN-SHU SO SELDOM SEE EACH OTHER.
THIS TOURNA-MENT'S LIKE A REUNION.
RAIHA VS. NOROI ...
GULP
FIGHT !!

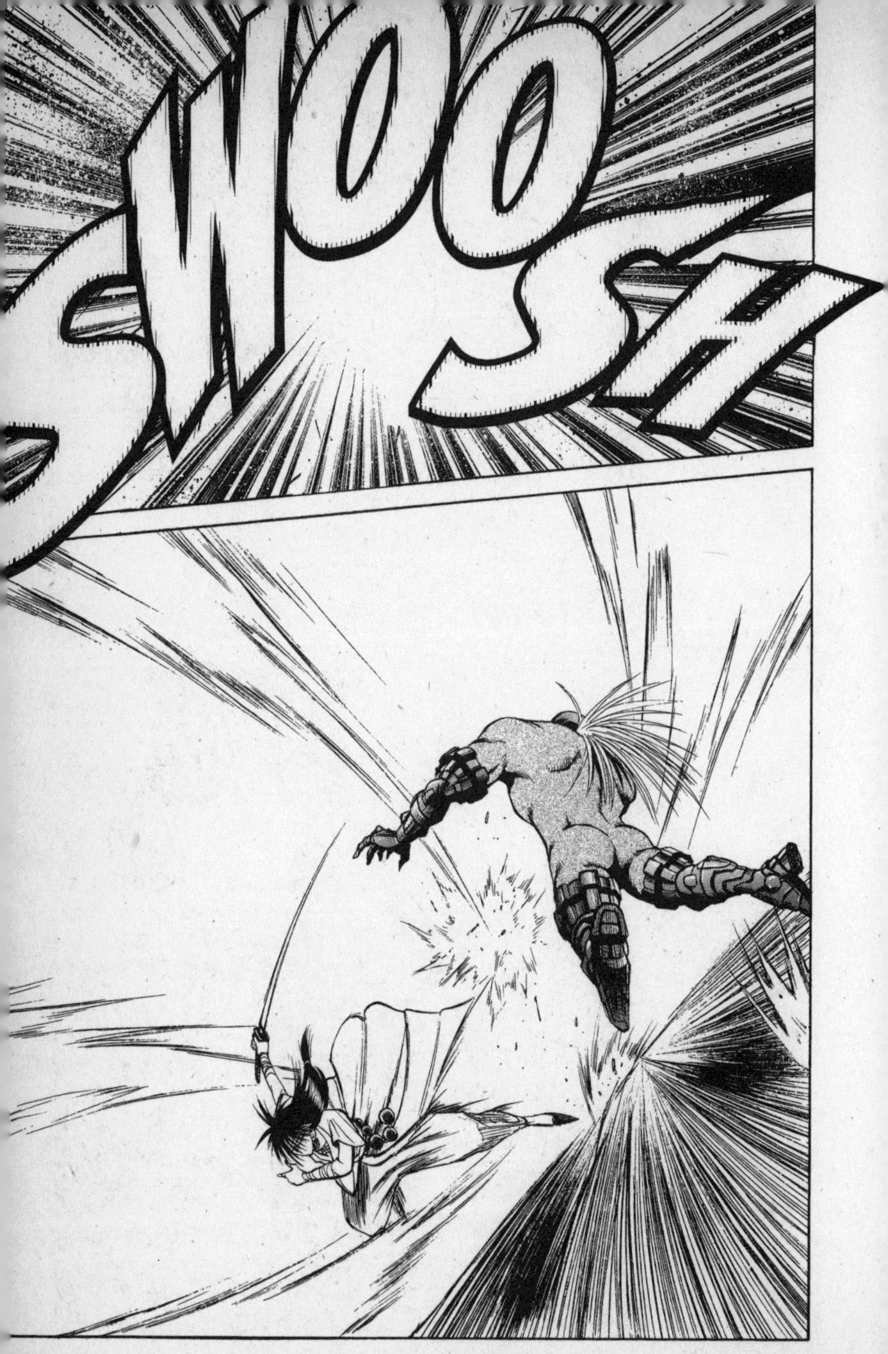
SHOOSH

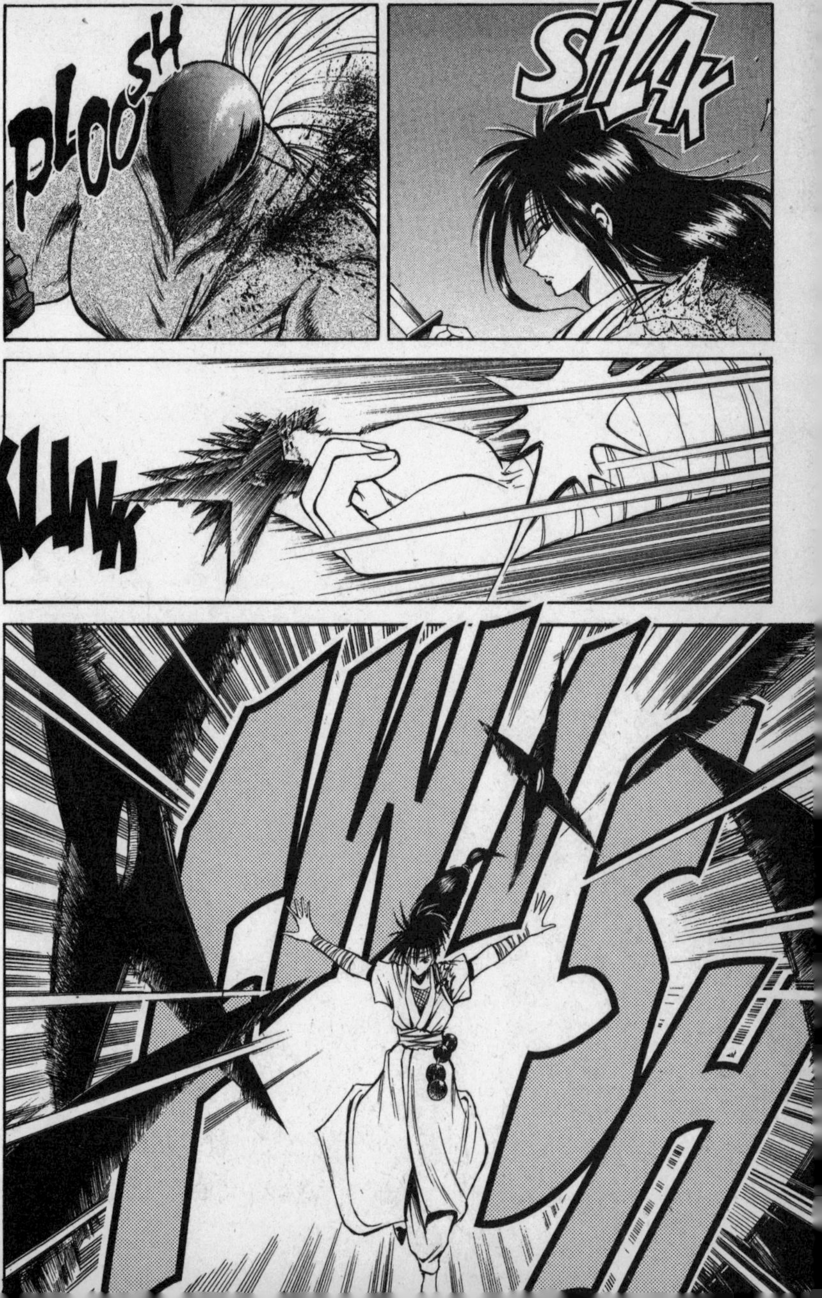
SHLAK
PLOOSH
KLINK

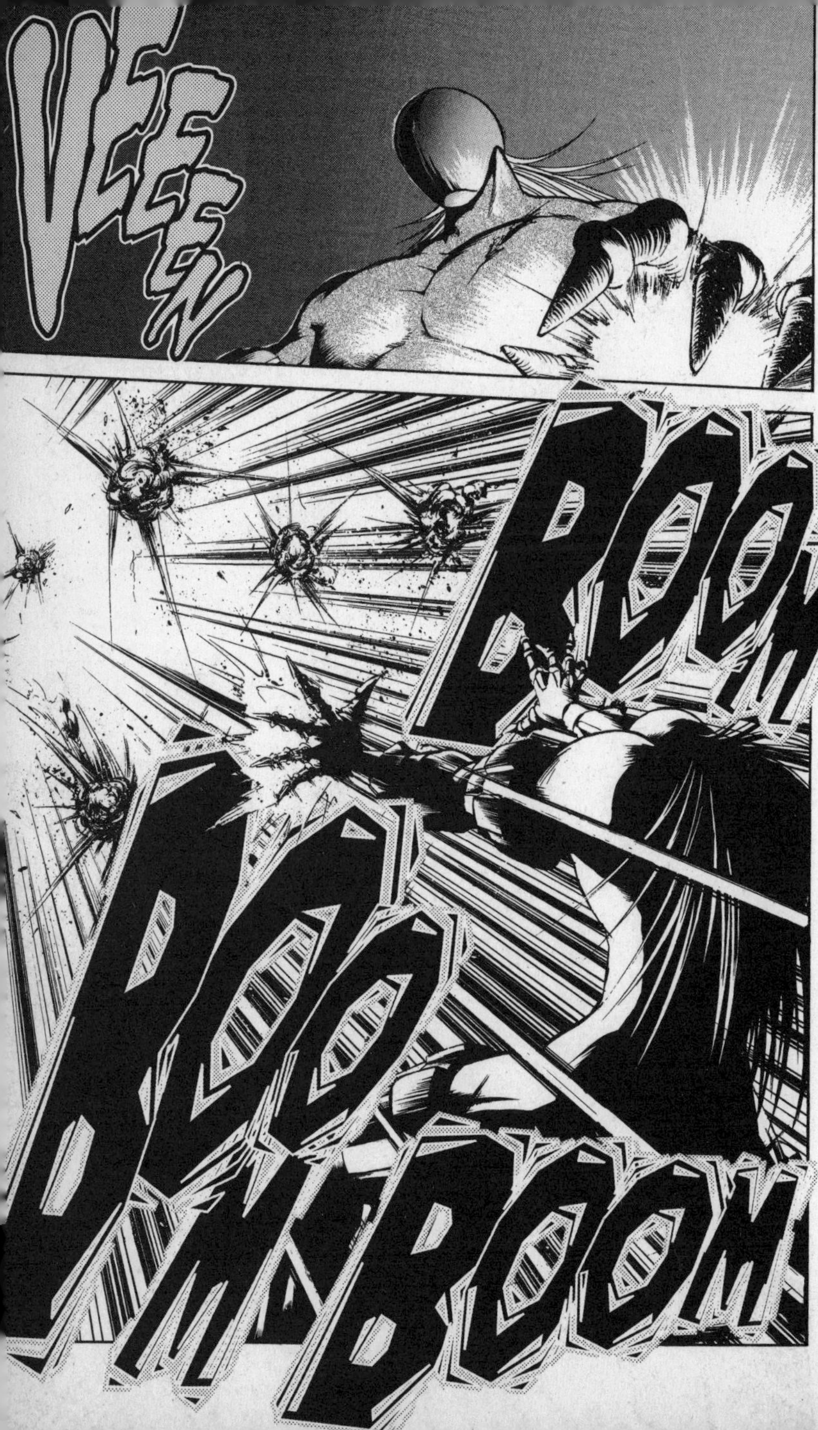
VEEEEN
BOOM
BOOM
BOOM

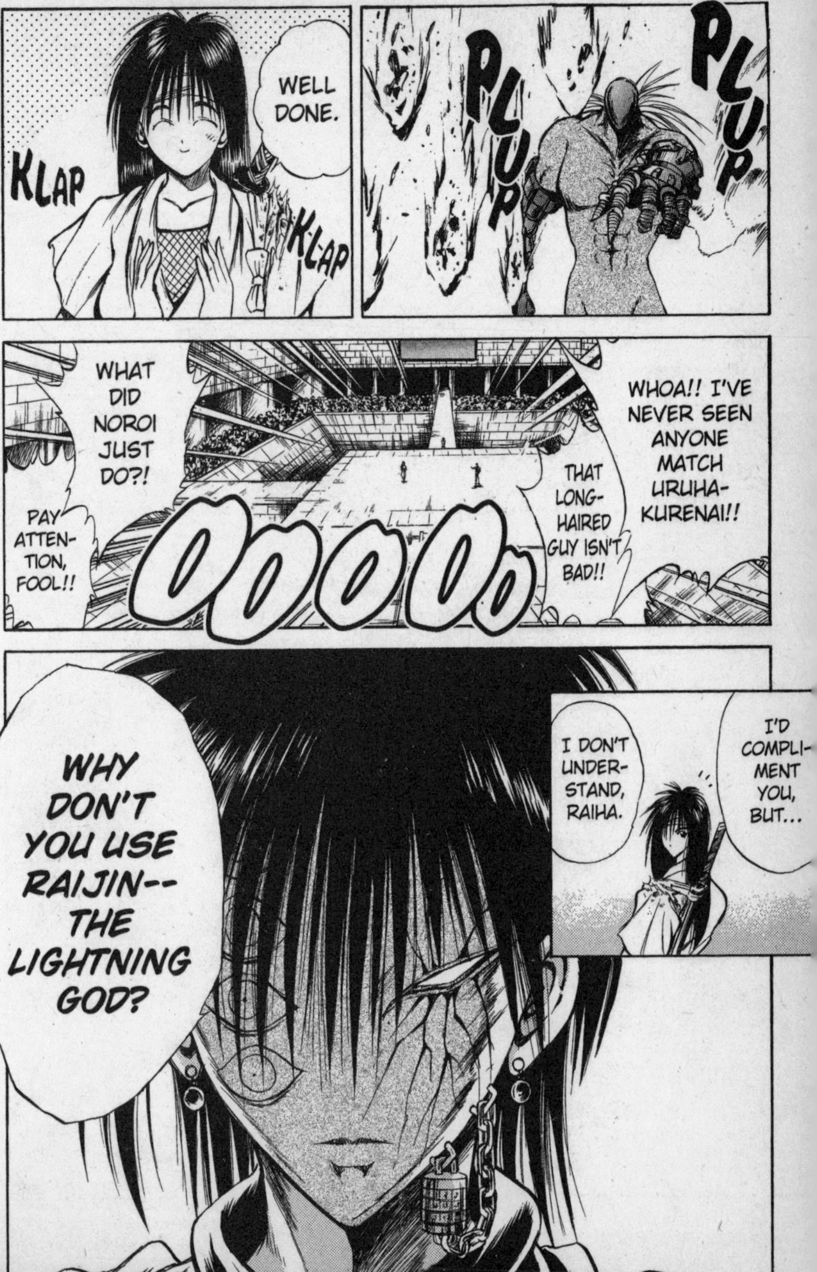
PLUP
PLUP
WELL DONE.
KLAP
KLAP
WHOA!! I'VE NEVER SEEN ANYONE MATCH URUHA-KURENAI!!
THAT LONG-HAIRED GUY ISN'T BAD!!
OOOO
WHAT DID NOROI JUST DO?!
PAY ATTENTION, FOOL!!
I'D COMPLIMENT YOU, BUT...
I DON'T UNDERSTAND, RAIHA.
WHY DON'T YOU USE RAIJIN-- THE LIGHTNING GOD?

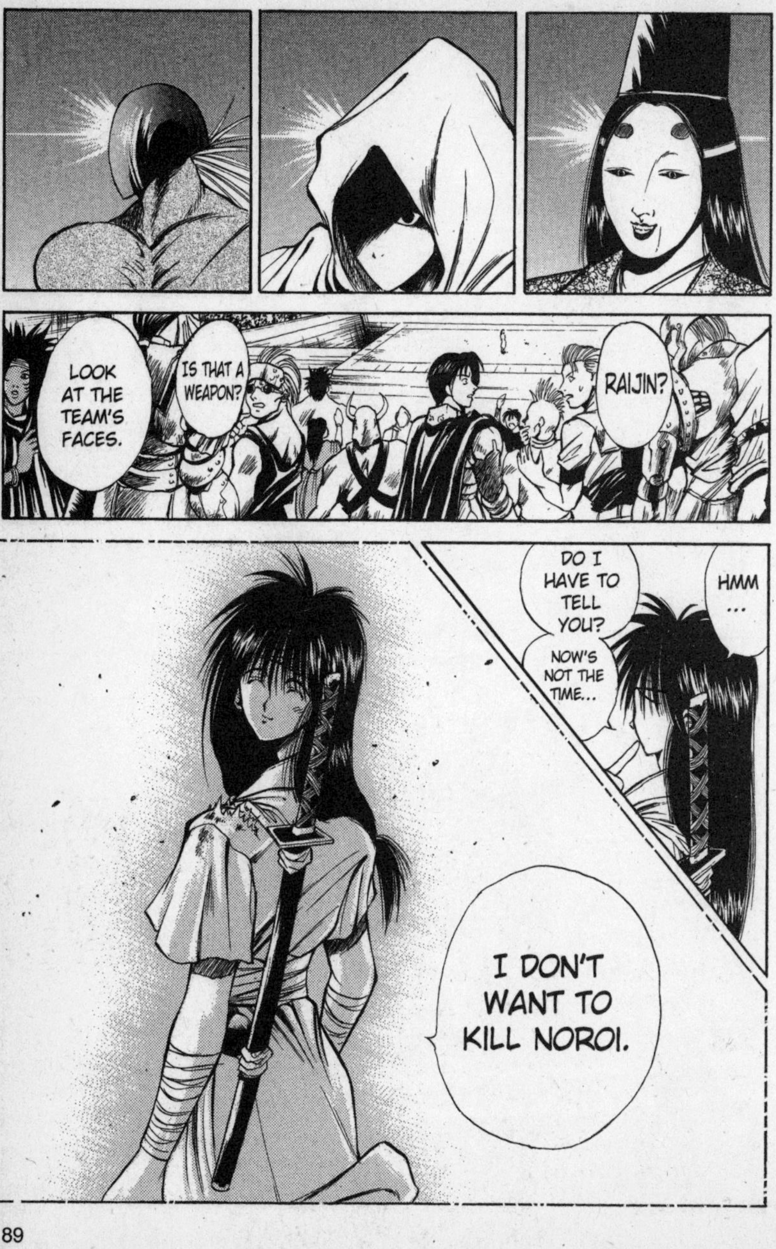
RAIJIN?
IS THAT A WEAPON?
LOOK AT THE TEAM'S FACES.
HMM ...
DO I HAVE TO TELL YOU?
NOW'S NOT THE TIME...
I DON'T WANT TO KILL NOROI.

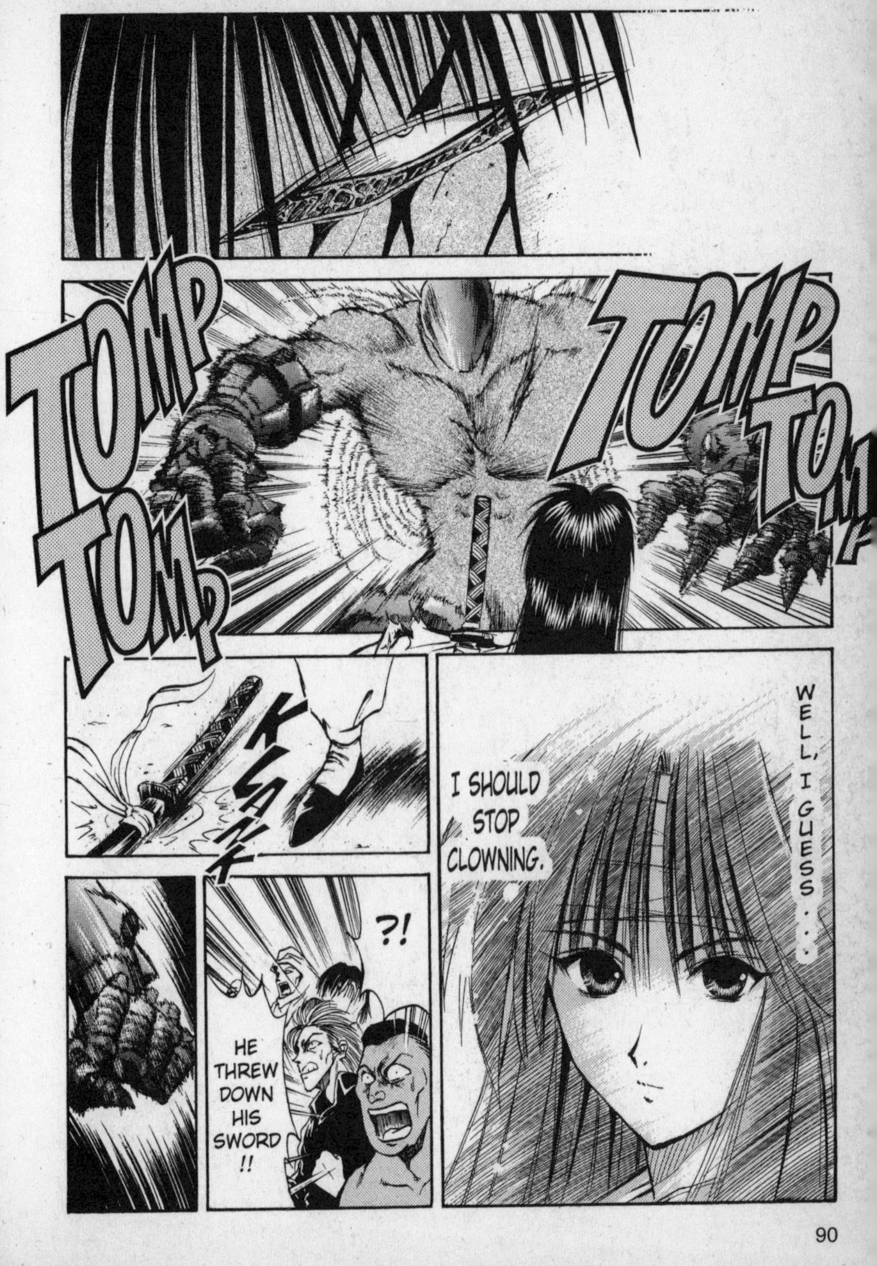
TOMP
TOM
TOMP
TOMP
WELL, I GUESS . . .
I SHOULD STOP CLOWNING.
KLANK
?!
HE THREW DOWN HIS SWORD !!

STOP, NOROI!!

WOOSH

HEH...

FWUMP

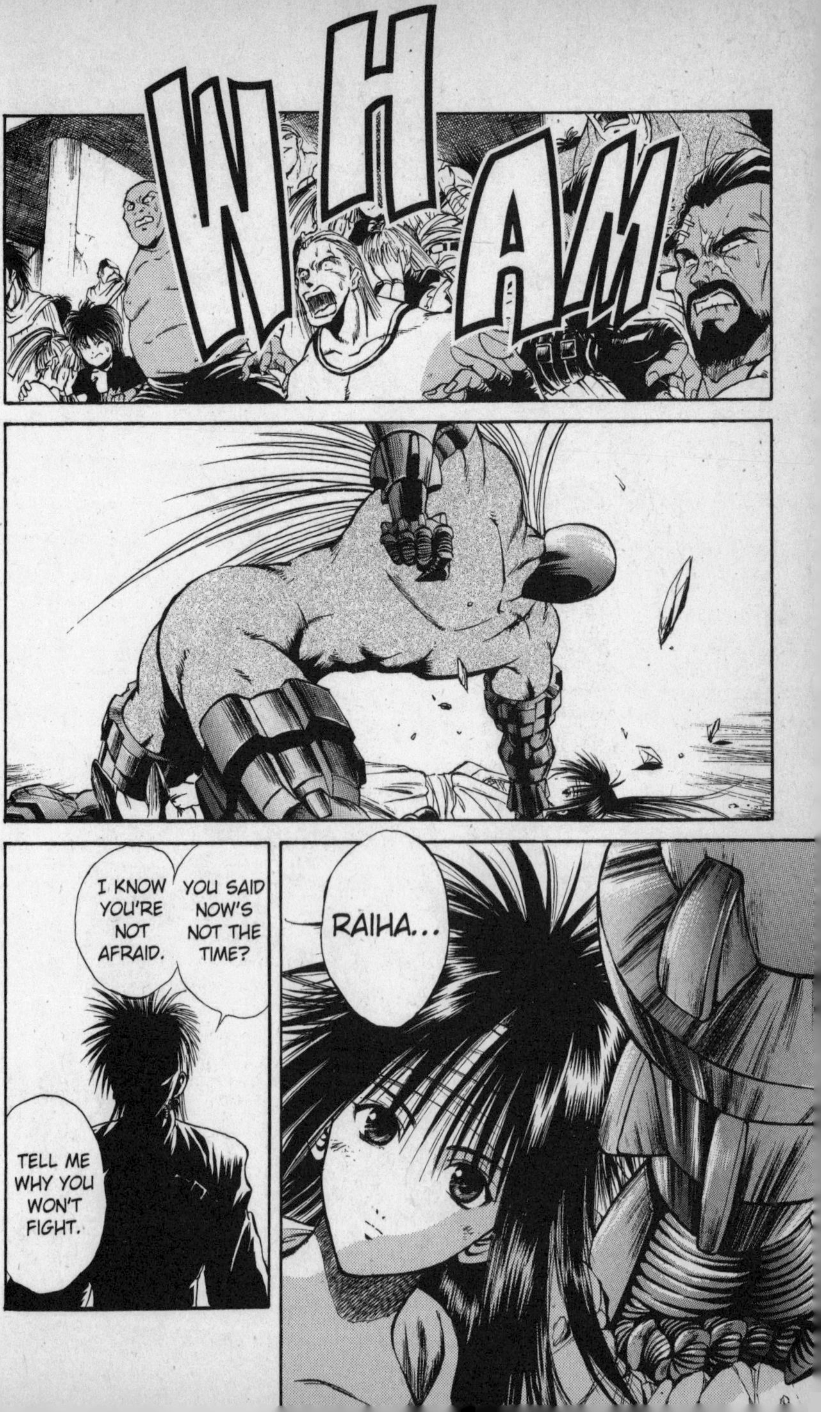
WHAM
RAIHA...
YOU SAID NOW'S NOT THE TIME?
I KNOW YOU'RE NOT AFRAID.
TELL ME WHY YOU WON'T FIGHT.

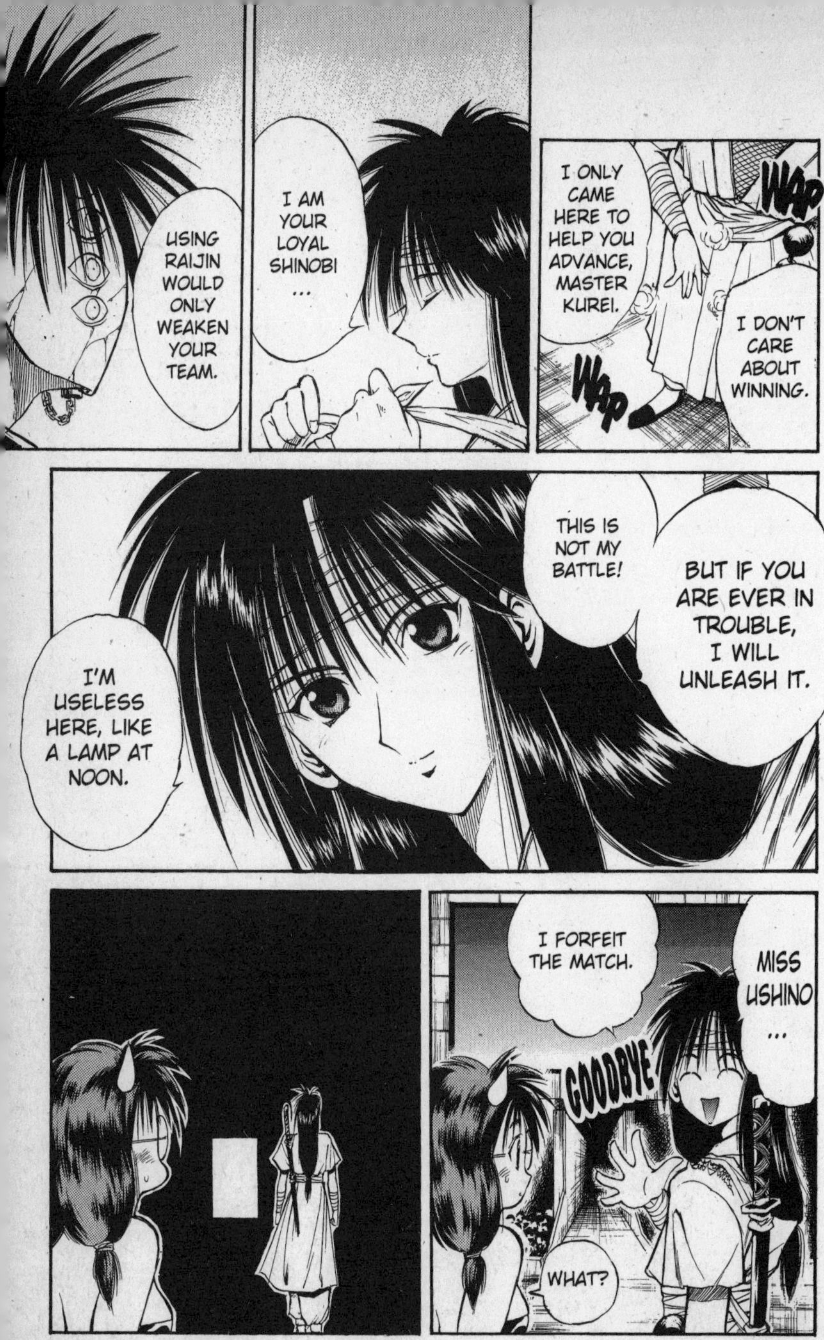
WAP
I DON'T CARE ABOUT WINNING.
I ONLY CAME HERE TO HELP YOU ADVANCE, MASTER KUREI.
WAP
I AM YOUR LOYAL SHINOBI ...
USING RAIJIN WOULD ONLY WEAKEN YOUR TEAM.
BUT IF YOU ARE EVER IN TROUBLE, I WILL UNLEASH IT.
THIS IS NOT MY BATTLE!
I'M USELESS HERE, LIKE A LAMP AT NOON.
MISS USHINO ...
I FORFEIT THE MATCH.
GOODBYE
WHAT?

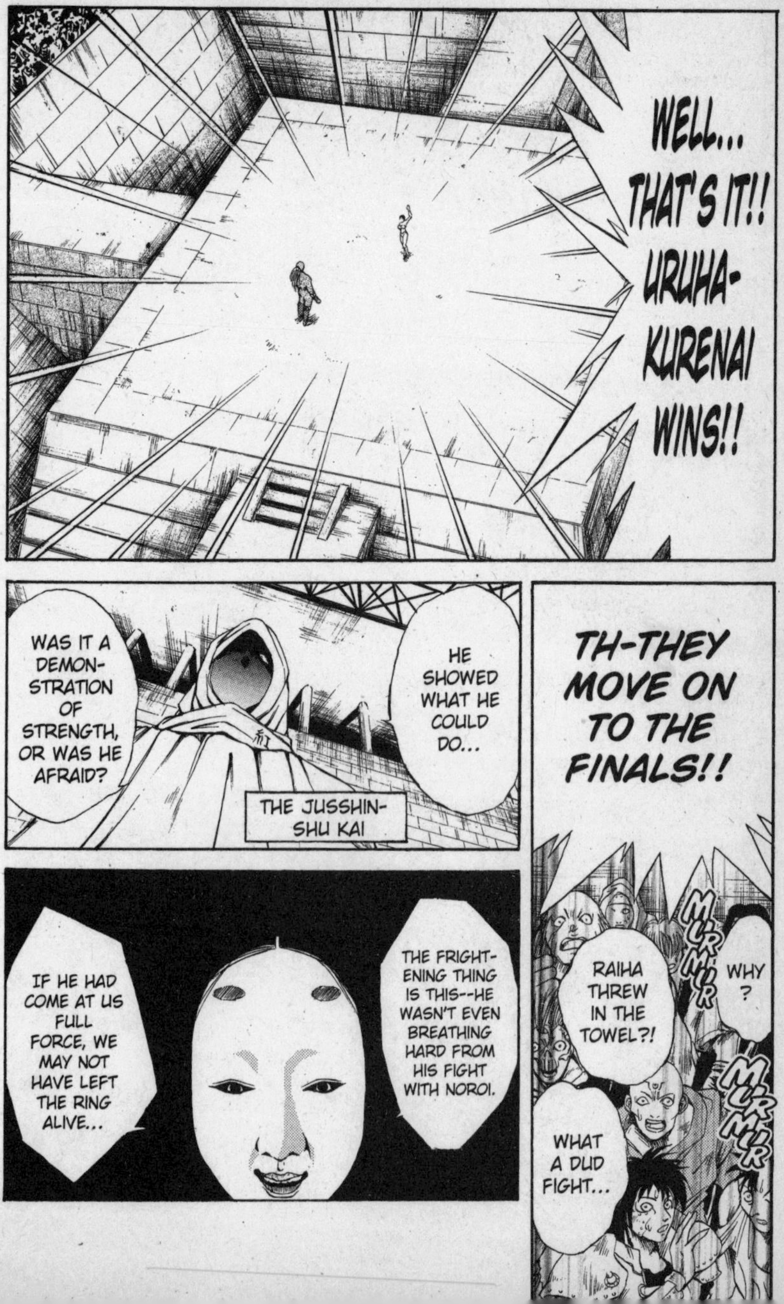
WELL... THAT'S IT!! URUHA-KURENAI WINS!!
TH-THEY MOVE ON TO THE FINALS!!
MURMUR
WHY?
RAIHA THREW IN THE TOWEL?!
MURMUR
WHAT A DUD FIGHT...
HE SHOWED WHAT HE COULD DO...
WAS IT A DEMON-STRATION OF STRENGTH, OR WAS HE AFRAID?
THE JUSSHIN-SHU KAI
THE FRIGHT-ENING THING IS THIS--HE WASN'T EVEN BREATHING HARD FROM HIS FIGHT WITH NOROI.
IF HE HAD COME AT US FULL FORCE, WE MAY NOT HAVE LEFT THE RING ALIVE...

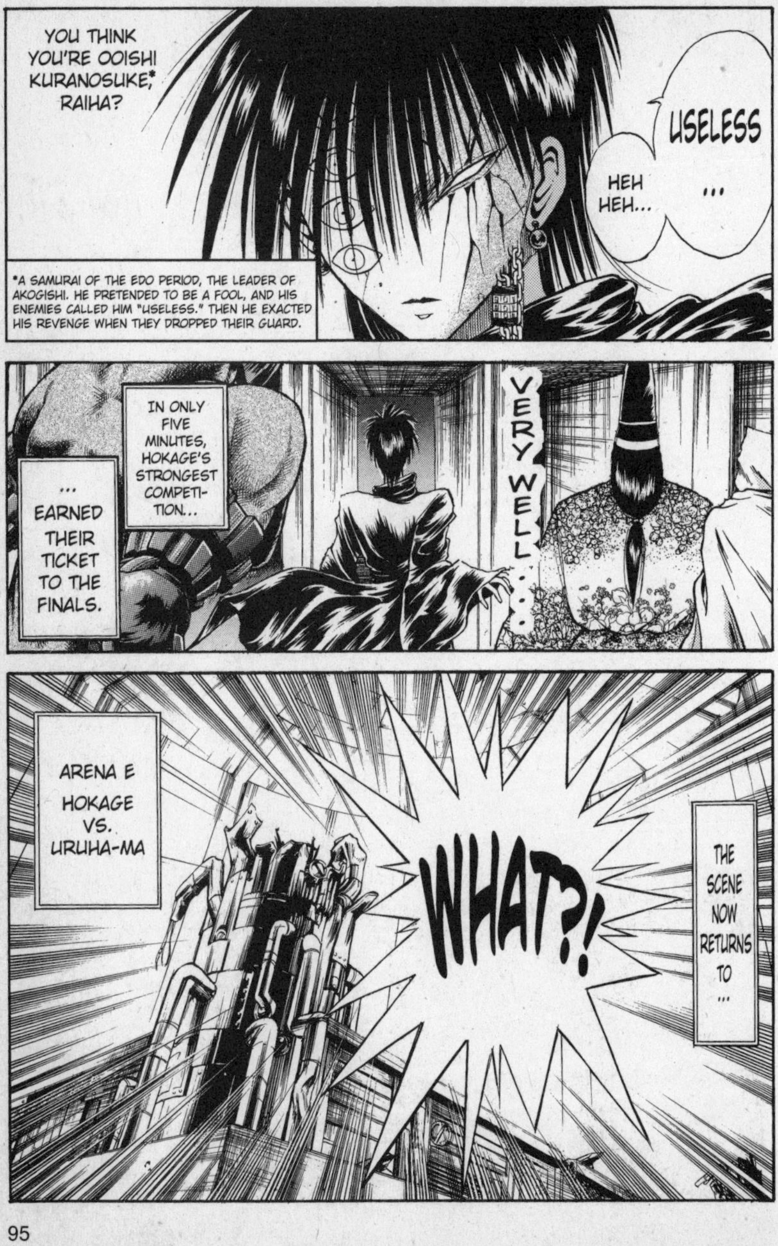
USELESS ...
HEH HEH...
YOU THINK YOU'RE OOISHI KURANOSUKE,* RAIHA?
*A SAMURAI OF THE EDO PERIOD, THE LEADER OF AKOGISHI. HE PRETENDED TO BE A FOOL, AND HIS ENEMIES CALLED HIM "USELESS." THEN HE EXACTED HIS REVENGE WHEN THEY DROPPED THEIR GUARD.
VERY WELL...
IN ONLY FIVE MINUTES, HOKAGE'S STRONGEST COMPETITION...
... EARNED THEIR TICKET TO THE FINALS.
THE SCENE NOW RETURNS TO ...
WHAT?!
ARENA E HOKAGE VS. URUHA-MA

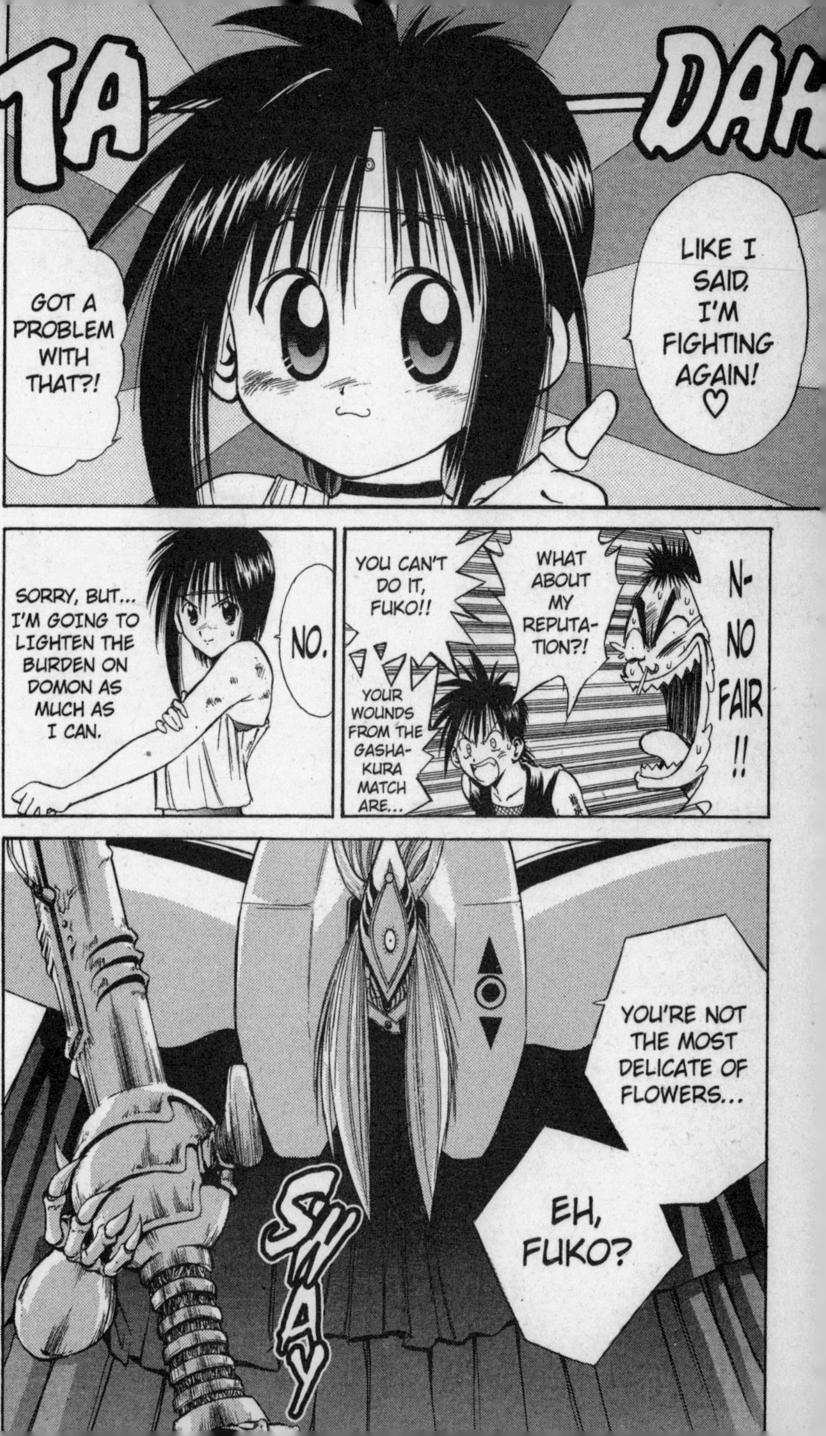
TA DAH
LIKE I SAID, I'M FIGHTING AGAIN! ♡
GOT A PROBLEM WITH THAT?!
N-NO FAIR!!
WHAT ABOUT MY REPUTATION?!
YOU CAN'T DO IT, FUKO!!
YOUR WOUNDS FROM THE GASHAKURA MATCH ARE...
NO.
SORRY, BUT... I'M GOING TO LIGHTEN THE BURDEN ON DOMON AS MUCH AS I CAN.
YOU'RE NOT THE MOST DELICATE OF FLOWERS...
EH, FUKO?
SHWAY

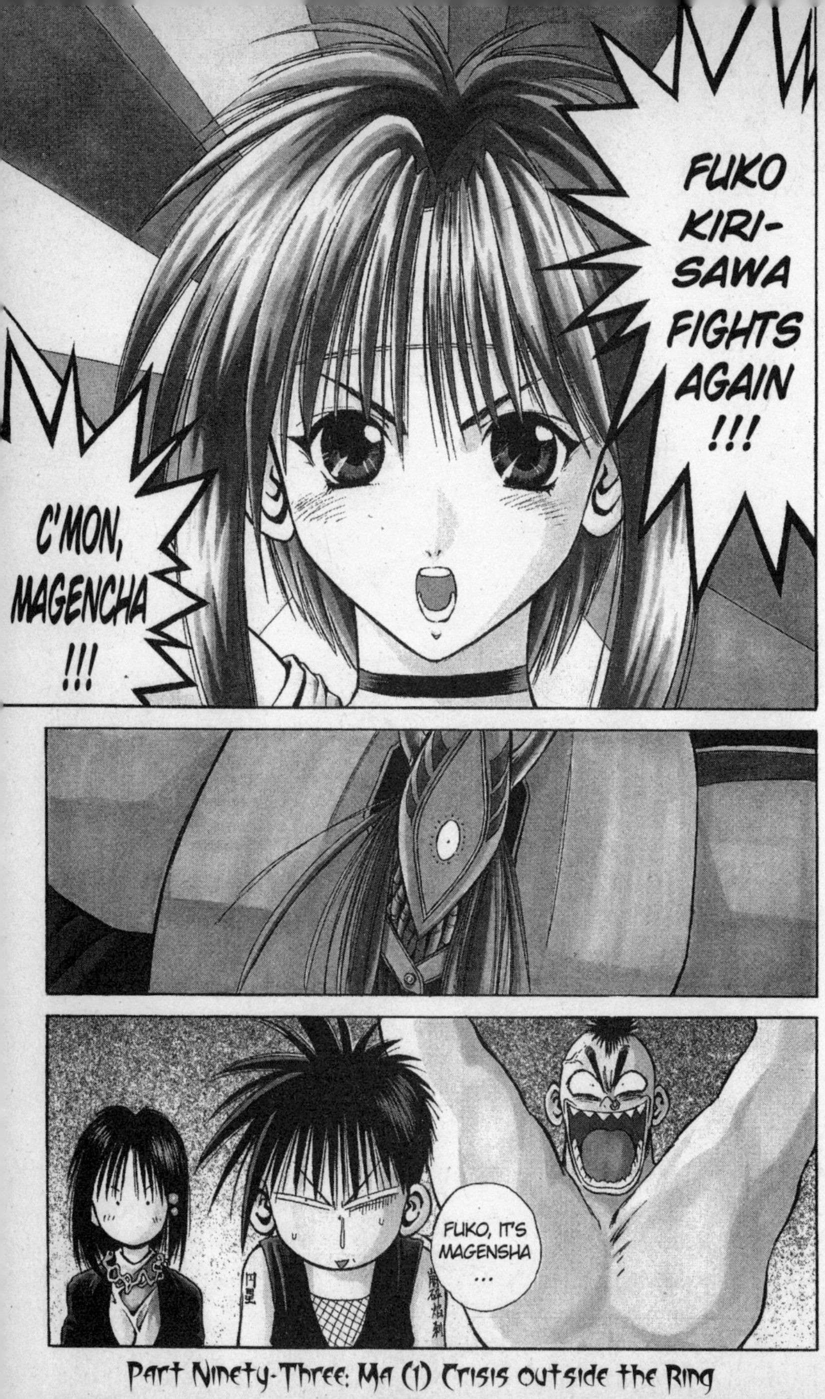
FUKO KIRI-SAWA FIGHTS AGAIN!!!
C'MON, MAGENCHA!!!
FUKO, IT'S MAGENSHA...

Part Ninety-Three: Ma (1) Crisis outside the Ring

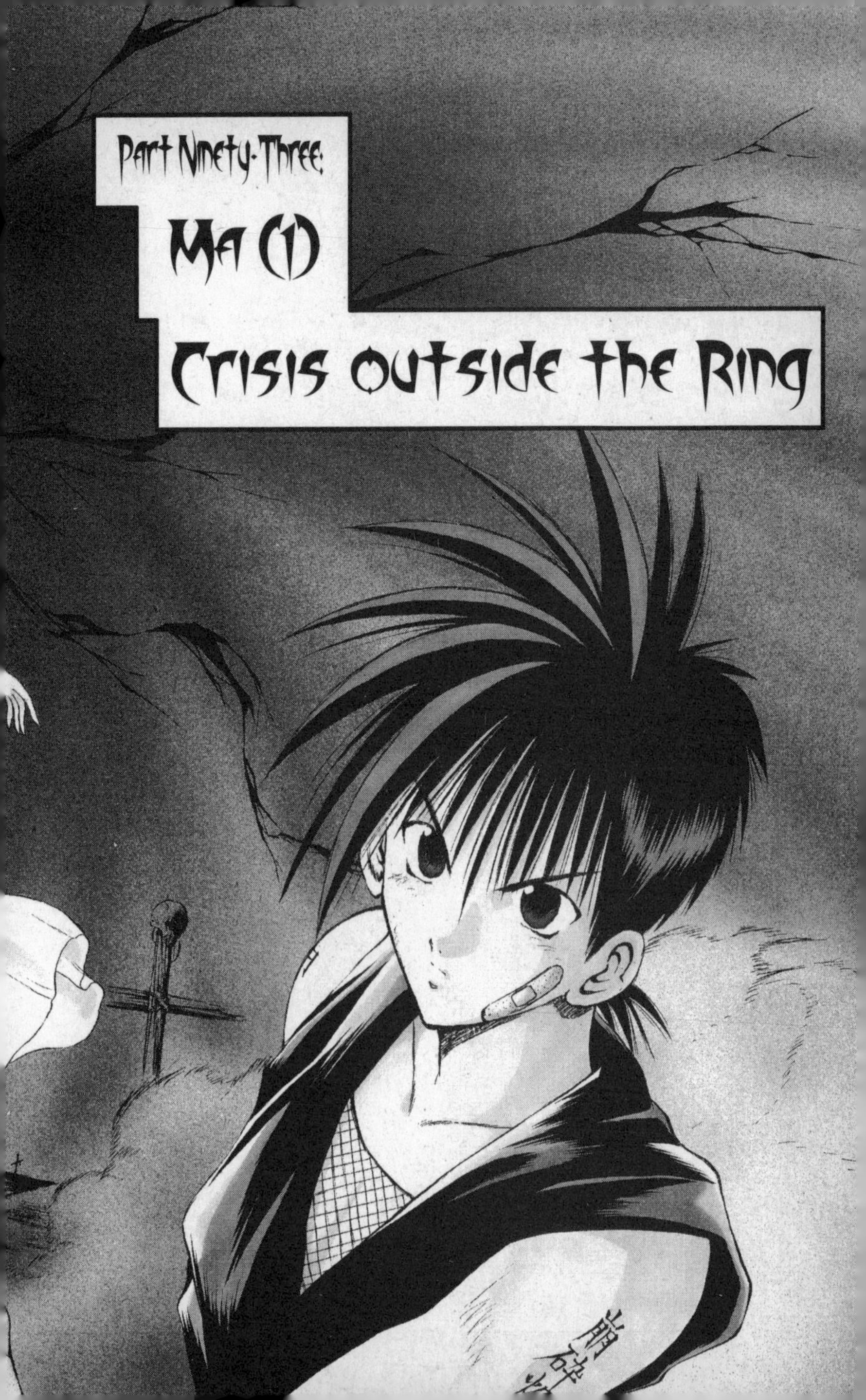
Part Ninety-Three:
Ma (1)
Crisis Outside the Ring

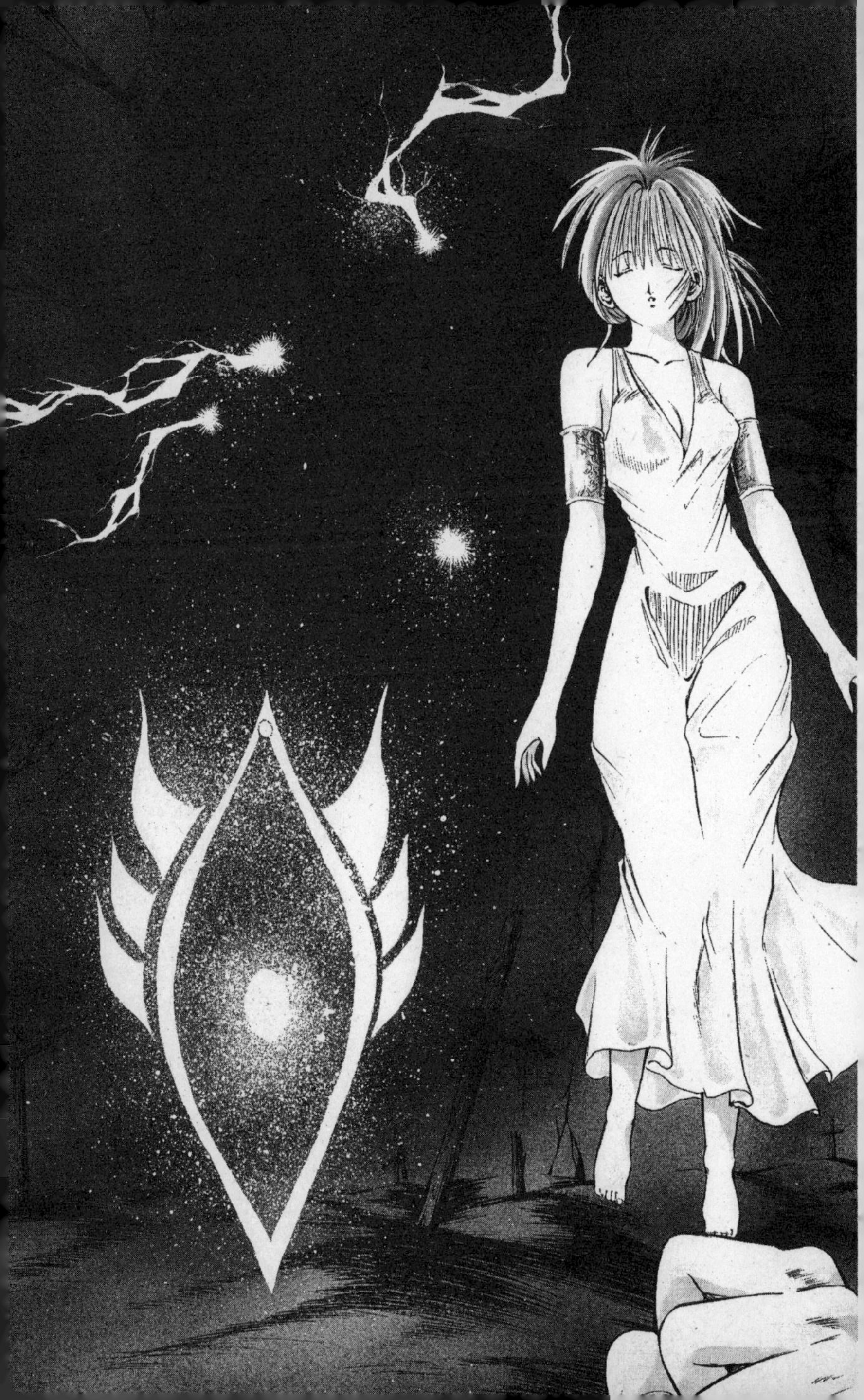

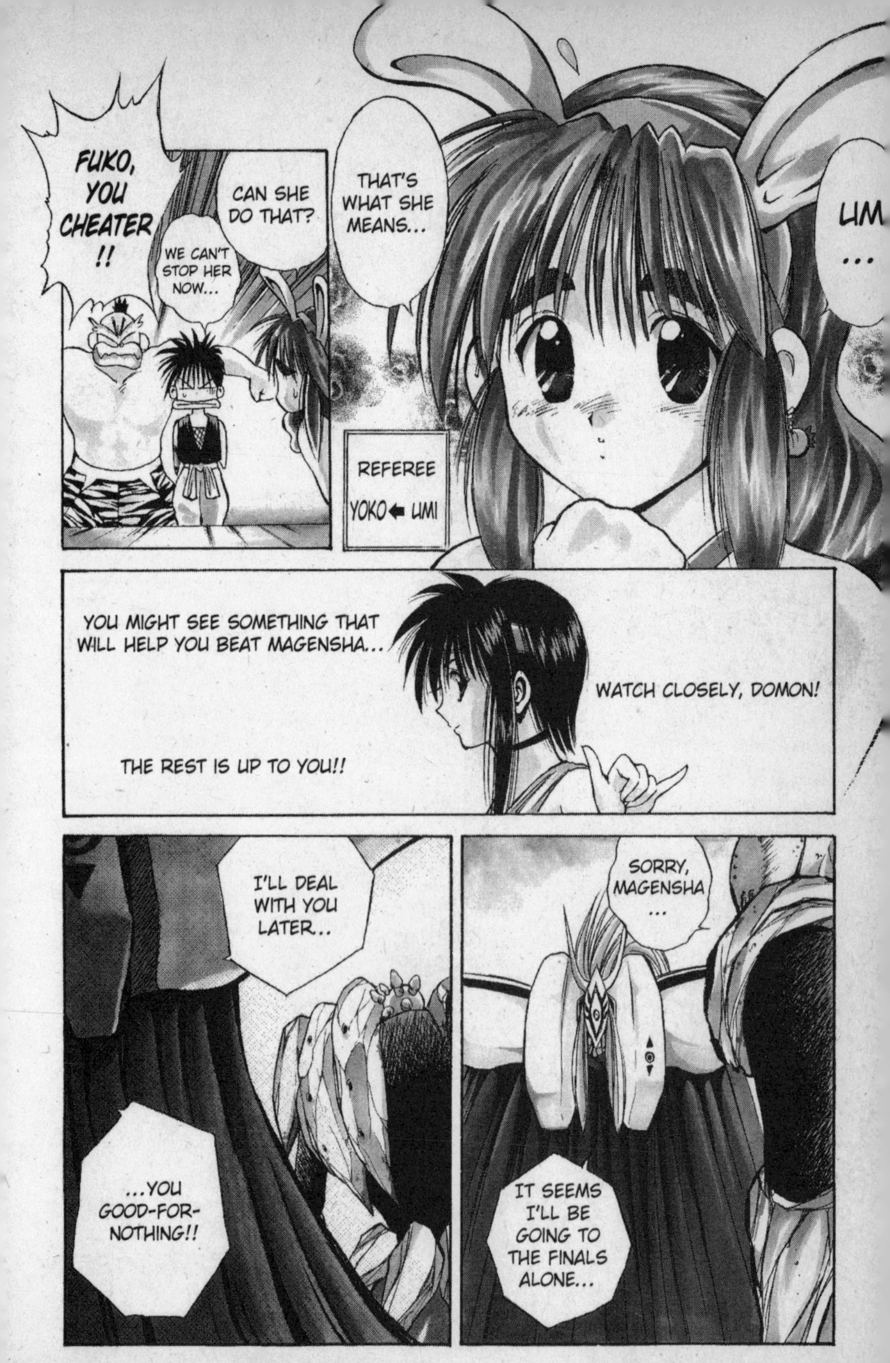
UM...
THAT'S WHAT SHE MEANS...
REFEREE
YOKO ← UMI
CAN SHE DO THAT?
WE CAN'T STOP HER NOW...
FUKO, YOU CHEATER!!
WATCH CLOSELY, DOMON!
YOU MIGHT SEE SOMETHING THAT WILL HELP YOU BEAT MAGENSHA...
THE REST IS UP TO YOU!!
SORRY, MAGENSHA...
IT SEEMS I'LL BE GOING TO THE FINALS ALONE...
I'LL DEAL WITH YOU LATER...
...YOU GOOD-FOR-NOTHING!!

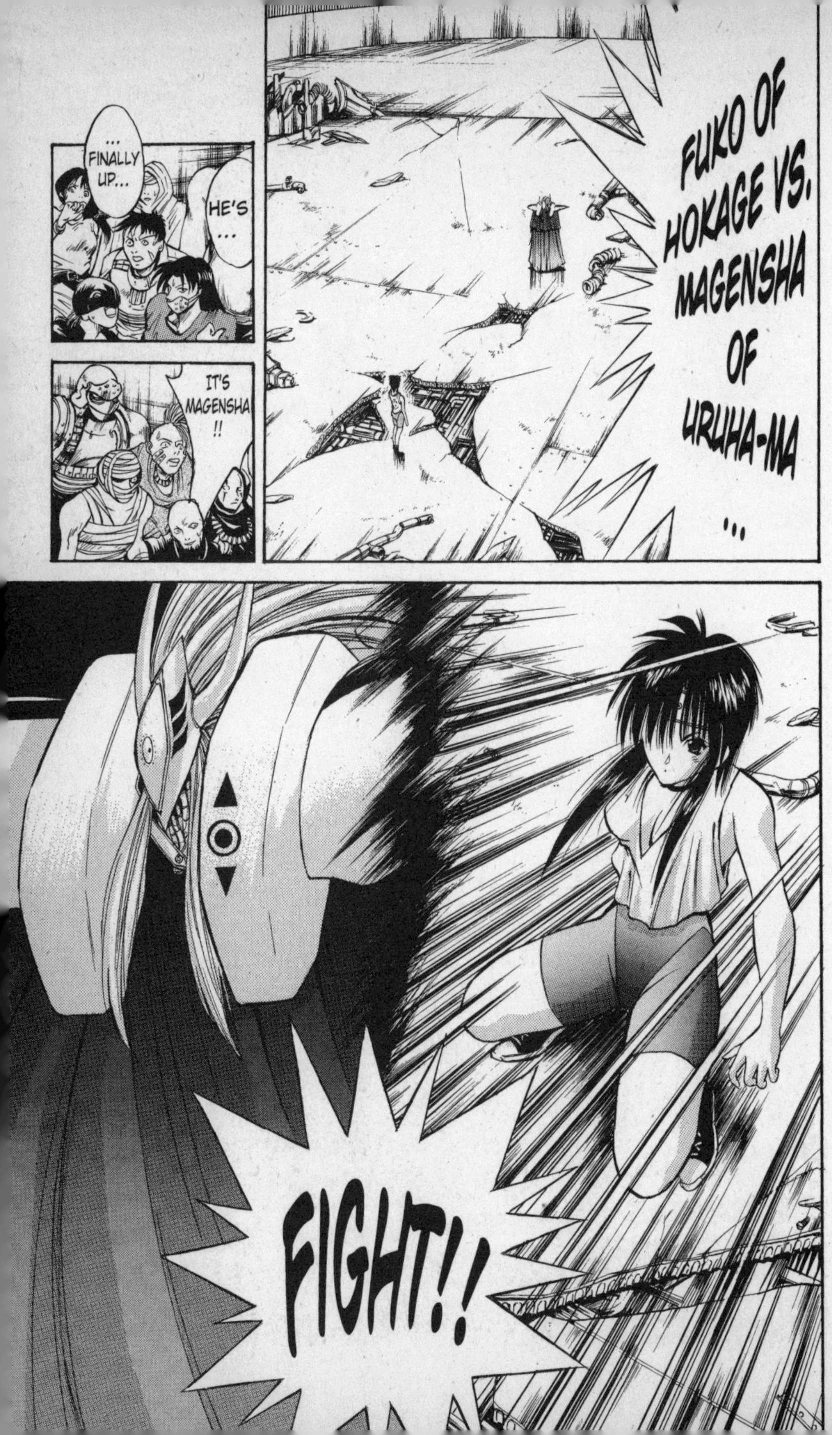
FUKO OF HOKAGE VS. MAGENSHA OF URUHA-MA ...
HE'S ...
... FINALLY UP...
IT'S MAGENSHA !!
FIGHT!!

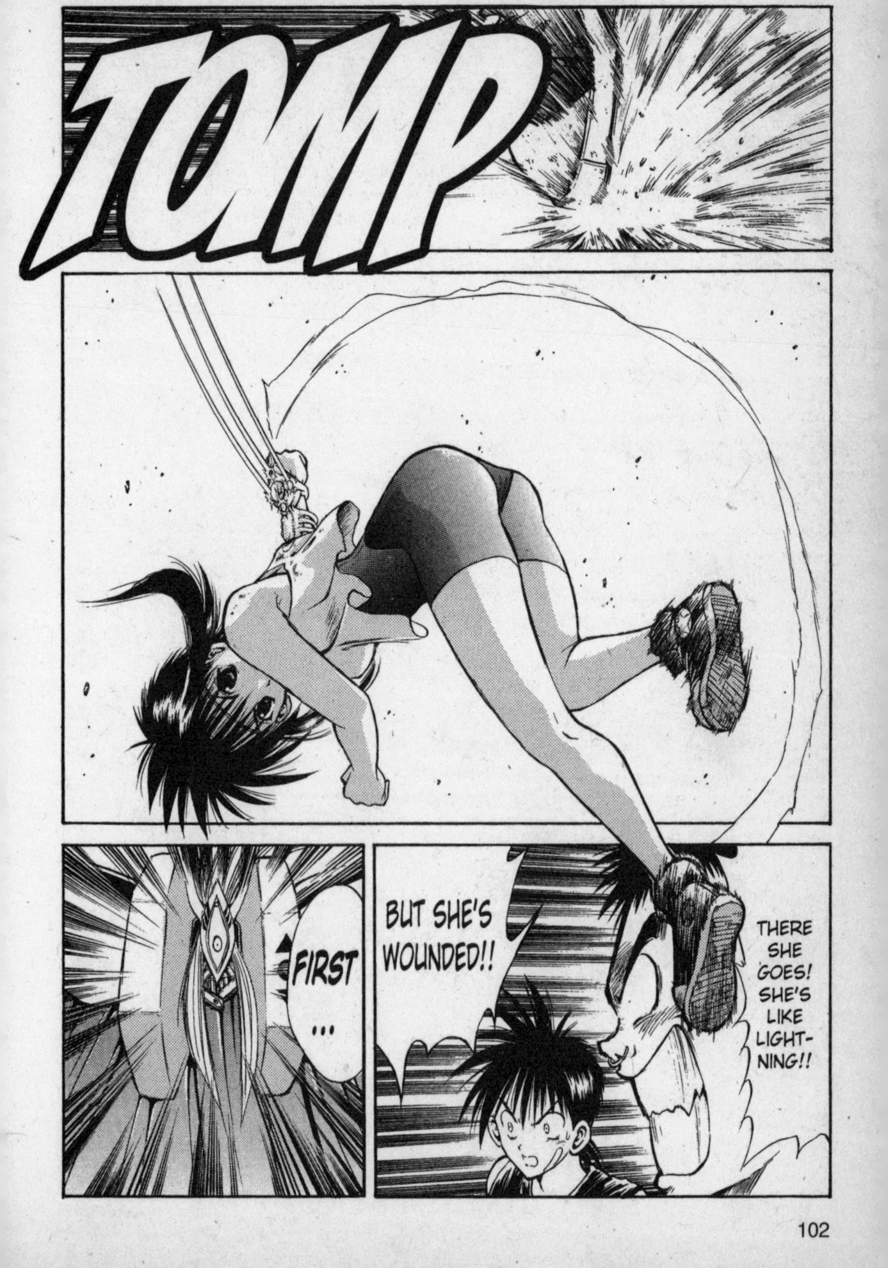
TOMP
THERE SHE GOES! SHE'S LIKE LIGHTNING!!
BUT SHE'S WOUNDED!!
FIRST ...

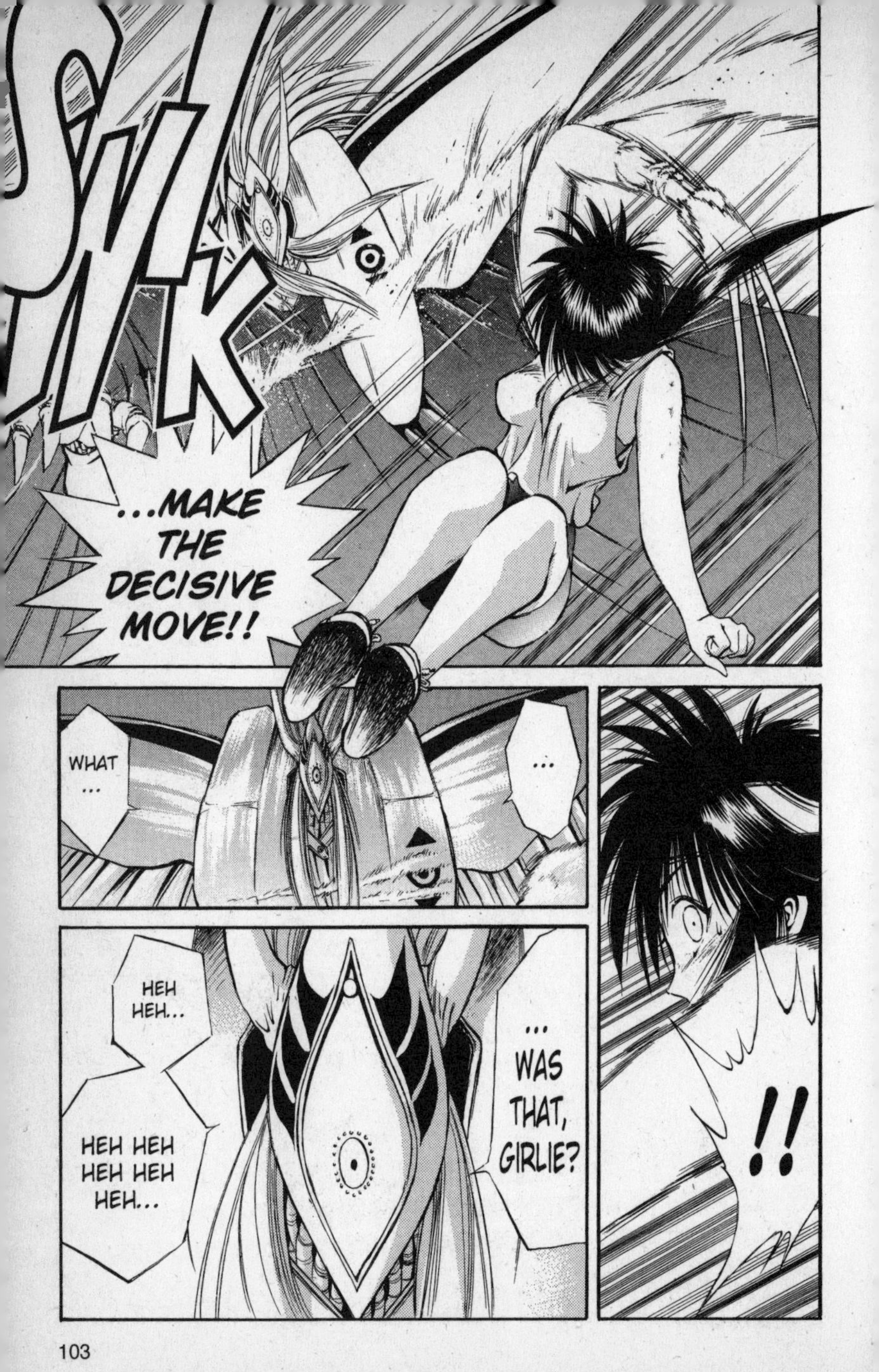
SHK
...MAKE THE DECISIVE MOVE!!
!!
...
WHAT ...
... WAS THAT, GIRLIE?
HEH HEH...
HEH HEH HEH HEH HEH...

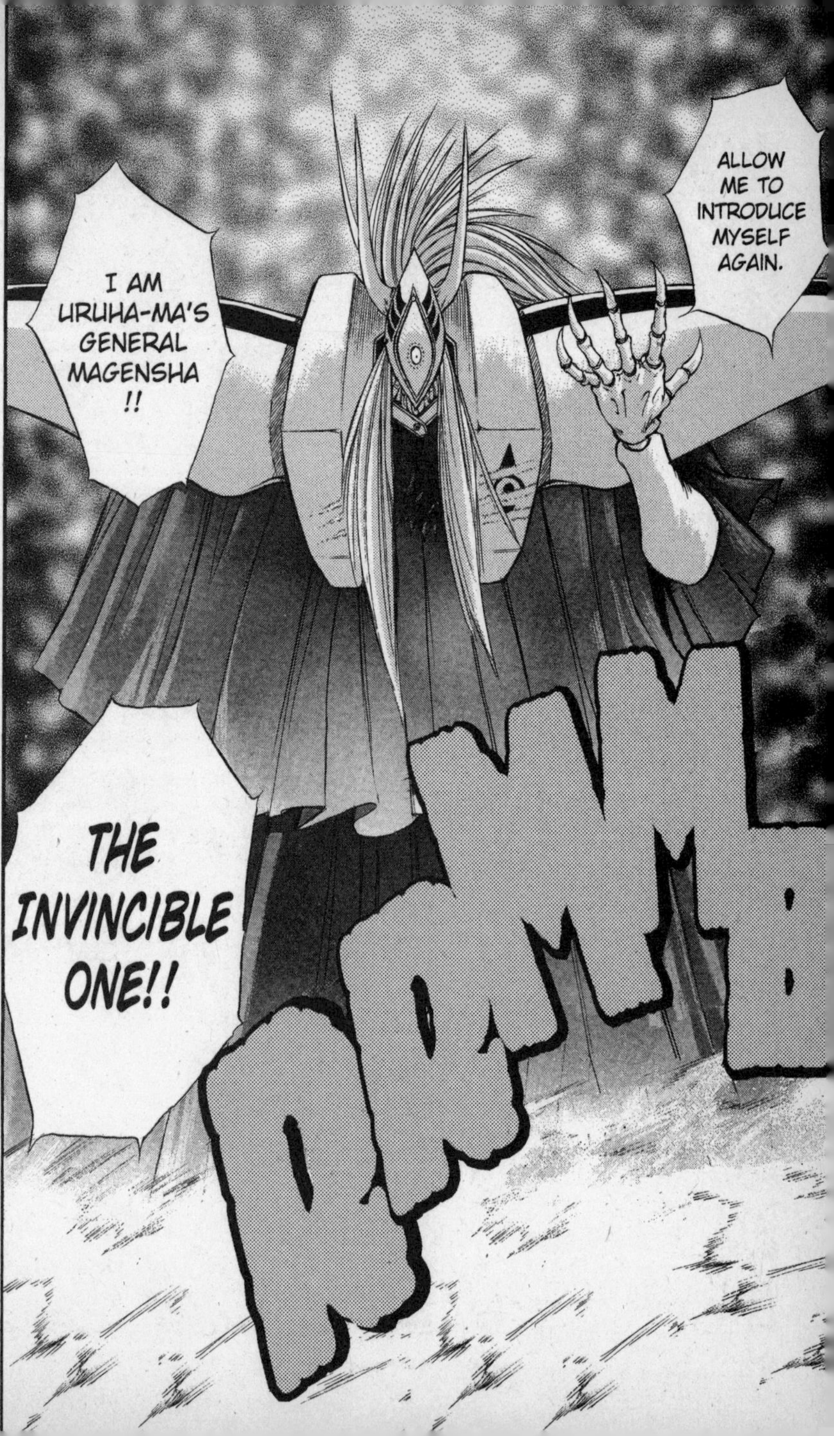
ALLOW ME TO INTRODUCE MYSELF AGAIN.
I AM URUHA-MA'S GENERAL MAGENSHA !!
THE INVINCIBLE ONE!!

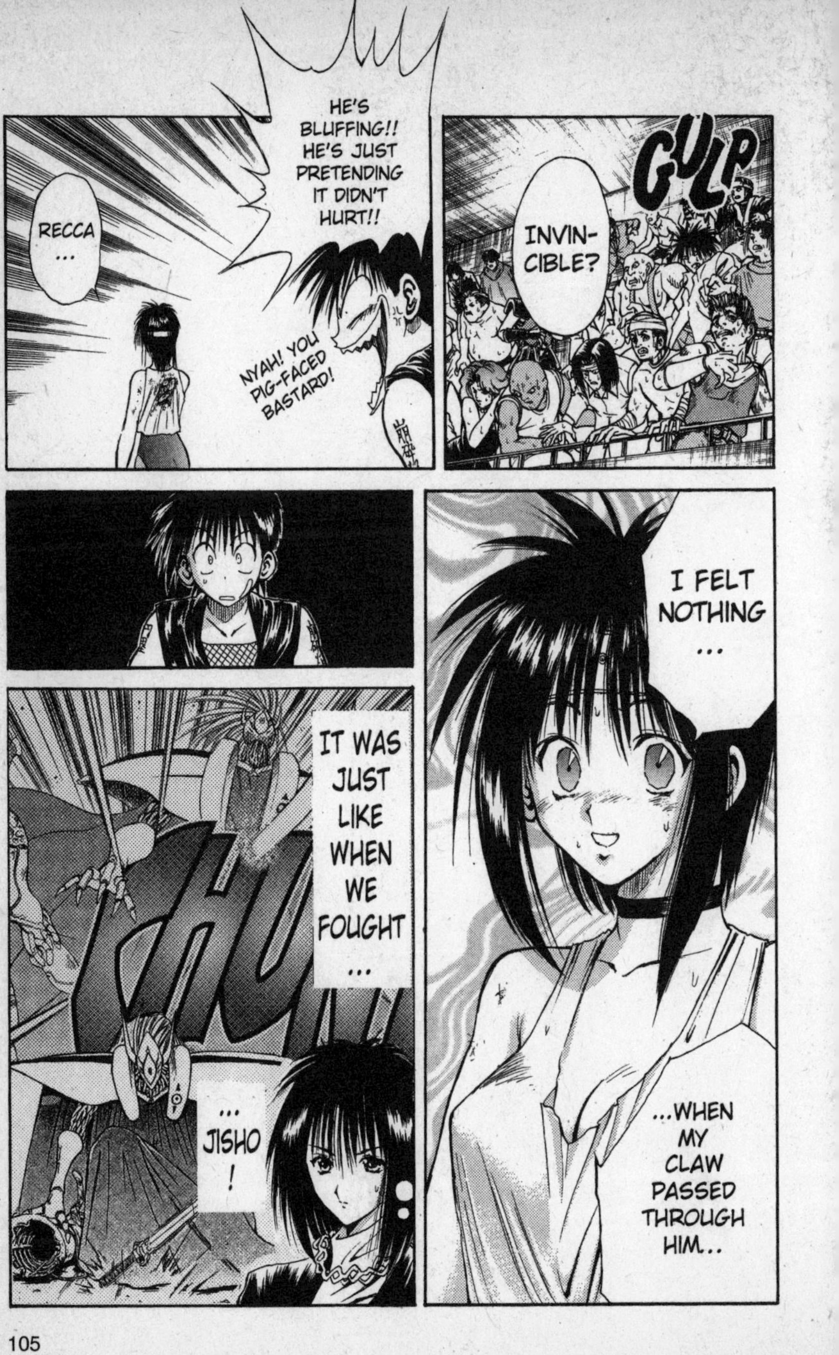
GULP
INVIN-CIBLE?
HE'S BLUFFING!! HE'S JUST PRETENDING IT DIDN'T HURT!!
NYAH! YOU PIG-FACED BASTARD!
RECCA ...
I FELT NOTHING ...
...WHEN MY CLAW PASSED THROUGH HIM..
IT WAS JUST LIKE WHEN WE FOUGHT ...
... JISHO !

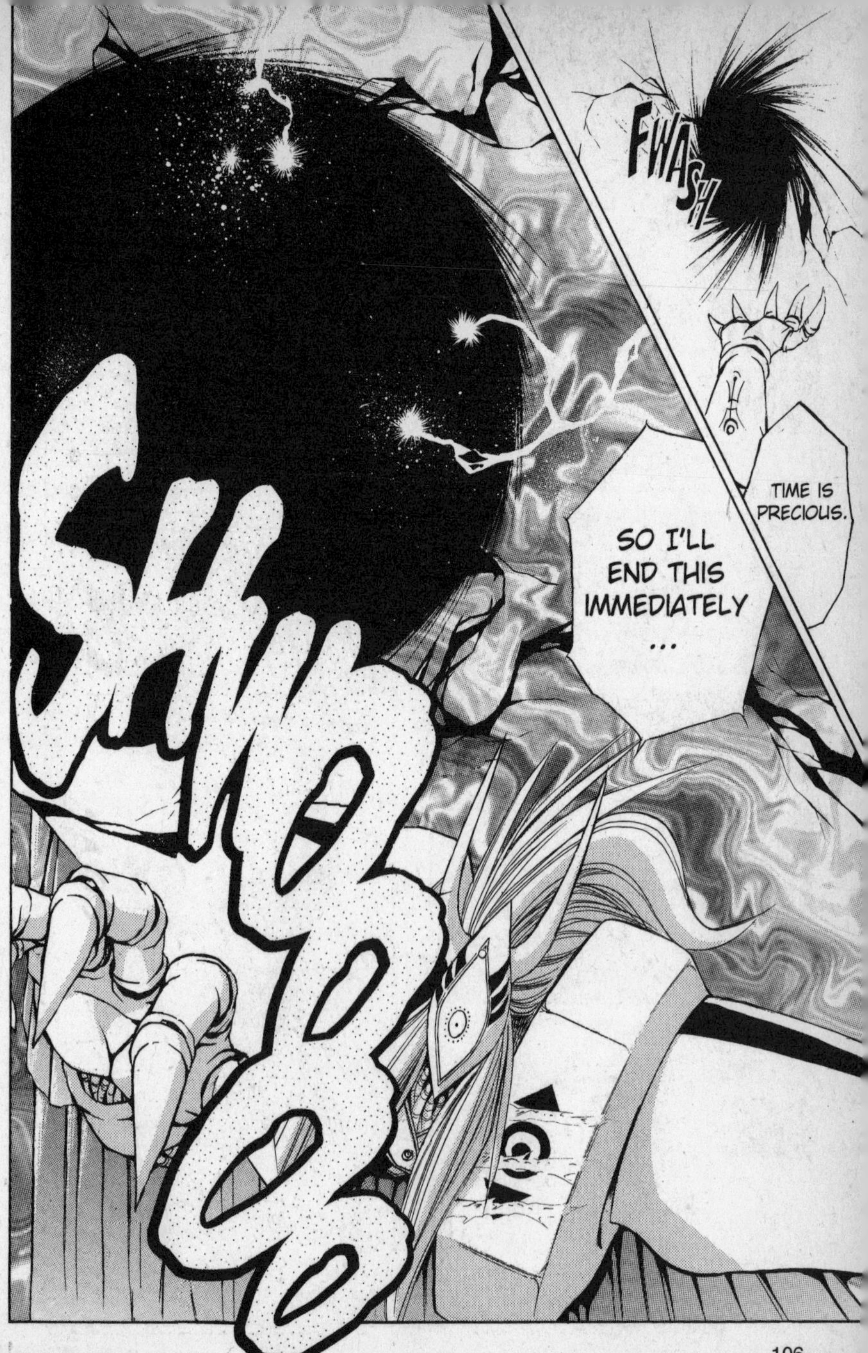
FWASH
TIME IS PRECIOUS.
SO I'LL END THIS IMMEDIATELY ...

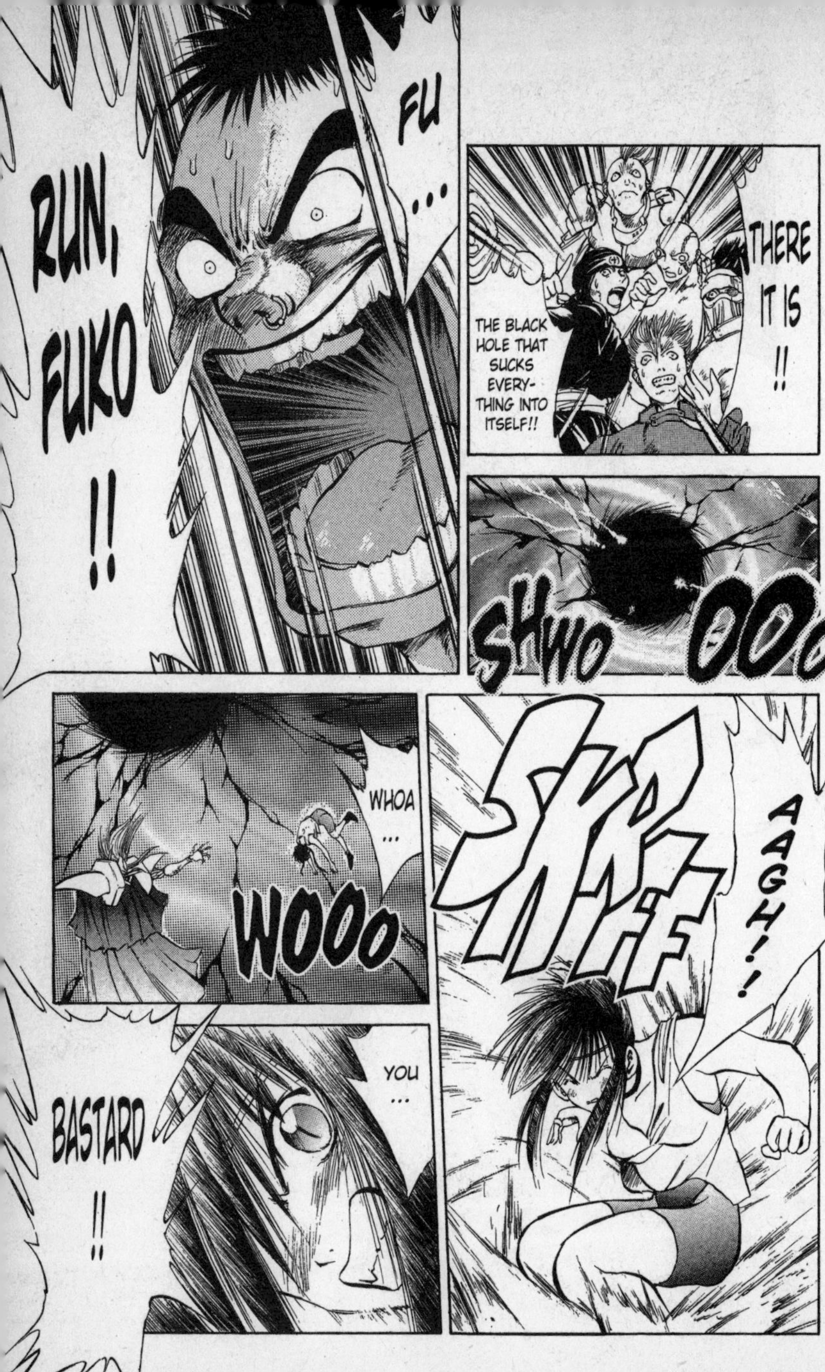
THERE IT IS!!
THE BLACK HOLE THAT SUCKS EVERYTHING INTO ITSELF!!
SHWOOOOo
FU...
RUN, FUKO!!
SKRFF
AAGH!!
WHOA...
WOOO
YOU...
BASTARD!!

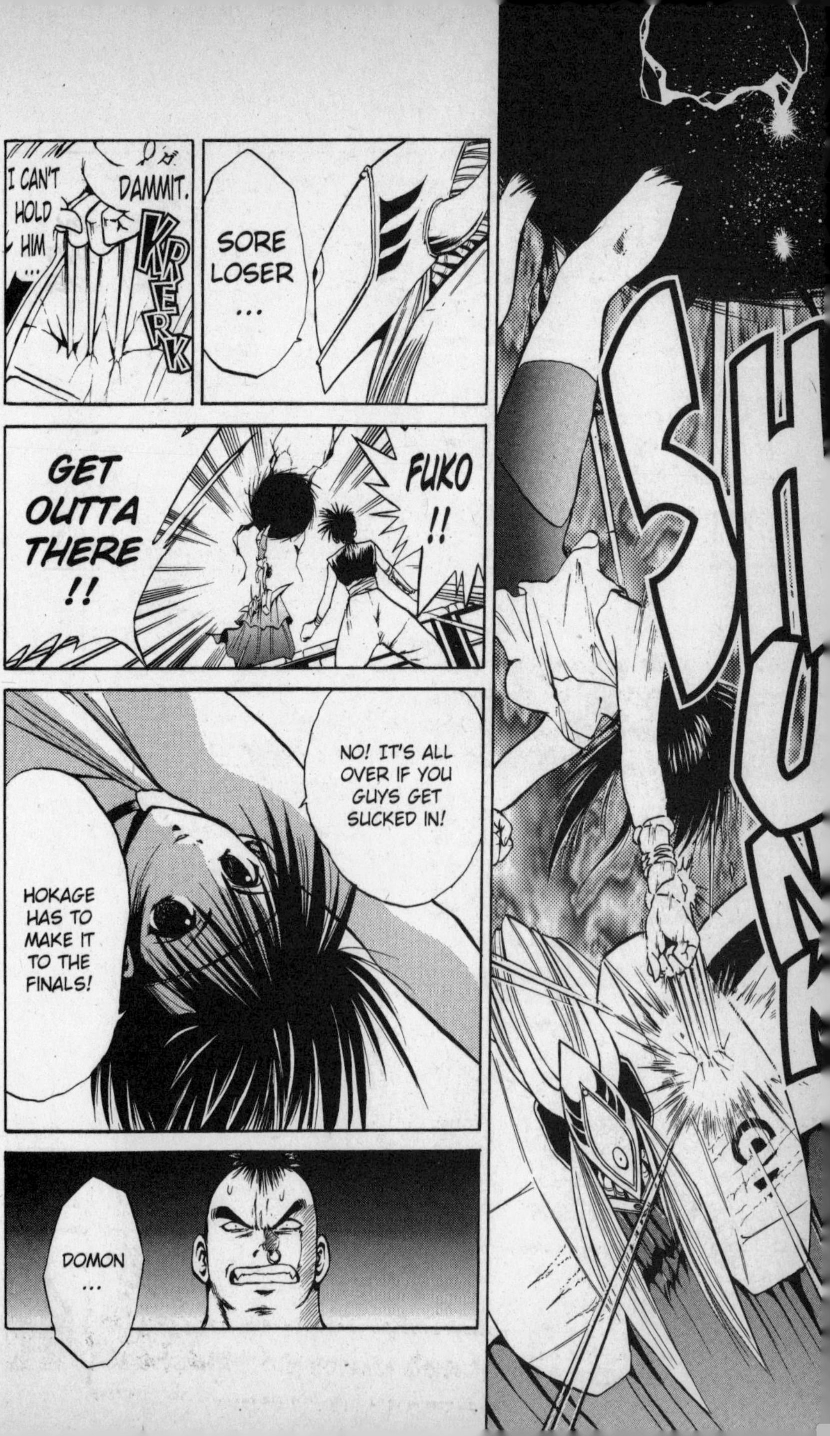
SHUNK
SORE LOSER ...
DAMMIT.
I CAN'T HOLD HIM ...
KRRERK
FUKO !!
GET OUTTA THERE !!
NO! IT'S ALL OVER IF YOU GUYS GET SUCKED IN!
HOKAGE HAS TO MAKE IT TO THE FINALS!
DOMON ...

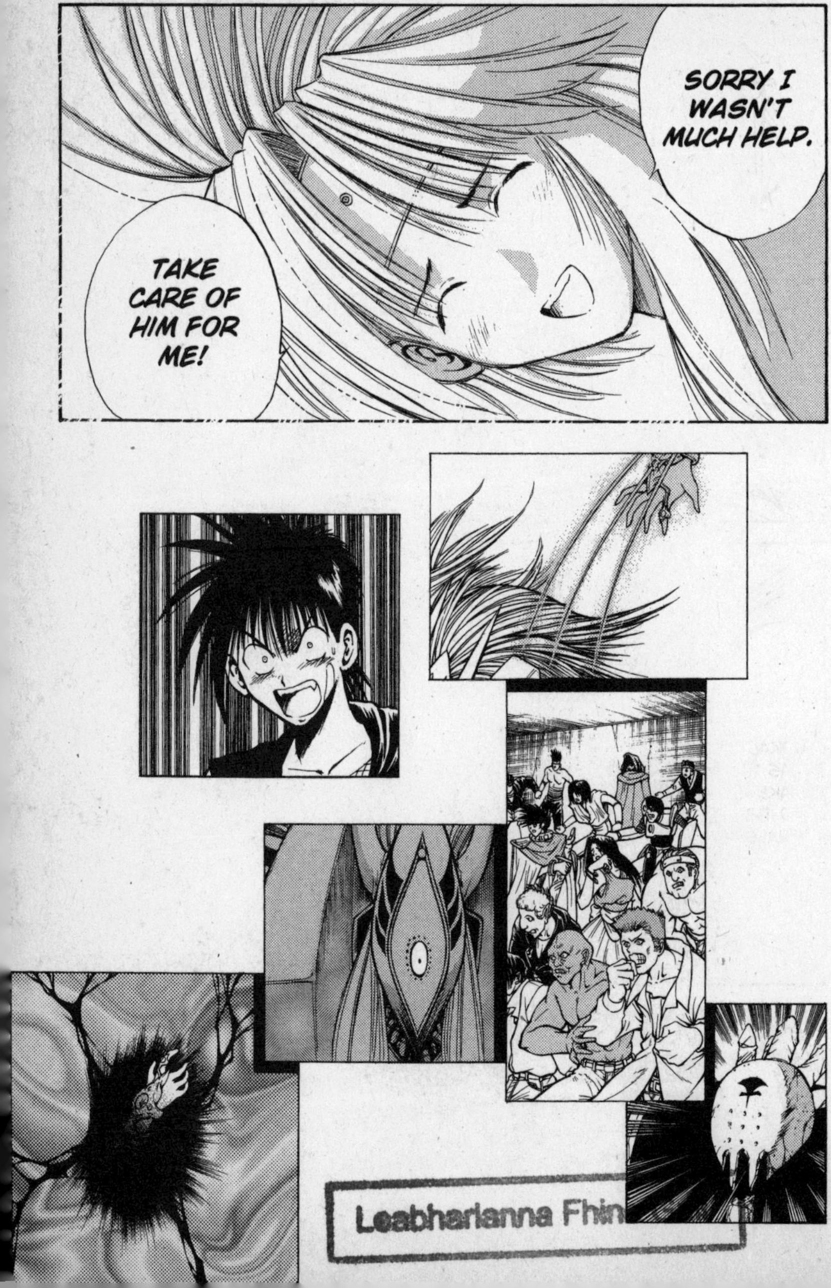
SORRY I WASN'T MUCH HELP.
TAKE CARE OF HIM FOR ME!

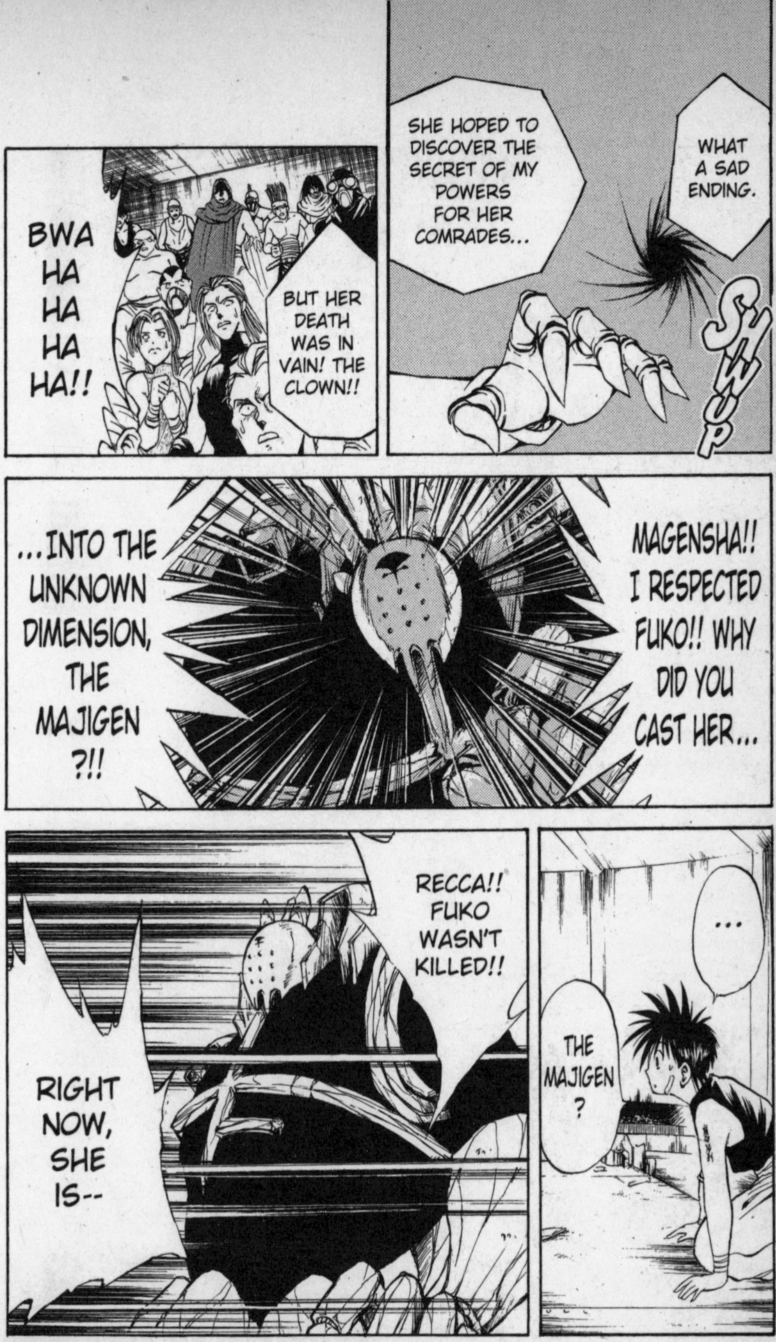
WHAT A SAD ENDING.
SHE HOPED TO DISCOVER THE SECRET OF MY POWERS FOR HER COMRADES...
SHWUP
BUT HER DEATH WAS IN VAIN! THE CLOWN!!
BWA HA HA HA HA!!
MAGENSHA!! I RESPECTED FUKO!! WHY DID YOU CAST HER...
...INTO THE UNKNOWN DIMENSION, THE MAJIGEN ?!!
...
THE MAJIGEN ?
RECCA!! FUKO WASN'T KILLED!!
RIGHT NOW, SHE IS--

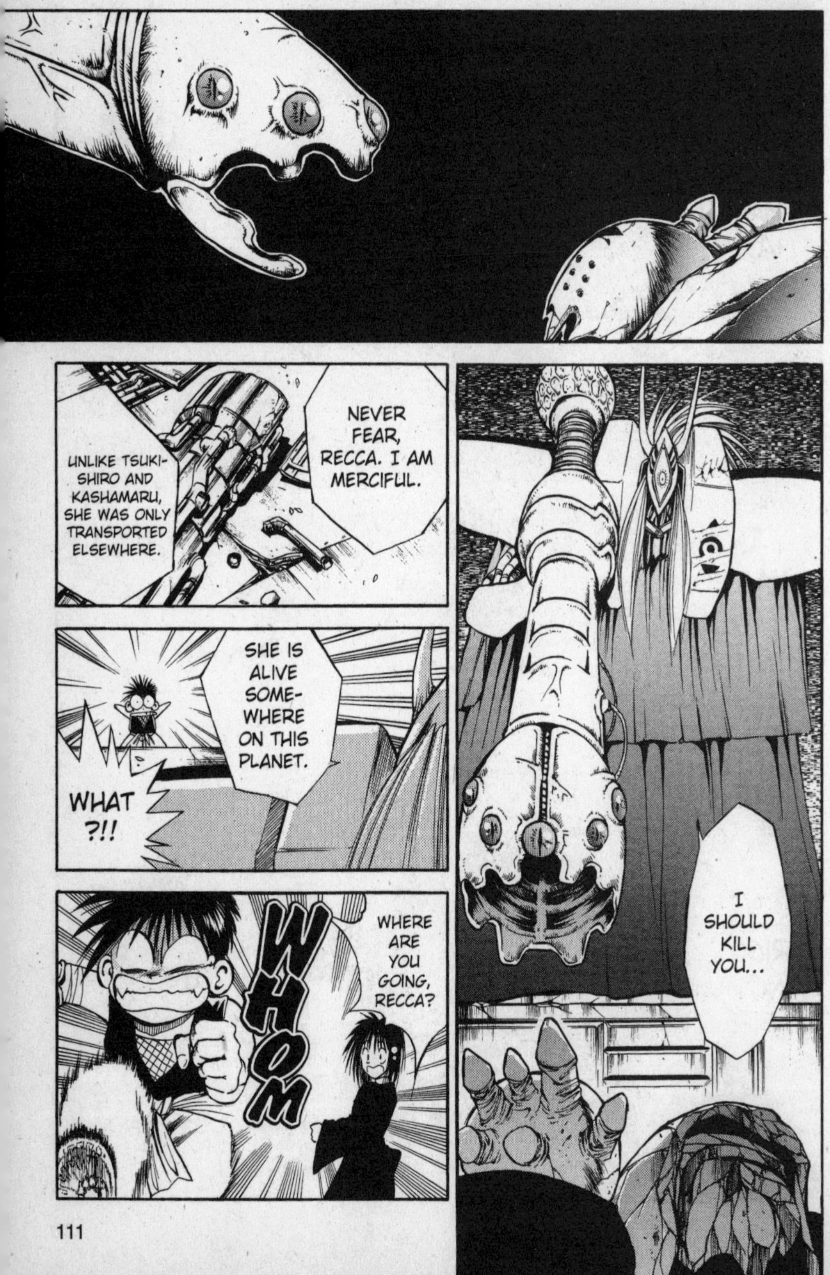
I SHOULD KILL YOU...
NEVER FEAR, RECCA. I AM MERCIFUL.
UNLIKE TSUKISHIRO AND KASHAMARU, SHE WAS ONLY TRANSPORTED ELSEWHERE.
SHE IS ALIVE SOMEWHERE ON THIS PLANET.
WHAT ?!!
WHERE ARE YOU GOING, RECCA?
WHOM

KEEP
SEARCHING
FOREVER!!
IT'S
HOPELESS
!!!

BWA
HA
HA!
FOOL
!!

FUKOOOOO...

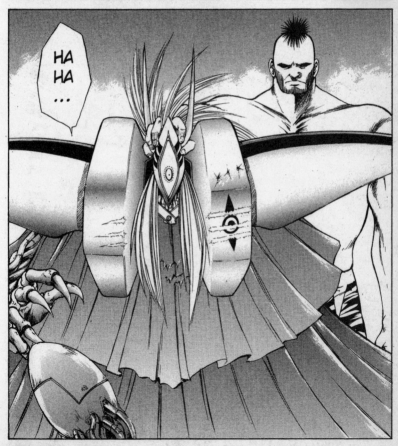

HA
HA
...

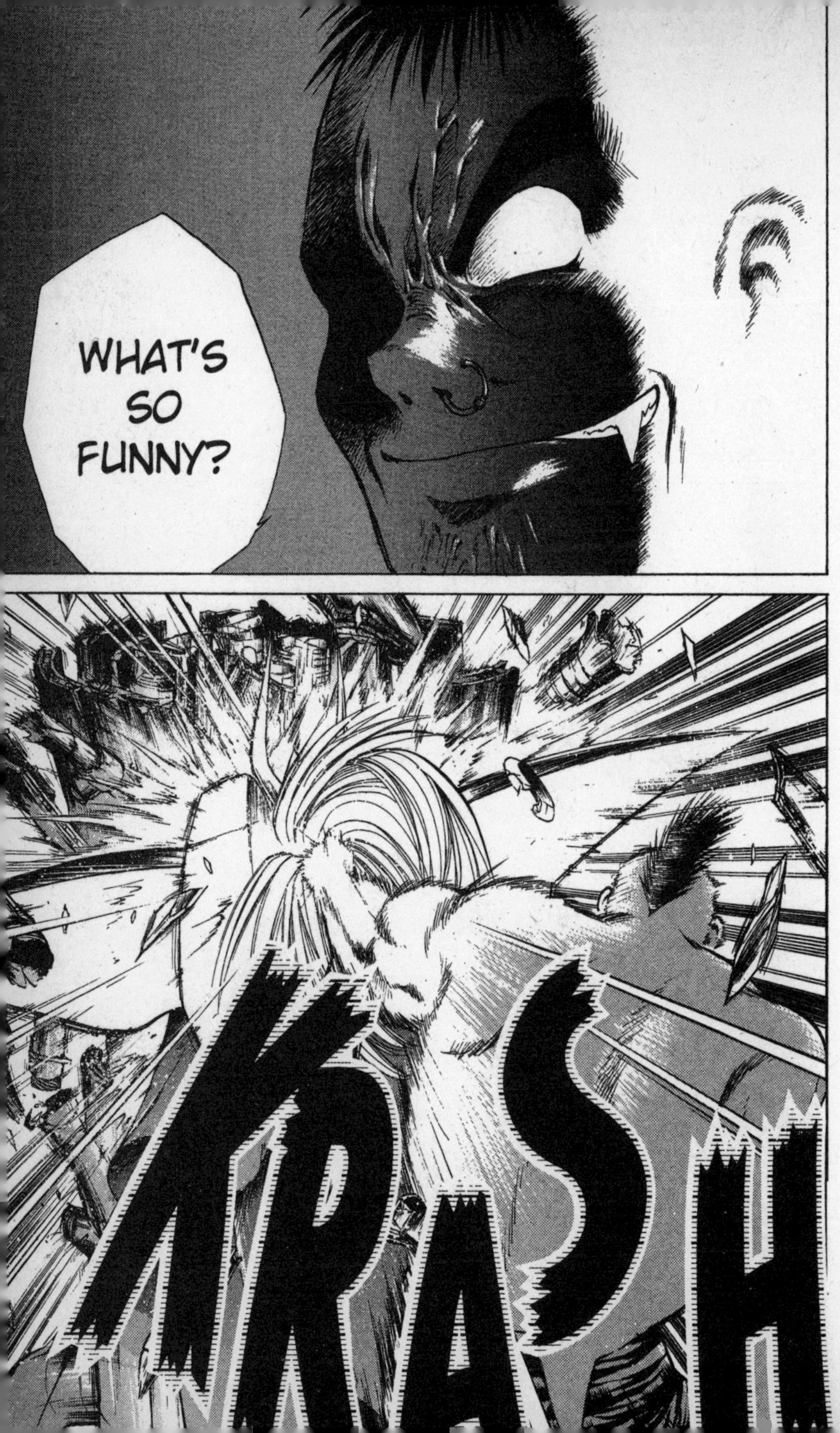
WHAT'S SO FUNNY?
KRASH

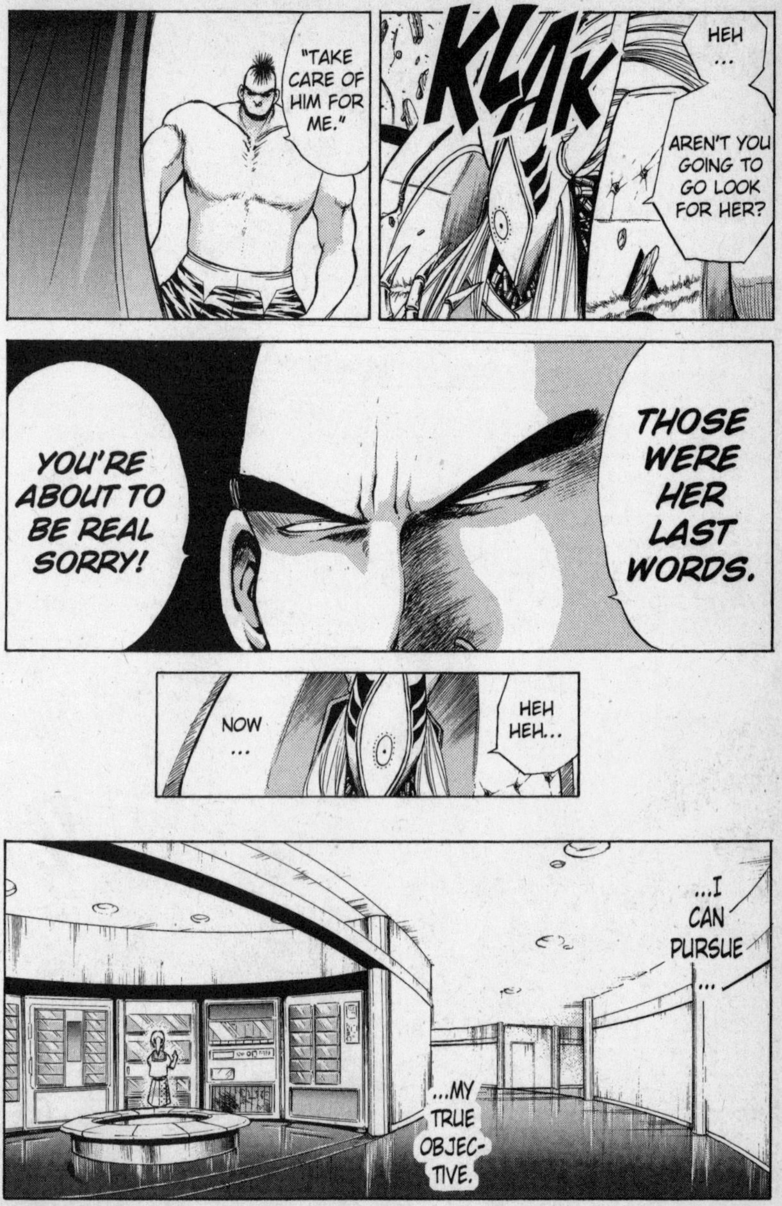
KLAK
HEH ...
AREN'T YOU GOING TO GO LOOK FOR HER?
"TAKE CARE OF HIM FOR ME."
THOSE WERE HER LAST WORDS.
YOU'RE ABOUT TO BE REAL SORRY!
HEH HEH...
NOW ...
...I CAN PURSUE ...
...MY TRUE OBJEC-TIVE.

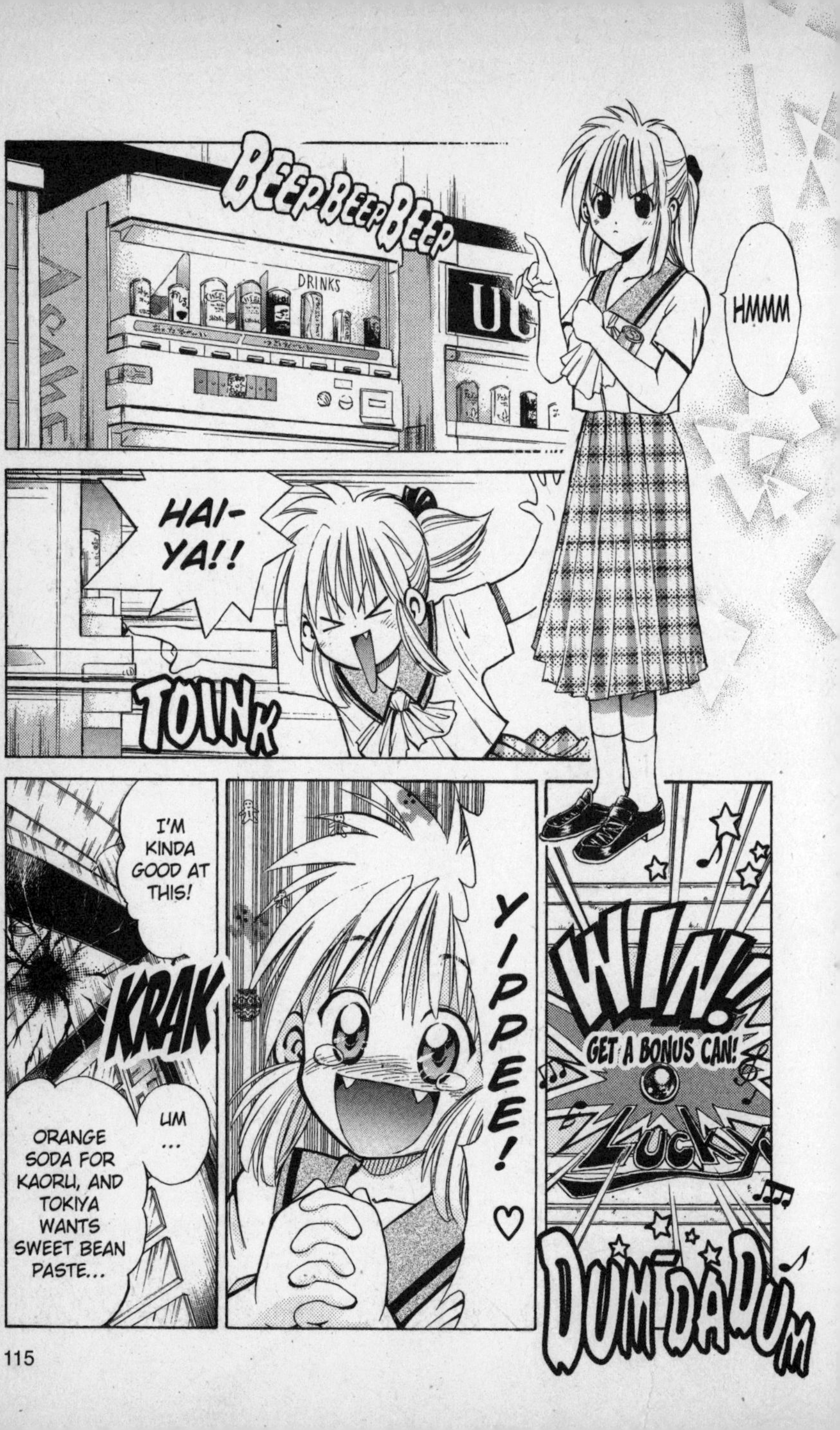
HMMM
BEEP BEEP BEEP
DRINKS
HAI-YA!!
TOINK
WIN!
GET A BONUS CAN!
Lucky
DUM DA DUM
YIPPEE! ♥
I'M KINDA GOOD AT THIS!
KRAK
UM ...
ORANGE SODA FOR KAORU, AND TOKIYA WANTS SWEET BEAN PASTE...

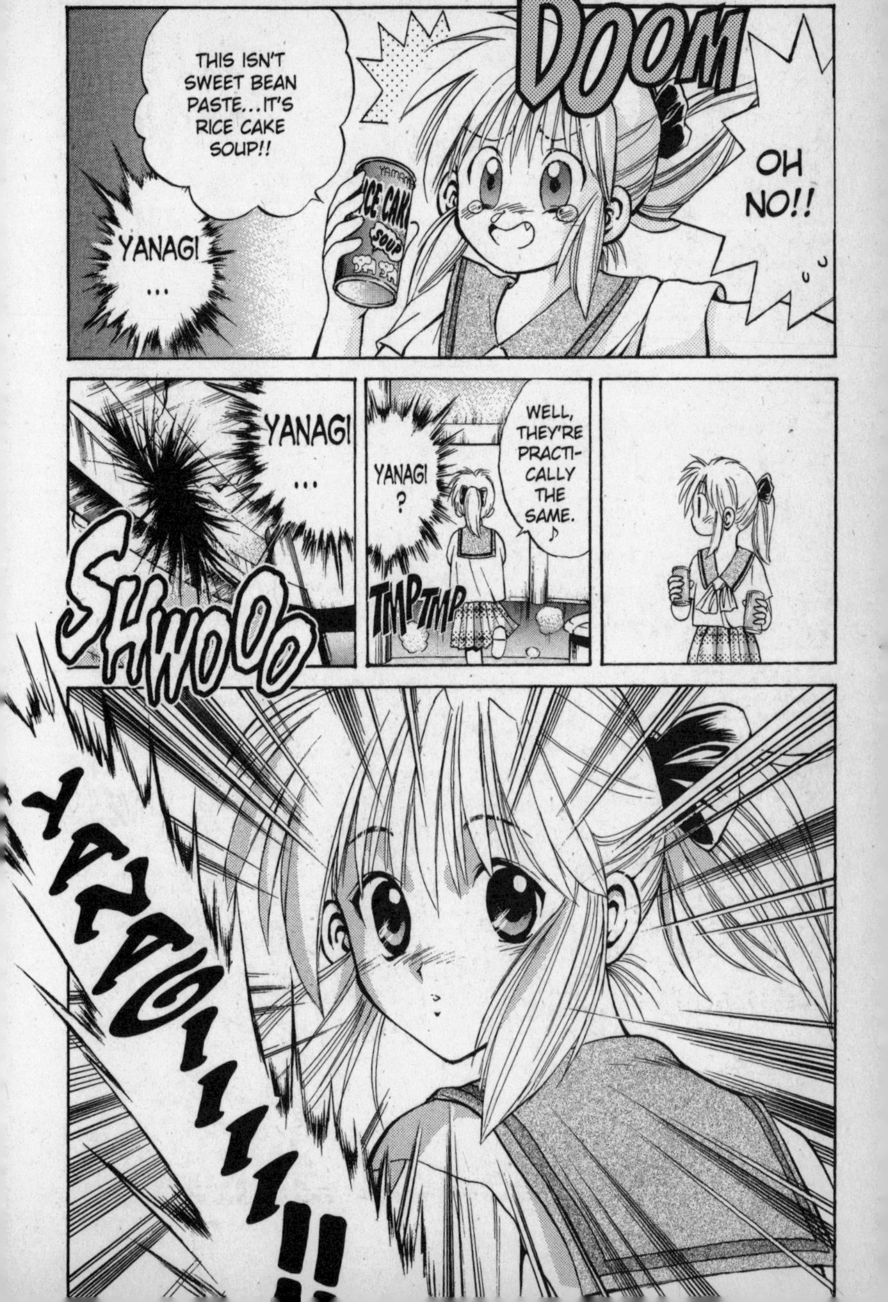
DOOM
OH NO!!
THIS ISN'T SWEET BEAN PASTE...IT'S RICE CAKE SOUP!!
YANAGI ...
WELL, THEY'RE PRACTI-CALLY THE SAME. ♪
YANAGI ?
TMP TMP
YANAGI ...
SHWOOO
YANAGIIIII!!

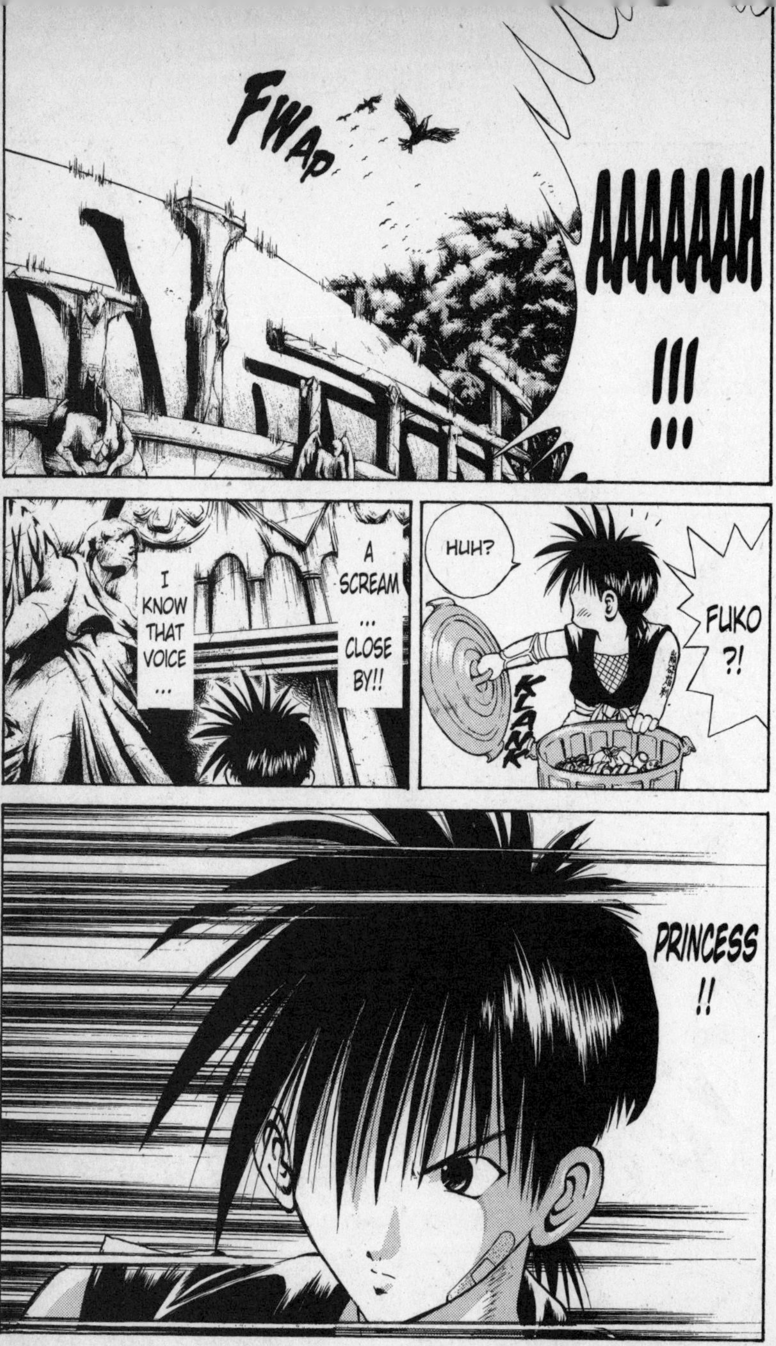
AAAAAH!!!!!!
FWAP
HUH?
FUKO?!
KLANK
A SCREAM ... CLOSE BY!!
I KNOW THAT VOICE ...
PRINCESS!!

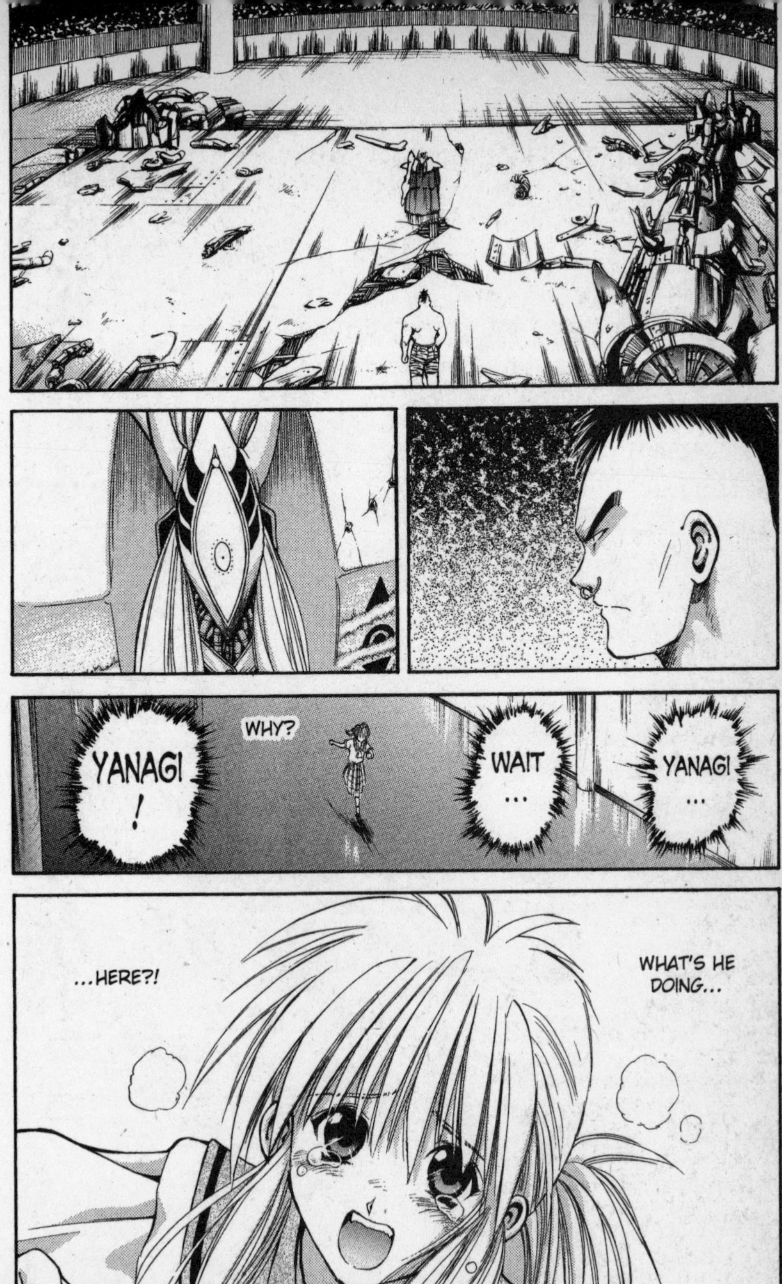
YANAGI ...
WAIT ...
WHY?
YANAGI !
WHAT'S HE DOING...
...HERE?!

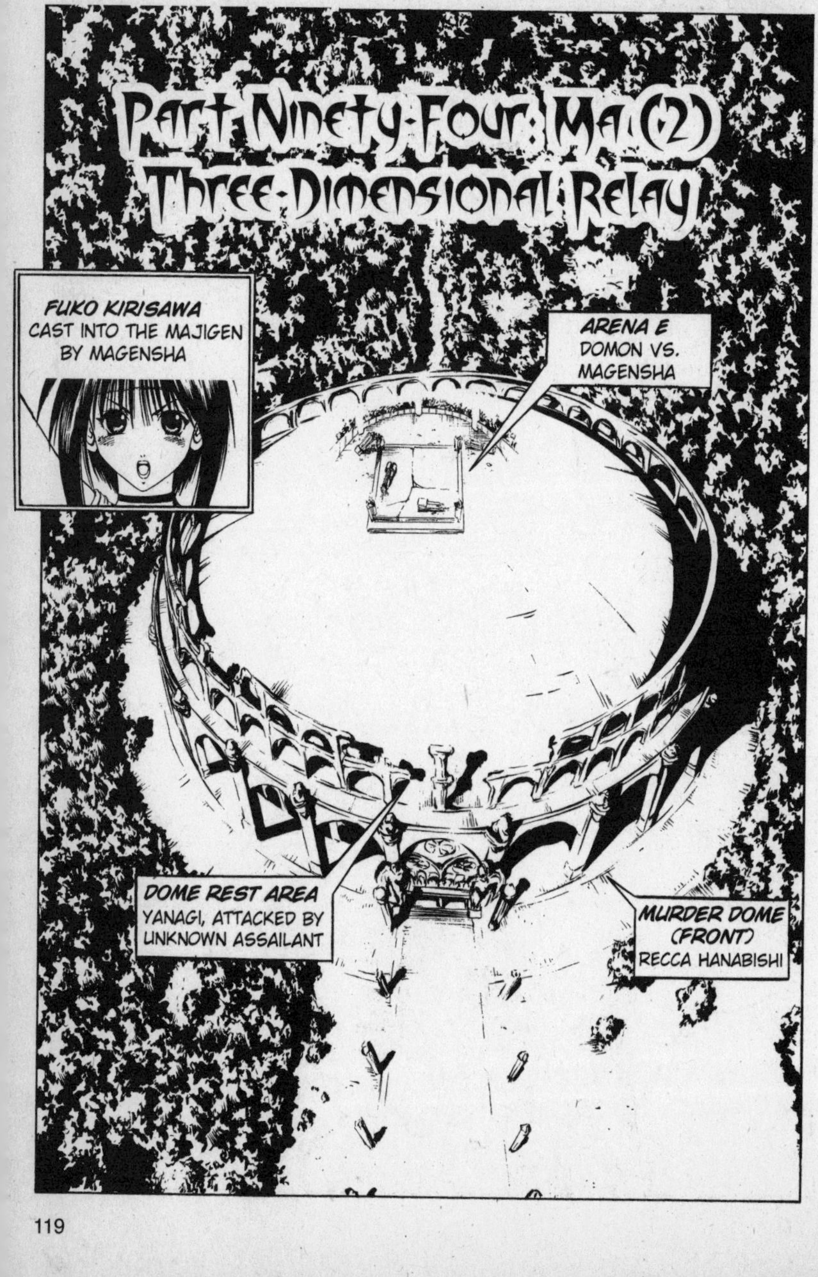
Part Ninety-Four: Ma (2)
Three-Dimensional Relay
ARENA E
DOMON VS. MAGENSHA
FUKO KIRISAWA
CAST INTO THE MAJIGEN BY MAGENSHA
MURDER DOME (FRONT)
RECCA HANABISHI
DOME REST AREA
YANAGI, ATTACKED BY UNKNOWN ASSAILANT

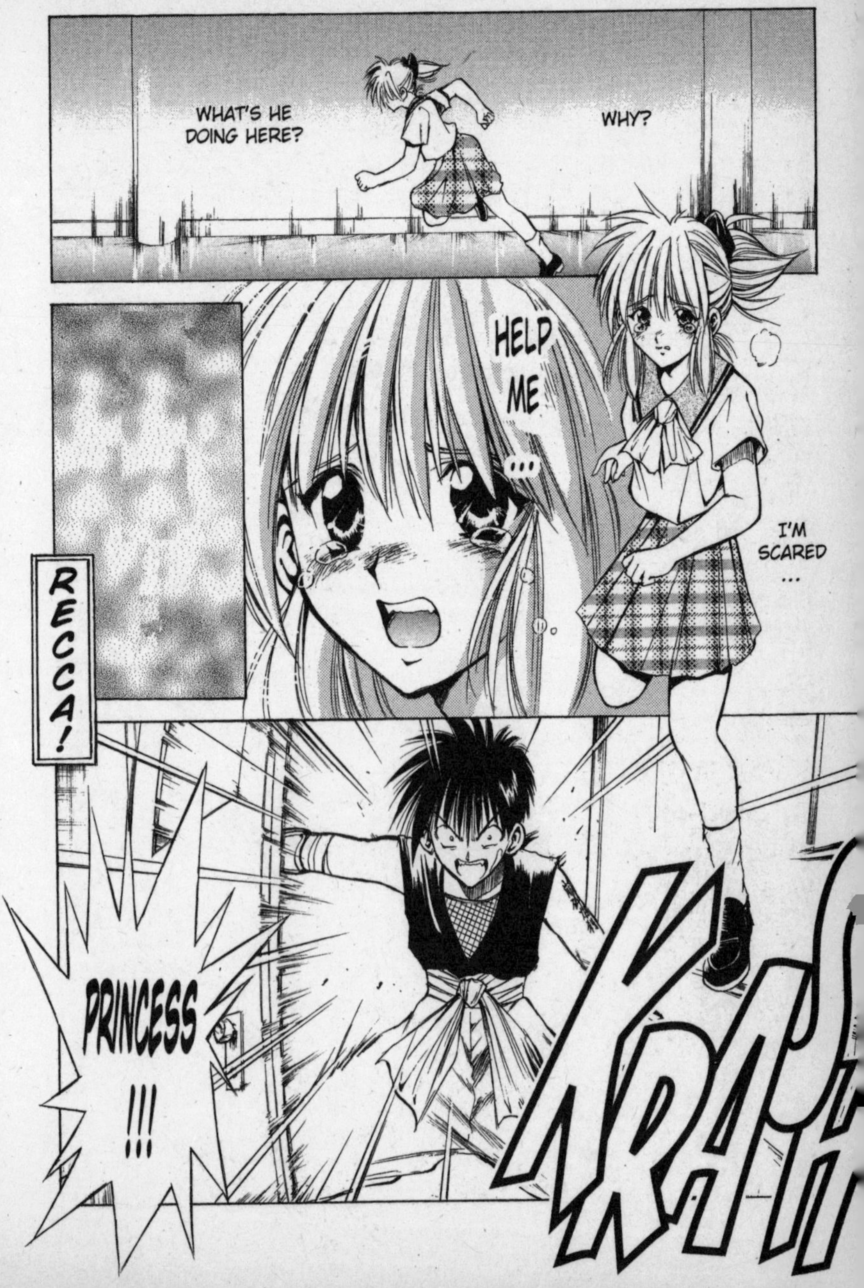
WHY?
WHAT'S HE DOING HERE?
I'M SCARED ...
HELP ME ...
RECCA!
PRINCESS !!!

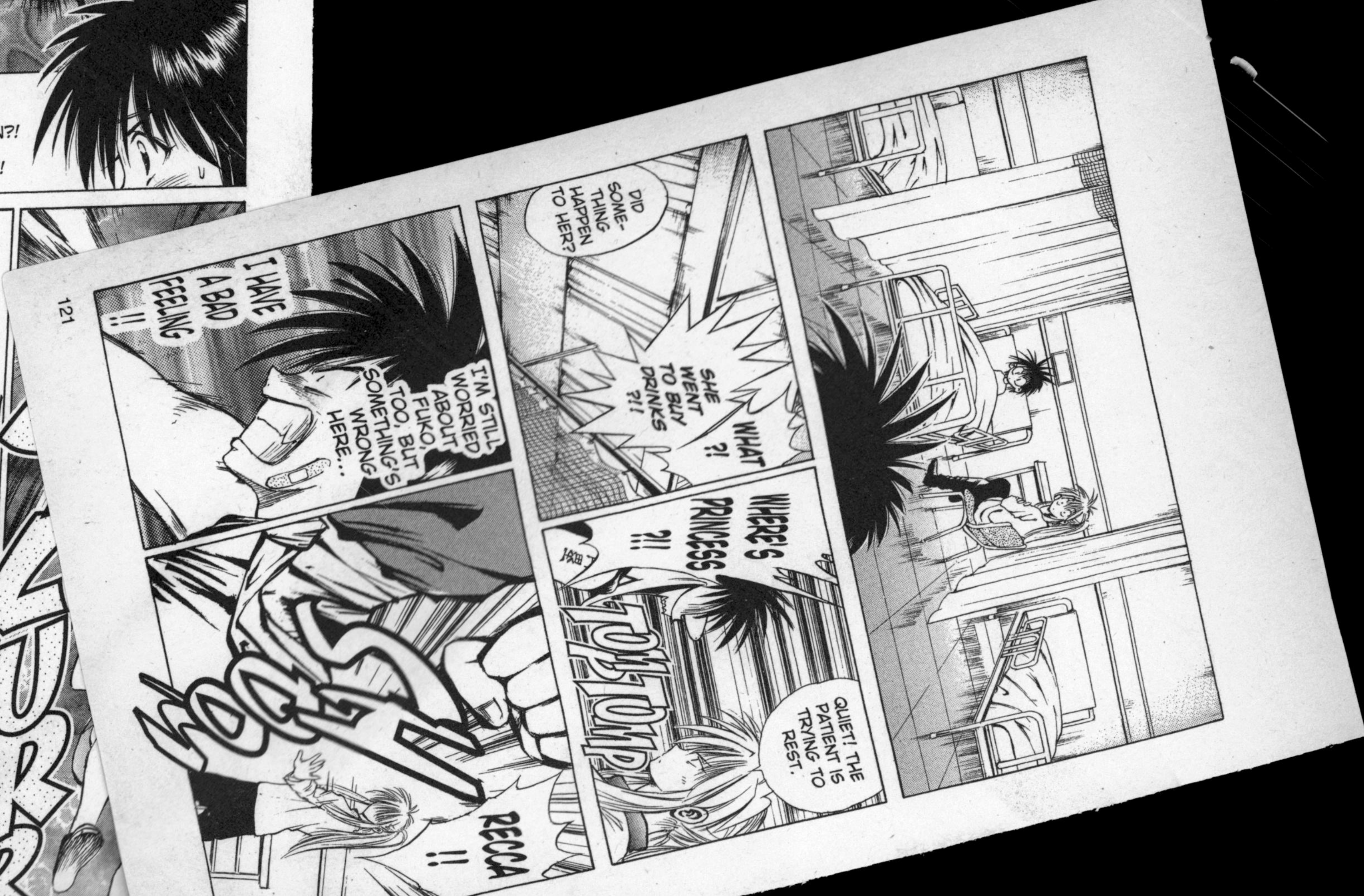

QUIET! THE PATIENT IS TRYING TO REST.
DID SOMETHING HAPPEN TO HER?
WHAT?!
SHE WENT TO BUY DRINKS?!
WHERE'S PRINCESS?!!
TOMP TOMP
I HAVE A BAD FEELING!!
I'M STILL WORRIED ABOUT FUKO, TOO, BUT SOMETHING'S WRONG HERE...
RECCA!!

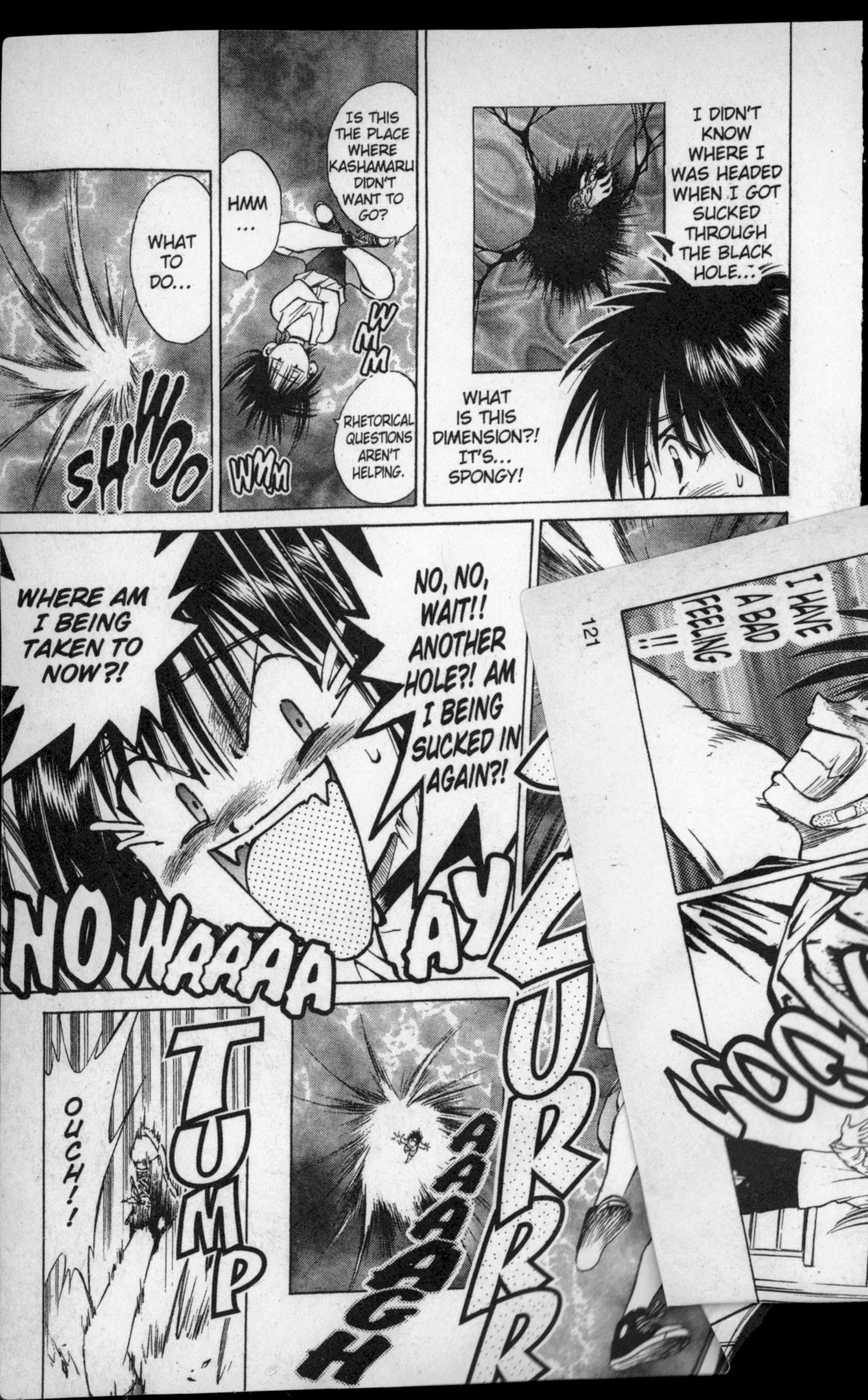

I DIDN'T KNOW WHERE I WAS HEADED WHEN I GOT SUCKED THROUGH THE BLACK HOLE...
WHAT IS THIS DIMENSION?! IT'S... SPONGY!
IS THIS THE PLACE WHERE KASHAMARU DIDN'T WANT TO GO?
HMM...
WMM
RHETORICAL QUESTIONS AREN'T HELPING.
WMM
WHAT TO DO...
SHWOO
NO, NO, WAIT!! ANOTHER HOLE?! AM I BEING SUCKED IN AGAIN?!
WHERE AM I BEING TAKEN TO NOW?!
NO WAAAAAY
ZURRR
AAAAAAGH
TUMP
OUCH!!

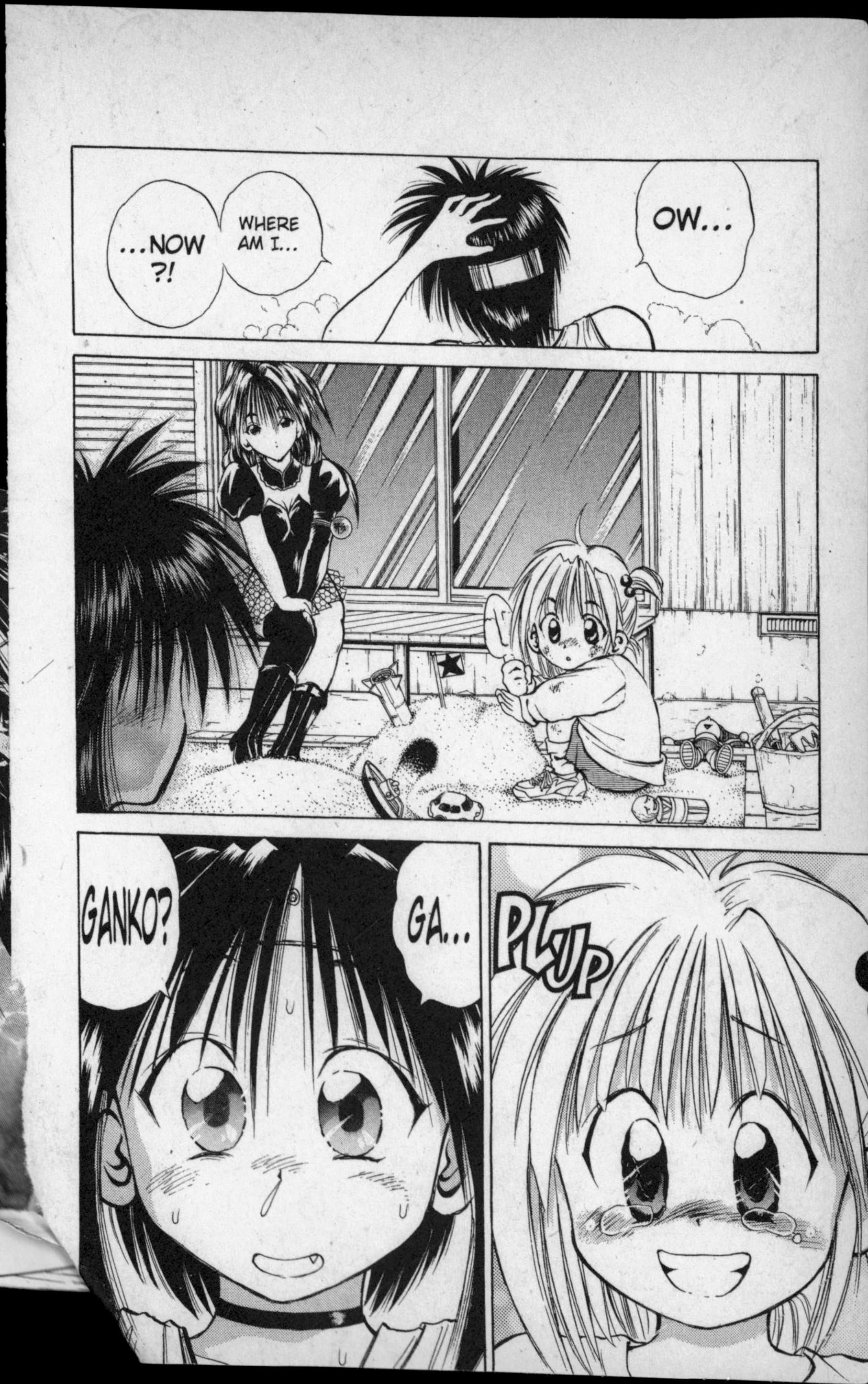
OW...
WHERE AM I...
...NOW ?!
PLUP
GA...
GANKO?

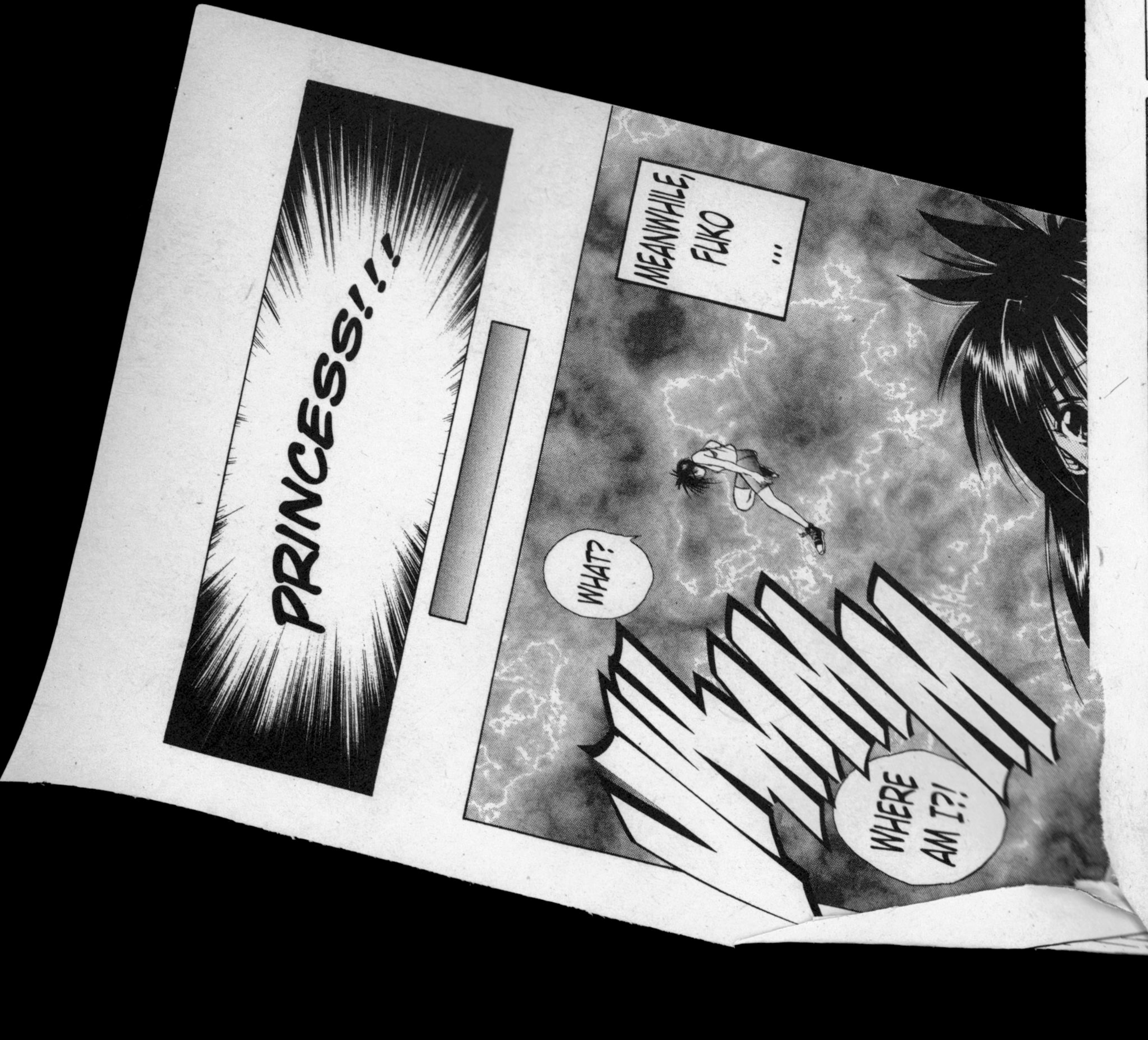
MEANWHILE, FUKO ...
WHERE AM I?!
WHAT?
PRINCESS!!!

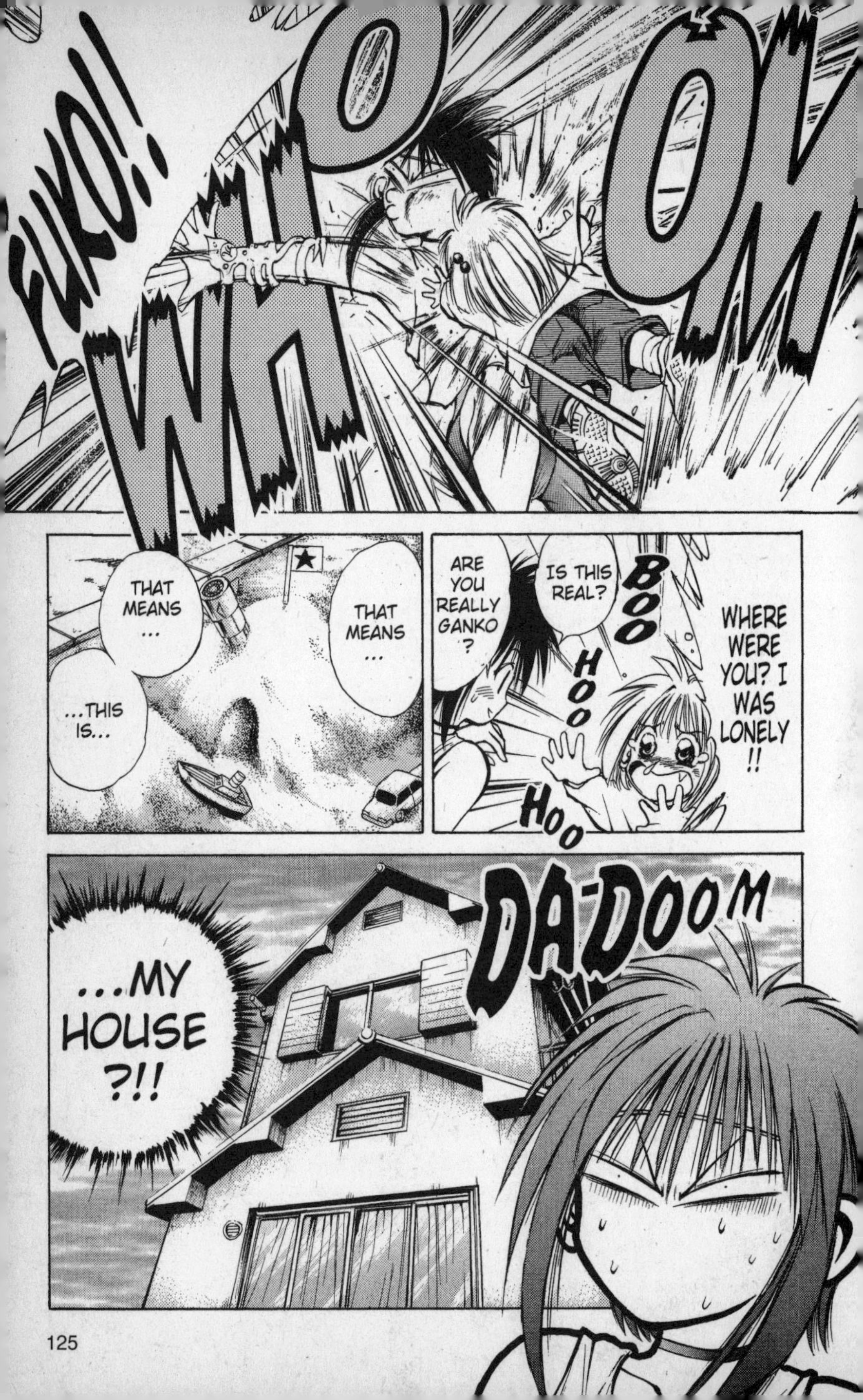
WHOOM
FUKO!!
WHERE WERE YOU? I WAS LONELY!!
BOO HOO HOO HOO
IS THIS REAL?
ARE YOU REALLY GANKO?
THAT MEANS...
THAT MEANS...
...THIS IS...
DA-DOOM
...MY HOUSE?!!

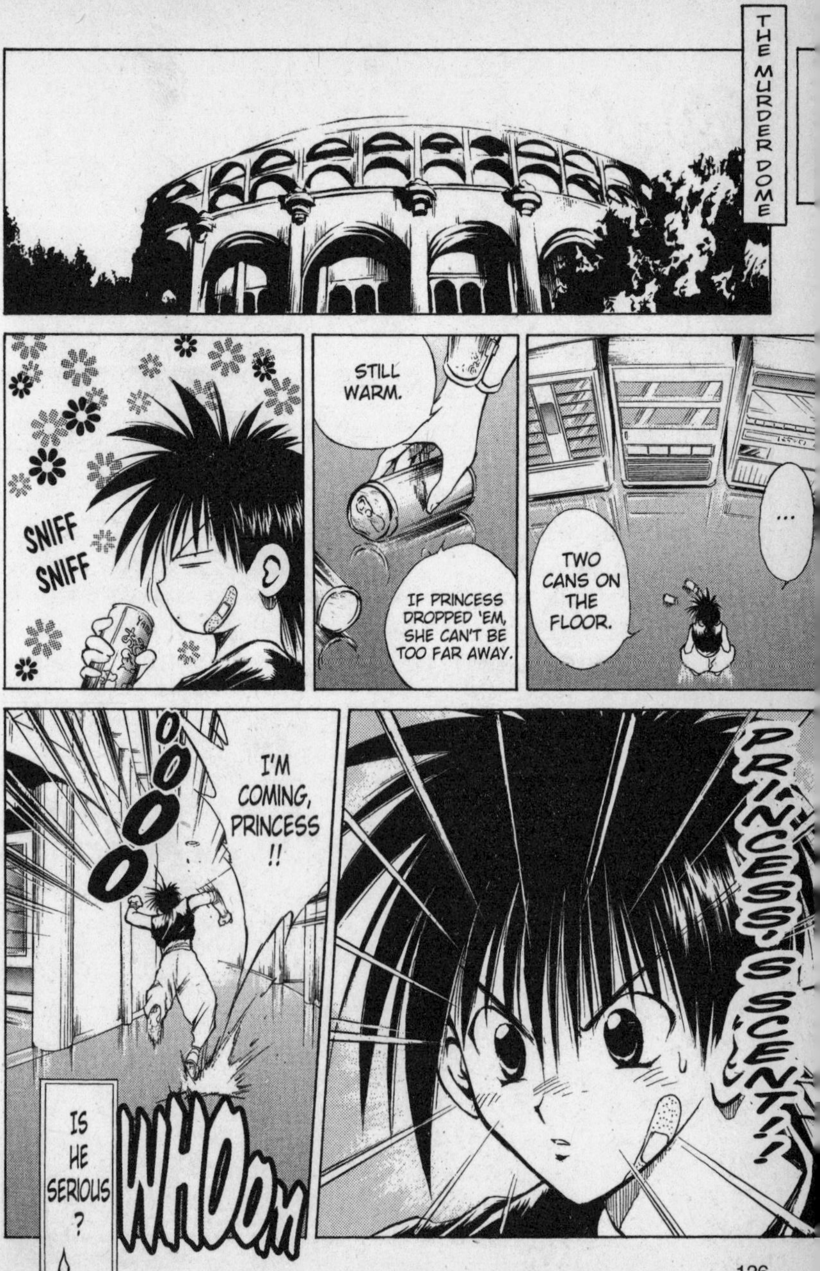
THE MURDER DOME
...
TWO CANS ON THE FLOOR.
STILL WARM.
IF PRINCESS DROPPED 'EM, SHE CAN'T BE TOO FAR AWAY.
SNIFF SNIFF
PRINCESS'S SCENT!!
I'M COMING, PRINCESS !!
OOOOO
WHOOM
IS HE SERIOUS ?

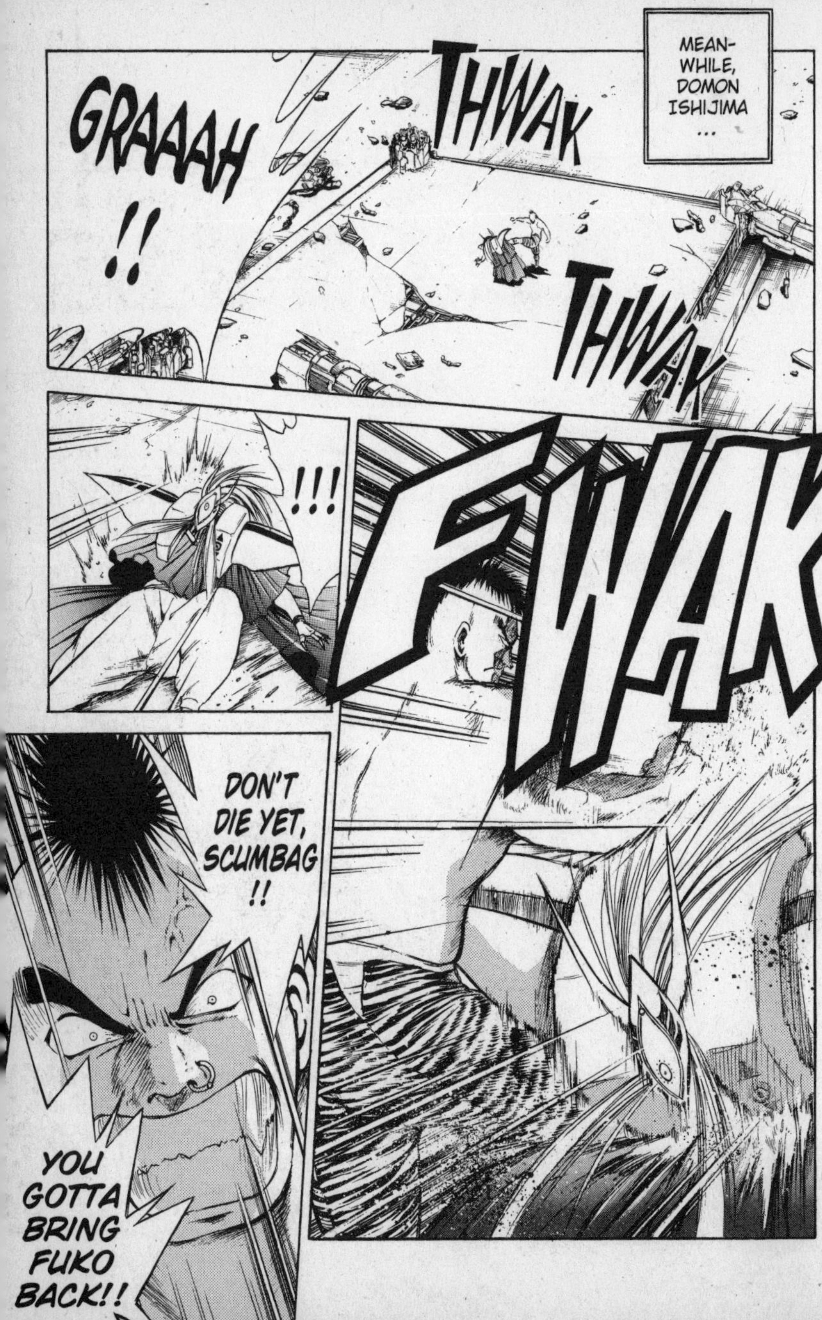
MEAN-WHILE, DOMON ISHIJIMA ...
THWAK
THWAK
GRAAAH!!
FWAK
!!!
DON'T DIE YET, SCUMBAG!!
YOU GOTTA BRING FUKO BACK!!

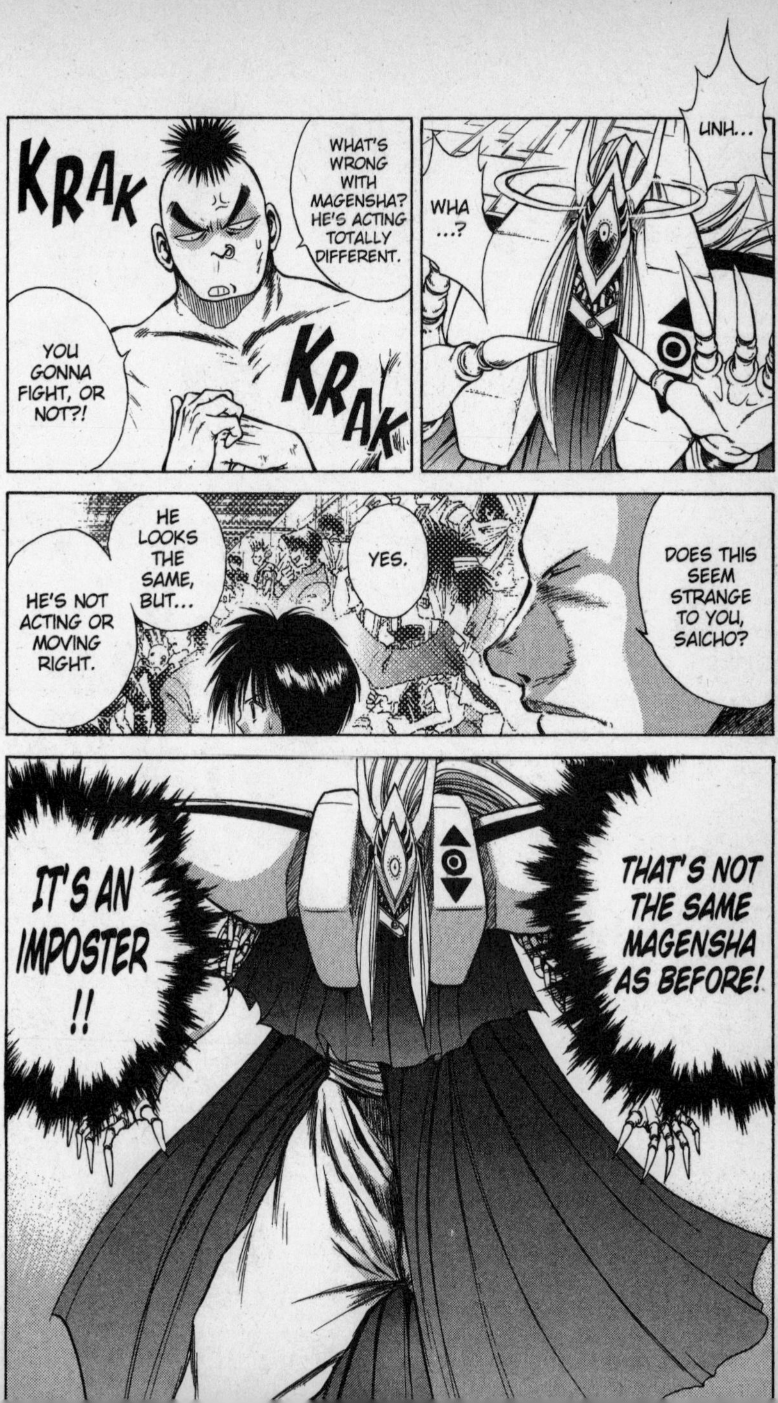
UNH...
WHA ...?
WHAT'S WRONG WITH MAGENSHA? HE'S ACTING TOTALLY DIFFERENT.
KRAK
KRAK
YOU GONNA FIGHT, OR NOT?!
DOES THIS SEEM STRANGE TO YOU, SAICHO?
YES.
HE LOOKS THE SAME, BUT...
HE'S NOT ACTING OR MOVING RIGHT.
THAT'S NOT THE SAME MAGENSHA AS BEFORE!
IT'S AN IMPOSTER !!

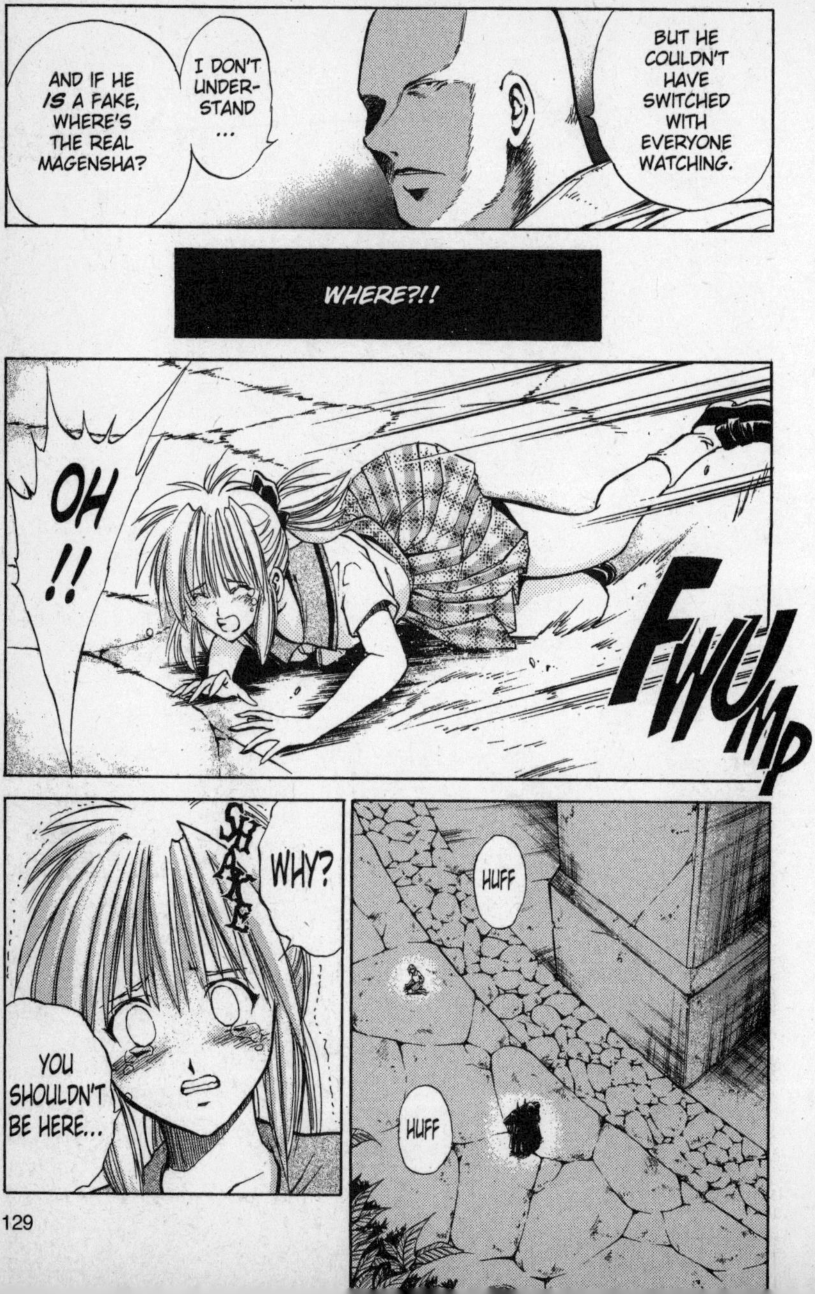
BUT HE COULDN'T HAVE SWITCHED WITH EVERYONE WATCHING.
I DON'T UNDER-STAND...
AND IF HE *IS* A FAKE, WHERE'S THE REAL MAGENSHA?
WHERE?!!
OH!!
FWUMP
HUFF
HUFF
SHAKE
WHY?
YOU SHOULDN'T BE HERE...

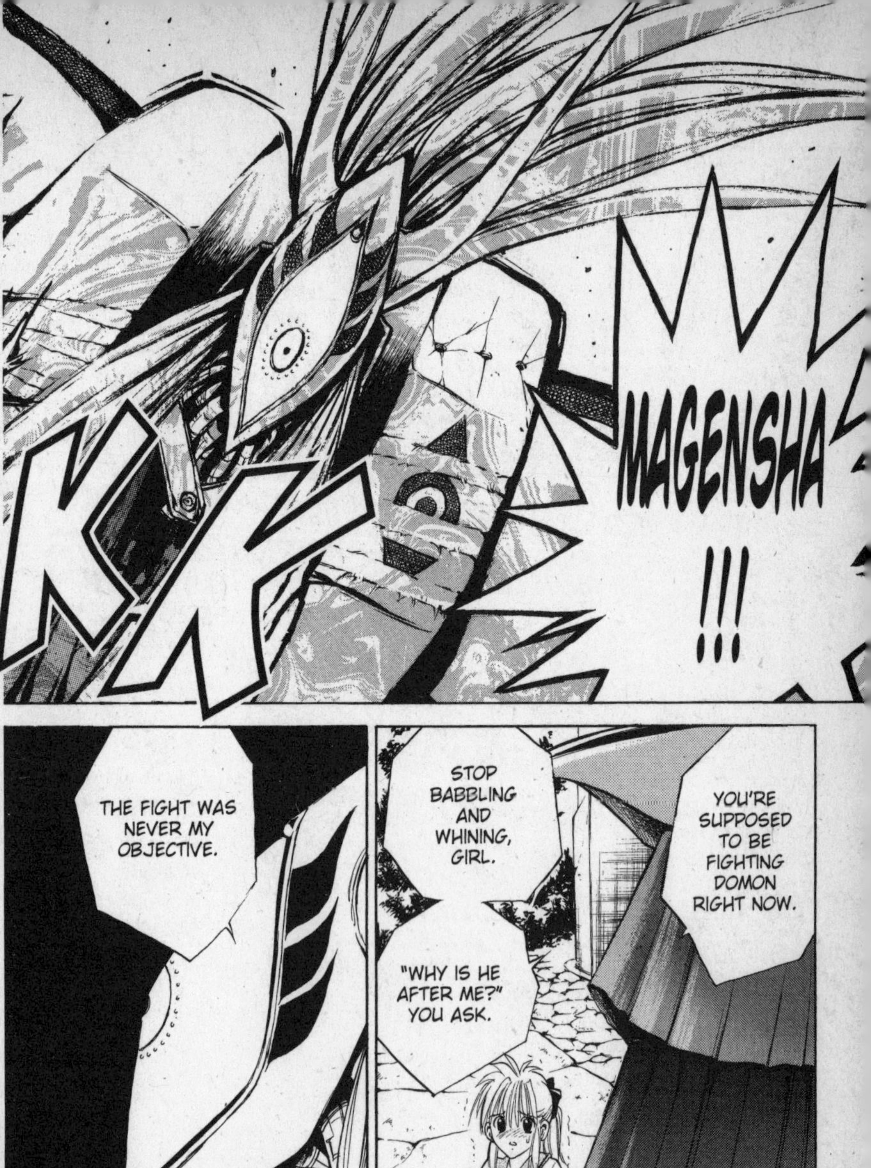
MAGENSHA !!!
KA
YOU'RE SUPPOSED TO BE FIGHTING DOMON RIGHT NOW.
STOP BABBLING AND WHINING, GIRL.
"WHY IS HE AFTER ME?" YOU ASK.
THE FIGHT WAS NEVER MY OBJECTIVE.
IT WAS ALWAYS YOU, YANAGI!!

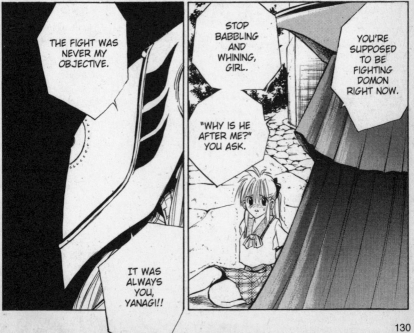

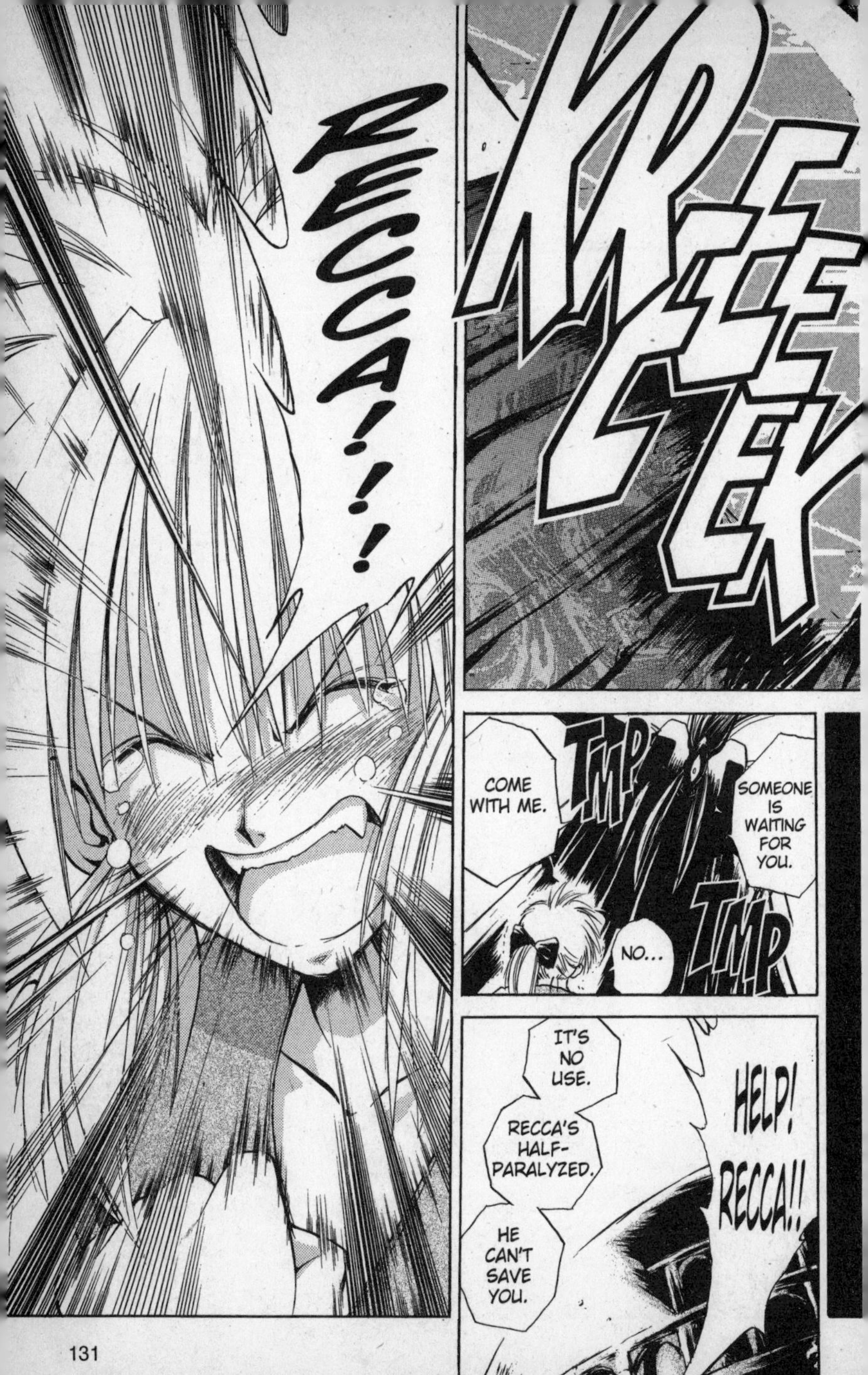
KREEEEK
SOMEONE IS WAITING FOR YOU.
TMP
COME WITH ME.
TMP
NO...
HELP! RECCA!!
IT'S NO USE.
RECCA'S HALF-PARALYZED.
HE CAN'T SAVE YOU.
RECCA!!!

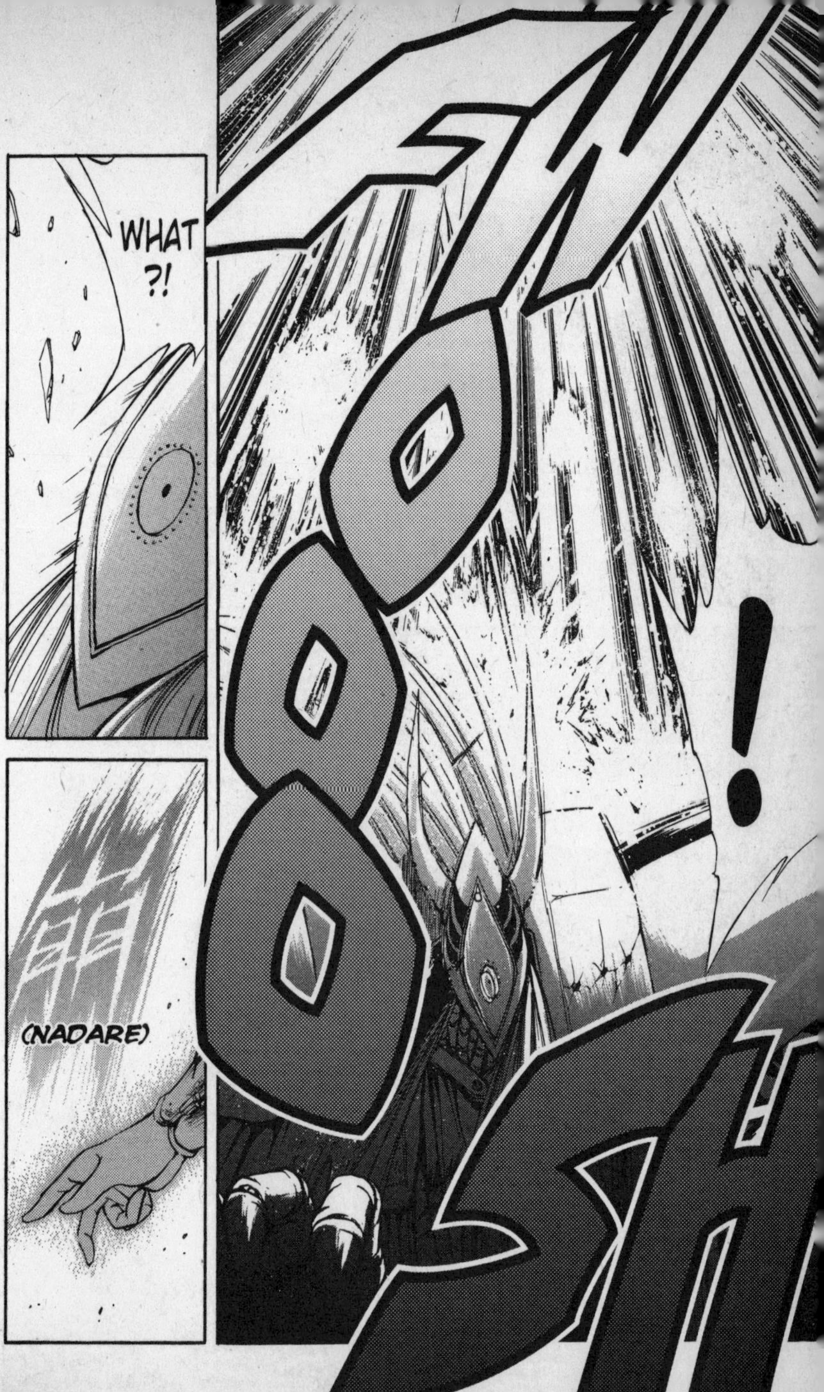
WHAT ?!
(NADARE)

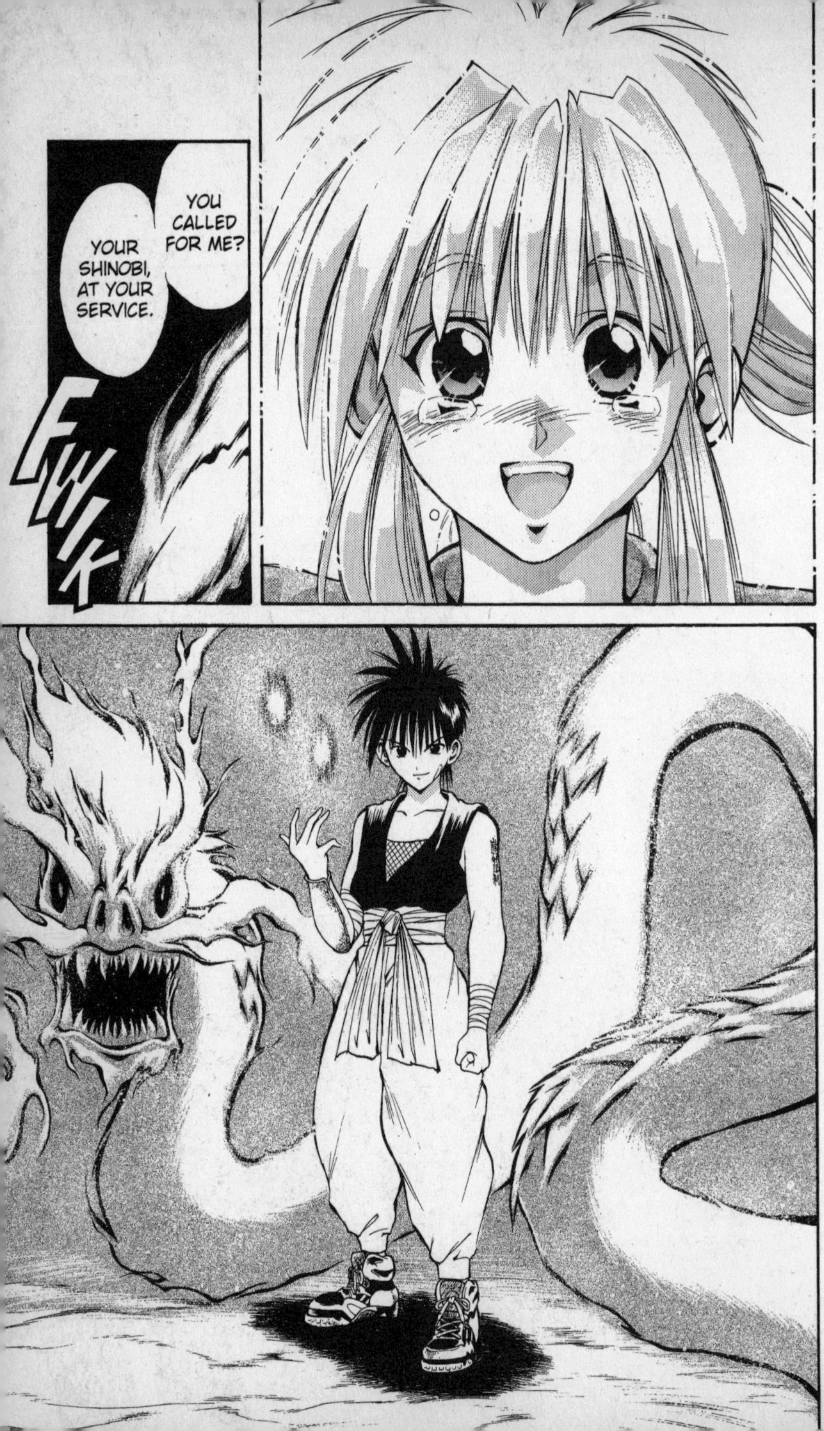
YOU CALLED FOR ME?
YOUR SHINOBI, AT YOUR SERVICE.
FWIK

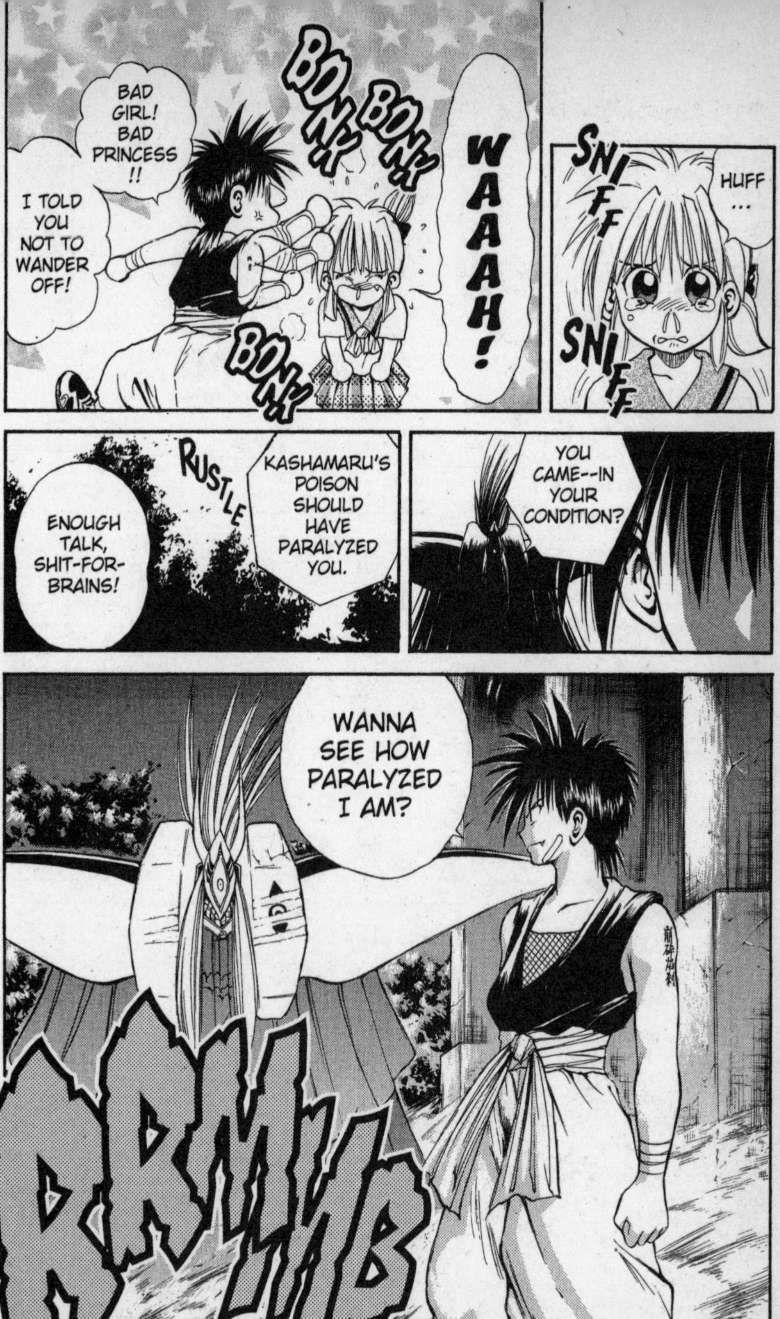
SNIFF
HUFF ...
SNIFF
WAAAAH!
BONK BONK
BAD GIRL! BAD PRINCESS !!
I TOLD YOU NOT TO WANDER OFF!
BONK
YOU CAME--IN YOUR CONDITION?
KASHAMARU'S POISON SHOULD HAVE PARALYZED YOU.
RUSTLE
ENOUGH TALK, SHIT-FOR-BRAINS!
WANNA SEE HOW PARALYZED I AM?

Part Ninety-Five: Ma (3) Ill-Met in Subspace

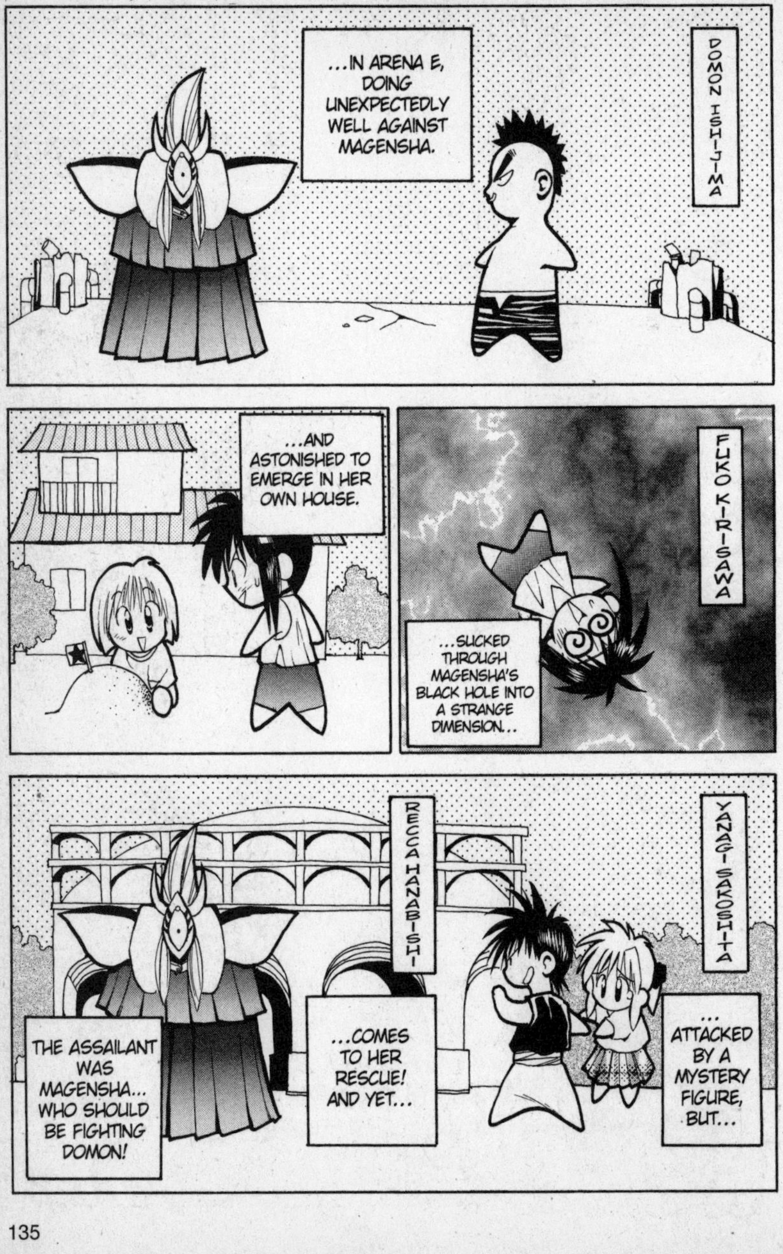
DOMON ISHIJIMA
...IN ARENA E, DOING UNEXPECTEDLY WELL AGAINST MAGENSHA.
FUKO KIRISAWA
...SUCKED THROUGH MAGENSHA'S BLACK HOLE INTO A STRANGE DIMENSION...
...AND ASTONISHED TO EMERGE IN HER OWN HOUSE.
YANAGI SAKOSHITA
... ATTACKED BY A MYSTERY FIGURE, BUT...
RECCA HANABISHI
...COMES TO HER RESCUE! AND YET...
THE ASSAILANT WAS MAGENSHA... WHO SHOULD BE FIGHTING DOMON!

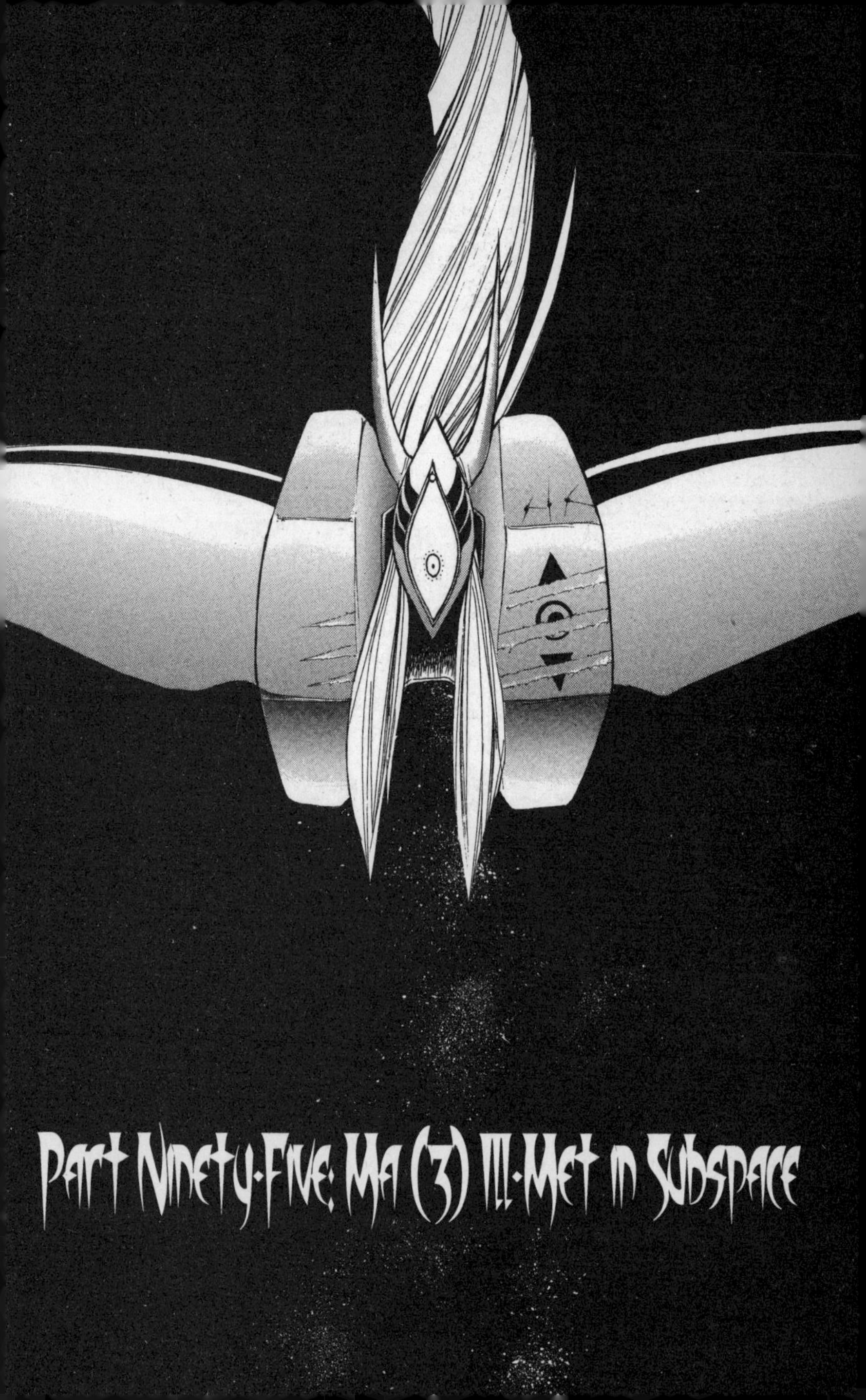

Part Ninety-Five: Ma (3) Ill-Met in Subspace

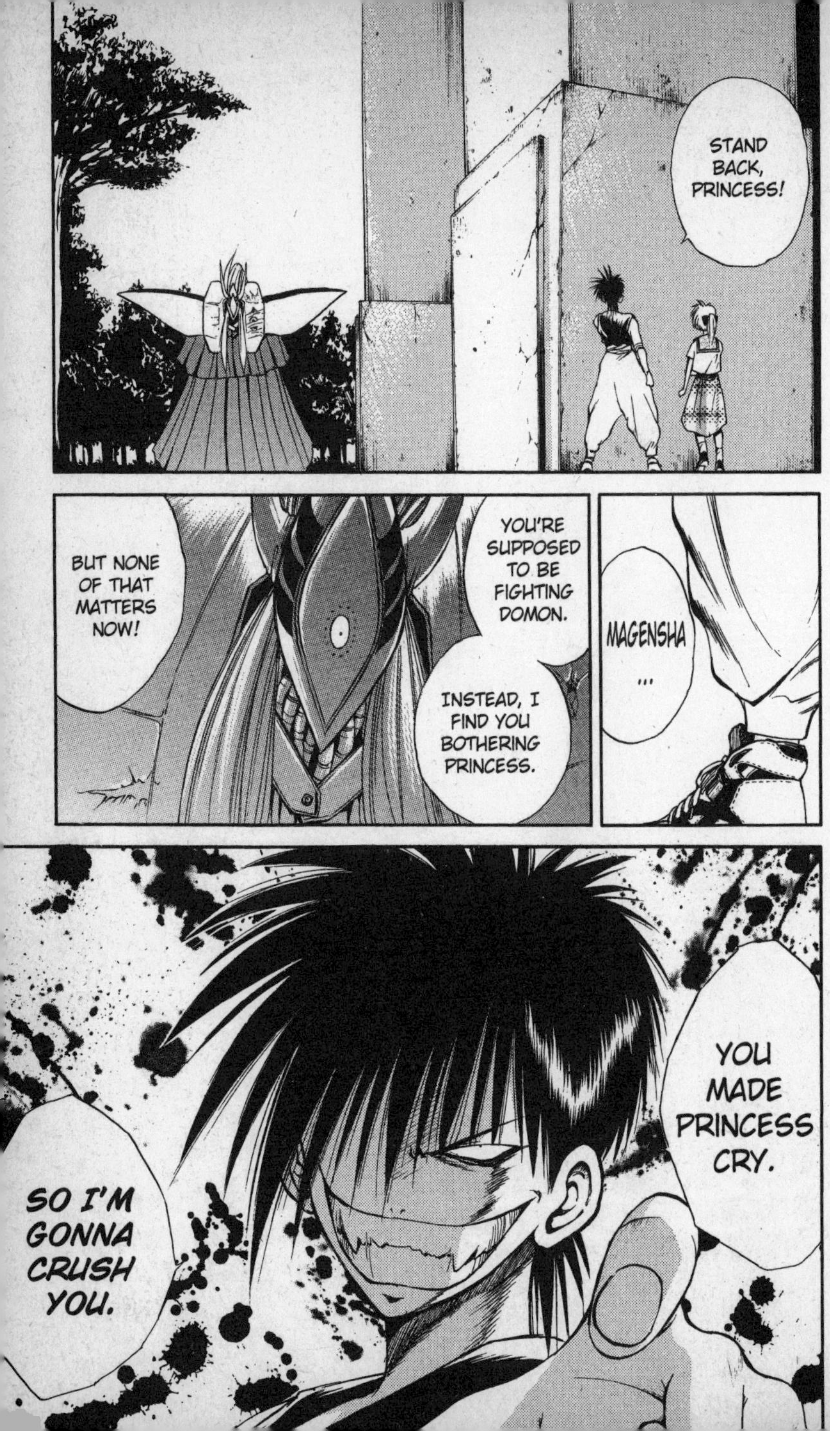
STAND BACK, PRINCESS!
MAGENSHA ...
YOU'RE SUPPOSED TO BE FIGHTING DOMON.
INSTEAD, I FIND YOU BOTHERING PRINCESS.
BUT NONE OF THAT MATTERS NOW!
YOU MADE PRINCESS CRY.
SO I'M GONNA CRUSH YOU.

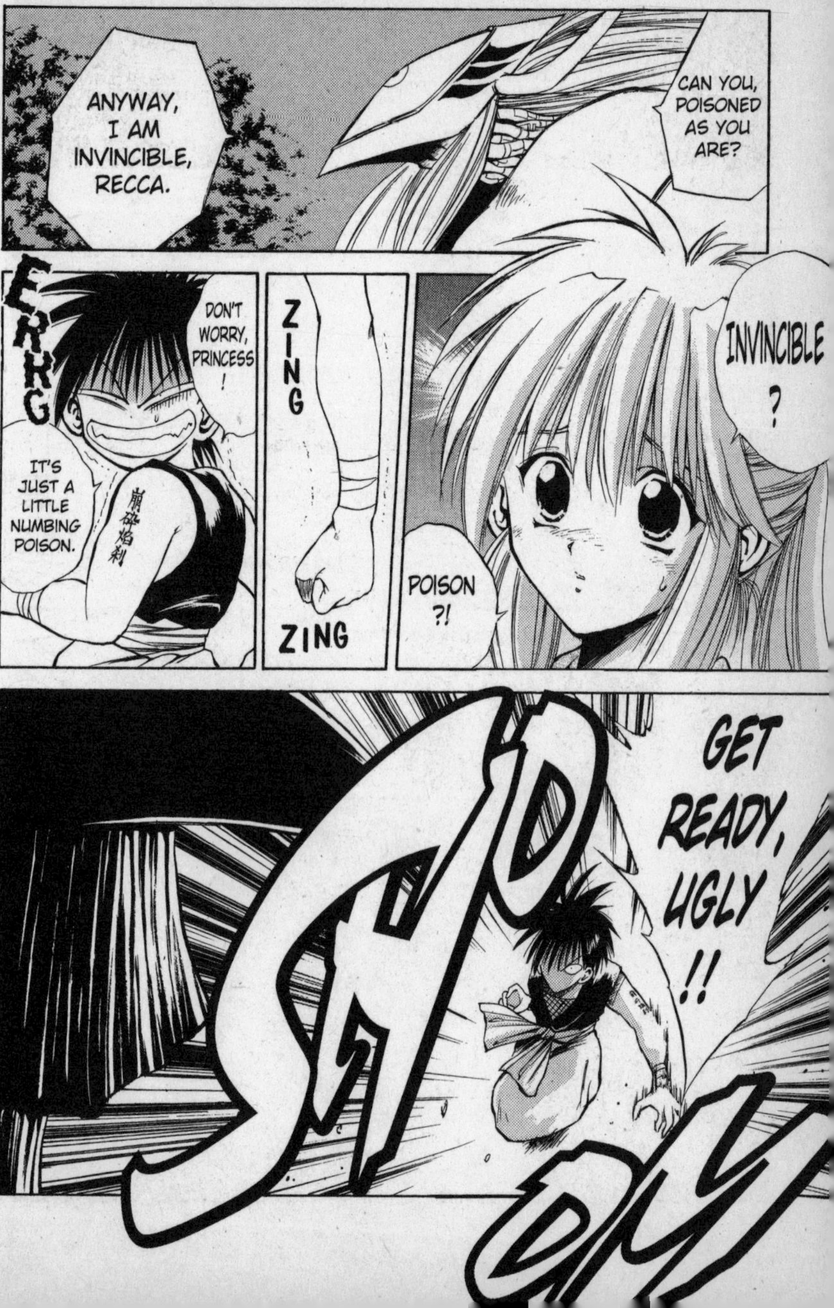
CAN YOU, POISONED AS YOU ARE?
ANYWAY, I AM INVINCIBLE, RECCA.
INVINCIBLE ?
POISON ?!
ZING
ZING
DON'T WORRY, PRINCESS !
ERKG
IT'S JUST A LITTLE NUMBING POISON.
GET READY, UGLY !!

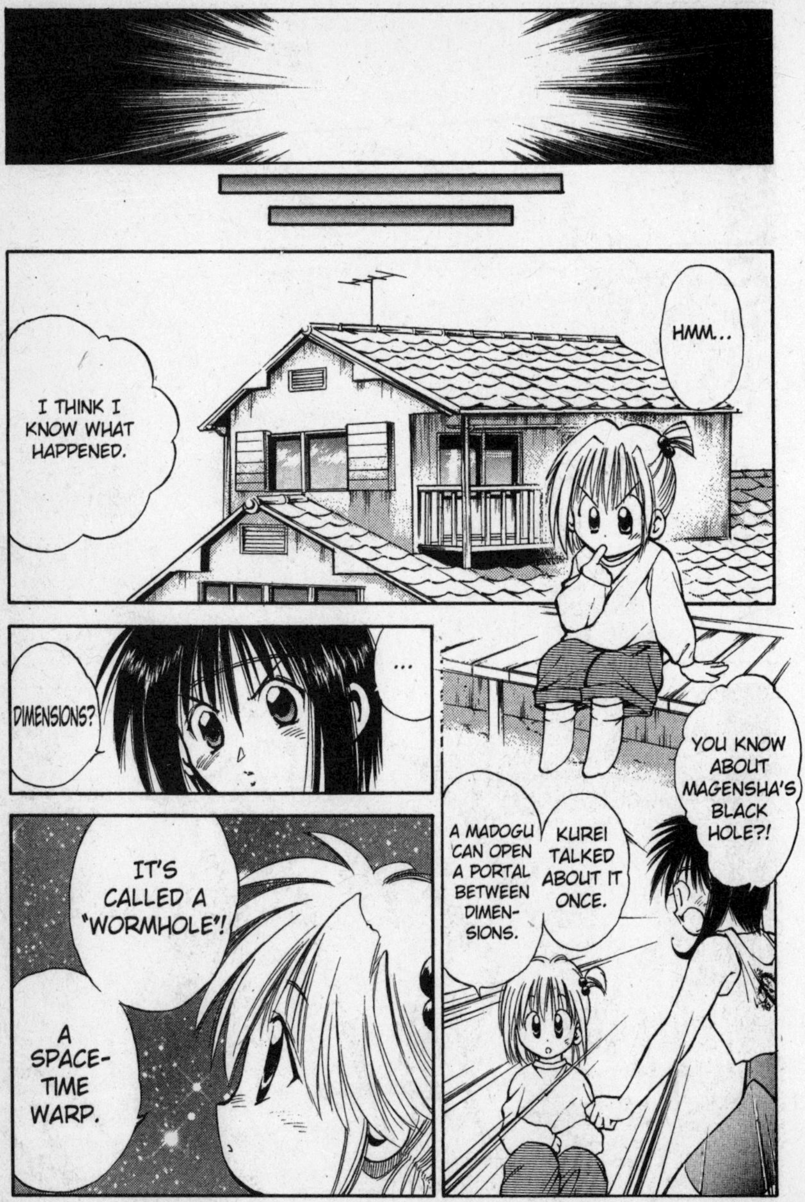
HMM...
I THINK I KNOW WHAT HAPPENED.
YOU KNOW ABOUT MAGENSHA'S BLACK HOLE?!
KUREI TALKED ABOUT IT ONCE.
A MADOGU CAN OPEN A PORTAL BETWEEN DIMENSIONS.
...
DIMENSIONS?
IT'S CALLED A "WORMHOLE"!
A SPACE-TIME WARP.

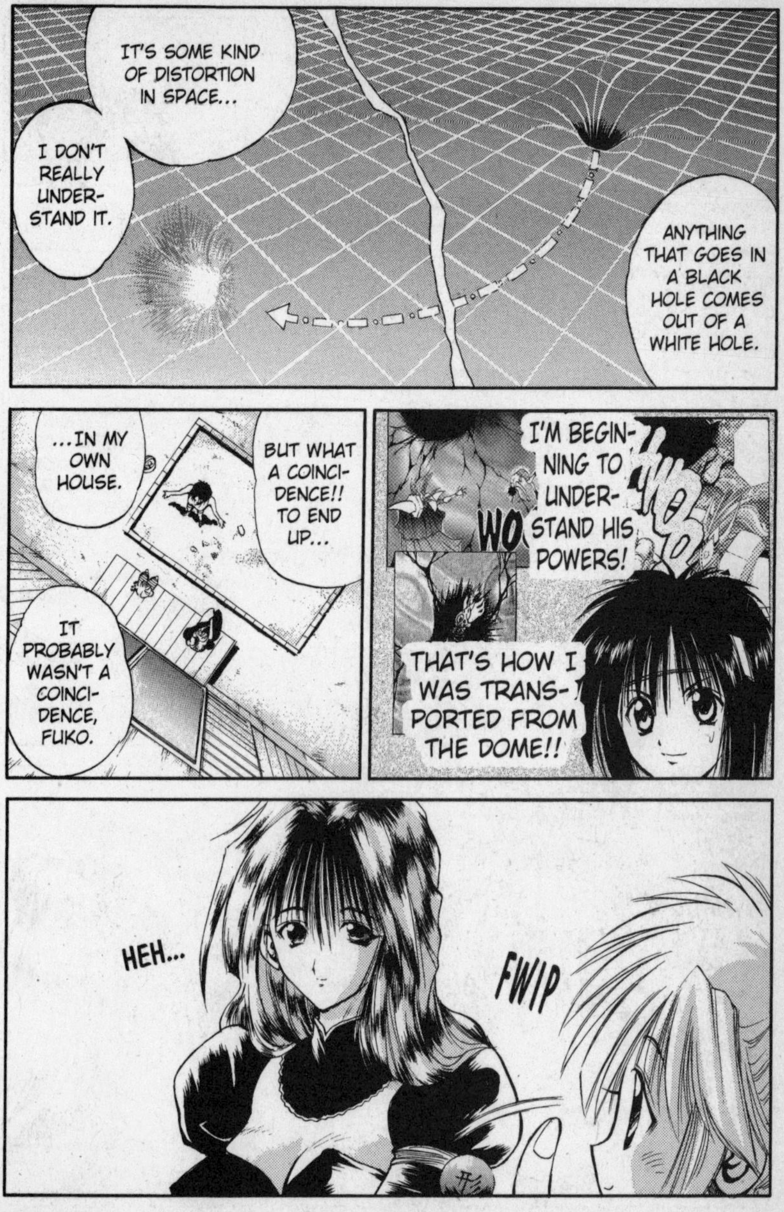
ANYTHING THAT GOES IN A BLACK HOLE COMES OUT OF A WHITE HOLE.
IT'S SOME KIND OF DISTORTION IN SPACE...
I DON'T REALLY UNDER-STAND IT.
I'M BEGIN-NING TO UNDER-STAND HIS POWERS!
THAT'S HOW I WAS TRANS-PORTED FROM THE DOME!!
BUT WHAT A COINCI-DENCE!! TO END UP...
...IN MY OWN HOUSE.
IT PROBABLY WASN'T A COINCI-DENCE, FUKO.
FWIP
HEH...

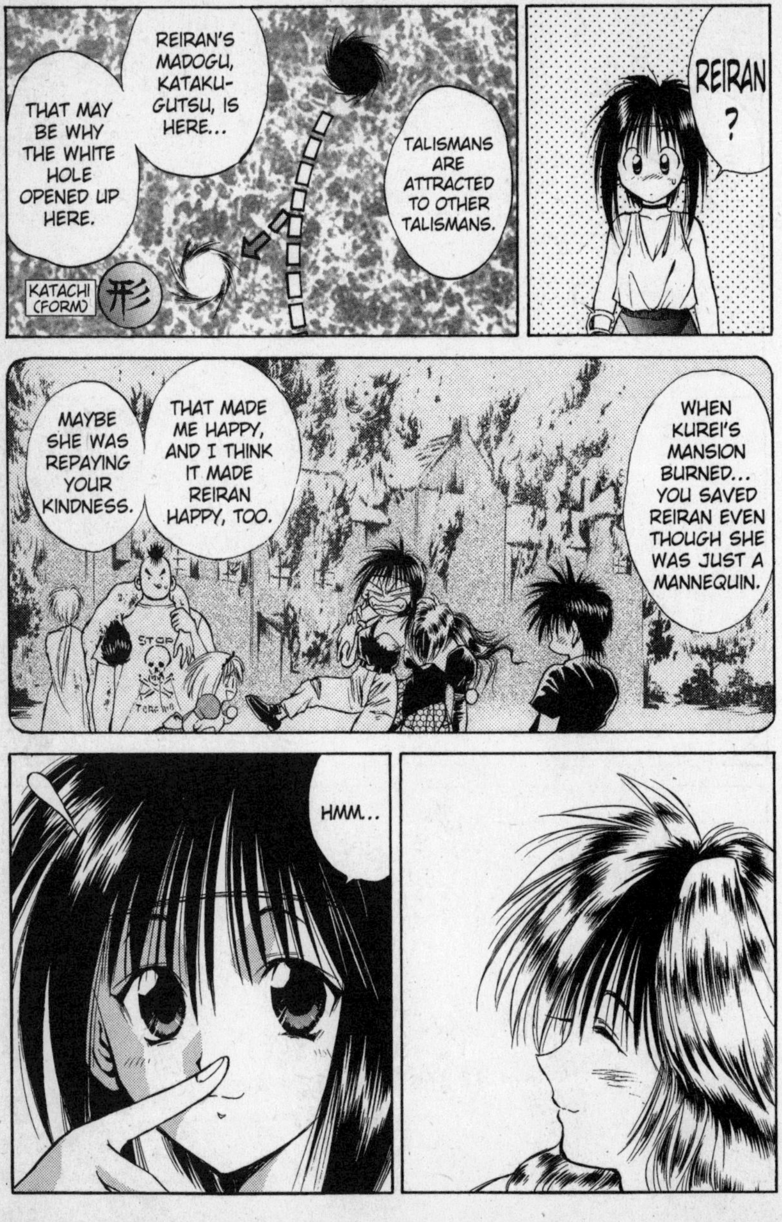
REIRAN?
TALISMANS ARE ATTRACTED TO OTHER TALISMANS.
REIRAN'S MADOGU, KATAKU-GUTSU, IS HERE...
THAT MAY BE WHY THE WHITE HOLE OPENED UP HERE.
KATACHI (FORM)
形
WHEN KUREI'S MANSION BURNED... YOU SAVED REIRAN EVEN THOUGH SHE WAS JUST A MANNEQUIN.
THAT MADE ME HAPPY, AND I THINK IT MADE REIRAN HAPPY, TOO.
MAYBE SHE WAS REPAYING YOUR KINDNESS.
STOP
HMM...

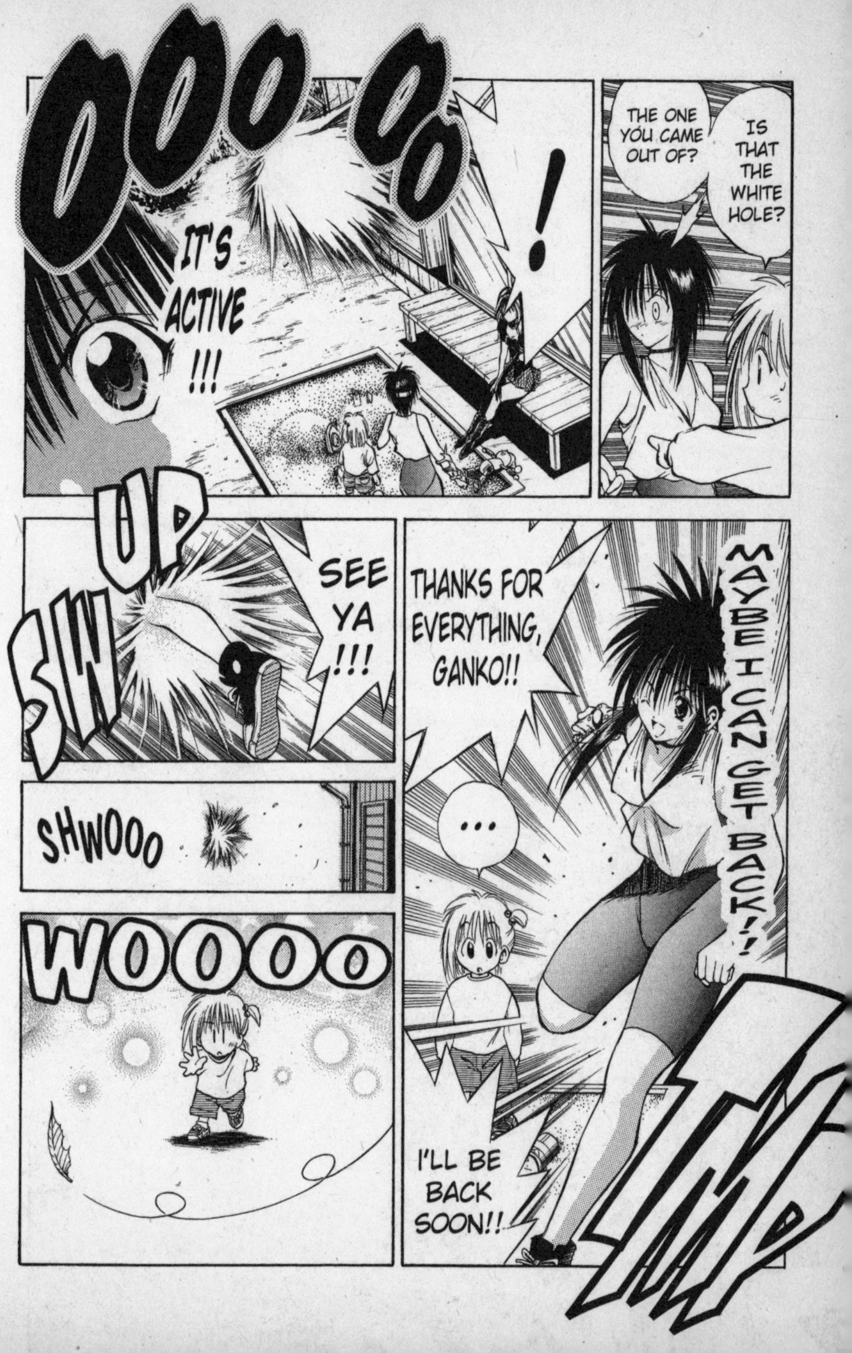
IS THAT THE WHITE HOLE?
THE ONE YOU CAME OUT OF?
OOOOO
!
IT'S ACTIVE !!!
MAYBE I CAN GET BACK!!
THANKS FOR EVERYTHING, GANKO!!
...
I'LL BE BACK SOON!!
SEE YA !!!
SWUP
SHWOOO
WOOOO

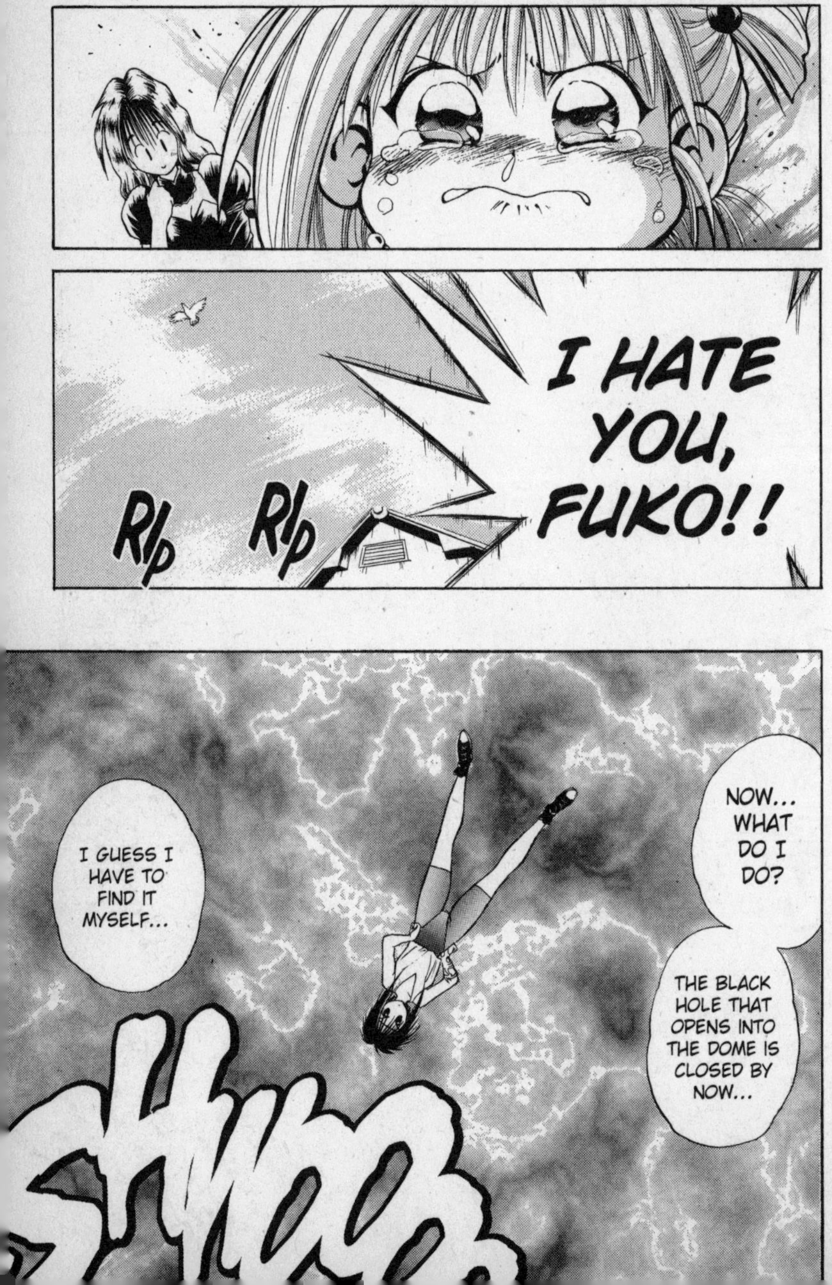
I HATE YOU, FUKO!!
RIP
RIP
NOW... WHAT DO I DO?
THE BLACK HOLE THAT OPENS INTO THE DOME IS CLOSED BY NOW...
I GUESS I HAVE TO FIND IT MYSELF...

...BEFORE I END UP LIKE HIM...

SHIVER

WUP WUP WUP WUP WUP WUP

WHO'S THERE ?!!

WP

A PRESENCE...!

TWO OF THEM ?

SHINK

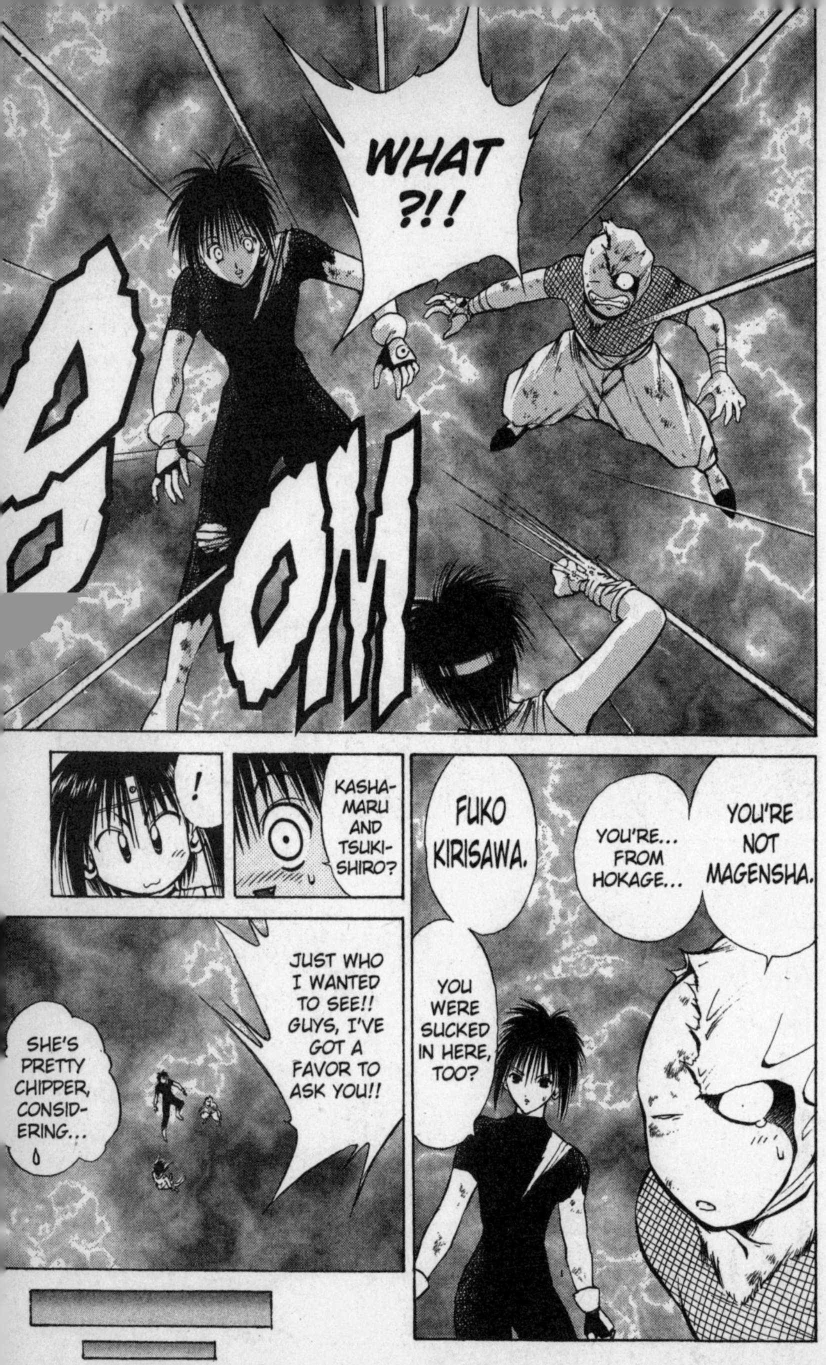
WHAT ?!!
BOOM
YOU'RE NOT MAGENSHA.
YOU'RE... FROM HOKAGE...
FUKO KIRISAWA.
YOU WERE SUCKED IN HERE, TOO?
KASHA-MARU AND TSUKI-SHIRO?
!
JUST WHO I WANTED TO SEE!! GUYS, I'VE GOT A FAVOR TO ASK YOU!!
SHE'S PRETTY CHIPPER, CONSID-ERING...

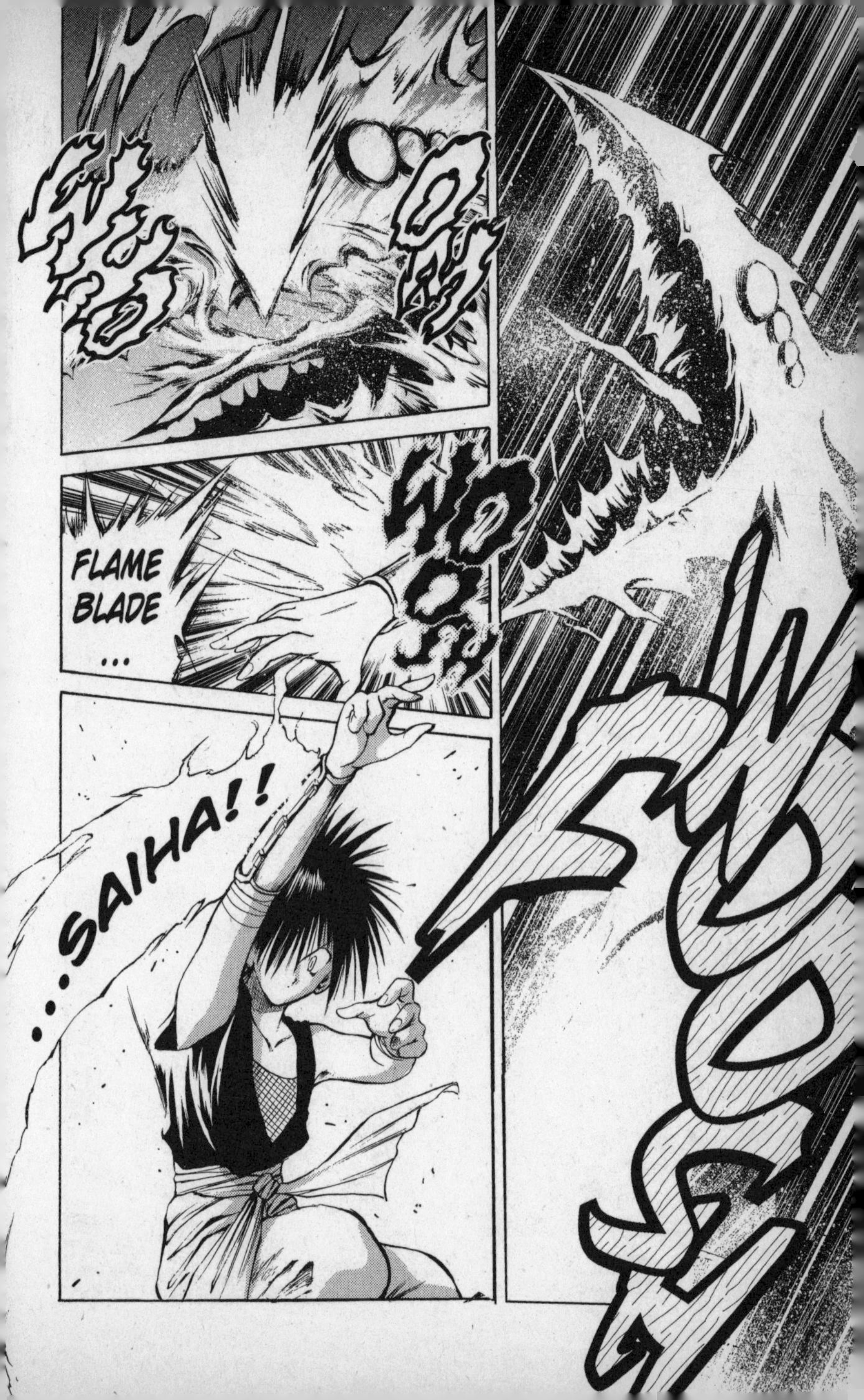
FLAME BLADE ...
...SAIHA!!

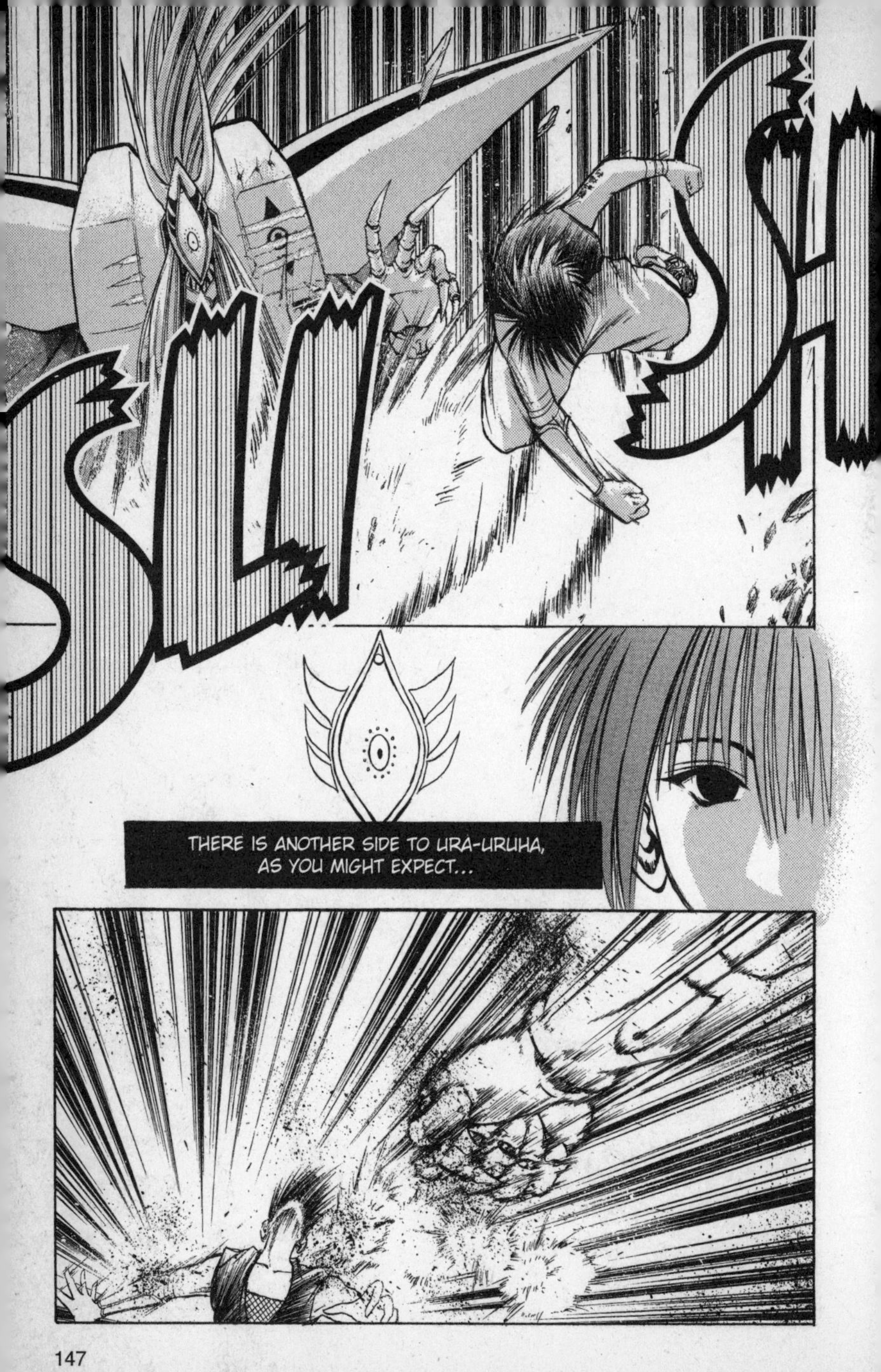
THERE IS ANOTHER SIDE TO URA-URUHA,
AS YOU MIGHT EXPECT...

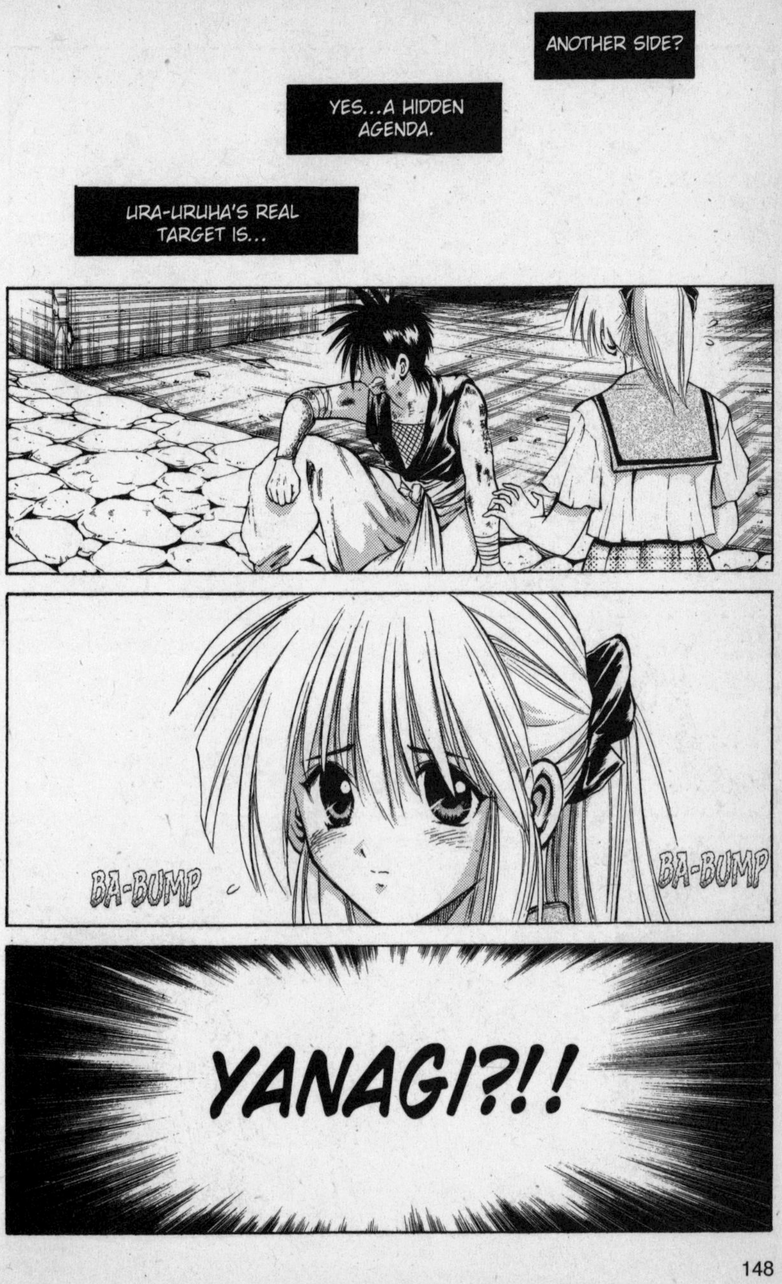
ANOTHER SIDE?
YES...A HIDDEN AGENDA.
URA-URUHA'S REAL TARGET IS...
BA-BUMP
BA-BUMP
YANAGI?!!

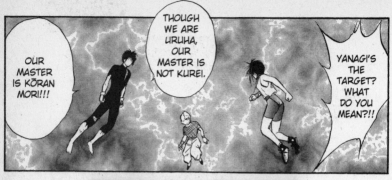

YANAGI'S THE TARGET? WHAT DO YOU MEAN?!!
THOUGH WE ARE URUHA, OUR MASTER IS NOT KUREI.
OUR MASTER IS KŌRAN MORI!!!
WE DID NOT ENTER THE CONTEST TO WIN...
OUR MISSION WAS TO HELP MAGENSHA CAPTURE YANAGI.
MASTER MORI IS INTERESTED IN THE GIRL'S HEALING POWERS.
SHOULD YOU BE TELLING HER THIS, TSUKISHIRO?
WHY SHOULDN'T I?!
I'M GOING TO TELL HER.
I DON'T OWE THEM! THEY SENT ME TO THIS PLACE.
I HAVE TO GET BACK TO THE MURDER DOME!
I HAVE TO WARN YANAGI.
WE WANT OUT, TOO.
I DON'T INTEND TO STARVE IN HERE.

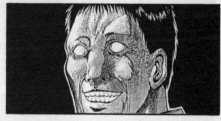

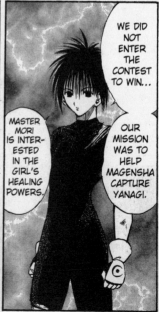

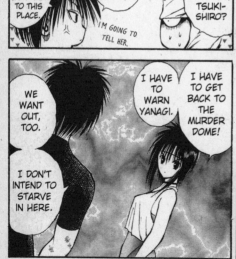

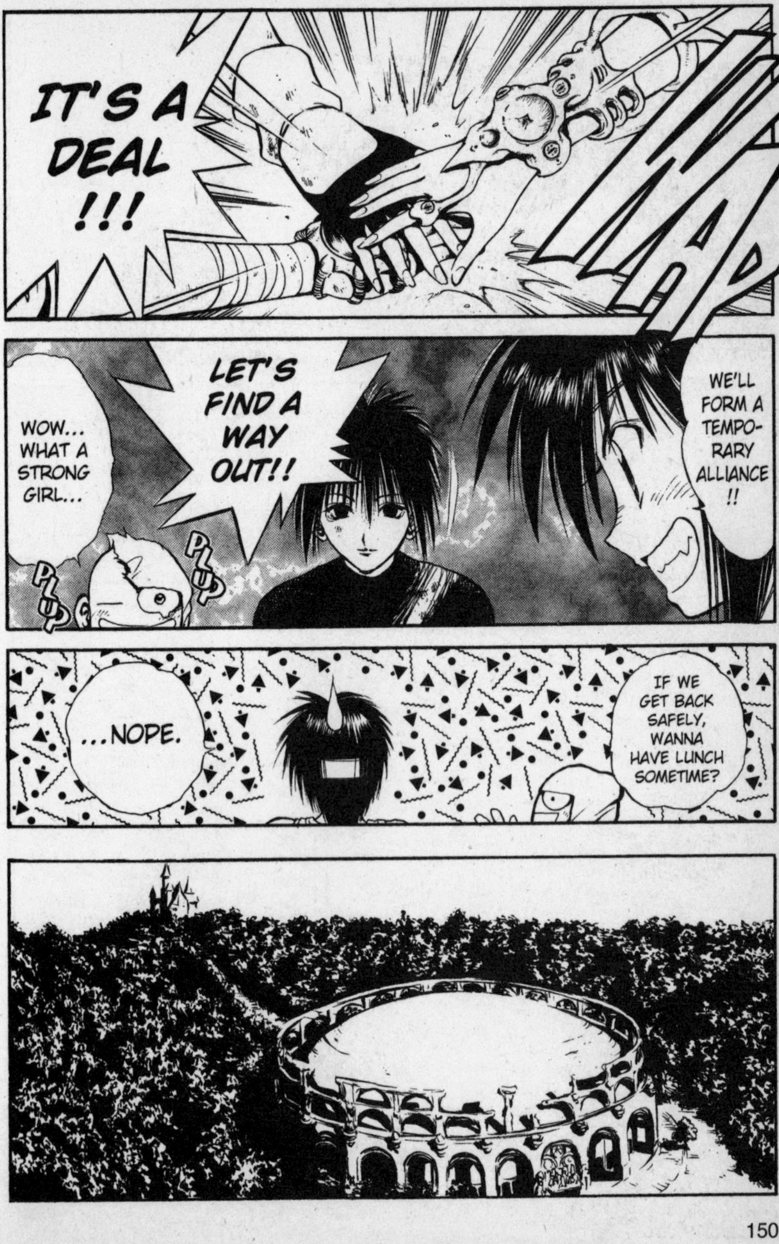
IT'S A DEAL!!!
WE'LL FORM A TEMPORARY ALLIANCE!!
LET'S FIND A WAY OUT!!
WOW... WHAT A STRONG GIRL...
PLUP
PLUP
IF WE GET BACK SAFELY, WANNA HAVE LUNCH SOMETIME?
...NOPE.

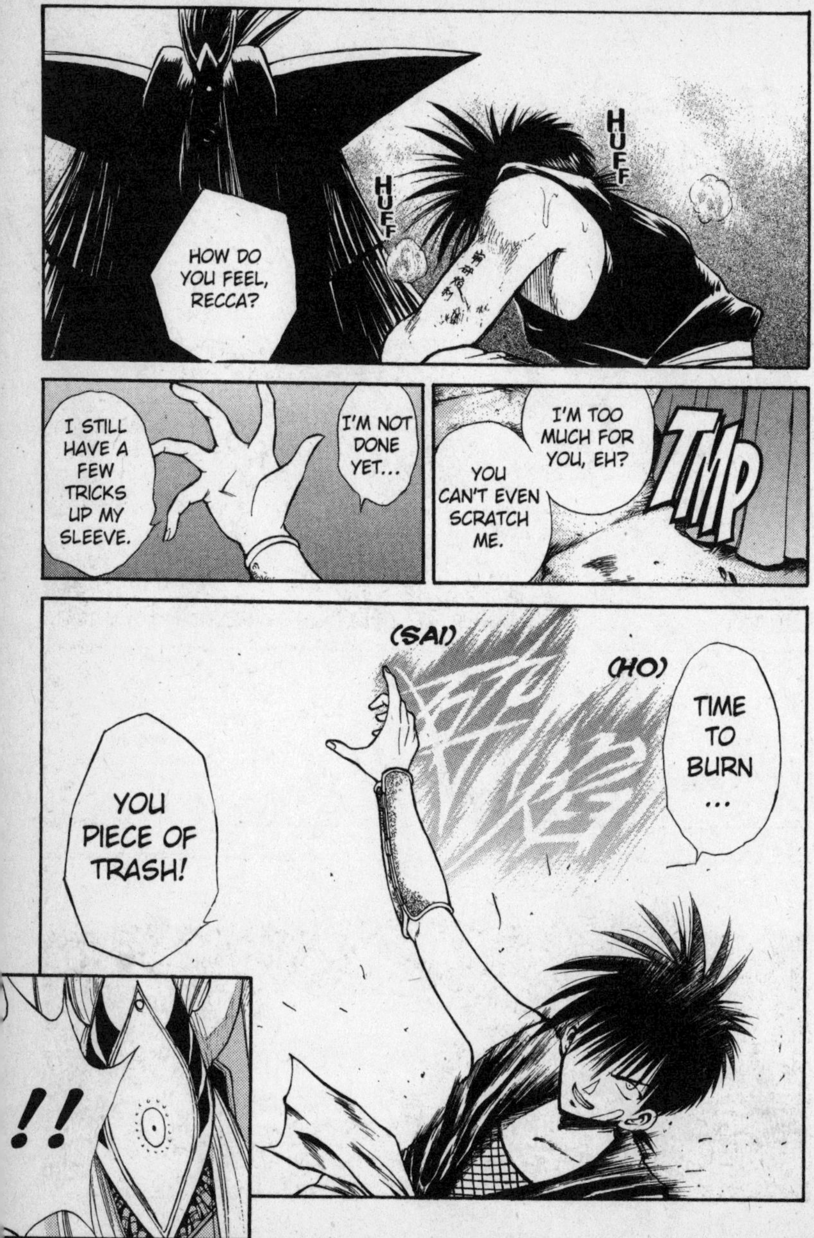
HUFF
HUFF
HOW DO YOU FEEL, RECCA?
TMP
I'M TOO MUCH FOR YOU, EH?
YOU CAN'T EVEN SCRATCH ME.
I'M NOT DONE YET...
I STILL HAVE A FEW TRICKS UP MY SLEEVE.
(SAI)
(HO)
TIME TO BURN ...
YOU PIECE OF TRASH!
!!

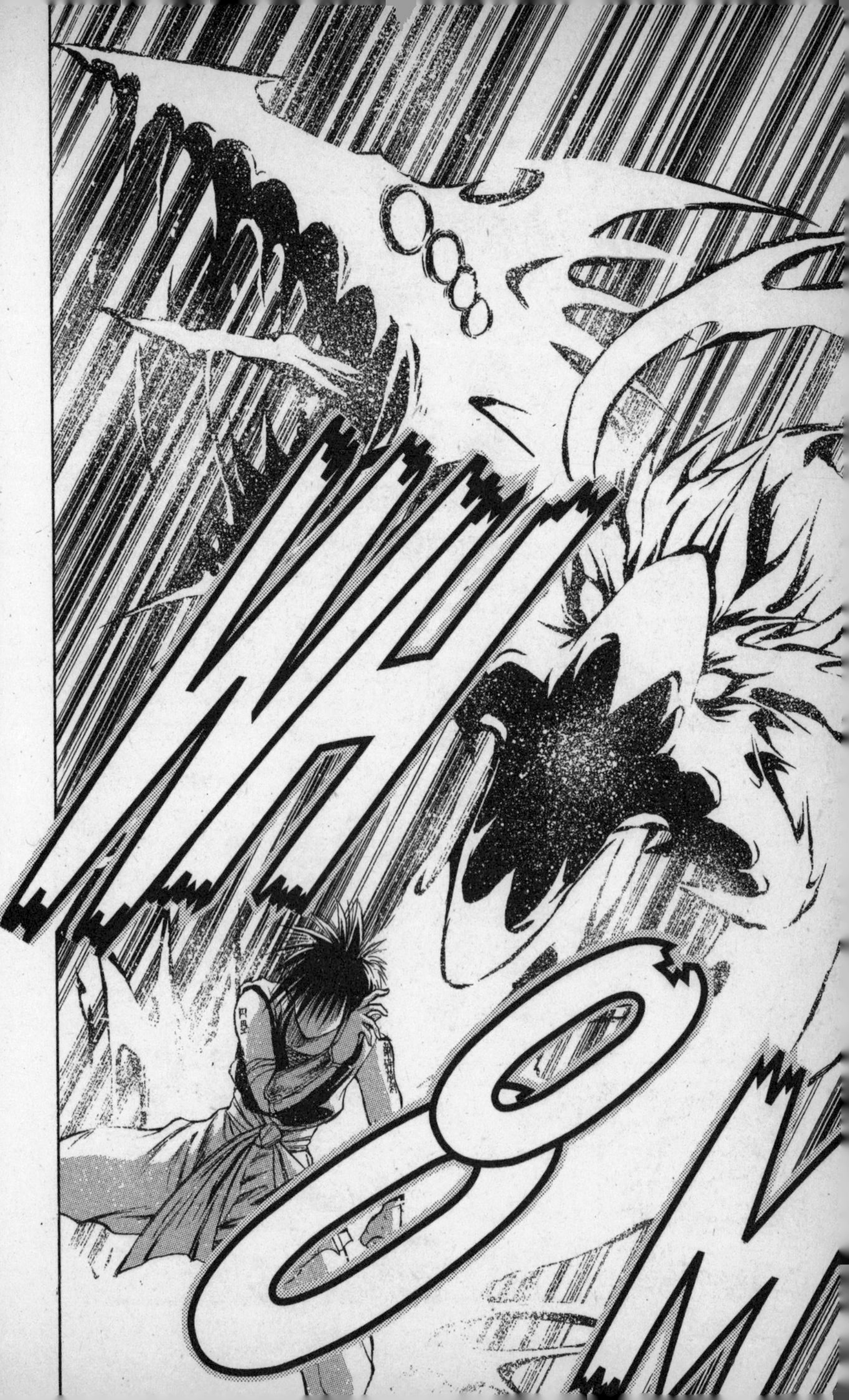
WHOOM

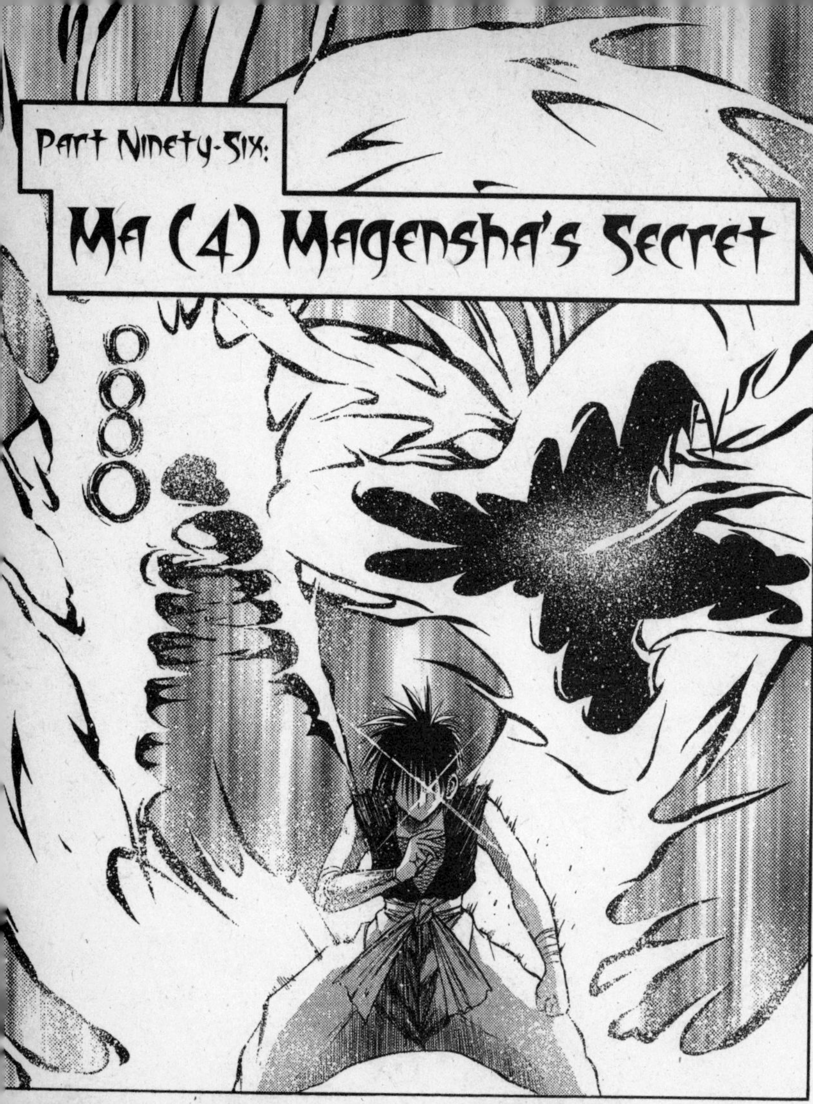
Part Ninety-Six:
Ma (4) Magensha's Secret

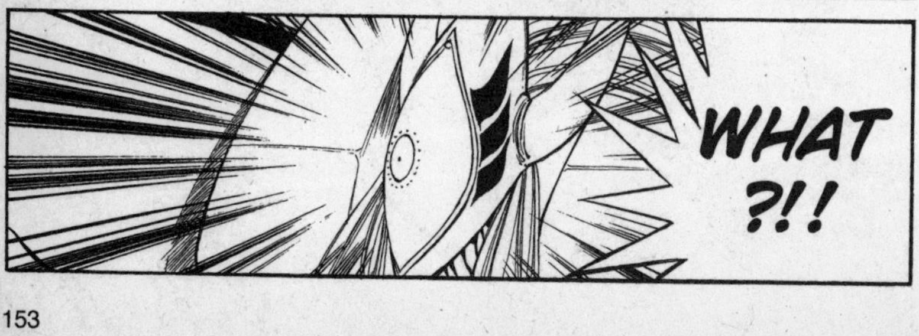
WHAT ?!!

GRAAR

FWOOM

HOMURA!!

SAIHA!!

I DIDN'T KNOW HE COULD SUMMON MORE THAN ONE DRAGON AT THE SAME TIME!!

FHA

FHA

IMPOSSIBLE?!!

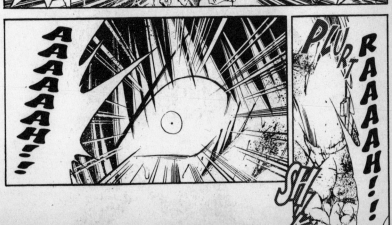

AAAAAAH!!!

PLURN

RAAAAH!!!

SH

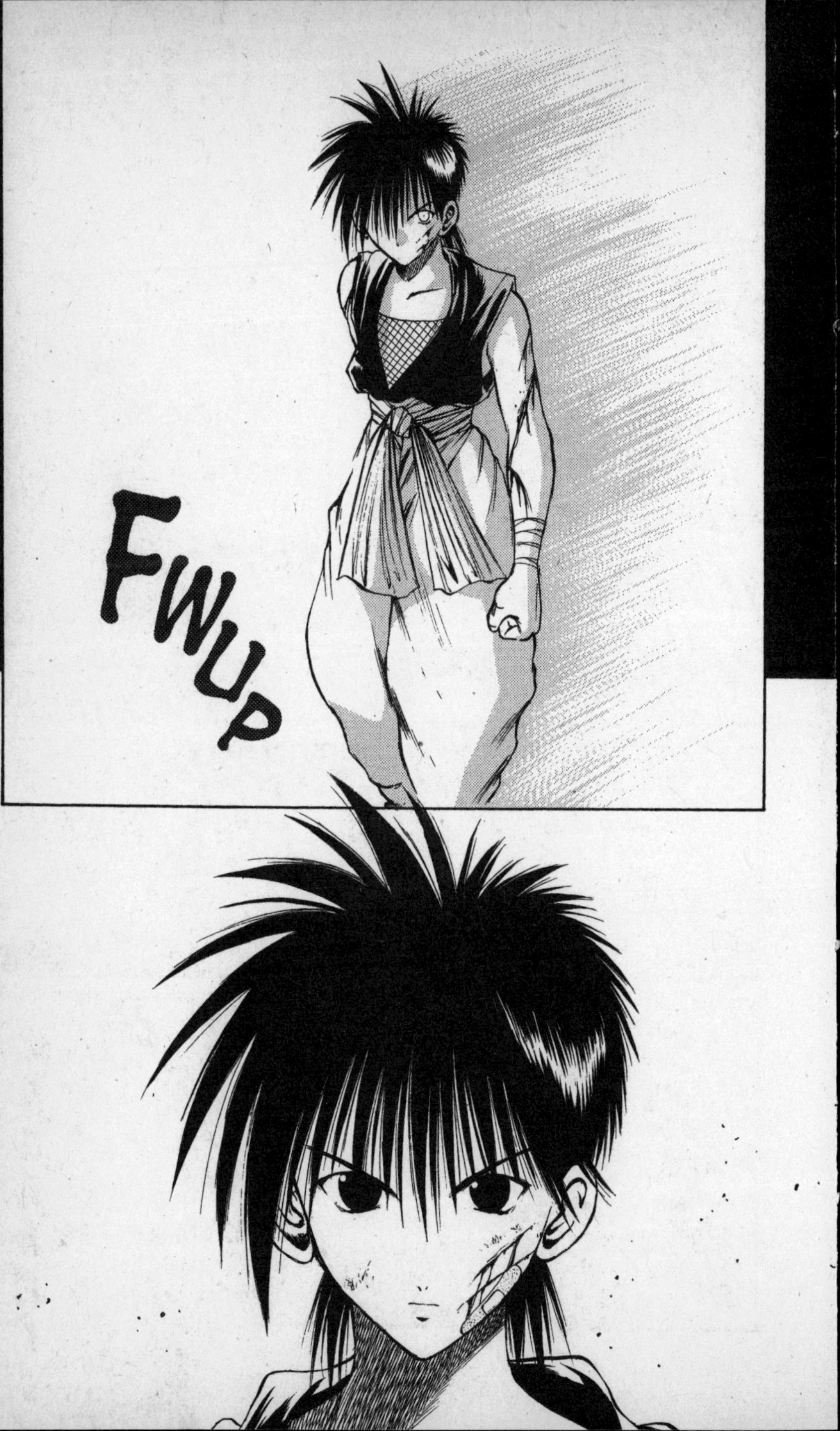
FWUP

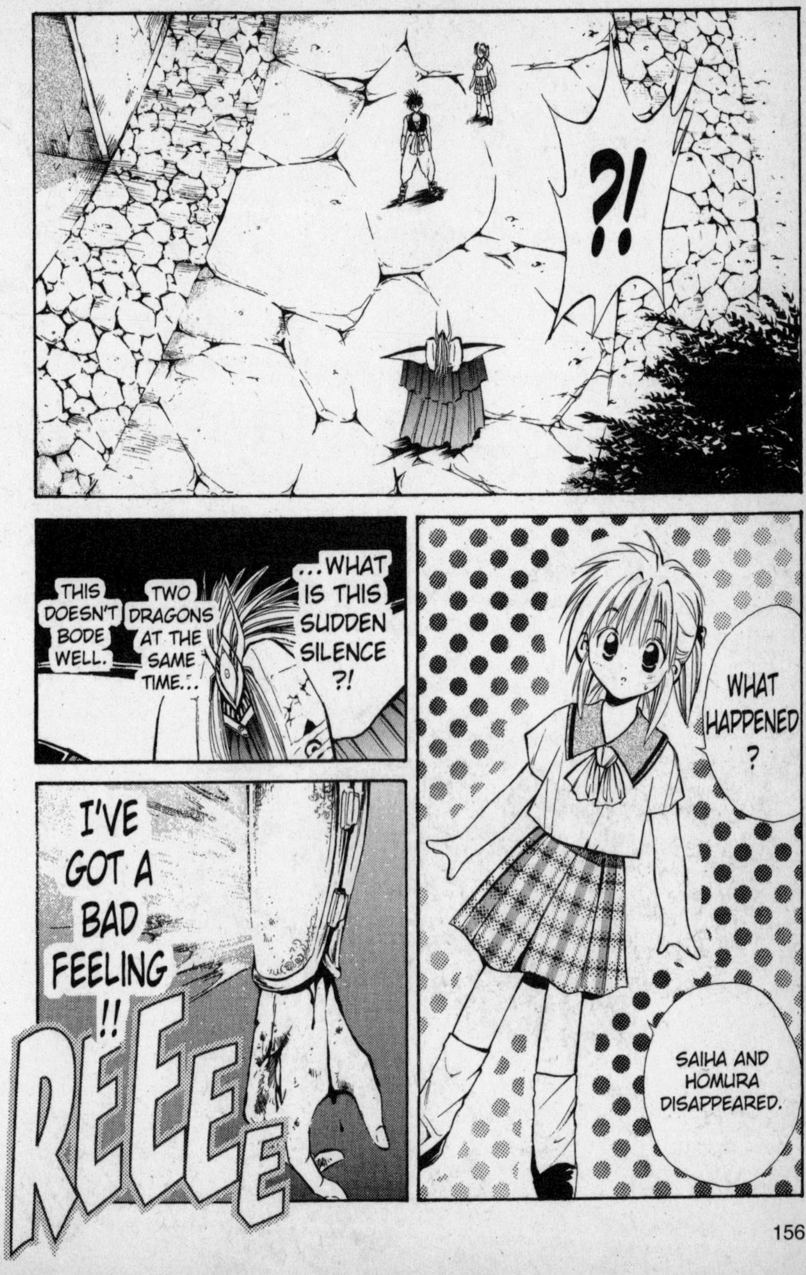
?!
WHAT HAPPENED ?
SAIHA AND HOMURA DISAPPEARED.
...WHAT IS THIS SUDDEN SILENCE ?!
TWO DRAGONS AT THE SAME TIME...
THIS DOESN'T BODE WELL.
I'VE GOT A BAD FEELING !!
REEEE

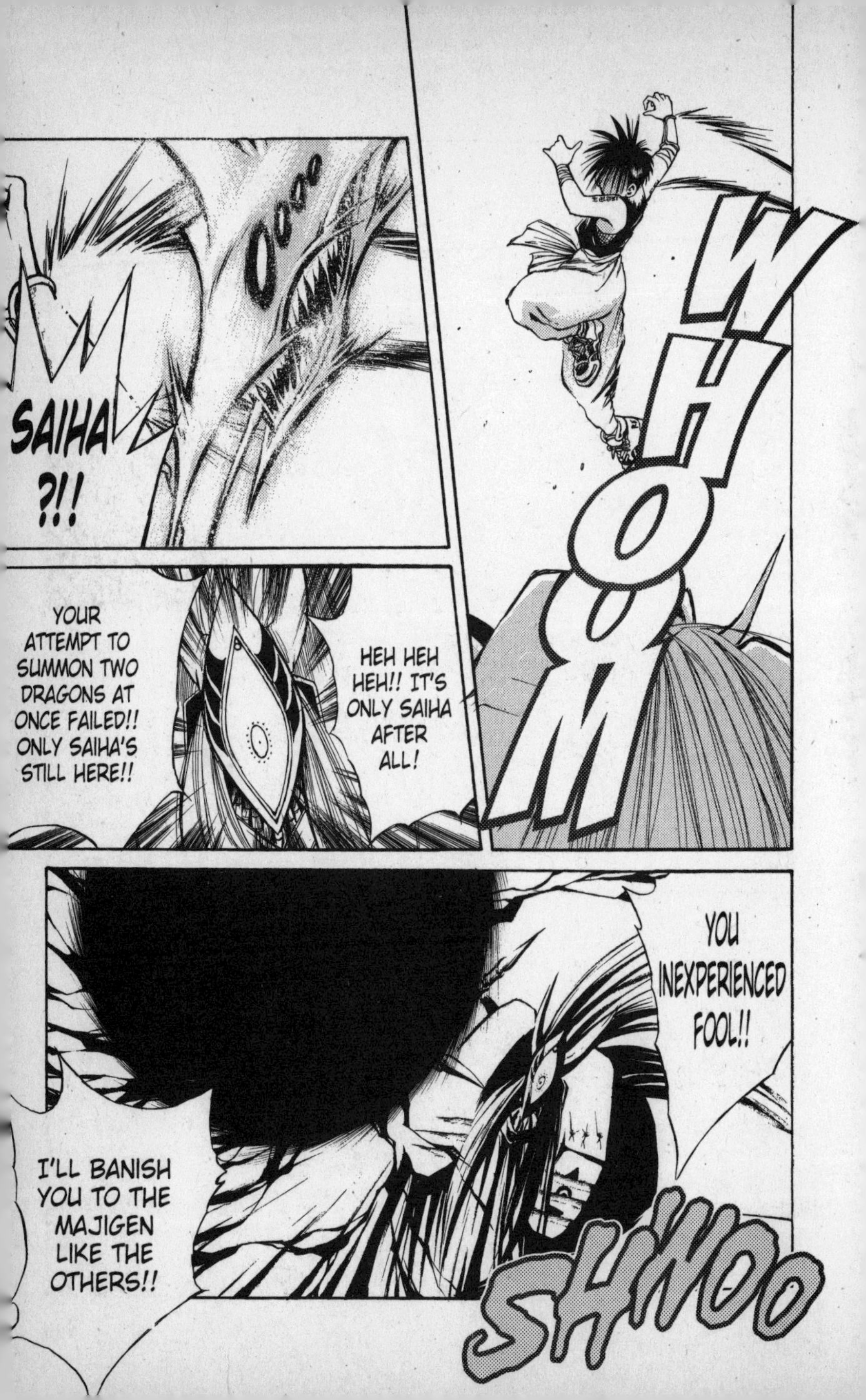
WHOOM
SAIHA ?!!
HEH HEH HEH!! IT'S ONLY SAIHA AFTER ALL!
YOUR ATTEMPT TO SUMMON TWO DRAGONS AT ONCE FAILED!! ONLY SAIHA'S STILL HERE!!
YOU INEXPERIENCED FOOL!!
I'LL BANISH YOU TO THE MAJIGEN LIKE THE OTHERS!!
SHHOO

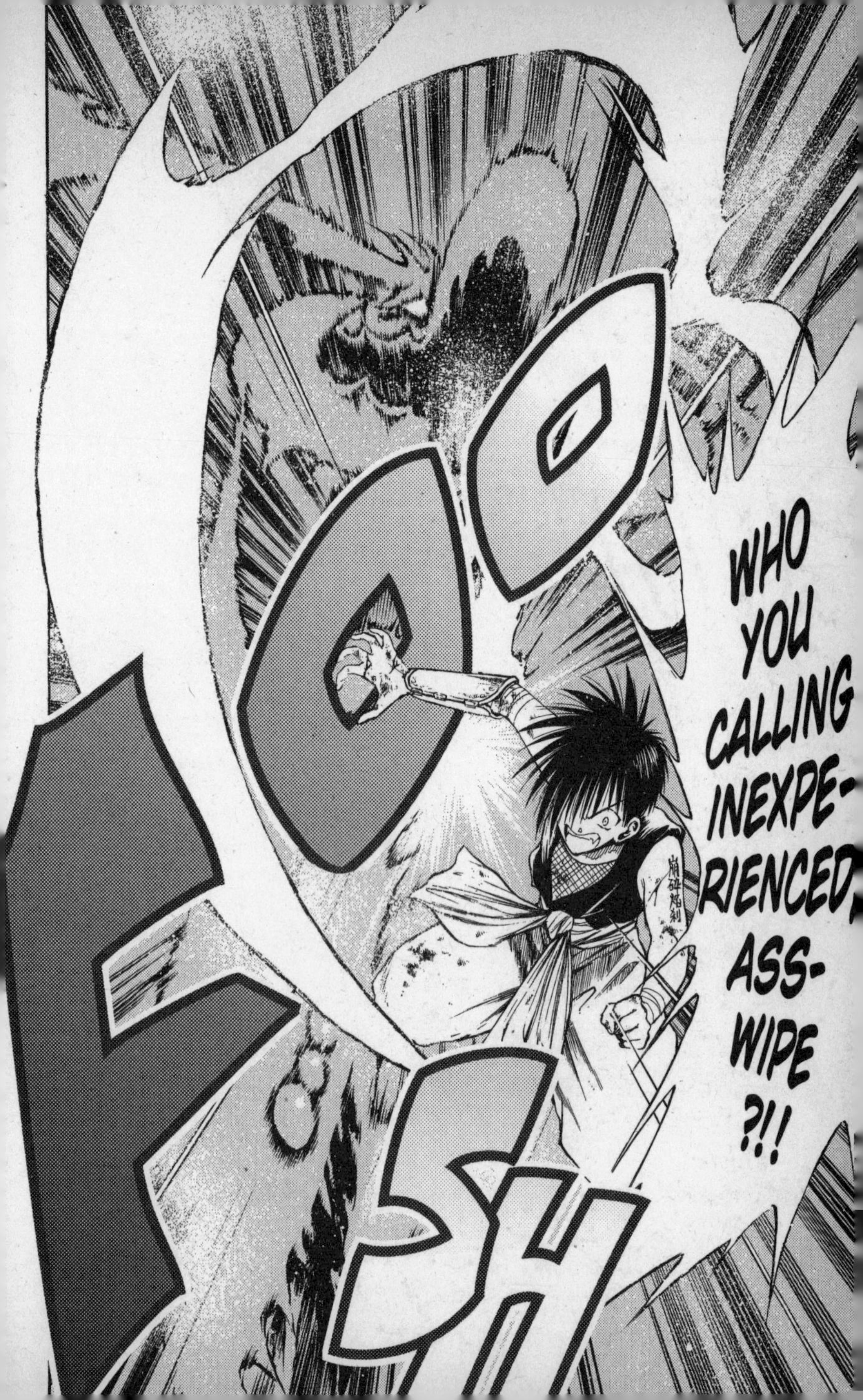
WHO YOU CALLING INEXPE-RIENCED, ASS-WIPE ?!!

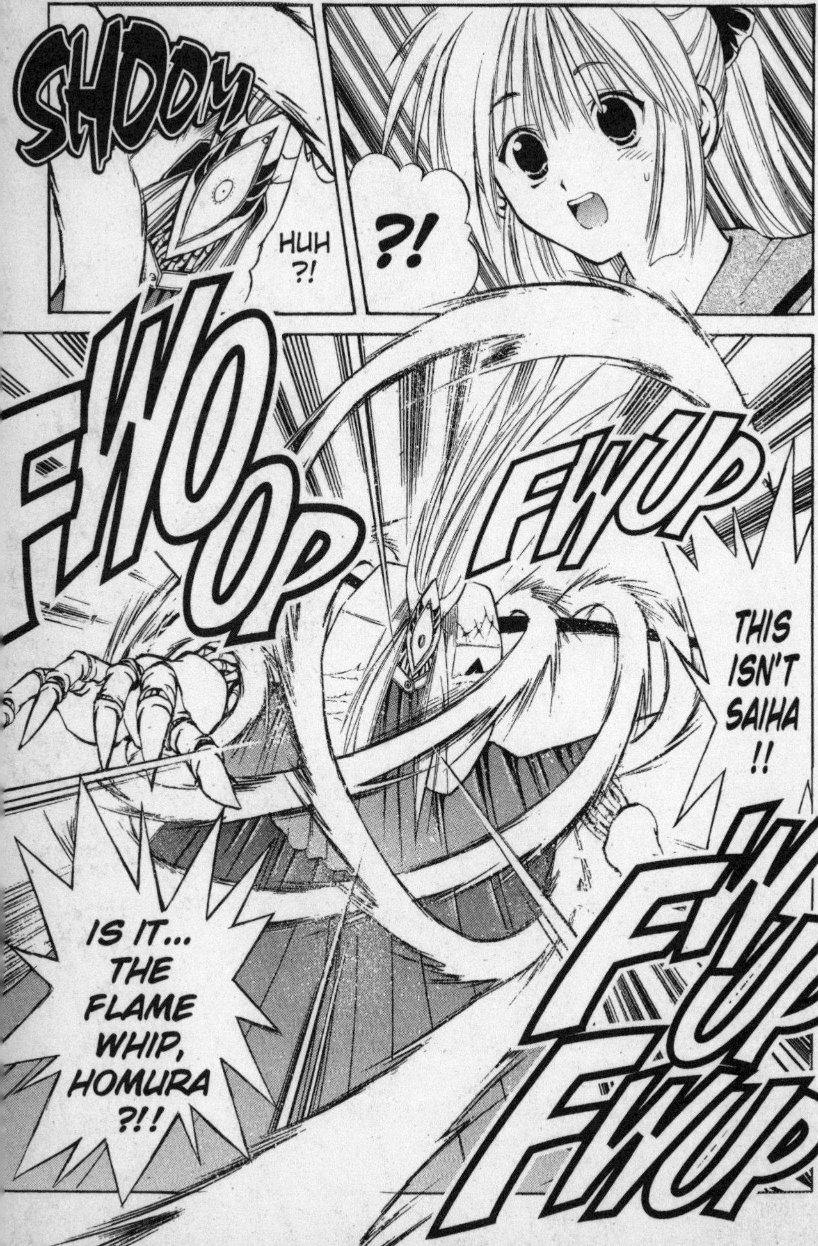
?!
SHOOM
HUH ?!
FWUP
THIS ISN'T SAIHA !!
FWOOP
FWUP FWUP
IS IT... THE FLAME WHIP, HOMURA ?!!

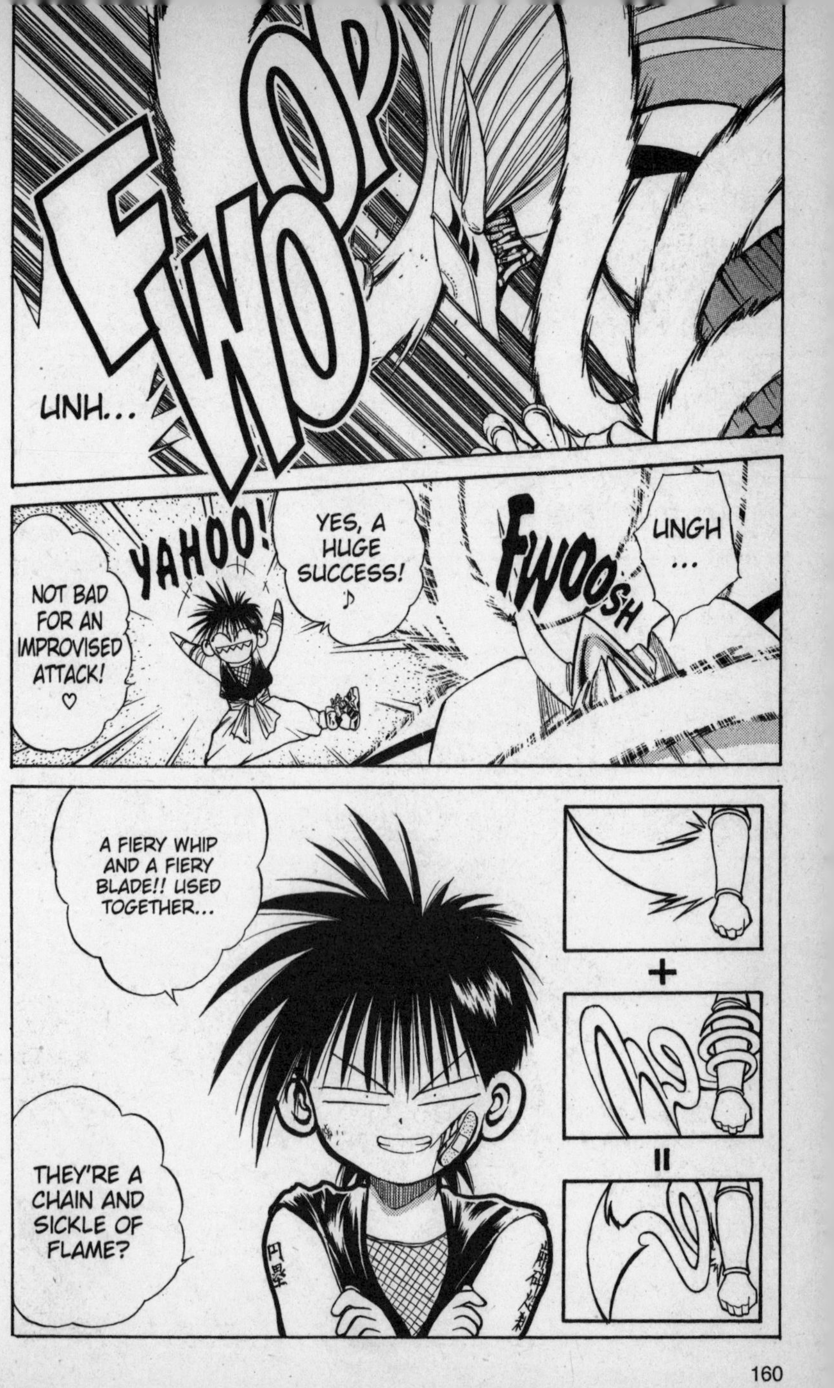
FWOOP
UNH...
UNGH ...
FWOOSH
YES, A HUGE SUCCESS! ♪
YAHOO!
NOT BAD FOR AN IMPROVISED ATTACK! ♡
+
=
A FIERY WHIP AND A FIERY BLADE!! USED TOGETHER...
THEY'RE A CHAIN AND SICKLE OF FLAME?

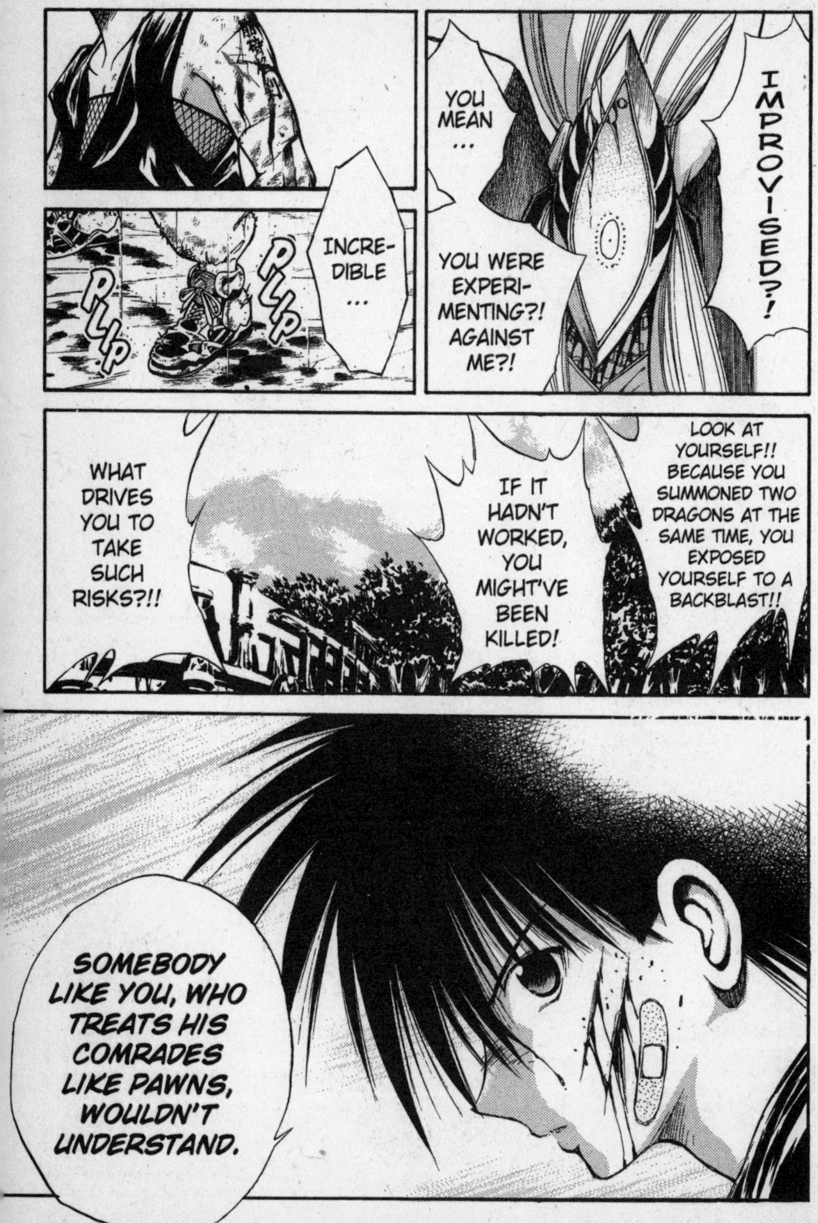
IMPROVISED?!
YOU MEAN ...
YOU WERE EXPERIMENTING?! AGAINST ME?!
INCREDIBLE ...
PLIP
PLIP
LOOK AT YOURSELF!! BECAUSE YOU SUMMONED TWO DRAGONS AT THE SAME TIME, YOU EXPOSED YOURSELF TO A BACKBLAST!!
IF IT HADN'T WORKED, YOU MIGHT'VE BEEN KILLED!
WHAT DRIVES YOU TO TAKE SUCH RISKS?!!
SOMEBODY LIKE YOU, WHO TREATS HIS COMRADES LIKE PAWNS, WOULDN'T UNDERSTAND.

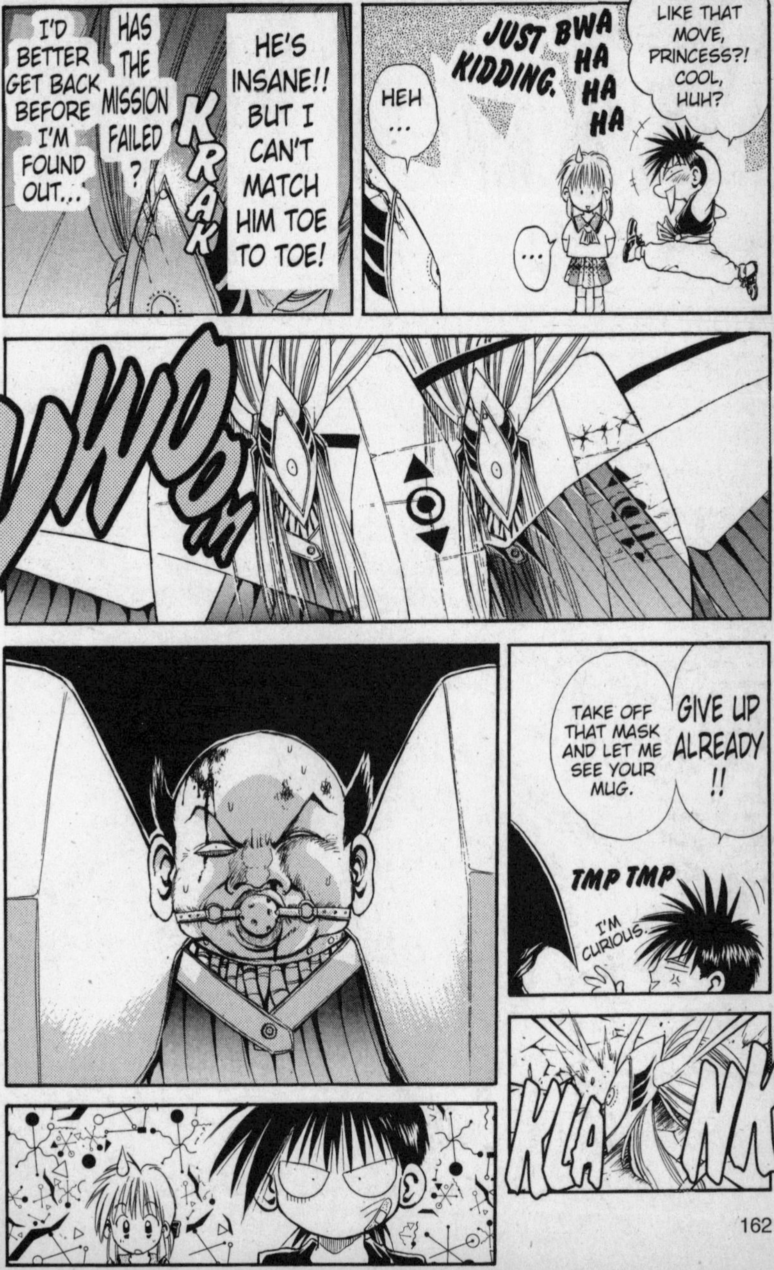
HEE HEE! LIKE THAT MOVE, PRINCESS?! COOL, HUH?
BWA HA HA HA
JUST KIDDING.
HEH ...
...
HE'S INSANE!! BUT I CAN'T MATCH HIM TOE TO TOE!
KRAK
HAS THE MISSION FAILED?
I'D BETTER GET BACK BEFORE I'M FOUND OUT...
VWOOM
GIVE UP ALREADY!!
TAKE OFF THAT MASK AND LET ME SEE YOUR MUG.
TMP TMP
I'M CURIOUS.
KLANK

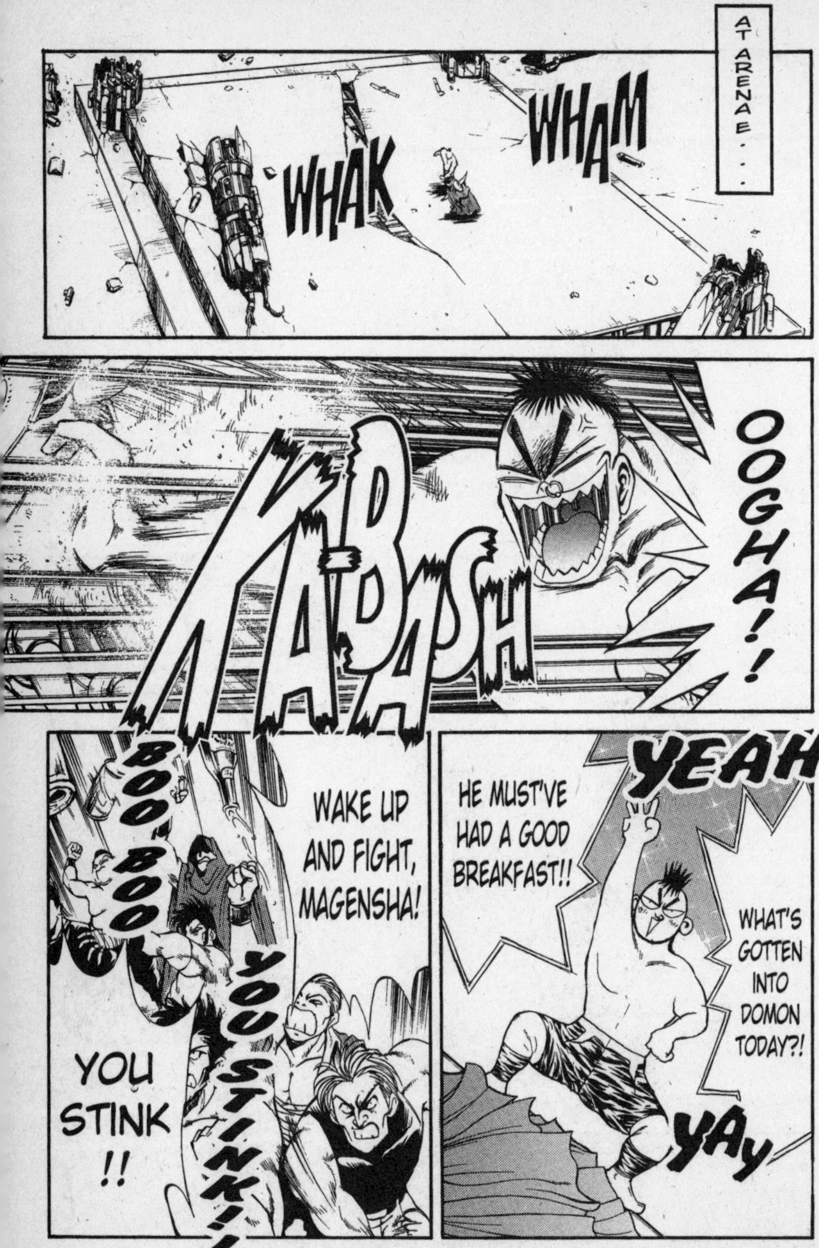
AT ARENAE . . .
WHAM
WHAK
OOGHA!!
KA-BASH
YEAH
HE MUST'VE HAD A GOOD BREAKFAST!!
WHAT'S GOTTEN INTO DOMON TODAY?!
YAY
WAKE UP AND FIGHT, MAGENSHA!
YOU STINK!!!
BOO BOO BOO
YOU STINK !!

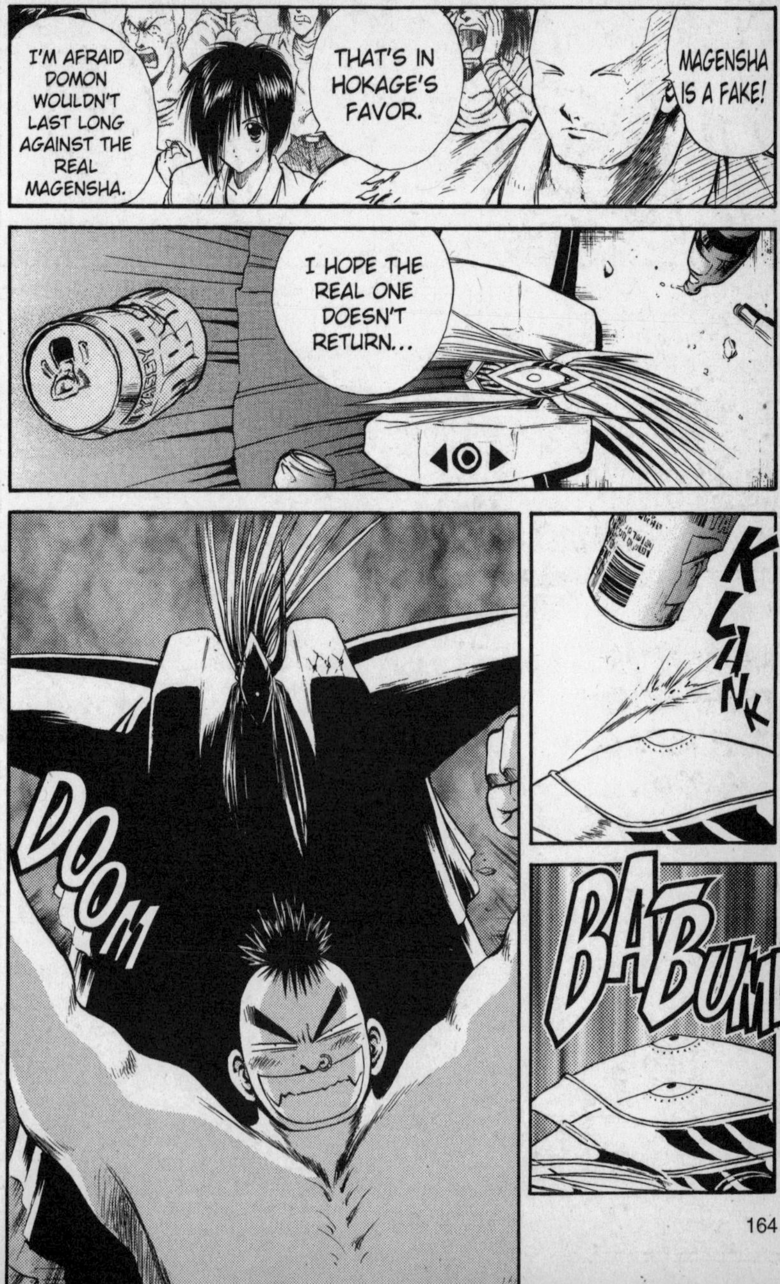
MAGENSHA IS A FAKE!
THAT'S IN HOKAGE'S FAVOR.
I'M AFRAID DOMON WOULDN'T LAST LONG AGAINST THE REAL MAGENSHA.
I HOPE THE REAL ONE DOESN'T RETURN...
KLANK
BABUMP
DOOM

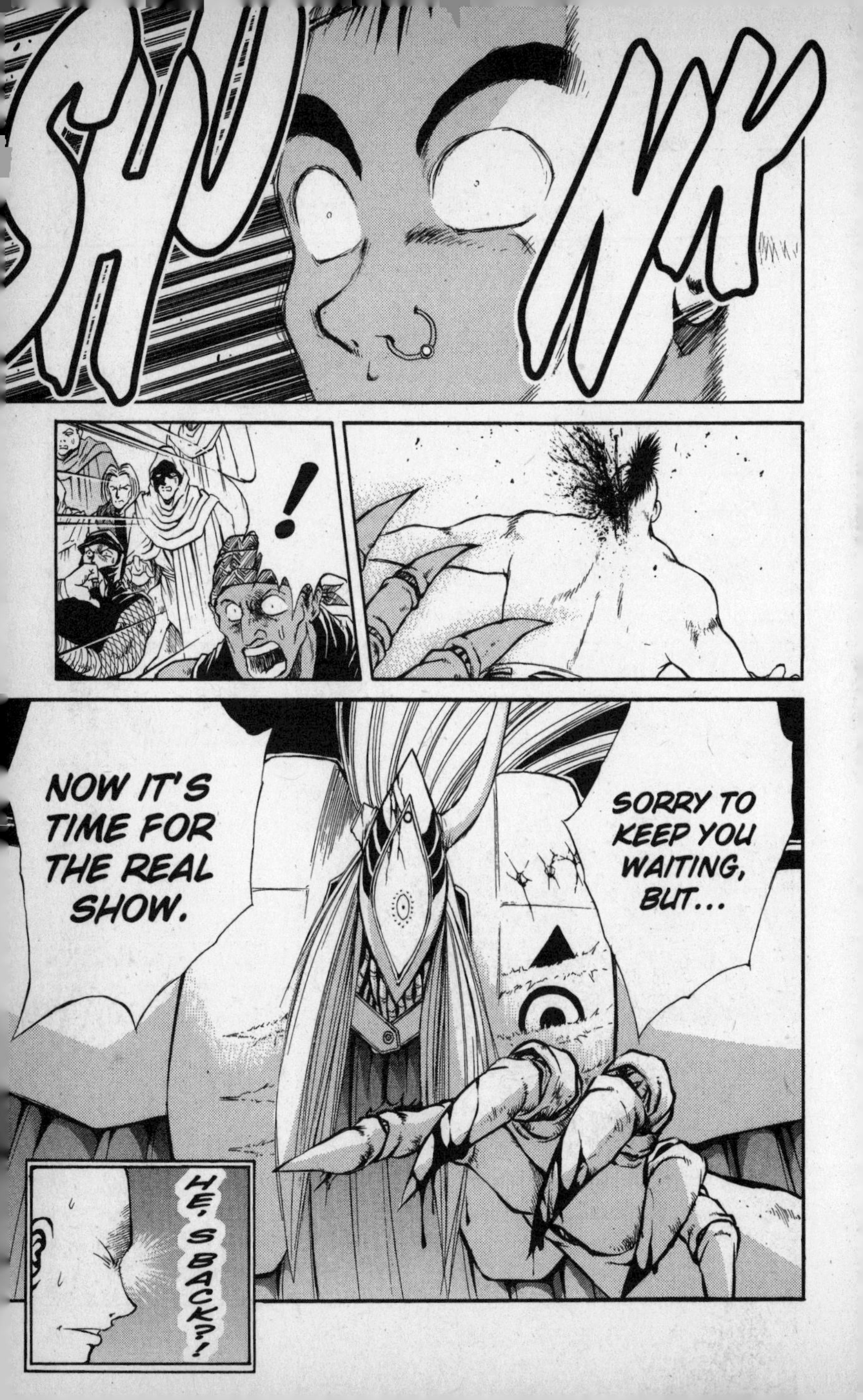
SHUNK
!
SORRY TO KEEP YOU WAITING, BUT...
NOW IT'S TIME FOR THE REAL SHOW.
HE'S BACK?!

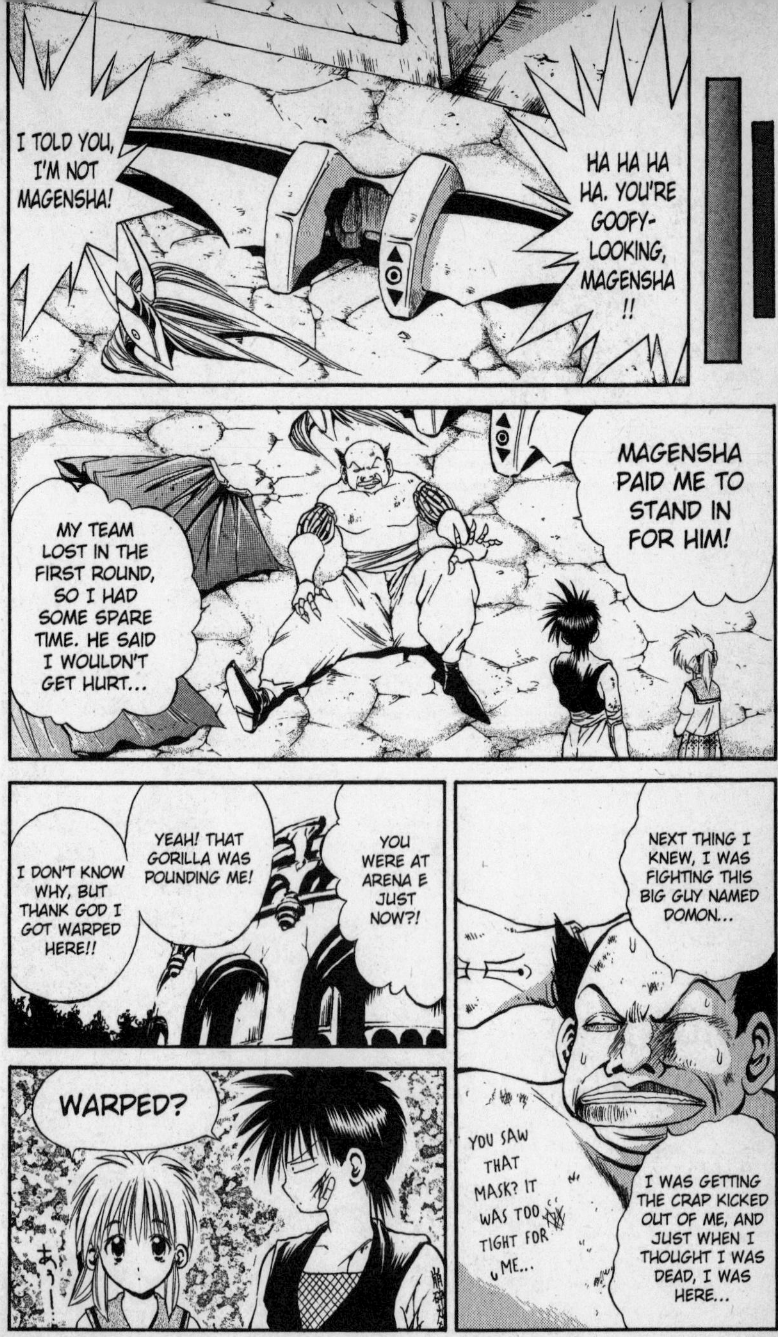
HA HA HA HA. YOU'RE GOOFY-LOOKING, MAGENSHA!!
I TOLD YOU, I'M NOT MAGENSHA!
MAGENSHA PAID ME TO STAND IN FOR HIM!
MY TEAM LOST IN THE FIRST ROUND, SO I HAD SOME SPARE TIME. HE SAID I WOULDN'T GET HURT...
NEXT THING I KNEW, I WAS FIGHTING THIS BIG GUY NAMED DOMON...
I WAS GETTING THE CRAP KICKED OUT OF ME, AND JUST WHEN I THOUGHT I WAS DEAD, I WAS HERE...
YOU SAW THAT MASK? IT WAS TOO TIGHT FOR ME...
YOU WERE AT ARENA E JUST NOW?!
YEAH! THAT GORILLA WAS POUNDING ME!
I DON'T KNOW WHY, BUT THANK GOD I GOT WARPED HERE!!
WARPED?

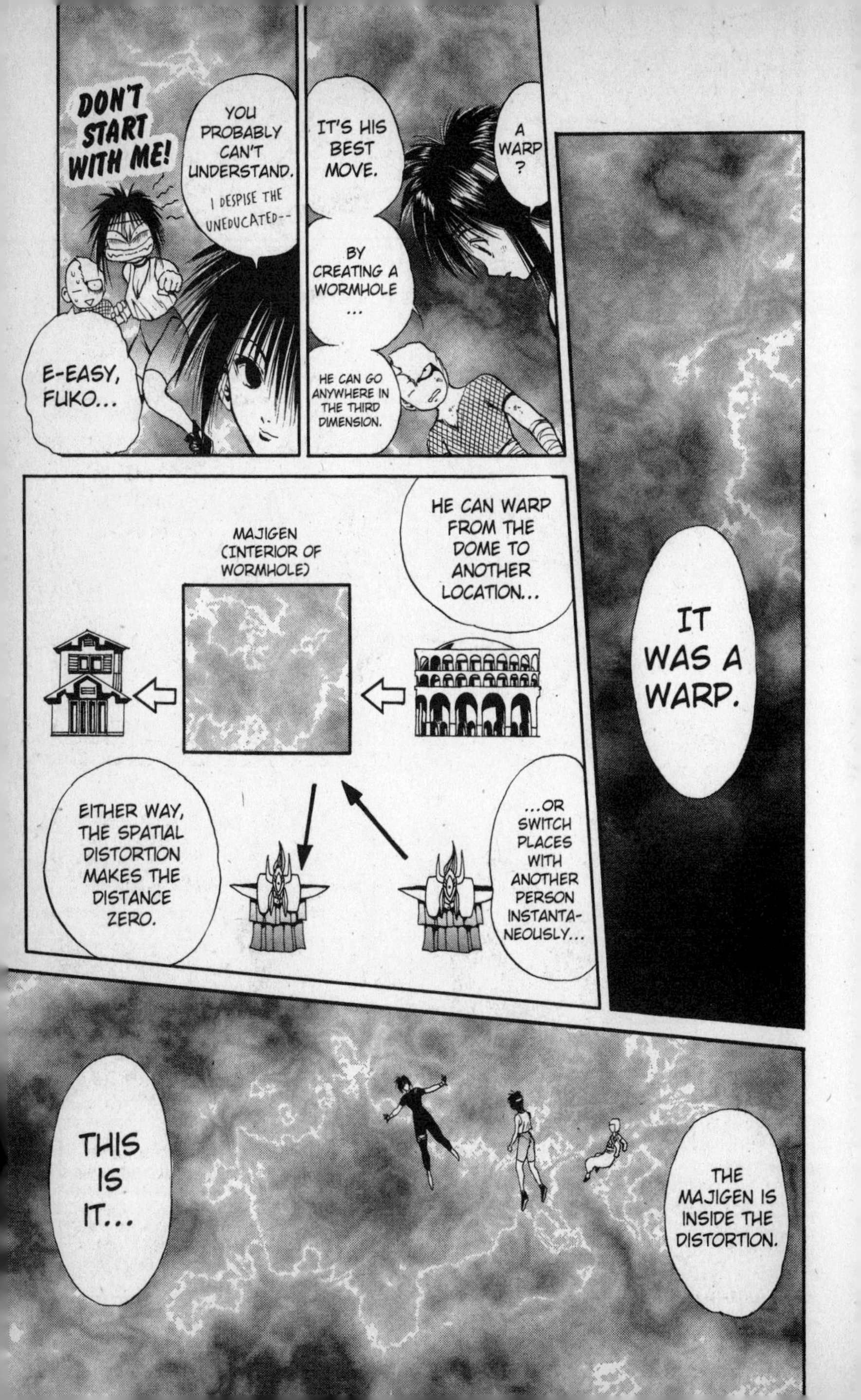
A WARP?
IT'S HIS BEST MOVE.
BY CREATING A WORMHOLE...
HE CAN GO ANYWHERE IN THE THIRD DIMENSION.
YOU PROBABLY CAN'T UNDERSTAND.
I DESPISE THE UNEDUCATED--
DON'T START WITH ME!
E-EASY, FUKO...
HE CAN WARP FROM THE DOME TO ANOTHER LOCATION...
MAJIGEN (INTERIOR OF WORMHOLE)
...OR SWITCH PLACES WITH ANOTHER PERSON INSTANTANEOUSLY...
EITHER WAY, THE SPATIAL DISTORTION MAKES THE DISTANCE ZERO.
IT WAS A WARP.
THE MAJIGEN IS INSIDE THE DISTORTION.
THIS IS IT...

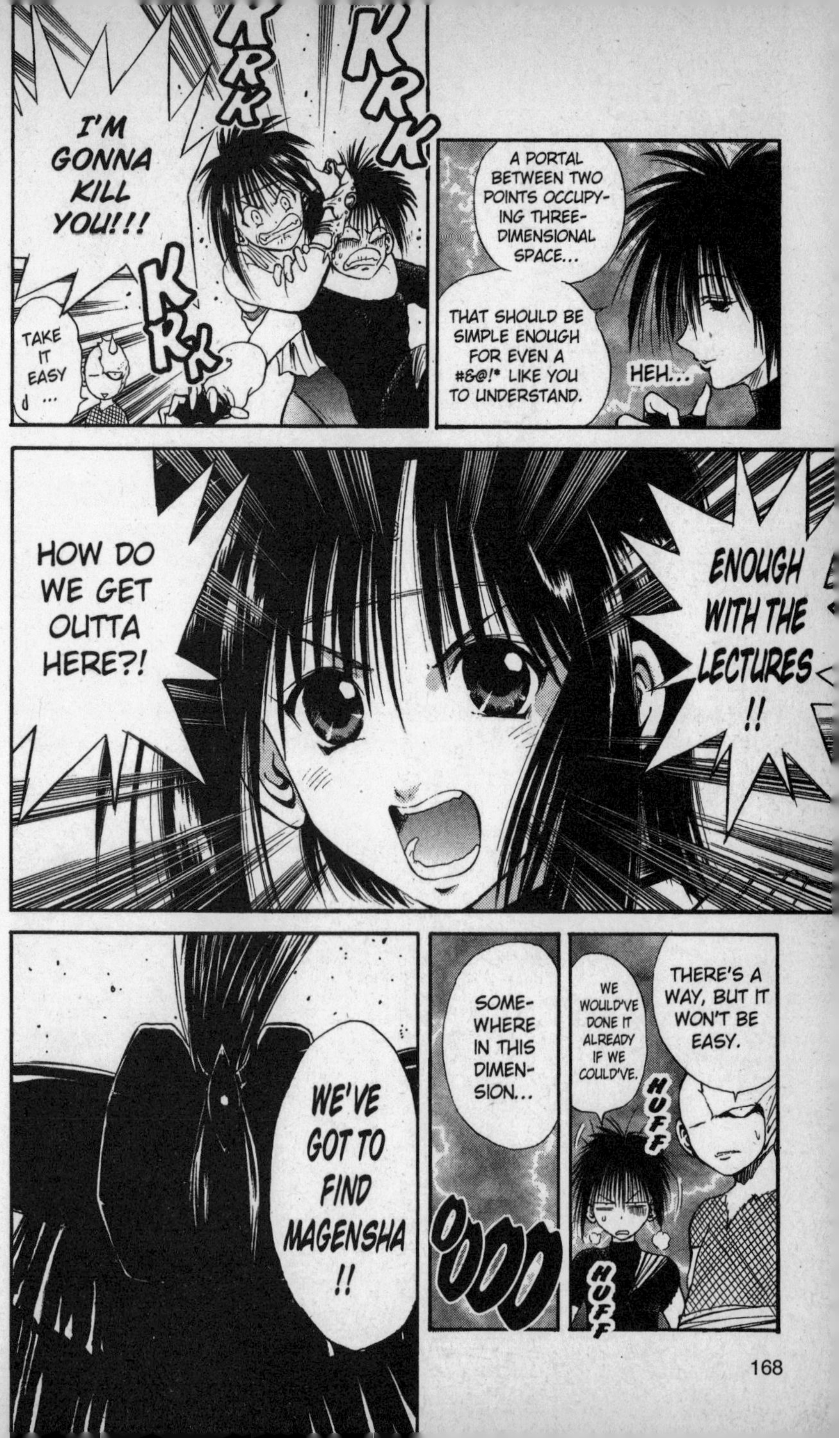
A PORTAL BETWEEN TWO POINTS OCCUPYING THREE-DIMENSIONAL SPACE...
THAT SHOULD BE SIMPLE ENOUGH FOR EVEN A #&@!* LIKE YOU TO UNDERSTAND.
HEH...
KRK
KRK
I'M GONNA KILL YOU!!!
KRK
TAKE IT EASY ...
ENOUGH WITH THE LECTURES !!
HOW DO WE GET OUTTA HERE?!
THERE'S A WAY, BUT IT WON'T BE EASY.
WE WOULD'VE DONE IT ALREADY IF WE COULD'VE.
HUFF
HUFF
SOME-WHERE IN THIS DIMEN-SION...
WE'VE GOT TO FIND MAGENSHA !!

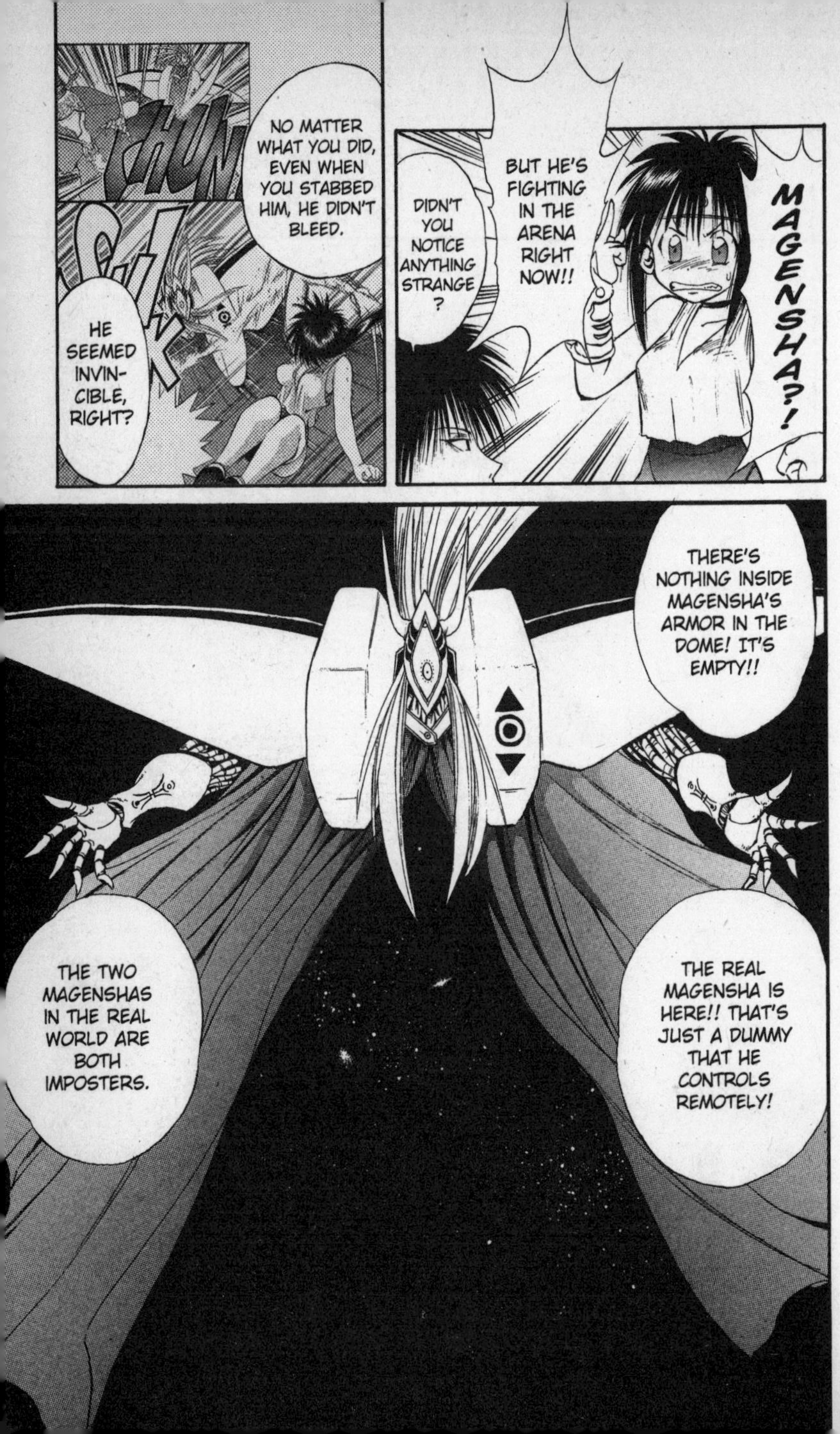
MAGENSHA?!
BUT HE'S FIGHTING IN THE ARENA RIGHT NOW!!
DIDN'T YOU NOTICE ANYTHING STRANGE?
CHUN
NO MATTER WHAT YOU DID, EVEN WHEN YOU STABBED HIM, HE DIDN'T BLEED.
HE SEEMED INVINCIBLE, RIGHT?
THERE'S NOTHING INSIDE MAGENSHA'S ARMOR IN THE DOME! IT'S EMPTY!!
THE REAL MAGENSHA IS HERE!! THAT'S JUST A DUMMY THAT HE CONTROLS REMOTELY!
THE TWO MAGENSHAS IN THE REAL WORLD ARE BOTH IMPOSTERS.

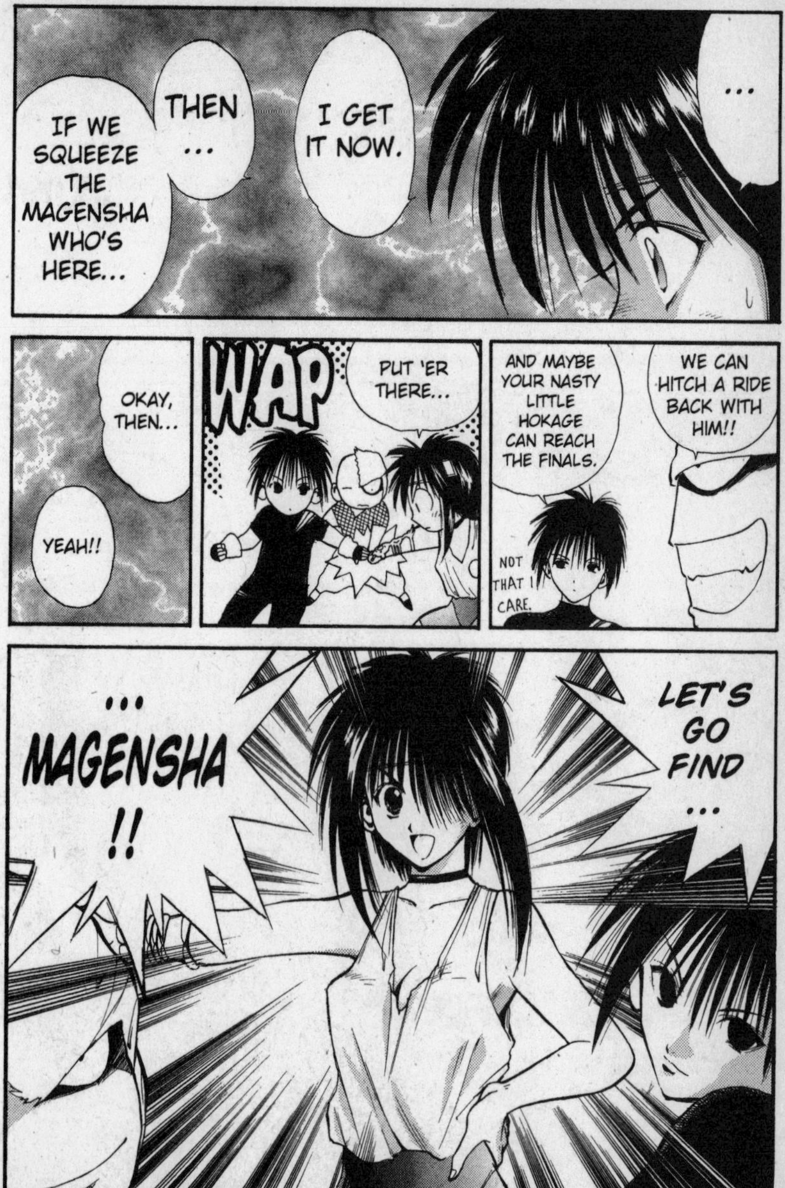
...
I GET IT NOW.
THEN ...
IF WE SQUEEZE THE MAGENSHA WHO'S HERE...
WE CAN HITCH A RIDE BACK WITH HIM!!
AND MAYBE YOUR NASTY LITTLE HOKAGE CAN REACH THE FINALS.
NOT THAT I CARE.
PUT 'ER THERE...
WAP
OKAY, THEN...
YEAH!!
LET'S GO FIND ...
... MAGENSHA !!

Part Ninety-Seven: Ma (5) The True Form Found

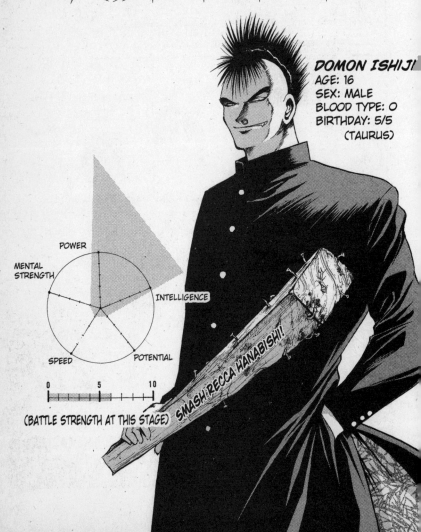

DOMON ISHIJI!
AGE: 16
SEX: MALE
BLOOD TYPE: O
BIRTHDAY: 5/5
(TAURUS)

POWER

MENTAL STRENGTH

INTELLIGENCE

SPEED

POTENTIAL

0　5　10

(BATTLE STRENGTH AT THIS STAGE)

SMASH!RECCA HANABISHI!!

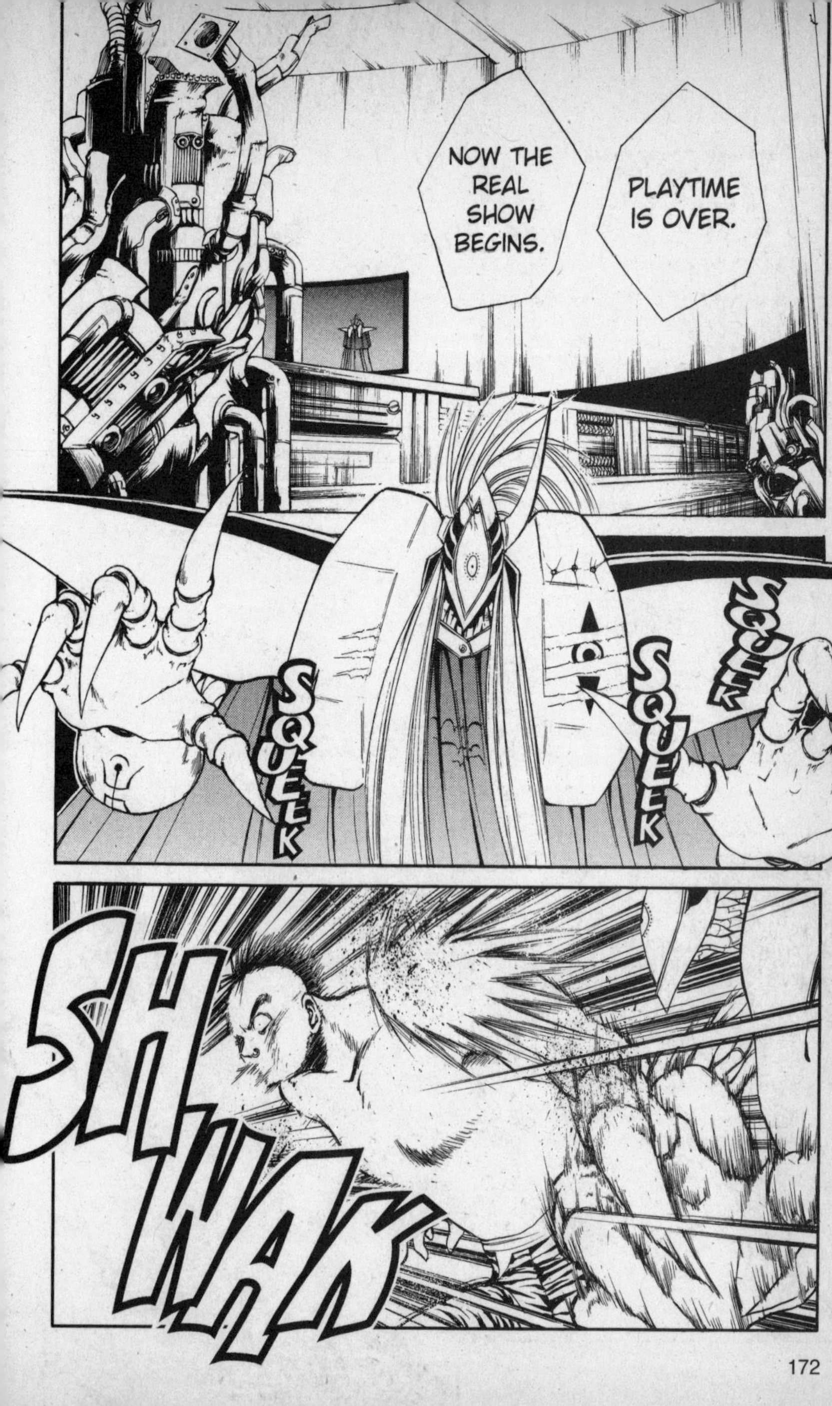
PLAYTIME IS OVER.
NOW THE REAL SHOW BEGINS.
SQUEEK
SQUEEK
SQUEEK
SHWAK

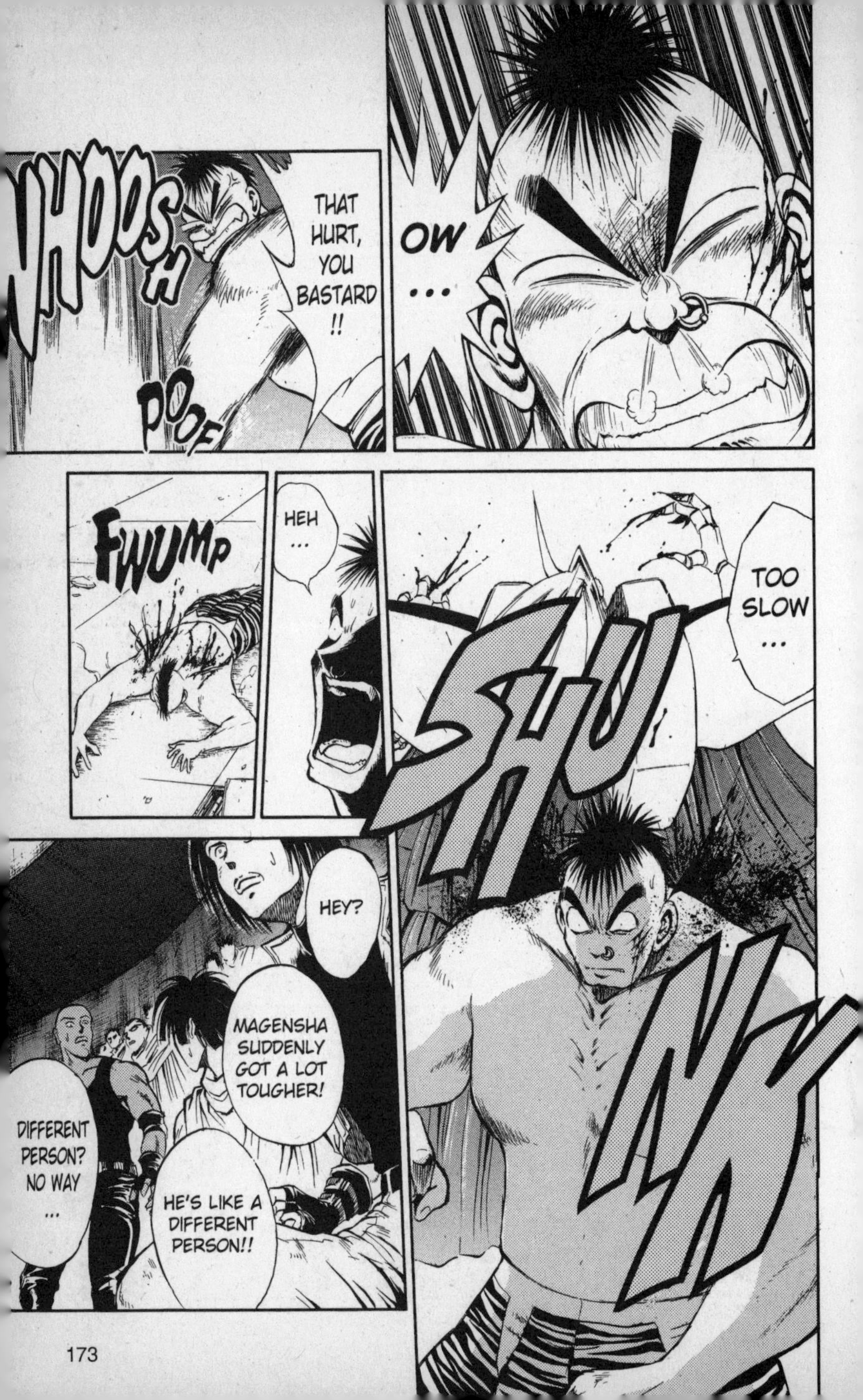
OW ...
WHOOSH
THAT HURT, YOU BASTARD!!
POOF
TOO SLOW ...
SHU
HEH ...
FWUMP
NK
HEY?
MAGENSHA SUDDENLY GOT A LOT TOUGHER!
HE'S LIKE A DIFFERENT PERSON!!
DIFFERENT PERSON? NO WAY ...

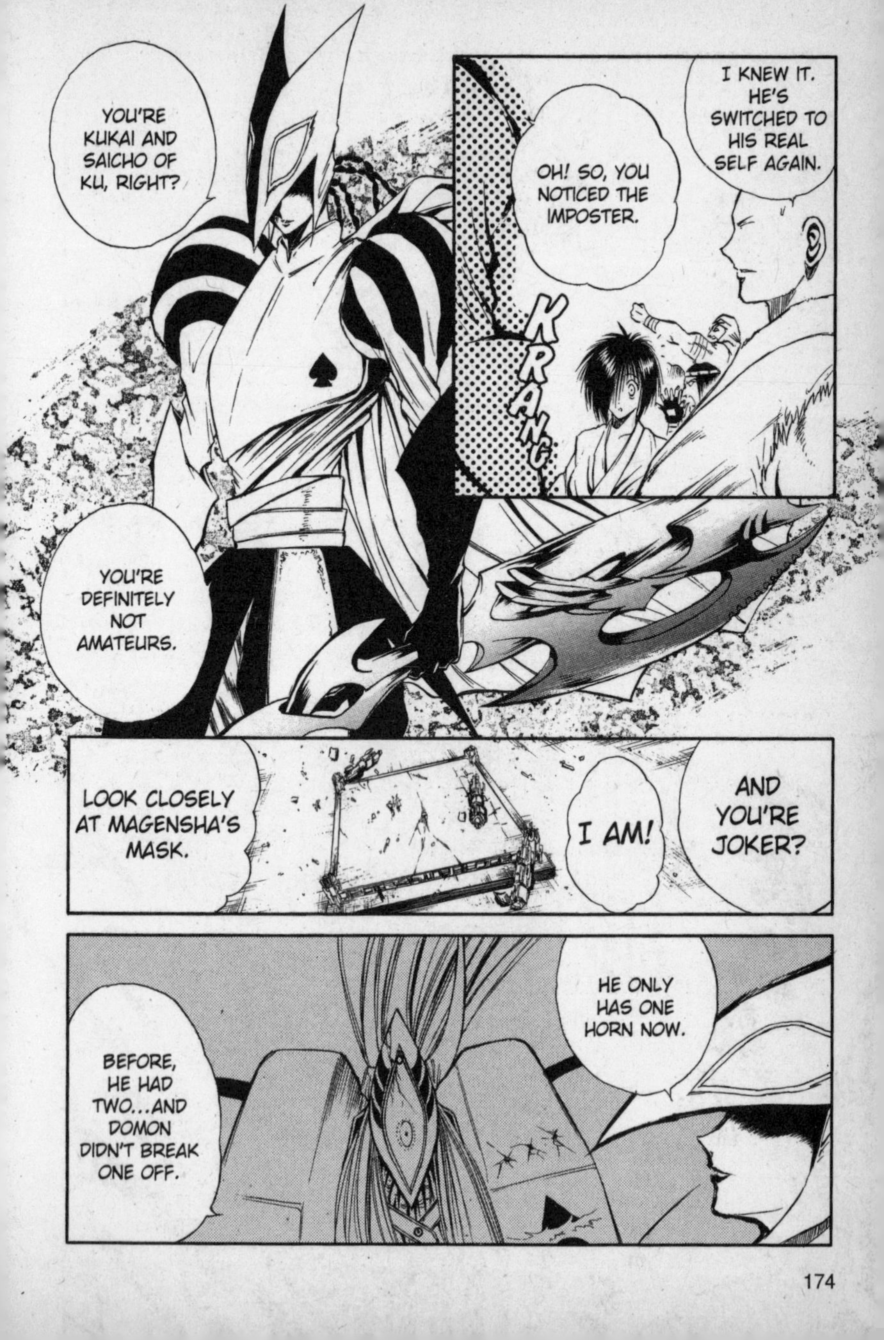
I KNEW IT. HE'S SWITCHED TO HIS REAL SELF AGAIN.
OH! SO, YOU NOTICED THE IMPOSTER.
KRANG
YOU'RE KUKAI AND SAICHO OF KU, RIGHT?
YOU'RE DEFINITELY NOT AMATEURS.
AND YOU'RE JOKER?
I AM!
LOOK CLOSELY AT MAGENSHA'S MASK.
HE ONLY HAS ONE HORN NOW.
BEFORE, HE HAD TWO...AND DOMON DIDN'T BREAK ONE OFF.

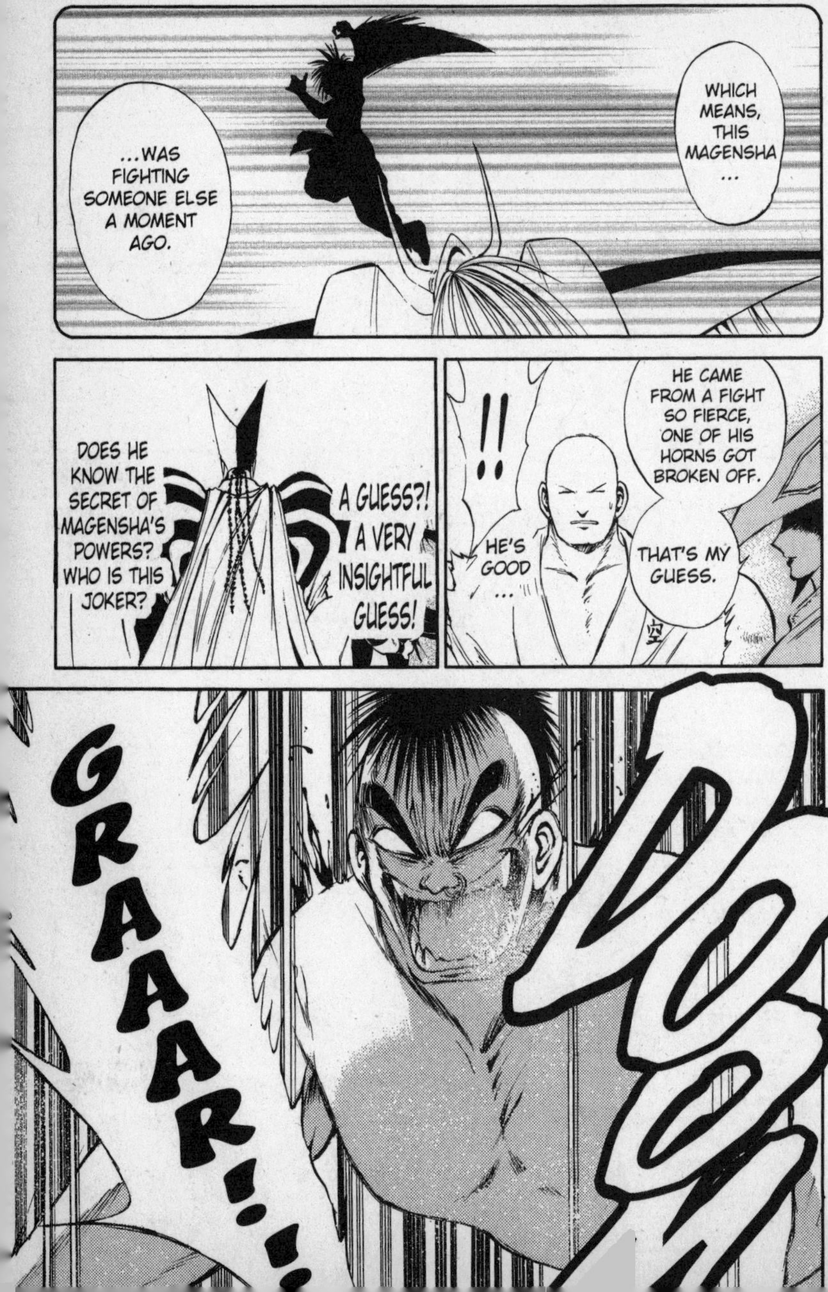
WHICH MEANS, THIS MAGENSHA ...
...WAS FIGHTING SOMEONE ELSE A MOMENT AGO.
HE CAME FROM A FIGHT SO FIERCE, ONE OF HIS HORNS GOT BROKEN OFF.
THAT'S MY GUESS.
!!
HE'S GOOD ...
A GUESS?! A VERY INSIGHTFUL GUESS!
DOES HE KNOW THE SECRET OF MAGENSHA'S POWERS? WHO IS THIS JOKER?
DOOM
GRAAAR!!!

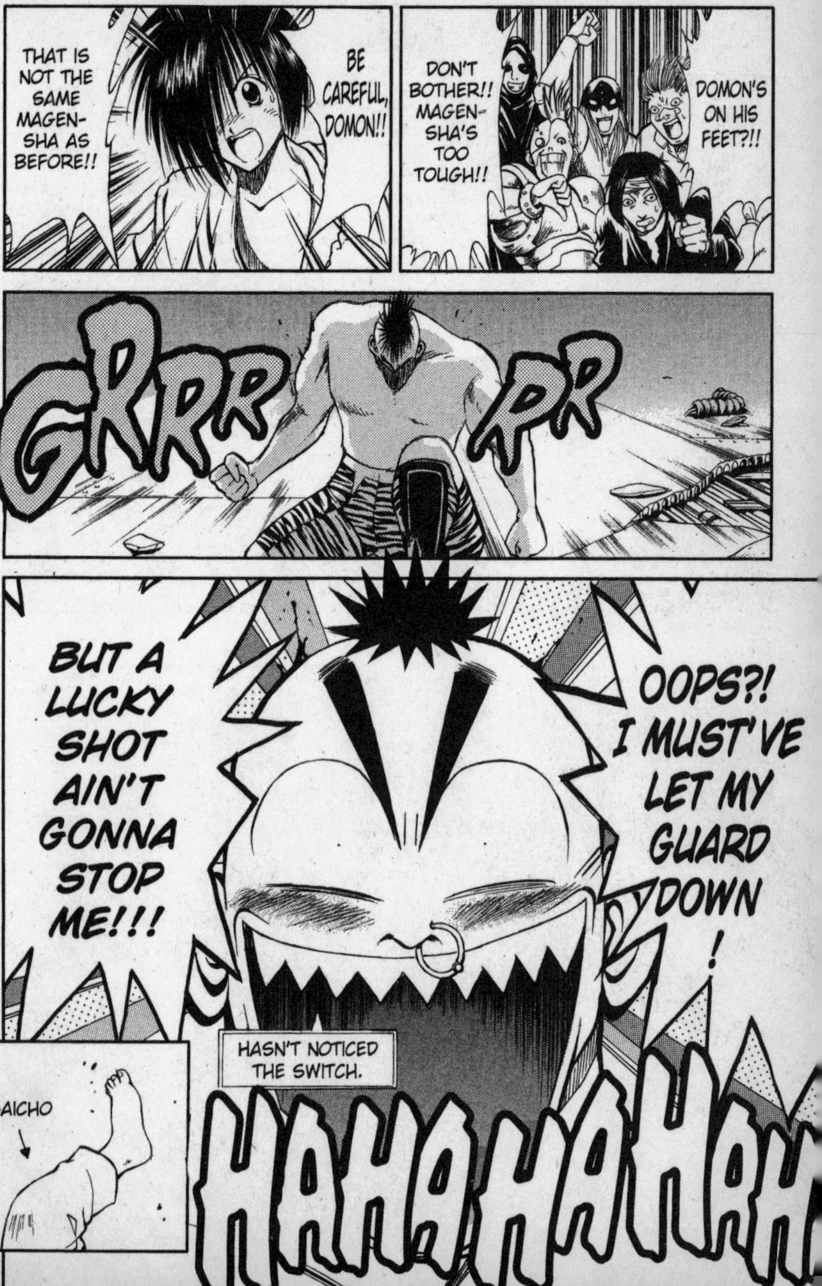
DOMON'S ON HIS FEET?!!
DON'T BOTHER!! MAGEN-SHA'S TOO TOUGH!!
BE CAREFUL, DOMON!!
THAT IS NOT THE SAME MAGEN-SHA AS BEFORE!!
GRRR PR
OOPS?! I MUST'VE LET MY GUARD DOWN!
BUT A LUCKY SHOT AIN'T GONNA STOP ME!!!
HASN'T NOTICED THE SWITCH.
HAHAHAHAH
SAICHO

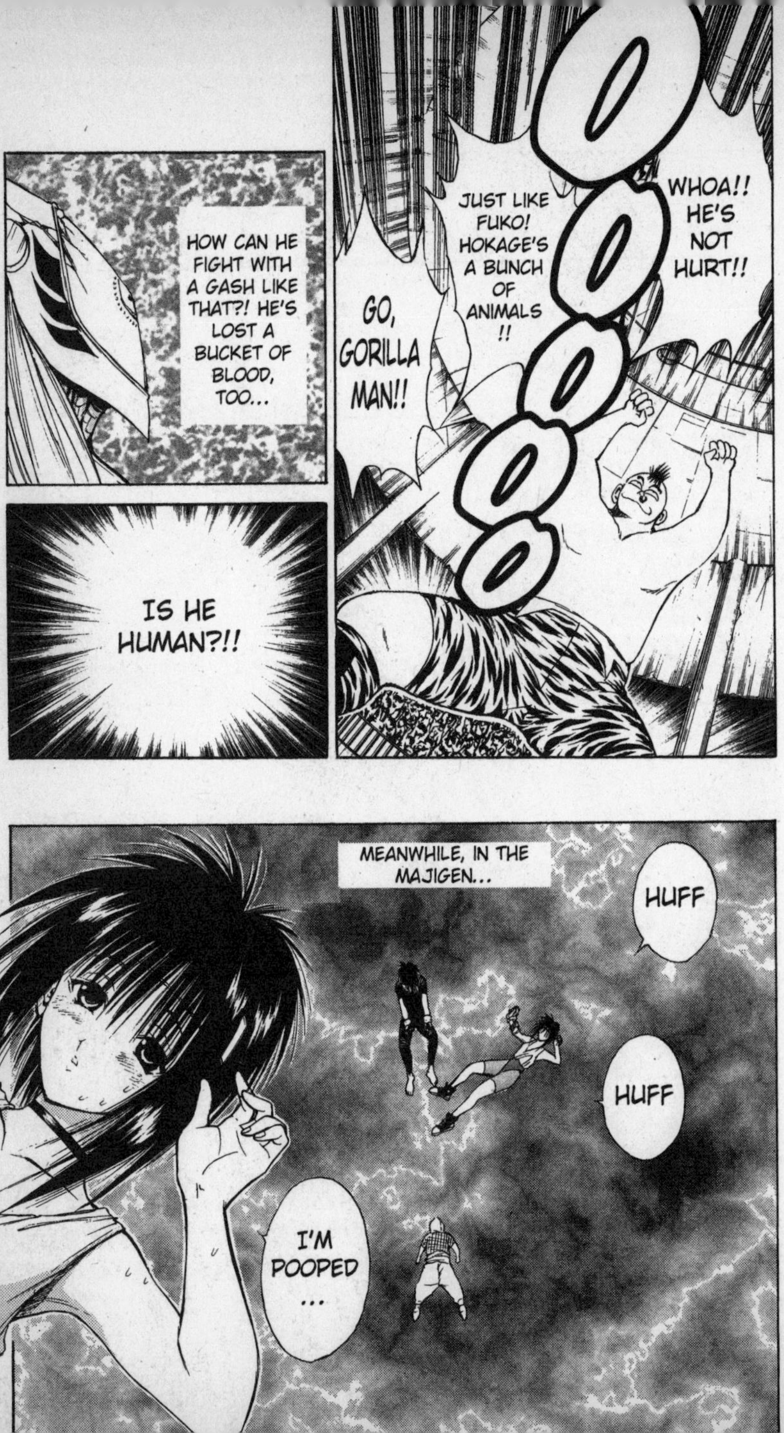
WHOA!! HE'S NOT HURT!!
JUST LIKE FUKO! HOKAGE'S A BUNCH OF ANIMALS!!
GO, GORILLA MAN!!
OOOOOOO
HOW CAN HE FIGHT WITH A GASH LIKE THAT?! HE'S LOST A BUCKET OF BLOOD, TOO...
IS HE HUMAN?!!
MEANWHILE, IN THE MAJIGEN...
HUFF
HUFF
I'M POOPED...

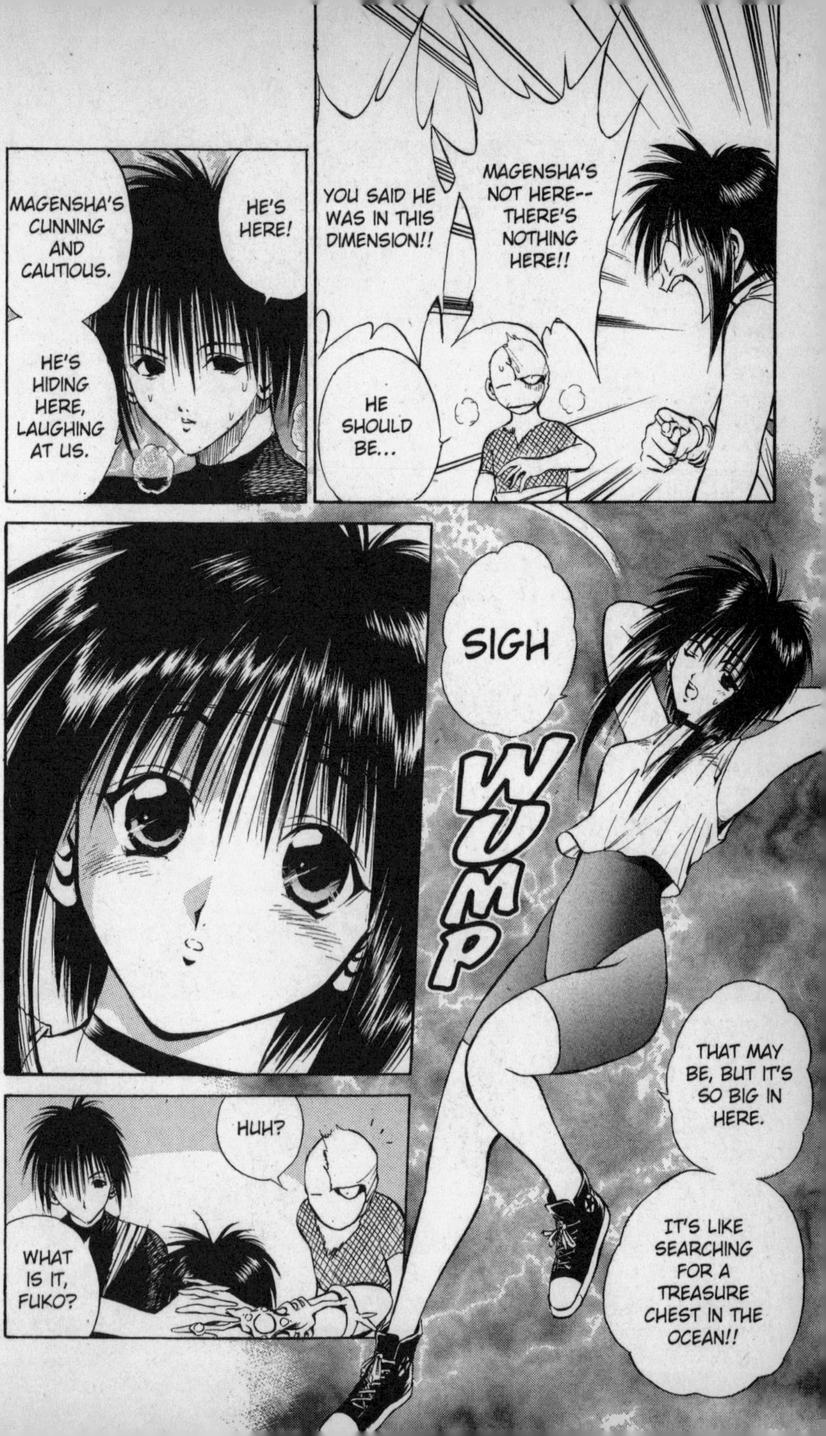
MAGENSHA'S NOT HERE-- THERE'S NOTHING HERE!!
YOU SAID HE WAS IN THIS DIMENSION!!
HE SHOULD BE...
HE'S HERE!
MAGENSHA'S CUNNING AND CAUTIOUS.
HE'S HIDING HERE, LAUGHING AT US.
SIGH
WUMP
THAT MAY BE, BUT IT'S SO BIG IN HERE.
IT'S LIKE SEARCHING FOR A TREASURE CHEST IN THE OCEAN!!
HUH?
WHAT IS IT, FUKO?

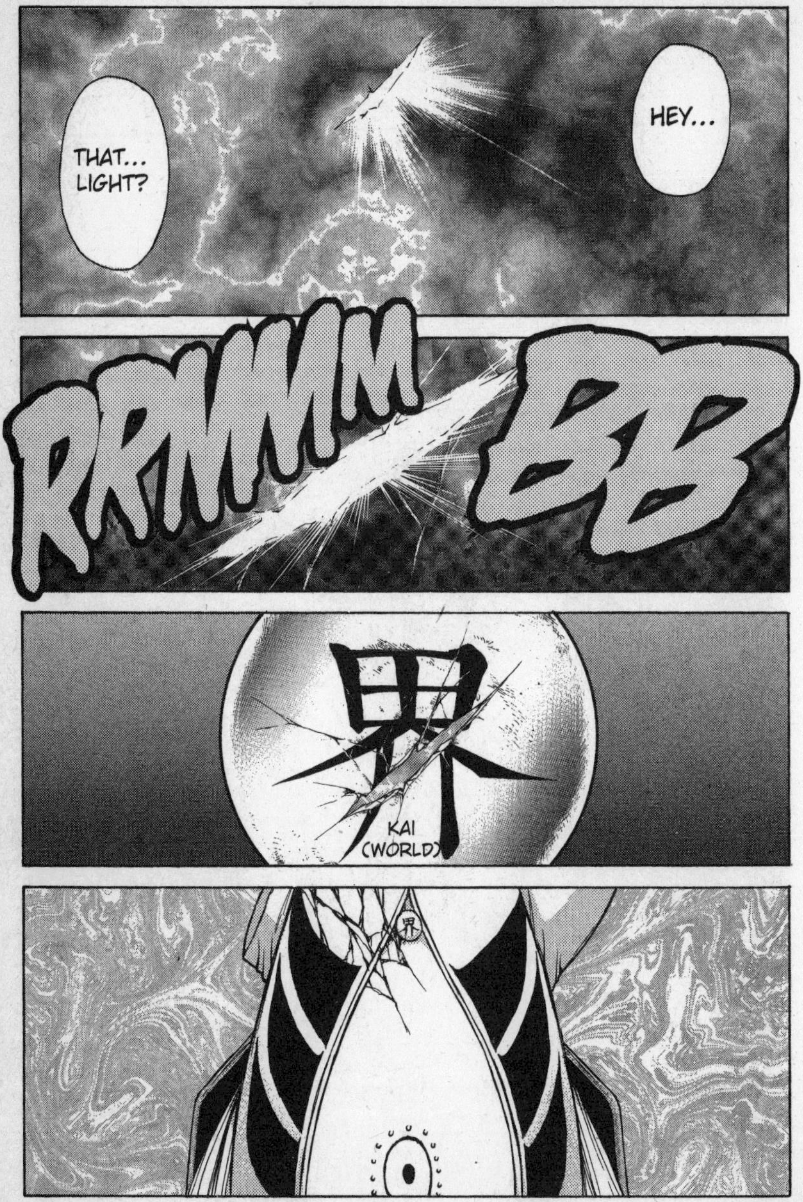
HEY...
THAT... LIGHT?
RRMMM BB
KAI (WORLD)

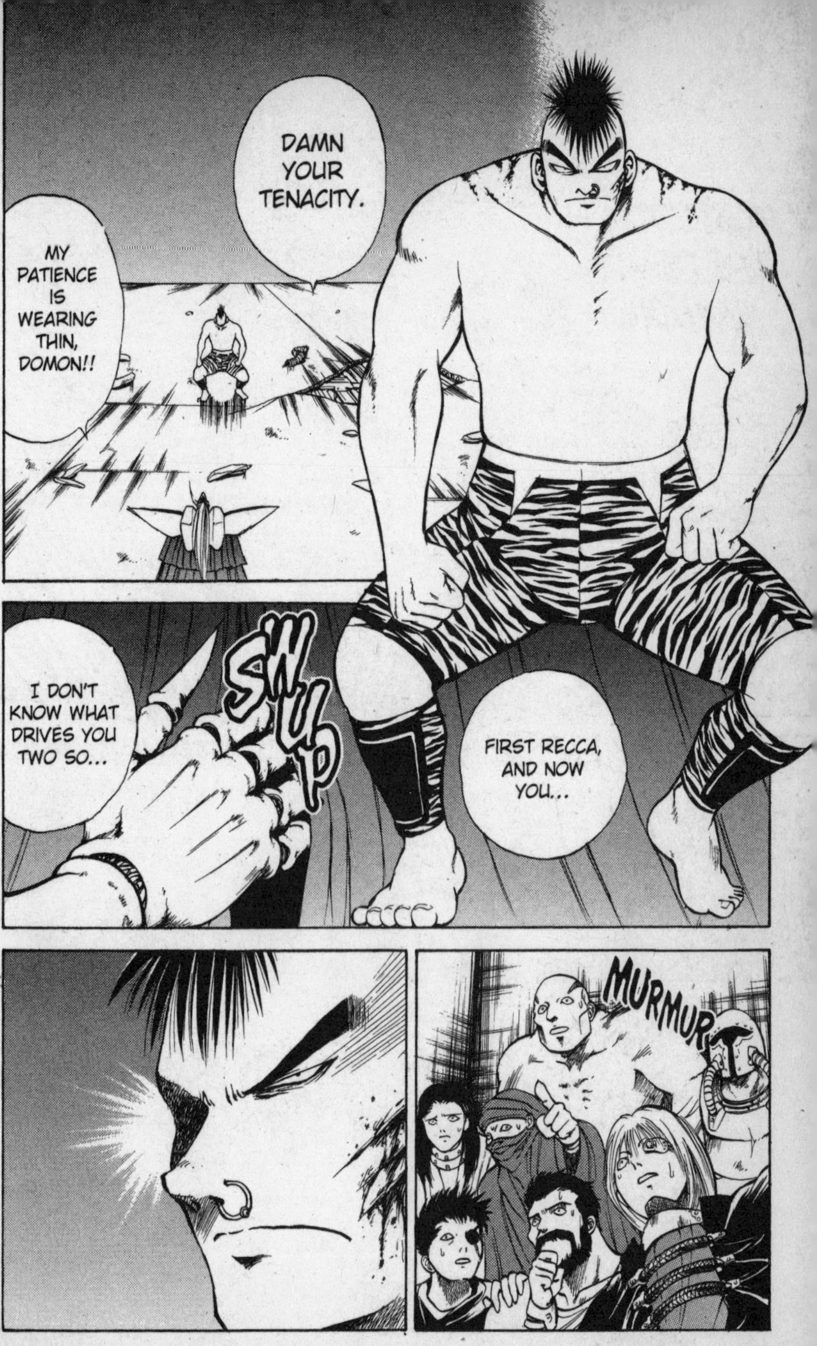
DAMN YOUR TENACITY.
MY PATIENCE IS WEARING THIN, DOMON!!
FIRST RECCA, AND NOW YOU...
S'HUP
I DON'T KNOW WHAT DRIVES YOU TWO SO...
MURMUR

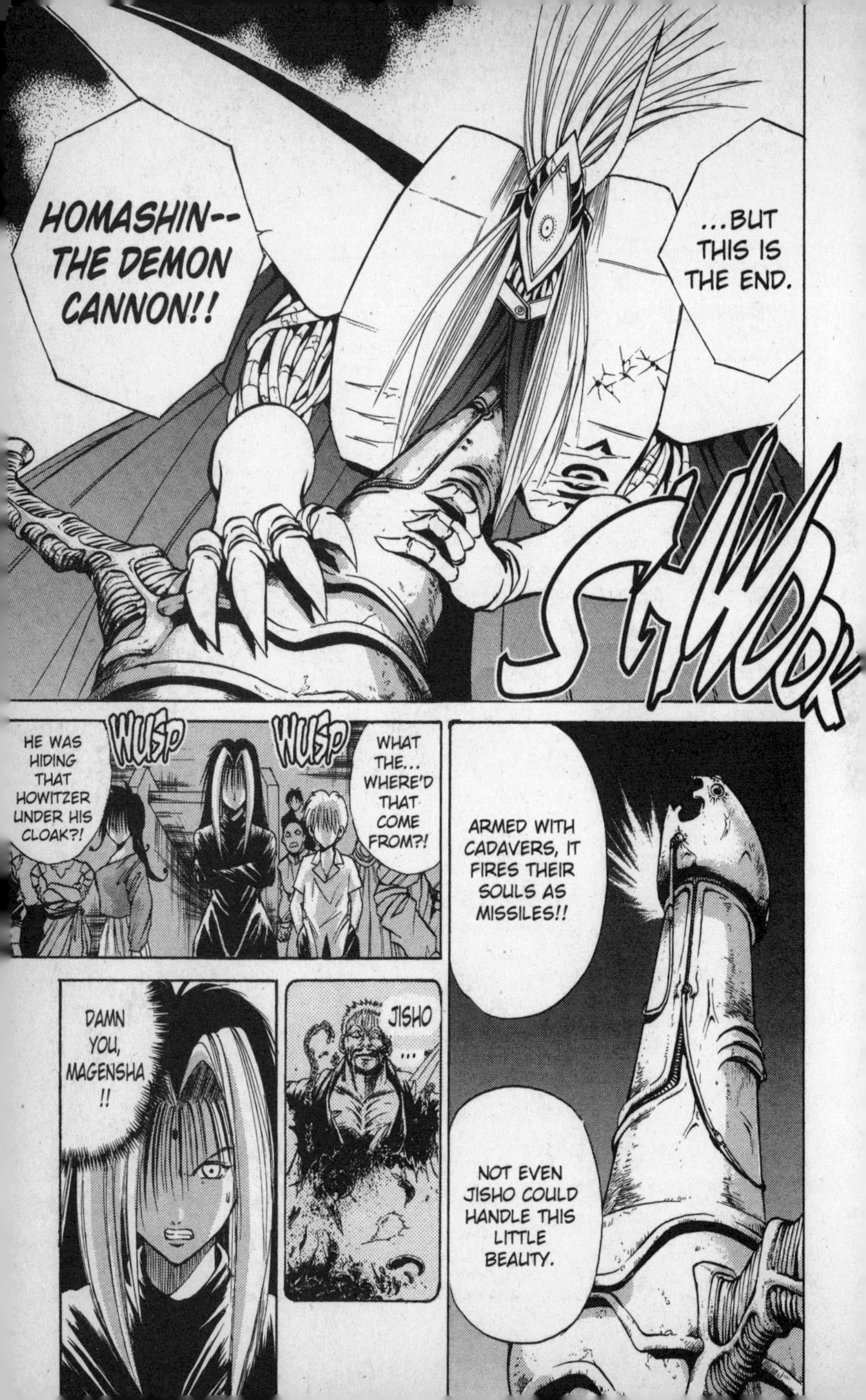

...BUT THIS IS THE END.
HOMASHIN-- THE DEMON CANNON!!
SCHLOK
ARMED WITH CADAVERS, IT FIRES THEIR SOULS AS MISSILES!!
NOT EVEN JISHO COULD HANDLE THIS LITTLE BEAUTY.
WHAT THE... WHERE'D THAT COME FROM?!
WUSP
WUSP
HE WAS HIDING THAT HOWITZER UNDER HIS CLOAK?!
JISHO...
DAMN YOU, MAGENSHA!!

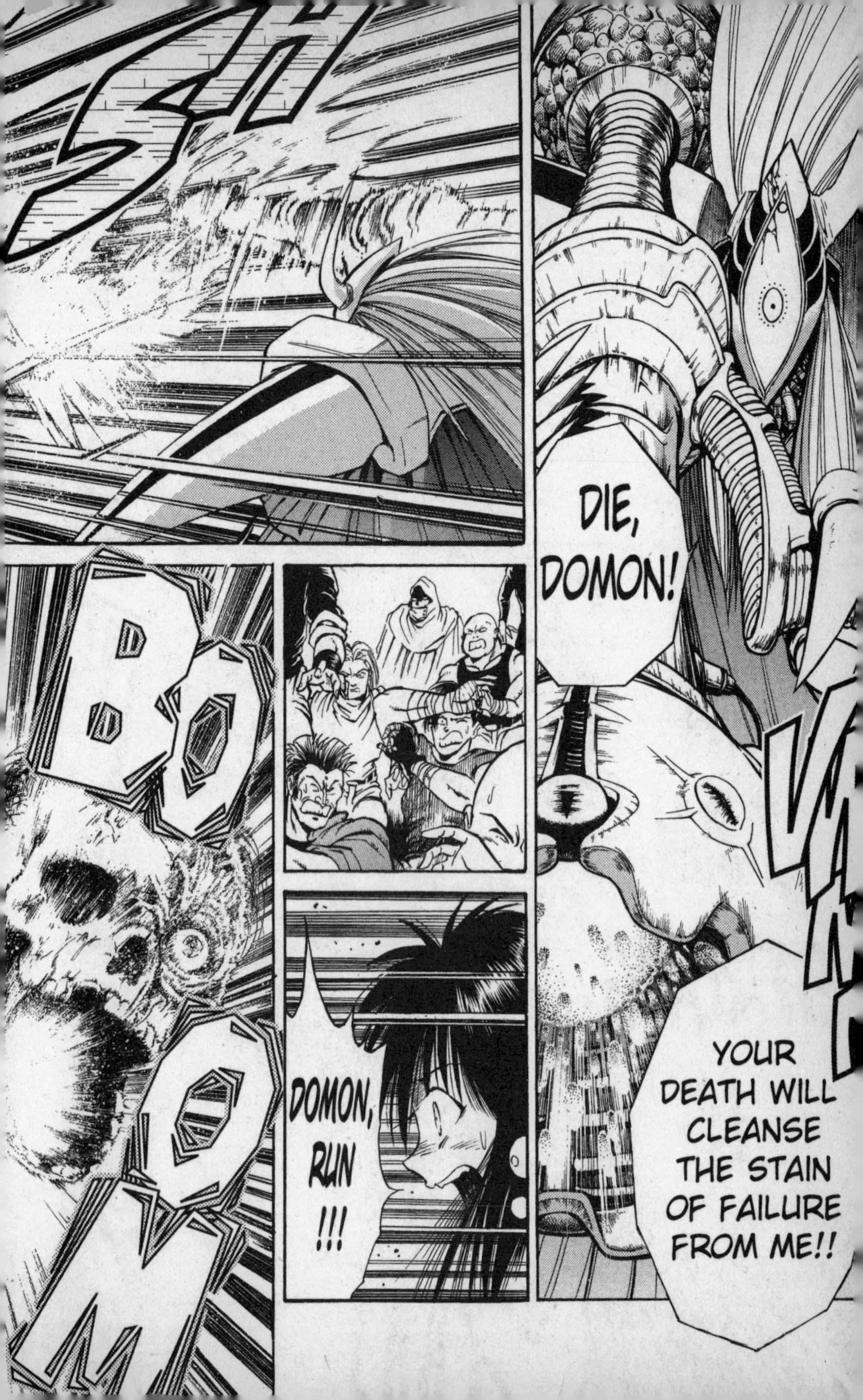
DIE, DOMON!
YOUR DEATH WILL CLEANSE THE STAIN OF FAILURE FROM ME!!
DOMON, RUN!!!

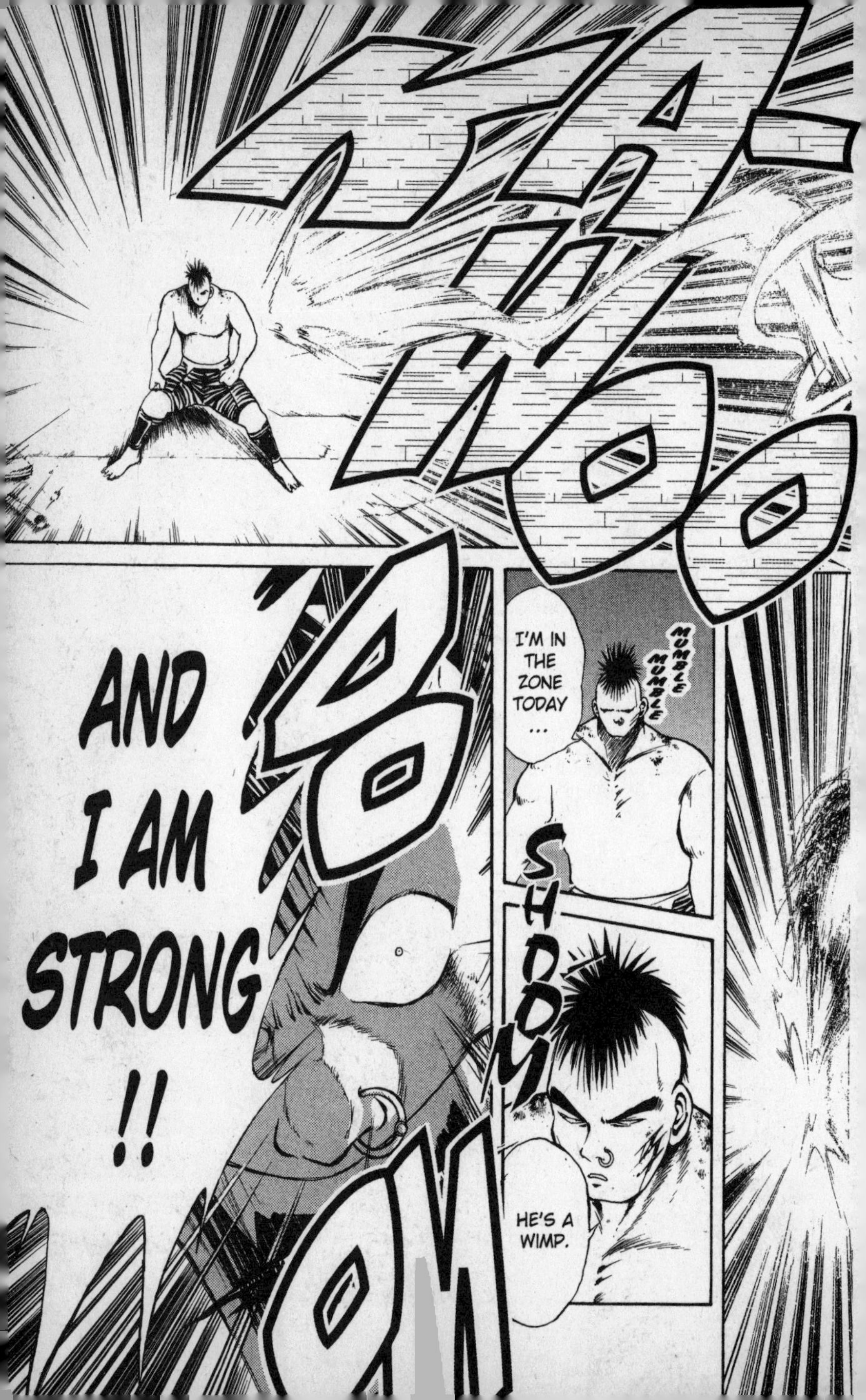

I'M IN THE ZONE TODAY ...
MUMBLE MUMBLE
SHOOM
HE'S A WIMP.
AND I AM STRONG !!

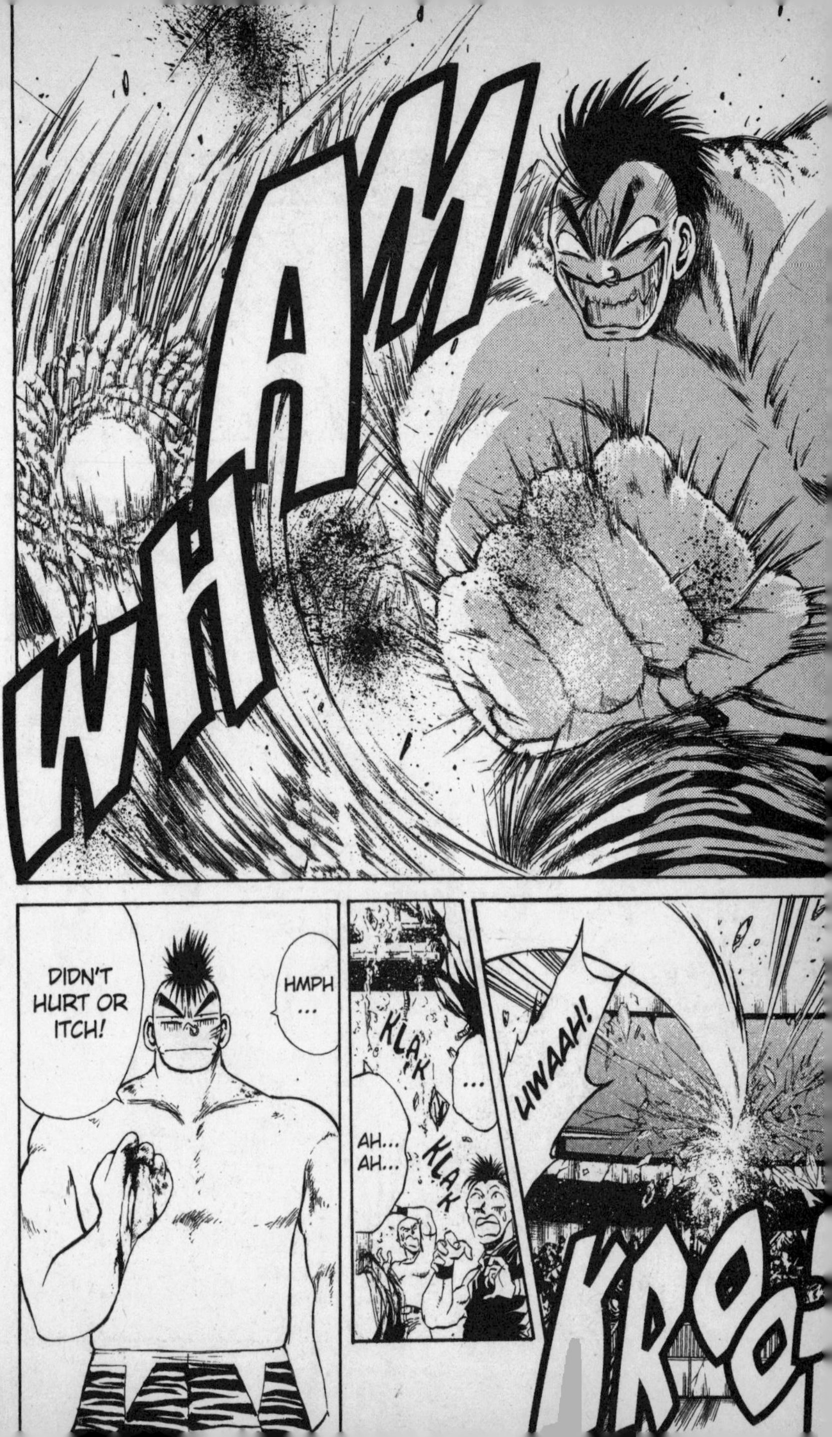
WHAM
UWAAH!
KROO
KLAK
...
AH... AH...
KLAK
HMPH ...
DIDN'T HURT OR ITCH!

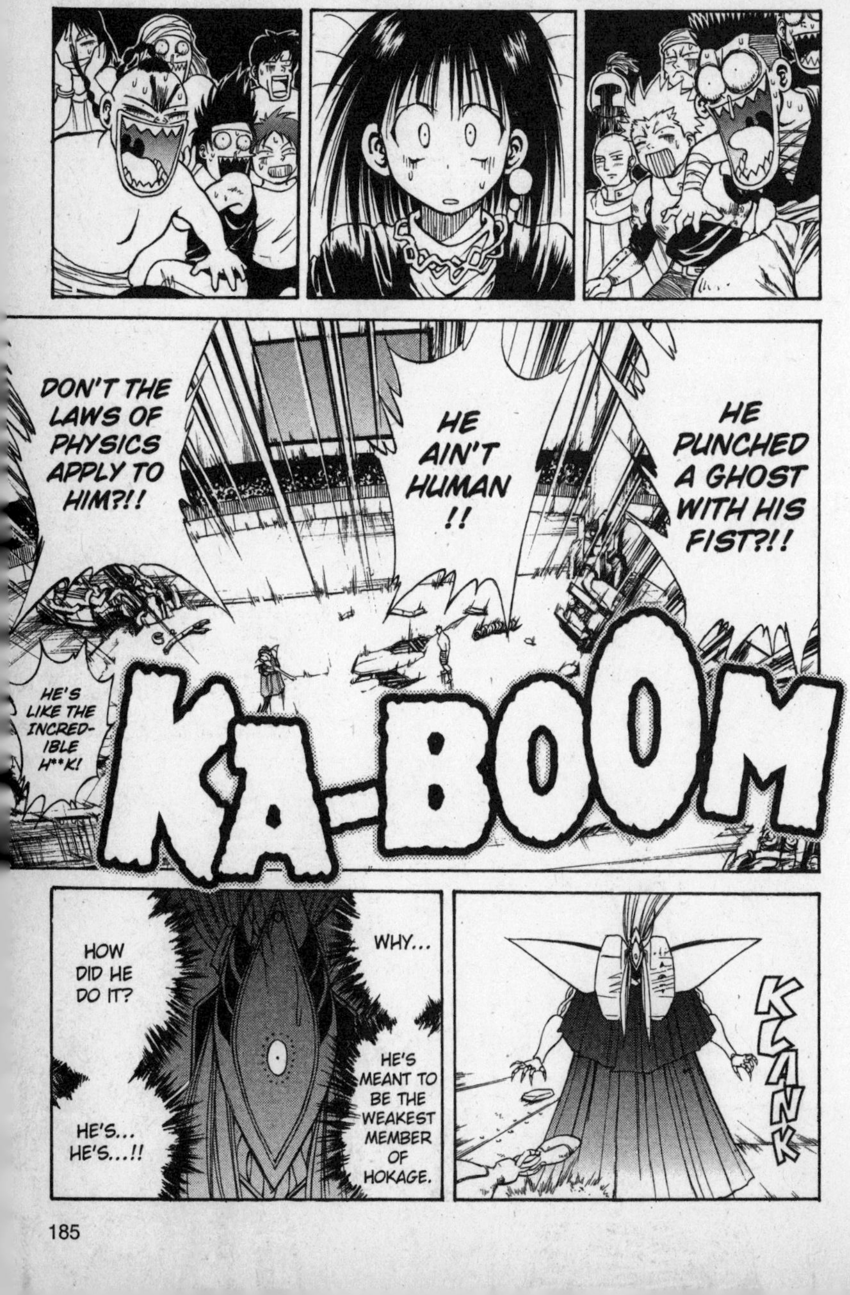
HE PUNCHED A GHOST WITH HIS FIST?!!
HE AIN'T HUMAN !!
DON'T THE LAWS OF PHYSICS APPLY TO HIM?!!
KA-BOOM
HE'S LIKE THE INCREDIBLE H**K!
KLANK
WHY...
HOW DID HE DO IT?
HE'S MEANT TO BE THE WEAKEST MEMBER OF HOKAGE.
HE'S... HE'S...!!

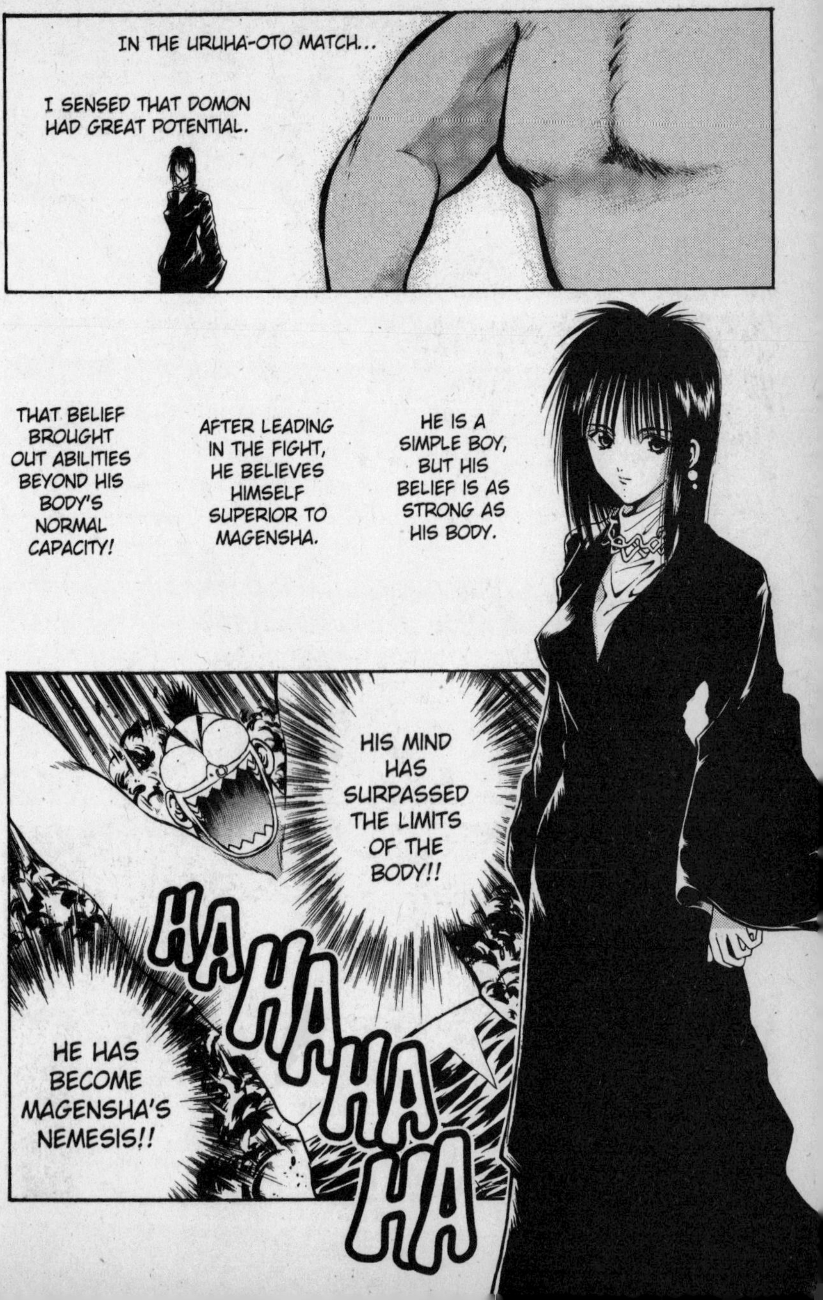
IN THE URUHA-OTO MATCH...
I SENSED THAT DOMON HAD GREAT POTENTIAL.
HE IS A SIMPLE BOY, BUT HIS BELIEF IS AS STRONG AS HIS BODY.
AFTER LEADING IN THE FIGHT, HE BELIEVES HIMSELF SUPERIOR TO MAGENSHA.
THAT BELIEF BROUGHT OUT ABILITIES BEYOND HIS BODY'S NORMAL CAPACITY!
HIS MIND HAS SURPASSED THE LIMITS OF THE BODY!!
HAHAHAHAHA
HE HAS BECOME MAGENSHA'S NEMESIS!!

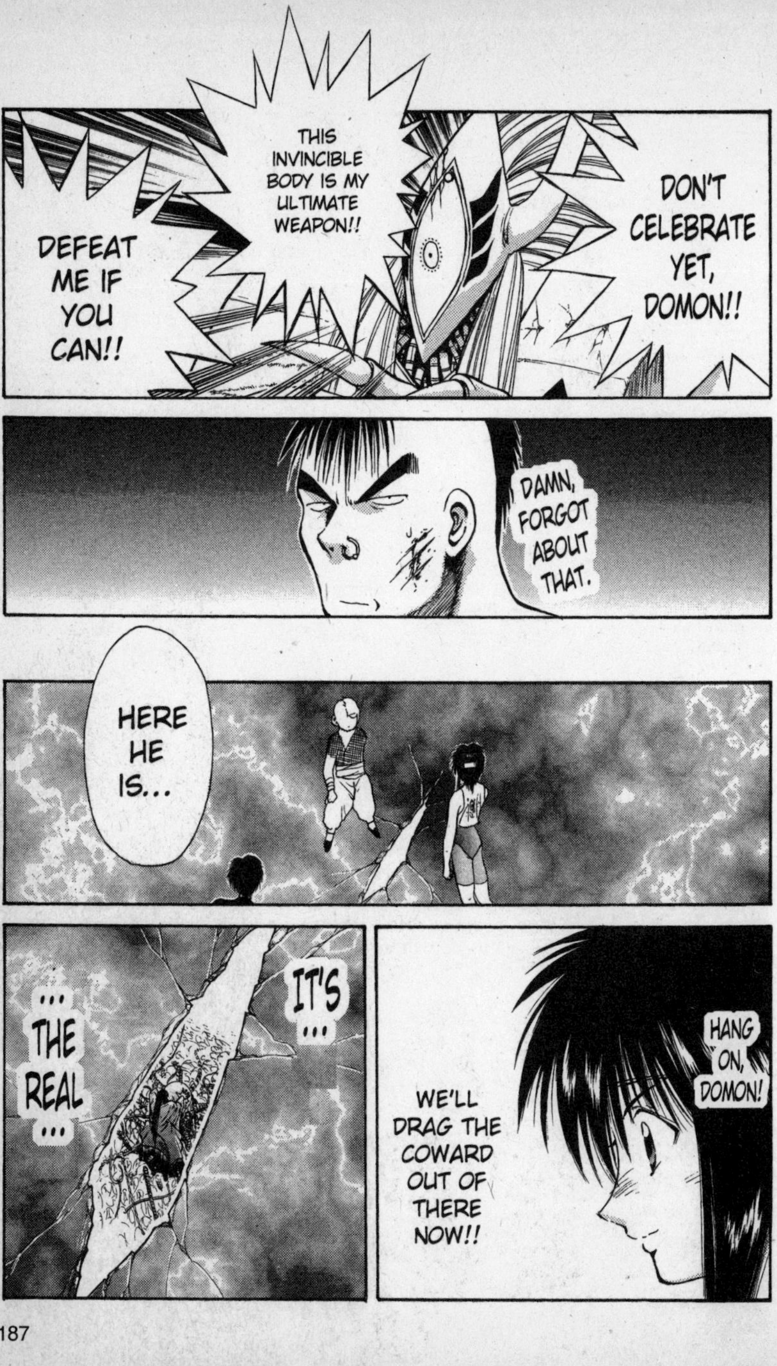
DON'T CELEBRATE YET, DOMON!!
THIS INVINCIBLE BODY IS MY ULTIMATE WEAPON!!
DEFEAT ME IF YOU CAN!!
DAMN, FORGOT ABOUT THAT.
HERE HE IS...
HANG ON, DOMON!
WE'LL DRAG THE COWARD OUT OF THERE NOW!!
IT'S...
...THE REAL...

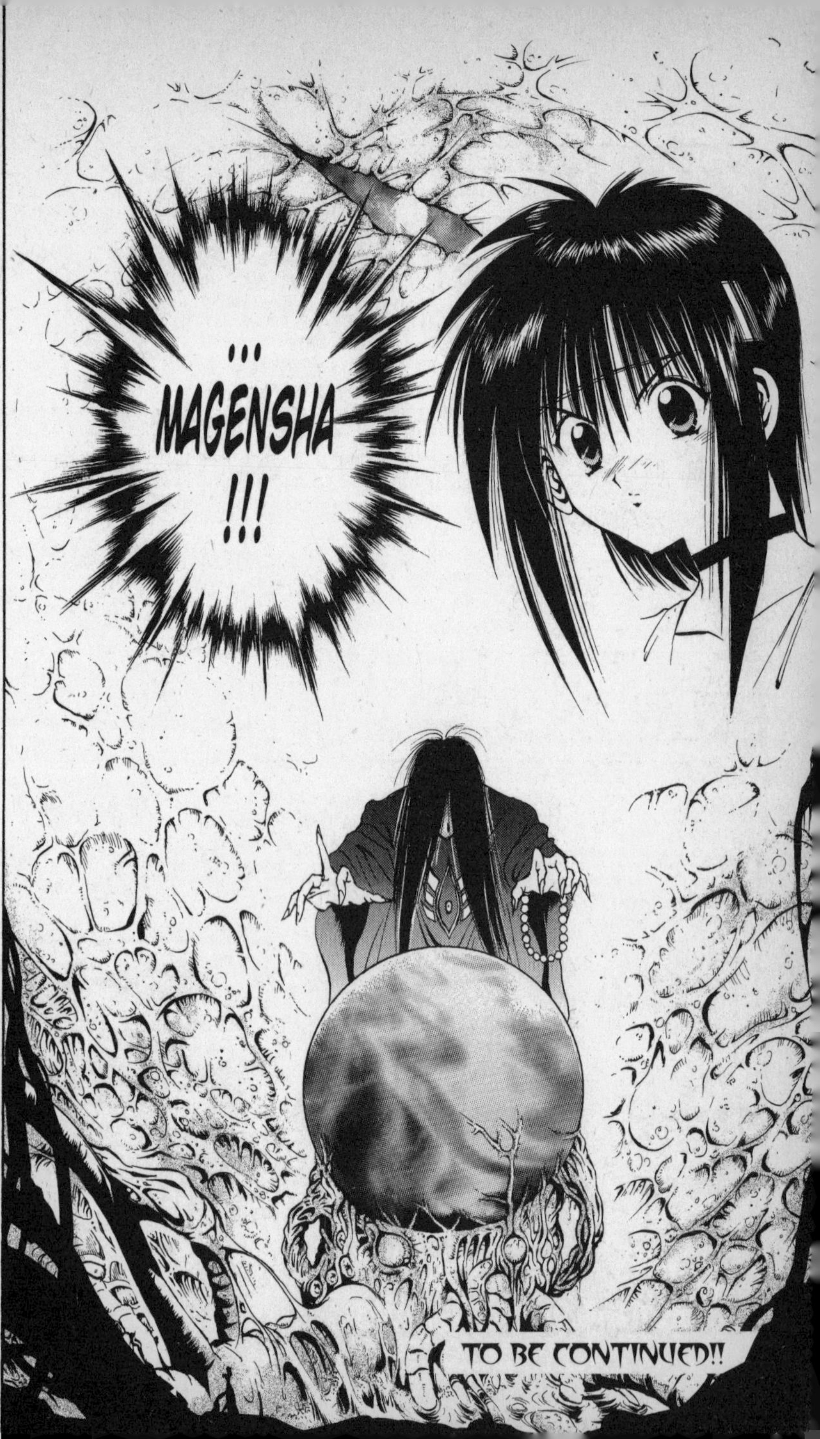
...
MAGENSHA
!!!
TO BE CONTINUED!!

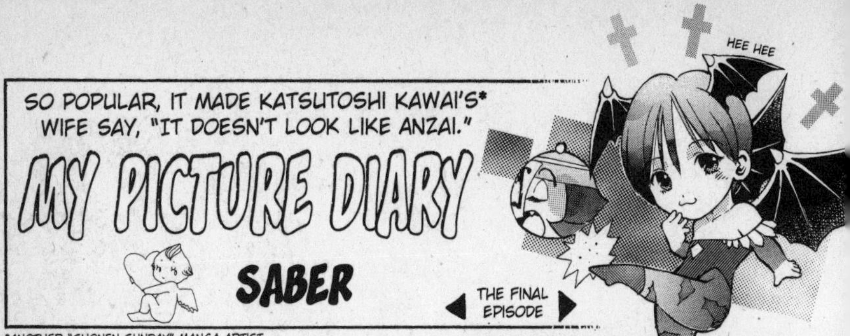
HEE HEE
SO POPULAR, IT MADE KATSUTOSHI KAWAI'S* WIFE SAY, "IT DOESN'T LOOK LIKE ANZAI."
MY PICTURE DIARY
SABER
THE FINAL EPISODE

*ANOTHER "SHONEN SUNDAY" MANGA ARTIST

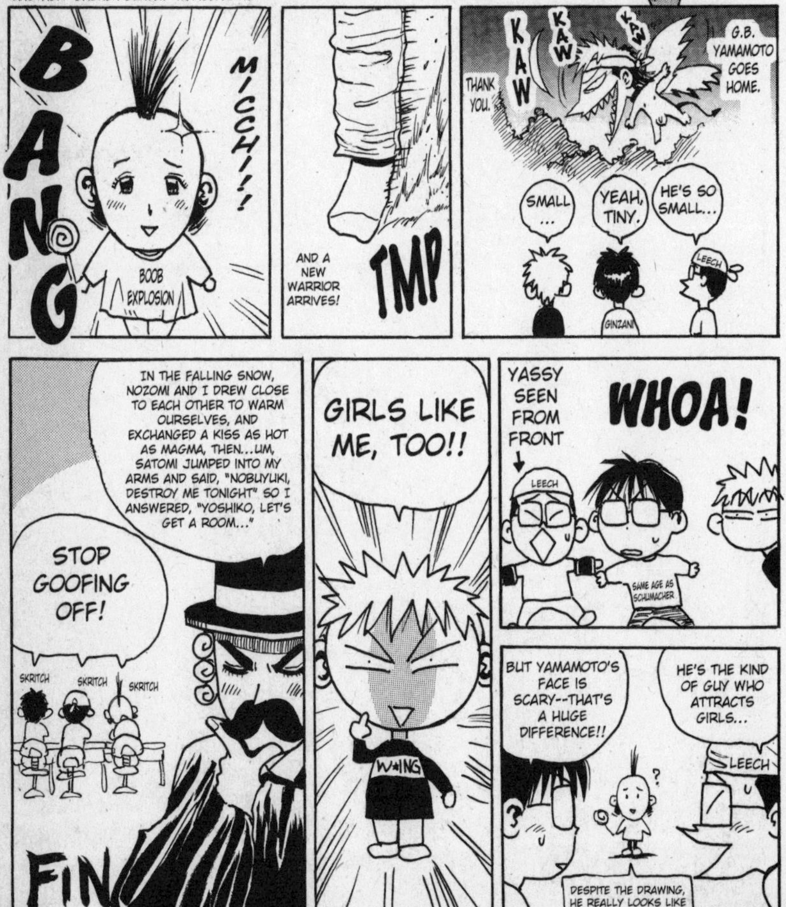
G.B. YAMAMOTO GOES HOME.
KAW
KAW
KAW
THANK YOU.
HE'S SO SMALL...
YEAH, TINY.
SMALL ...
LEECH
GINZANI
AND A NEW WARRIOR ARRIVES!
TMP
MICCHI!!
BANG
BOOB EXPLOSION
WHOA!
YASSY SEEN FROM FRONT
LEECH
SAME AGE AS SCHUMACHER
HE'S THE KIND OF GUY WHO ATTRACTS GIRLS...
BUT YAMAMOTO'S FACE IS SCARY--THAT'S A HUGE DIFFERENCE!!
LEECH
DESPITE THE DRAWING, HE REALLY LOOKS LIKE KOJI ISHIZAKA.*
GIRLS LIKE ME, TOO!!
W*ING
IN THE FALLING SNOW, NOZOMI AND I DREW CLOSE TO EACH OTHER TO WARM OURSELVES, AND EXCHANGED A KISS AS HOT AS MAGMA, THEN...UM, SATOMI JUMPED INTO MY ARMS AND SAID, "NOBUYUKI, DESTROY ME TONIGHT" SO I ANSWERED, "YOSHIKO, LET'S GET A ROOM..."
STOP GOOFING OFF!
SKRITCH
SKRITCH
SKRITCH
FIN

*A POPULAR AND VERSATILE JAPANESE ACTOR

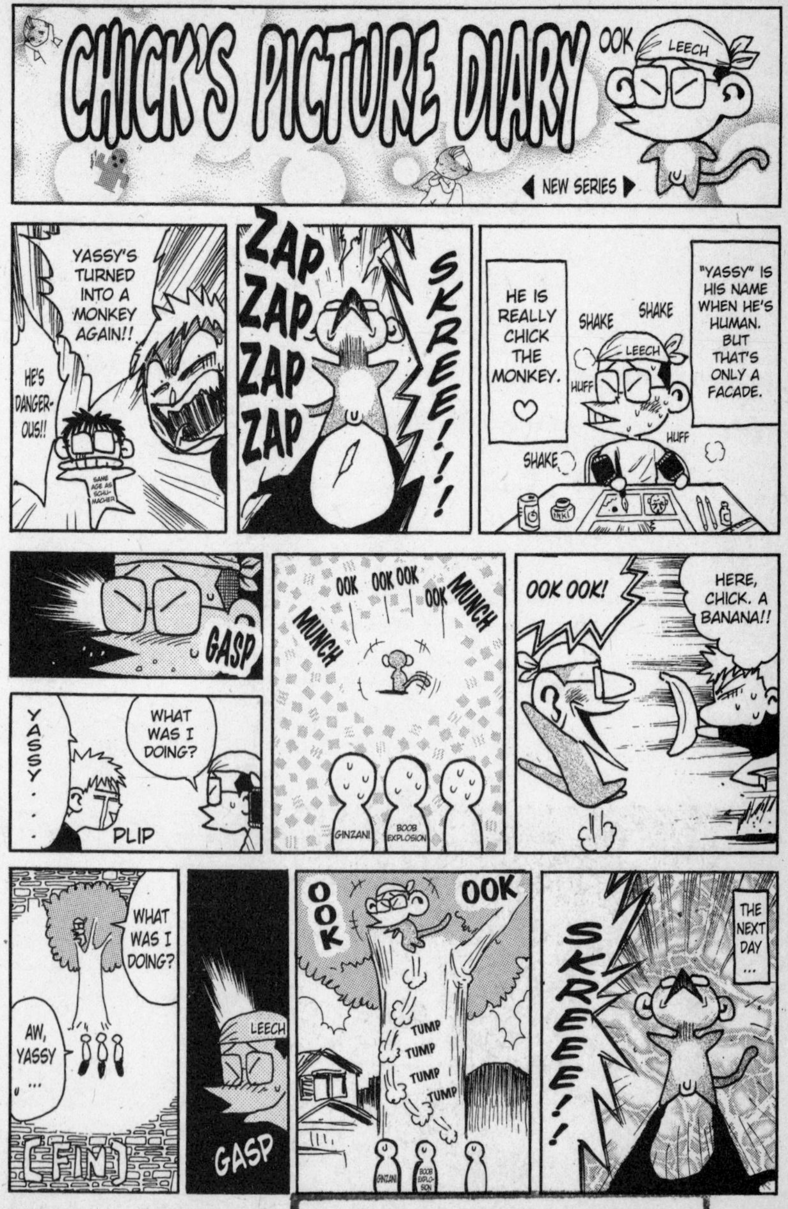
CHICK'S PICTURE DIARY
OOK
LEECH
NEW SERIES
"YASSY" IS HIS NAME WHEN HE'S HUMAN. BUT THAT'S ONLY A FACADE.
HE IS REALLY CHICK THE MONKEY. ♡
SHAKE
SHAKE
LEECH
HUFF
HUFF
SHAKE
INK
ZAP ZAP ZAP ZAP
SKREE!!!
YASSY'S TURNED INTO A MONKEY AGAIN!!
HE'S DANGER-OUS!!
SAME AGE AS SCHU-MACHER
HERE, CHICK. A BANANA!!
OOK OOK!
OOK
OOK OOK
OOK
MUNCH
MUNCH
GINZANI
BOOB EXPLOSION
GASP
WHAT WAS I DOING?
YASSY...
PLIP
THE NEXT DAY...
SKREEE!!
OOK
OOK
TUMP
TUMP
TUMP
TUMP
GINZANI
BOOB EXPLO-SION
LEECH
GASP
WHAT WAS I DOING?
AW, YASSY...
[FIN]

IF YOU ENJOYED THIS VOLUME OF "FLAME OF RECCA," THEN HERE'S SOME MORE MANGA YOU MIGHT BE INTERESTED IN.

Editor's Recommendations

© 1999 Hiroyuki Nishimori/Shogakukan, Inc.

© 1996 Masahito Soda/Shogakukan, Inc.

© 1992 Yuu Watase/Shogakukan, Inc.

Cheeky Angel
What happens when a genie mishears your wish to be "the manliest man on earth" and turns you into "the womanliest woman" instead?! Find out in this gender-bending, slapstick comedy about a boy named Megumi who grows up to be the hottest girl in his high school!

Firefighter! Daigo of Fire Company M
Rookie firefighter Daigo Asahina can't believe his bad luck when he's assigned to the district with the fewest fires on record! But now that Daigo has joined Fire Company M, things won't stay quiet for long. His offbeat methods and uncanny instincts soon have his fellow firefighters wondering whether he's a hero or a menace!

Fushigi Yûgi
From the author of *CERES: CELESTIAL LEGEND* and *IMADOKI! NOWADAYS* comes the story of a teenage girl who is whisked away into the world of a book set in ancient China. There, she must gather seven rambunctious Celestial Warriors and summon the god Suzaku to save the nation of Hong-Nan and be granted her deepest wish!

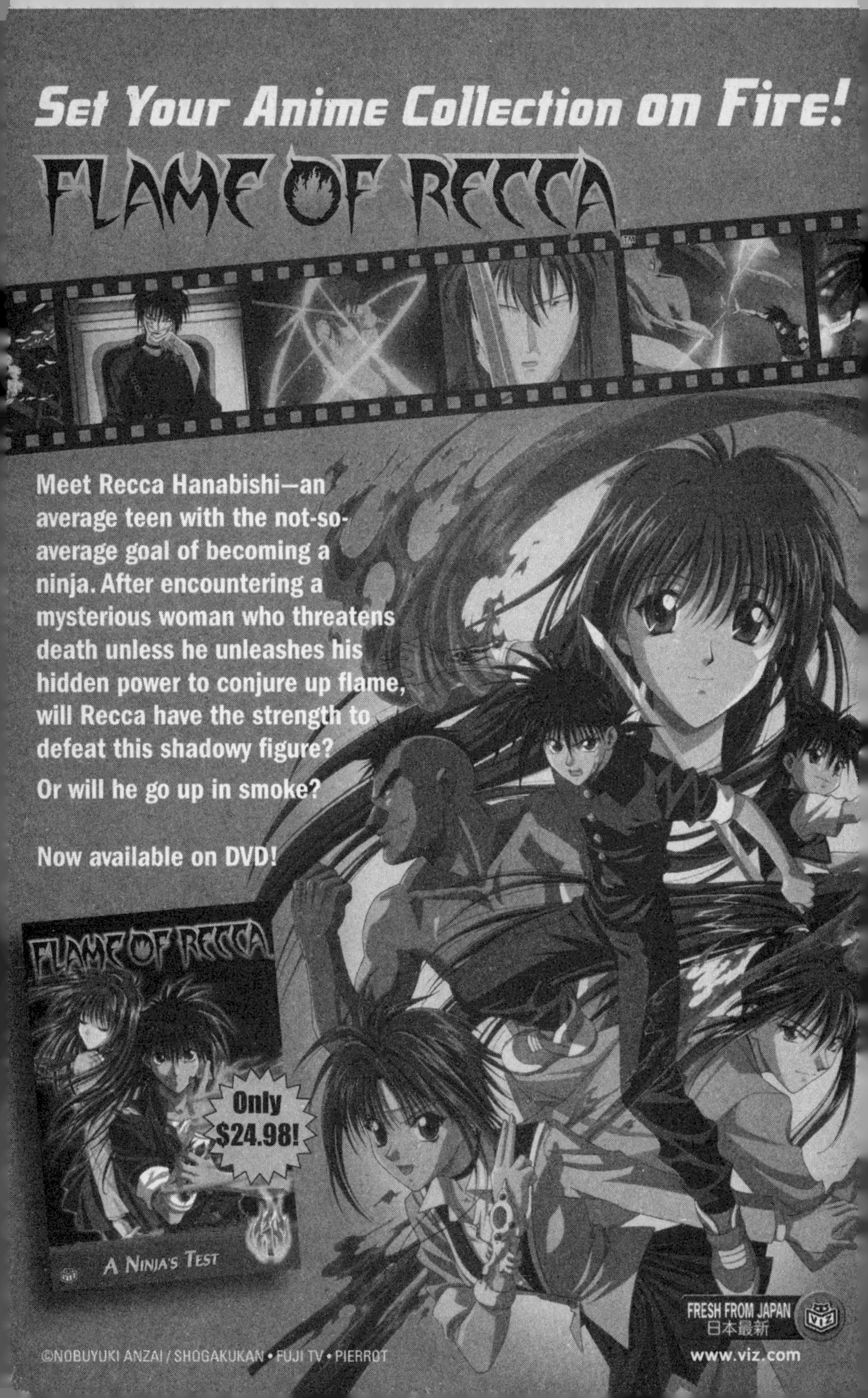
Set Your Anime Collection on Fire!
FLAME OF RECCA
TM
Meet Recca Hanabishi—an average teen with the not-so-average goal of becoming a ninja. After encountering a mysterious woman who threatens death unless he unleashes his hidden power to conjure up flame, will Recca have the strength to defeat this shadowy figure?
Or will he go up in smoke?
Now available on DVD!
FLAME OF RECCA
A NINJA'S TEST
Only $24.98!
FRESH FROM JAPAN
日本最新
VIZ
©NOBUYUKI ANZAI / SHOGAKUKAN • FUJI TV • PIERROT
www.viz.com

Half Human, Half

When Kagome discovers a well that transports her to feudal era Japan, she unwittingly frees a half-demon, Inuyasha, and shatters the sacred Jewel of Four Souls. Now they must work together to restore the jewel before it falls into the wrong hands...

INUYASHA

The manga that inspired a phenomenon!

FULL COLOR adaptation of the TV series!

Only $9.95!

Only $11.95!

action

Prepare For Battle!

Tyson is a boy with a passion for Beyblades. His enemies are the militant Blade Sharks, who want to win at any cost! Can Tyson get the skills and training to beat them in a Beyblade battle?

From the #1 rated series on ABC Family and the popular HASBRO toys —
Start your graphic novel collection today!

Only
$7.99!

Story and art by
Takao Aoki

BEYBLADE™

FRESH FROM JAPAN
日本最新

action   www.viz.com

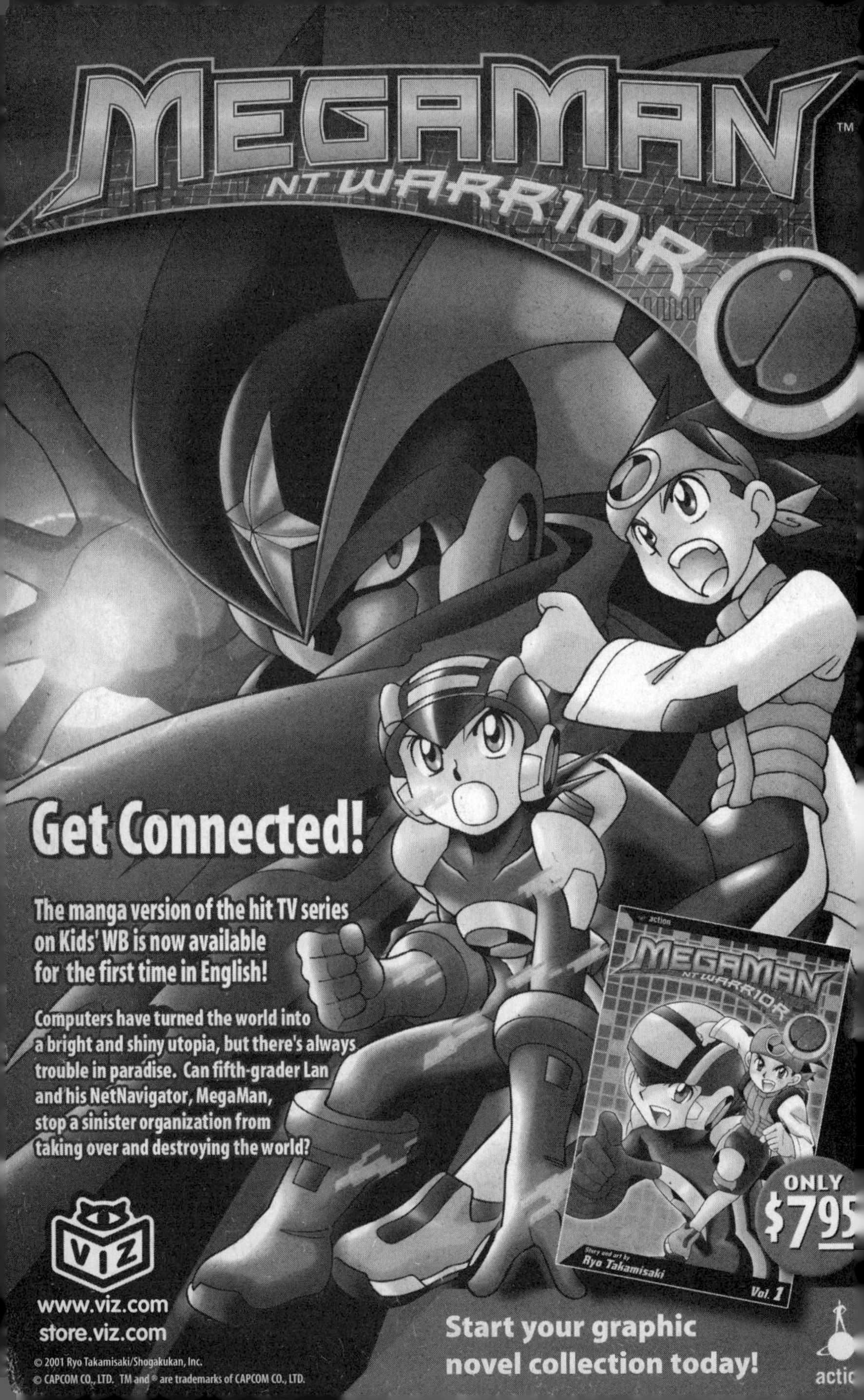

COMPLETE OUR SURVEY AND LET
US KNOW WHAT YOU THINK!

☐ Please do NOT send me information about VIZ products, news and events, special offers, or other information.

☐ Please do NOT send me information from VIZ's trusted business partners.

Name: _____

Address: _____

City: _____ **State:** _____ **Zip:** _____

E-mail: _____

☐ Male ☐ Female **Date of Birth** (mm/dd/yyyy): ___ / ___ / ___ (Under 13? Parental consent required)

What race/ethnicity do you consider yourself? (please check one)

☐ Asian/Pacific Islander ☐ Black/African American ☐ Hispanic/Latino

☐ Native American/Alaskan Native ☐ White/Caucasian ☐ Other: _____

What VIZ product did you purchase? (check all that apply and indicate title purchased)

☐ DVD/VHS _____

☐ Graphic Novel _____

☐ Magazines _____

☐ Merchandise _____

Reason for purchase: (check all that apply)

☐ Special offer ☐ Favorite title ☐ Gift

☐ Recommendation ☐ Other _____

Where did you make your purchase? (please check one)

☐ Comic store ☐ Bookstore ☐ Mass/Grocery Store

☐ Newsstand ☐ Video/Video Game Store ☐ Other: _____

☐ Online (site: _____)

What other VIZ properties have you purchased/own? _____

_____

How many anime ... **How many were VIZ titles?** (please c...

ANIME	MANGA	VIZ
☐ None	☐ None	☐ None
☐ 1-4	☐ 1-4	☐ 1-4
☐ 5-10	☐ 5-10	☐ 5-10
☐ 11+	☐ 11+	☐ 11+

I find the pricing of VIZ products to be: (please check one)

☐ Cheap ☐ Reasonable ☐ Expensive

What genre of manga and anime would you like to see from VIZ? (please check two)

☐ Adventure ☐ Comic Strip ☐ Science Fiction ☐ Fighting

☐ Horror ☐ Romance ☐ Fantasy ☐ Sports

What do you think of VIZ's new look?

☐ Love It ☐ It's OK ☐ Hate It ☐ Didn't Notice ☐ No Opinion

Which do you prefer? (please check one)

☐ Reading right-to-left

☐ Reading left-to-right

Which do you prefer? (please check one)

☐ Sound effects in English

☐ Sound effects in Japanese with English captions

☐ Sound effects in Japanese only with a glossary at the back

THANK YOU! Please send the completed form to:

... sell or otherwise